HOLLYWOOD AND
Hitler 1933–1939

—

FILM AND CULTURE
JOHN BELTON, EDITOR

FILM AND CULTURE • A SERIES OF COLUMBIA UNIVERSITY PRESS
FOR THE LIST OF TITLES IN THIS SERIES, SEE PAGE 431

HOLLYWOOD AND
Hitler 1933–1939

THOMAS DOHERTY

COLUMBIA UNIVERSITY PRESS
NEW YORK

Columbia University Press
Publishers Since 1893
New York   Chichester, West Sussex
cup.columbia.edu

Library of Congress Cataloging-in-Publication Data

Doherty, Thomas Patrick.
Hollywood and Hitler, 1933–1939 / Thomas Doherty
pages cm. — (Film and culture)
Includes bibliographical references and index.
ISBN 978-0-231-16392-7 (cloth : alk. paper) —ISBN 978-0-231-53514-4 (ebook)
1. National socialism and motion pictures. 2. Motion picture industry—
United States—History—20th century. 3. Motion pictures—Political
aspects—United States—History—20th century. 4. Motion picture
industry—Germany—History—20th century. 5. Motion pictures—Political
aspects— Germany—History—20th century. 6. Motion pictures in propaganda—Germany—History—20th century. 7. Motion pictures, American—
Germany—History—20th century. 8. Motion pictures, German—United
States—History—20th century. 9. Nazis in motion pictures.
I. Title.

PN1995.9.N36D65   2013
791.43094309'04—dc23   2012046863

Columbia University Press books are printed on permanent
    and durable acid-free paper.

This book is printed on paper with recycled content.
Printed in the United States of America

c 10 9 8 7 6 5 4 3 2 1
p 10 9 8 7 6 5 4 3 2 1

Cover image: "Song of Songs" © 1933 Paramount Productions Inc.
    Courtesy of Universal Studios Licensing LLC
Cover design: Lisa Hamm

References to Internet Web sites (URLs) were accurate at the time of writing.
    Neither the author nor Columbia University Press is responsible for URLs
    that may have expired or changed since the manuscript was prepared.

To Sandra—Again

CONTENTS

HOLLYWOOD AND
Hitler 1933–1939

HEIL! HEIL!

All Germans and Aryans of Pure Nordic Blood!

We Have the JEWS on the Run!
Let Us Keep Up the Good Work!

DO NOT ATTEND

Any Theater showing pictures with any of these Jews or Jew Lovers:

Claudette Colbert is married to a Jew; Norma Shearer was married to a Jew; Margaret Sullivan was married to a Jew; Eddie Cantor is a Jew; Al Jolson is a jew; Sylvia Sydney is a Jew; Ruby Keeler is married to a Jew; and Ricardo Cortez is a Jew.

This is only the Beginning to an End:

WATCH ALL FUTURE DEVELOPMENTS

Join any one of our country wide organizations and clubs chartered for the purpose of eliminating the enemy – the JEW from all Industry!

Become a member of this Legion to make this great country of ours safe from the Jew and Russia.

HEADQUARTERS: San Francisco, California
Charter No. 12

The CCC Camps would make good Concentration Camps for the Jews!

Homegrown antisemitism: a leaflet denouncing Hollywood Jews, 1936.

PROLOGUE
Judenfilm!

Hollywood first confronted Nazism when a mob of brownshirts barged into a motion picture theater and trashed a film screening—a resonant enough curtain-raiser, if a bit heavy-handed on symbolism.

On December 4, 1930, *All Quiet on the Western Front* (1930), Universal Pictures' spectacular screen version of the international best seller by Erich Maria Remarque, premiered at the Mozart Hall, a showpiece venue in Berlin, the true capital of the Weimar Republic, the democratic federation founded in 1920 and hanging on by a slim thread ten years later. The antiwar epic was the first must-see film, not starring Al Jolson, of the early sound era. Only a few years earlier, Jolson had shattered the mute solemnity of the silent screen with the soulful racket of *The Jazz Singer* (1927), a technological marvel and cultural bellwether about an ethnic, religious, and racial chameleon—a Jewish boy in blackface—who hits the big time in America, actually becomes American, by singing jazz and shaking his hips on the Broadway stage.

Only the clash of ignorant armies filled the soundtrack of *All Quiet on the Western Front*. Directed by Lewis Milestone, a Russian-born veteran of the U.S. Army Signal Corps, the somber death march kept faith with Remarque's bitter perspective on the Great War, a wrenching tale of blithe cannon fodder led to the slaughter by dreams of glory and the lies of cynical old men. The film won top honors from a professional guild founded just two years earlier, the Academy of Motion Picture Arts and Sciences, garnering a pair of trophies not yet dubbed Oscar for Best Director and Best Production.

Remarque's sentiments were shared by most of the people so lately in each other's crosshairs: the real enemy was war, not Germany, England, or France, still less the United States, a tardy combatant who had emerged from the bloodbath relatively unscathed, the body count for its entire hitch in service not matching the deaths suffered by the British, French, and Germans at the Somme, or Verdun, or Pachendale. With a presold story and a heartfelt message, the international market for what critics and audiences alike hailed as a cinematic masterpiece seemed auspicious, nowhere more so than in Germany, the war-ravaged home of the author.

Yet since the January 1929 publication of Remarque's novel, a *bildungsroman* steeped in the antiwar atmospherics of the Weimar Republic, a rival zeitgeist had swept over Germany. Led by a former corporal on the Western front, the most extreme of the right-wing militarist groups continued to fight for a noble cause lost only because the gallant warriors had been stabbed in the back by the Armistice of November 11, 1918, and crushed underfoot by the Versailles Treaty. For the Nazis, the Great War remained a festering wound and a powerful recruitment tool. The party's paramilitary wing, the *Sturmabteilung* (storm troopers, or S.A.)—street thugs known by the brown color of their uniform—stood ready to do battle, Armistice or not.

Anticipating a turbulent reception in Germany, Universal tried to head off trouble by soliciting prior clearance from Baron Otto von Hentig, the German consul general in San Francisco, who flew down to Los Angeles for a private screening at Universal Pictures.[1] Under his editorial guidance, and with the approval of the German Chargé d'Affaires in Washington, D.C., Universal prepared a special print for German release, sanitizing the stench of life in the trenches—the foul mud, the rancid food, the vulgar griping—and muting the antiwar rhetoric, notably a patch of dialogue blaming the Kaiser for the war. On November 22, 1930, given the go-ahead from the foreign office, the German censors in Berlin cleared *All Quiet on the Western Front* for exhibition in the nation that had inspired the source material.[2]

The first public screening in Berlin augured well. Mirroring the reactions of American, British, and French audiences, the opening-night crowd at the Mozart Hall watched in quiet reverie. After all, like the book, the film was a deeply German story: of a patriotic young *Gymnasium* student, blazing with fervor for the Fatherland, who marches into carnage, disillusionment, and ultimately, inevitably, death, felled by a sniper's bullet as he reaches over a parapet to touch a fluttering butterfly. The final image plays taps for the dead on all sides: a double exposure of fresh-faced, smiling recruits, looking back into the camera, not accusingly, just oblivious to what awaits them, over a field of graveyard crosses.

When the lights came up, the Berliners sat still for a long moment, as if shell-shocked, "too stirred and moved to either disapprove or applaud," according to a Hollywood reviewer in the crowd.[3] A beat later, the patrons filed out in stricken silence. A relieved reporter for the *Film Daily*, the New York–based trade paper, cabled back an optimistic prediction to the home office. "Considerable interest and apprehension has been aroused over the picture due to its war theme, but it does not appear likely that any untoward demonstrations will result."[4]

A film for the ages: a German solder (Lew Ayres) and a dying French soldier (Raymond Griffith) share a night in a bomb crater in Universal Pictures' antiwar epic *All Quiet on the Western Front* (1930), directed by Lewis Milestone from the novel by Erich Maria Remarque.

In fact, the first day's screening was uneventful; the police, tipped off to the potential for violence, had come out in force. The next day, however, the authorities let down their guard, or perhaps looked away. Led by Dr. Paul Joseph Goebbels, the media impresario for the Nazi Party, a cadre of burly brownshirts had infiltrated the theater's interior. As the film unspooled, the Nazis stood up and howled invective at the screen, railing against the perfidy of the Hollywood Jews who had bankrolled this slur on German honor. Above the din, a shrill epithet rang out. "Judenfilm!" screeched Goebbels. "Judenfilm!" Along with the rhetoric, other noxious elements—stink bombs and sneezing powder—permeated the air, and white mice, released at the same time, scurried down the aisles. As patrons gagged and women stood on their seats screaming, the management was forced to stop the show and clear the house. Amid the chaos, several moviegoers, taken for Jews by the brownshirts, were savagely beaten.

"Within ten minutes, the cinema was a madhouse," Goebbels gloated in his diary that night. "The police are powerless. The embittered masses are violently against the Jews."[5] Over the next evenings, Goebbels mounted a series of nighttime rallies and torchlit parades to protest *All Quiet on the Western Front*. Assembling in the nearby Nollendorf Plaza, hordes of brownshirts, with Goebbels in the lead, descended on the Mozart Hall and demanded that the theater doors be shuttered and the film print destroyed.

As similar riots erupted across Germany, Dr. Alfred Hugenburg, owner of Ufa, Germany's flagship motion picture studio, beseeched President Paul von Hindenburg, the geriatric leader of the wheezing Weimar Republic, to revoke the permit for exhibition issued by the German film censors. The German Motion Picture Theater Owners passed a resolution refusing to exhibit *All Quiet on the Western Front* and regretting "exceedingly that Carl Laemmle, a German-American, should present, twelve years after the war, a war film in which the German version differs from those shown throughout the world."[6] That is, after insisting on alterations in the original American version for the German release, the Germans now objected to the alterations.

Carl Laemmle, president and founder of Universal Pictures, was indeed a native son of Germany, but his national heritage was not the problem. Born in 1867 in the municipality of Laupheim, in the blue Danube district of Württemberg, Germany, he was the son of precariously bourgeois Jewish merchants, Julius and Rebekka Laemmle. At seventeen, he immigrated to America to live out a scenario scripted by Benjamin Franklin: up the ladder a rung at a time, working hard, living modestly, and keeping an eye out for the main chance, rising from $4-a-week messenger, to clerk, to store manager, to store owner. In 1906, Laemmle moved to Chicago with plans to invest his savings in a five-and-dime store—until he noticed a long line of customers, nickels in hand, waiting to enter a storefront to gawk at the entertainment revolution launched with the new century.

Opening his own nickelodeon, Laemmle got in on the ground floor of a business that would never again be small change. As an exhibitor, he needed a reliable film broker, so he expanded into distribution. As a distributor, he needed a steady stream of product, so he moved into production—financing his own films and fighting the monopolistic film trusts that controlled the supply chain. In 1912, flush with an infusion of cash from a white-slavery exposé entitled *Traffic in Souls* (1912), he transferred his operation to the city soon to become synonymous with the budding industry, opening the first Universal Pictures in an old brewery on the corner of Sunset Boulevard and Gower Street. On March 15, 1915, he expanded the operation to a 230-acre lot in the San Fernando Valley and christened the grounds Universal City—already declaring his global aspirations for the universal medium.

As Laemmle built his American dream factory, he maintained warm kinship ties and close commercial links with his native Germany, frequently vacationing there and mixing business and pleasure with his extended family. In 1920, returning to Germany for the first time since the Great War, he was heartsick at the appalling destitution in a once prosperous land. Taking to the pages of the *Saturday Evening Post*, he made impassioned pleas for the fortunate people of America to relieve the sufferings of the stricken people of Germany. "Possibly many of you haven't forgotten the war and maybe some hatred still lingers in your hearts, yet it is an American trait to forget and forgive, to soften and sympathize, when real distress steps over the threshold," he wrote, imploring his readers to give aid and comfort to their former enemy—not the bestial Hun leering from the Great War propaganda posters but fellow human beings in desperate need of relief. "Will you send me any kind of help you can afford—food, clothing, hats, shoes, money?" he begged. "All the employees of Universal are contributing and weekly we are sending cases of supplies to Germany."[7] Laemmle paid the shipping costs for the donations out of his own pocket.

A product of late-nineteenth-century Germany, Laemmle was a generation and a culture removed from the newer Jewish arrivals in Hollywood, descendents of Eastern European and Russian Jews mostly, who occupied the executive suites of his rivals at Warner Bros., MGM, Paramount, and Fox. An avuncular figure known—universally—as "Uncle Carl," he had a weakness for the ponies (he was a regular at the racetrack at Santa Anita) and poker (he wryly described himself as "the unluckiest poker player in the United States," knowing how lucky he was in other ways).[8] If Laemmle adhered to any stereotype, it was the stock image of the kindly German burgher—white-haired, well-fed, and warm-hearted.

The idea for a motion picture version of *All Quiet on the Western Front* was the brainchild of his son, Carl Laemmle Jr., known as "Junior Laemmle" around town, whom Laemmle Senior appointed as head of production for Universal in 1929 when his son was just twenty-one years old. Both Laemmles visited Germany that year to negotiate the film rights with Remarque and to reassure the wary author that the Hollywood version would remain true to the spirit of the book. On the centrality of the antiwar theme, father, son, and author were all on the same page. "The picture will bring home the useless wastefulness of war," declared Laemmle Senior, pledging to infuse the film with "the spirit that moved so many to read the volume."[9]

Laemmle Jr. was even more emphatic. Having botched his first big assignment as executive producer, a film version of the hit play *Broadway* (1929), by meddling with the original formula, he resolved not to make the same mistake with the more valuable screen property. "It gave me the courage to okay *All Quiet* exactly as written, when that seemed an utterly foolhardy and iconoclastic thing to do," he recalled in 1932. "There was no love story in *All Quiet*, and none was added. Its success shattered the legend that no picture can succeed without love interest. At least that's one less picture taboo."[10] To the Laemmles, the project was more than a commercial investment. "If there is anything in my life I am proud of, it is this picture," the elder Laemmle told his associates at the Universal Sales Convention in 1930. "It is, to my mind, a picture that will live forever."[11]

Genuinely shocked by the uproar in Germany, Laemmle responded from Hollywood with a 1,000-word cable published as a paid advertisement in the German newspapers. Still eloquent in his native tongue, he

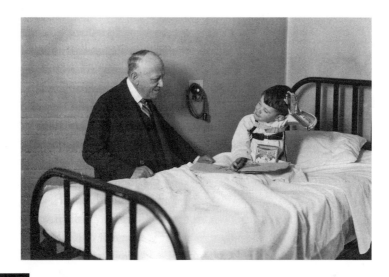

"Uncle Carl": Universal Pictures founder Carl Laemmle in 1927, visiting a child with polio, the first patient convalescing in a room donated to the Los Angeles Orthopedic Hospital by the employees of Universal in Laemmle's honor. Laemmle brought along a radio set for the boy.

asserted that the film, like the book, in no way insulted Germany.[12] "The real heart and soul of Germany has never been shown to the world in all its fineness and honor as it is shown in this picture," Laemmle wrote. "The civilized world, outside of Germany, has seen [*All Quiet on the Western Front*] and accepted it as anything but anti-German. If you, the German people say it is not all I claim for it, I shall withdraw it from exhibition in Germany. I yield to no one in my love for the Fatherland. The fact that I came to America as a boy and built my future in America has never for a moment caused any cessation of my love for the land of my birth." He expressed amazement "that a film which has done more to create friendship for Germany than any other single agency since the War, should receive an adverse reception in Berlin."[13]

In truth, the adverse reception was not confined to Berlin. In Vienna, the training ground for the man spearheading the movement, the Nazis incited an even more tumultuous scene when *All Quiet on the Western Front* premiered at the Apollo Theater. A cordon of 1,500 police surrounded the theater to beat back a mob of several thousand Nazis determined to halt the screening. Here too stink bombs—concealed in seat cushions—forced an evacuation of the house. After the air was cleared, the show went on, but outside in the streets the mob wreaked havoc, torching streetcars, smashing shop windows, and scuffling with mounted policemen.[14]

Shaken by the civic disorder and terrified of the brownshirts, the Supreme Board of Censors in Germany reversed its original decision and banned *All Quiet on the Western Front* on the grounds that it was "endangering Germany's reputation." Besides, the Germans were reportedly "so depressed by economic adversity and so excited by Nationalistic agitation that further provocation must be avoided."[15]

With the cancellation of *All Quiet on the Western Front*, the Nazis had won victories real and symbolic—over the Weimar Republic, exposed as a paper tiger cowed by street violence; over the cultural memory of the Great War, redefined as a patriotic cause sabotaged by enemies within; and over American cinema, branded as an infection spread by Hollywood Jews. "All of this indicates that films are now in politics for good as far as Germany is concerned," read a postmortem filed by the Foreign Department of the Motion Picture Producers and Distributors of America (MPPDA).[a] "The trouble over *All Quiet* had a tremendous effect in Germany. This of course has little to do with the nature of the film itself. It is simply that the film is the thing that precipitated a fundamental internal conflict within Germany."[16]

At the production site, the violence in Germany was monitored with mounting anxiety. "This adverse decision has been hailed as a great victory by the National Socialists and their supporters, and has led to a series of other demonstrations against theatrical and film productions to which they take exception," read a confidential U.S. government report filed in Berlin and passed on to the MPPDA office in New York. In Munich, emboldened Nazis turned to another subversive import from Hollywood, King Vidor's all-black musical *Hallelujah* (1929). "The National Socialists claim this is a blow at Germanic civilization," explained the dispatch, "because it was in the English language and portrayed Negro culture."

---

[a] The edited version of *All Quiet on the Western Front* was quietly rereleased in Germany in 1931. By then, the film had served its purpose for the Nazis. In 1933, however, the Nazis took special delight in an act of cinematic suppression that was also sweet payback. The single print of *All Quiet on the Western Front*, still circulating in Germany three years after its historic Berlin premiere, was confiscated by party zealots in Prussia. After protests on behalf of Universal by the U.S. Embassy, the print was deported to Paris.

More bad news was on the horizon. "There is no doubt that this wave of intense national prejudice, which is now going on, will continue and that any pictures, particularly foreign pictures, which offend the sensibilities of the National Socialists will be a signal for riots and demonstrations."[17]

In America, Hollywood cinema may have appalled Victorian matrons and bluenose clerics, but it did not incite riots by armed militias. Whether in the cathedral-like expanse of a grand motion picture palace or a cozy seat at the neighborhood Bijou, the movie theater was a privileged zone of safety and fantasy—a place to escape, to dream, to float free from the worries of the world beyond the Art Deco lobby, a world that, in the first cold winter of the Great Depression, was harder and harder to keep at bay. All the more reason to view the Nazi-instigated violence as the desecration of a sacred space.

A few in Hollywood tried to shrug off the vandalism. Hearing that Germany had banned "that splendid film, *All Quiet on the Western Front,* on account of it showing Germany losing the war," the cowboy philosopher and motion picture star Will Rogers joshed that the Germans should just tack on a different ending for domestic consumption. "Well, they can show us losing it and they won't be far wrong, and I am sure there will be no kick," he drawled.[18]

Unlike the good-humored Rogers, W. R. "Billy" Wilkerson, editor-publisher of the *Hollywood Reporter,* found nothing funny in the news from Berlin. Introducing a new word to his motion picture-wise but foreign affairs–deficient readership, he fretted over the omens. "Certainly the Nazis—as the National Socialists are called—and their leaders would not create and foster so much dissatisfaction for so puerile a reason," he pointed out, scoffing at Nazi claims that the film had been maliciously doctored solely for German release. "The real force back of these demonstrations apparently is the revived military spirit of a large part of the German people." Wilkerson was old enough to remember where German militarism had once led, and he feared it might lead there again. "People cannot be spurred to another war if they see on the screens of the country representations of their armies retreating, of their soldiers going hungry, becoming discouraged, losing their courage at the sight of battle or the imminence of death. Such depictions bring things too close to home."

Wilkerson, who usually devoted his columns to studio intrigues and box office tallies, concluded his diagnosis of the German psyche with a gloomy prediction:

The military spirit of the German people, created through years of training, is only dormant, not dead. Such a spirit, with centuries of growth
behind it, cannot be killed even through such a lesson as the Great War.
It is comparatively easy to revive—much easier than one would imagine. But—to revive it successfully, to fan it again into flame, cannot be
done if the horrors of war are to be spread before the eyes of the people
so dramatically and realistically as in *All Quiet.*[19]

The Nazis were well off the beat covered by the *Film Daily*, the *Hollywood Reporter*, and the rest of the motion picture trade press, but stink
bombs, street violence, and death threats incited by American movies
were hard to ignore. At first irregularly and glibly, and then more avidly
and grimly as the brutality of the regime hit home, Nazism and its featured players garnered banner headlines and copious ink in the pages of
Hollywood's required reading. After January 30, 1933, when Adolf Hitler was appointed Reich Chancellor of Germany and began his reign as
omnipotent *führer* (another word soon to enter the American vocabulary), geopolitical concerns and moral calculations vied with commercial
considerations in Hollywood's relations with Germany.

Sweeping away a long-standing and mutually profitable bilateral relationship, the Third Reich forced Hollywood to face an unwelcome set
of economic, cinematic, and moral problems. As Hollywood films were
banned from German screens and Hollywood employees run out of the
country, studio executives had to decide whether to cut their losses or
bargain with the devil. Inevitably, the behind-the-scenes negotiations
with Nazism bled into more public spaces. The terrain of the Hollywood feature film, by long reputation and official billing a fantasyland
for the weary masses, a leisure product devoted to "mere entertainment," became a battleground for fierce political fights. Some Americans
wanted Hollywood to indict the Nazis and sound the alarm; others coun-
seled neutrality and aloofness. Even the newsreels, the ostensible screen
journalism of the day, were uncertain about whether the Nazis were fit
subjects for the news of the day or best left on the cutting-room floor so
as not to upset fragile moviegoers.

Percolating not too far under the surface of the controversies over
trade relations and film content was the issue that for the Nazis over-
rode all others. During the trashing of *All Quiet on the Western Front*,
after all, Goebbels and his henchmen had screamed "Judenfilm!" not

The first day of the Third Reich:
Hitler reviews his brownshirted
Sturmabteilung ("storm troopers")
on January 30, 1933. S.A. Chief
of Staff Ernst Röhm marches
directly behind him.

"Amerikanfilm!" In the streets of Berlin, Jews were Hitler's preferred victims. In Hollywood, Jews were titans of industry, respected artists, and
adored stars. The disproportionately Jewish backgrounds of the executives of the studios and the workers on the payroll shaded reactions to
what was never simply a business decision. The term that in the 1920s
came to describe the Hollywood studio heads—*moguls*—had an echo that
cut two ways for the strangers in the land of plenty: powerful but alien,
exotic transplants not yet firmly rooted in the American soil. A decade
of unparalleled prosperity, influence, and visibility for American Jews,
the 1930s was also, not coincidentally, a decade of festering antisemitism. On radio, domestic demagogues snarled the medieval slurs and
spat out newly coined insults: that Jews were a fifth column in league
with godless Bolsheviks, that the reformist New Deal was in fact a nefarious Jew Deal, and that Hollywood was a nest of smut merchants bent
on corrupting Christian America with a foul product line. Pro-Nazi
outfits like the German American Bund and the Silver Shirts agitated
openly for an American-style Reich. Might the virus in Germany jump to

America? Should Hollywood's Jews lie low—or stand tall and denounce their sworn enemy?

Popular histories of the American motion picture industry rhapsodize over the 1930s as the Golden Age of Hollywood, the decade that saw the well-oiled studio system firing on all cylinders, a glitzy machineworks delivering reel after reel of graceful, cheek-to-cheek musicals, sleek screwball comedies, and lavish Technicolor pageants. It is a storied epoch capped by the mother lode struck in the most glittering of all movie years, 1939: *Gone With the Wind, The Wizard of Oz, Mr. Smith Goes to Washington, Ninotchka, Stagecoach*, and on and on.

The list of greatest hits from that vintage year usually omits *Confessions of a Nazi Spy*, Hollywood's first marquee posting of a four-letter word that had blackened newspaper headlines since 1933. The story of Hollywood and Nazism—the behind-the-scenes business deals and the images shown and shunned on the screen—is more apt to tarnish than polish the luster of the Golden Age mythos. Yet the motion picture industry was no worse than the rest of American culture in its failure of nerve and imagination, and often a good deal better in the exercise of both. In the nearly seven years between Hitler's seizure of power and the outbreak of war in Europe, the meaning of Nazism came slowly to Hollywood, like a picture just out of focus—fuzzy and dimly lit at first, sharp and fully outlined only at the end.

1

HOLLYWOOD–BERLIN–HOLLYWOOD

Soon after discovering the movies, Hollywood and Berlin discovered each other. Linked by business interests, ethno-religious affinities, and family ties, the filmmakers in the two cities competed, cooperated, and kibitzed over the great art of the twentieth century. There was magic to conjure, product to peddle, and money to be made.

The codependency was encouraged by the state of the art. Before synchronous dialogue turned the universal medium into a babel of indigenous tongues, film of whatever national origin spoke a common language to a global consumer base. Silent pictures crossed borders with no fuss, no dubbing: merely translate the intertitles and ship the 35mm canisters to ports worldwide. The currency collected at the ticket windows—francs, pence, pfennigs—was all coin of the realm.

The tricks of the trade were also assets to be shared, refined, and stolen. An art-cum-technology still in embryo, the motion picture medium underwent daily improvements and innovations. Artists and technicians kept a keen eye out for hot new developments, lifting each other's styles and knocking off the latest equipment with minimal regard for patent law.

The flashiest cinematic moves earned international acclaim. In 1926 the film event of the season in Berlin was an import from Moscow, Sergei Eisenstein's *Battleship Potemkin* (1925), a vessel brimming with Bolshevik agitprop and kinetic energy. After years of expressionist lighting and balletic camera movements, the jagged montage and slashing suture of the Russian provocateur dazzled a generation of German filmmakers, including a sinewy dancer-turned-actress named Leni Riefenstahl. Also spellbound were the brightest stars in Hollywood's firmament, Mary Pickford, Douglas Fairbanks, and Charles Chaplin, three-fourths of the founders of United Artists, who swooned over Eisenstein's revolutionary style. Returning the favor, Eisenstein called D. W. Griffith, the fourth partner in United Artists, the man responsible for "all that is best in the Soviet film."[1]

The tastes of the average American moviegoer were more provincial, but even when foreign films failed to impress the public, Hollywood craftsmen marveled at the technical wizardry of European artisans, especially the sorcerers at Ufa, the only company logo on the planet that ranked with the MGM lion or the Warner Bros. shield. Located south of Berlin in Neubabelsberg, Ufa was the hothouse for the great flowering of German Expressionism that took root in the afterburn of the Great War. The psychosomatic dreamwork of Robert Weine's *The Cabinet of Dr. Caligari* (1920), the bloodcurdling horror of F. W. Murnau's *Nosferatu* (1922), and the gravity-defying camerawork of E. A. Dupont's *Variety* (1925) may not have dimmed the stars of the Little Tramp, Valentino, or Rin Tin Tin, but studio executives understood the appeal of high-quality product differentiation and fretted over the contrast. "No American producer could have made a better picture of *Variety* than this picture is, and that may be letting down the Americans easily," admitted Sime Silverman, the esteemed editor-publisher of the trade paper *Variety* in a rave review of Dupont's felicitously titled tour de force. "Many an American director may be only too eager to watch it a second time."[2] More ominously, unlike *Battleship Potemkin*, *Variety* drew crowds. At the Rialto on Times Square, an area Hollywood usually owned, New Yorkers flocked to the Ufa import. "Almost unbelievable," gasped a report on the first week's grosses. "Constant lines at the theater . . . indicated that the picture is a veritable riot."[3]

The impact of German cinema was powerful enough to alert the Hollywood moguls (a word that by the late 1920s was common parlance for the mainly Jewish businessmen who ruled the studios like tribal potentates) to the commercial threat posed by such skillful rivals. Wary of the competition, they opened their checkbooks and raided the European workshops. Why compete when you could buy out?

Director Ernst Lubitsch caught the eye of Hollywood early and gladly succumbed in 1922 when beckoned by Mary Pickford, the hard-nosed businesswoman disguised as America's sweetheart. Lubitsch—former

agile clog dancer on the German stage and orchestrator of grand historical epics such as *Anna Boleyn* (1920) and *The Loves of Pharaoh* (1922)—
was the German import who yielded the highest return on investment
as the master chef behind Hollywood's most sophisticated comedies of
manners. Unlike Europeans, American audiences "must have a happy
ending to be satisfied," he said after directing Pickford in the jaunty *Ros-
ita* (1923), plans to cast her against type as the doomed Marguerite in
Faust having fallen through (husband Douglas Fairbanks joked about
playing Mephistopheles). Besides a fat paycheck, the industrial support
network compensated Lubitsch for the need to leave 'em smiling.[4] "The
studio equipment is far superior to that of Europe and beyond doubt
American photography and lighting are the best in the world," he admitted. "And also the excellent developing and printing facilities make for
perfection in motion picture projection."[5]

In 1926, F. W. Murnau, the moody genius behind *Nosferatu, The
Last Laugh* (1924), and *Faust* (1926), was plucked from Ufa by the Fox
Film Corporation to direct *Sunrise* (1927), a Germanic tone poem whose
rhythms and lighting were unlike anything seen on home turf. Just as
the influx of immigrants at Ellis Island added fresh blood to the American melting pot, the marriage of Berlin artistry and Hollywood commerce was thought to generate a superior strain of moviemaking. *Sunrise*
"was adapted from *A Trip to Tilsit,* written by a German, Hermann Suder-
mann; the scenario was mapped out by another German, Carl Mayer, and
still another German, Murnau, directed it," enthused Winfield R. Sheehan, vice president and general production manager at Fox. "The production was made in Hollywood with Janet Gaynor and George O'Brien in
the principal roles. And this picture is to have its world premiere in Berlin this month [September 1927] at the Capitol Theatre."[6]

Luminaries like Lubitsch and Murnau had plenty of company. "American producers are bringing over foreign directors, mostly German, as
fast as they can pry them loose," reported *Moving Picture World* in 1926,
likening Ufa to a farm team training talent for the World Series in Hollywood. "Whenever a college baseball nine develops a Frisch or a Gehrig,
the big leagues grab him.[a] That's what we do to Germany."[7]

---

[a] A pair of future baseball Hall of Famers, slugger Frankie Fisch played second base for the New
York Giants and the durable Lou Gehrig played first base for the New York Yankees.

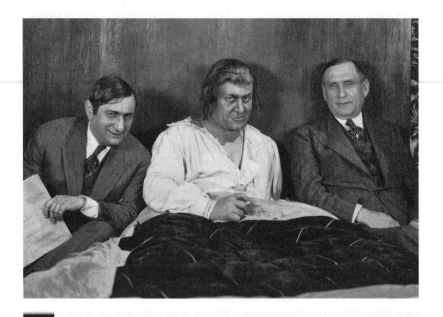

The German invasion: director Ernst Lubitsch and film star Emil Jannings welcome Alexander P. Moore, former ambassador to Spain, to the set of Paramount's *The Patriot* (1928).

By the late 1920s, the Hollywood-Berlin link was a roundtrip, with the passage marked by single degrees of separation. In 1927, *Variety* star Emil Jannings arrived in Hollywood to topline a string of pictures for Paramount, including *The Patriot* (1928), directed by his former countryman Lubitsch, and *The Last Command* (1928), directed by the Austrian-born Josef von Sternberg. Jannings was so pleased with the latter that he recommended von Sternberg for the directing assignment on *The Blue Angel* (1930), filmed at Ufa in both English- and German-language versions. Von Sternberg was so bewitched by his star Marlene Dietrich that he brought her back to Paramount, where they collaborated on a streak of eight smoldering melodramas trailing the scent of Weimar decadence.

Another fortuitous collaboration was between Paul Leni, director of the German hit *Das Wachsfigurenkabinett* (1924), released in the United States as *Waxworks*, and Universal, a corporate entity that married Hollywood and Berlin in the name of the studio's German branch, Deutsche

Universal. In *The Cat and the Canary* (1927) and *The Man Who Laughs* (1928), Leni's "Continental touch" and "weird lighting and unusual camera angles" were kept in check by "the American technique of picture production."[8] Critics and moguls alike agreed that cinematic opposites made beautiful films together.

When the German personnel could not be coaxed to California, the locals borrowed or stole outright from the Ufa playbook. King Vidor's *The Crowd* (1928) was a virtual homage to the geometric framing and spatial mobility that defined the house style at Ufa. Vidor trapped the mundane Everyman in *Caligari*-esque staircases and took his cameras out to Coney Island for giddy slide rides and dizzying whirligigs. Looking over at Murnau's light show on the Fox lot, director John Ford breathed in the atmospherics of dappled chiaroscuro, but even when Ufa alumni were not on the set, the Ufa style permeated Hollywood aesthetics—in the play of the light, the embroidery of the set design, and the contrapuntal rhythms of the editing.

Actually, few in Germany—or Sweden, Hungary, and England for that matter—resisted the siren call of the Hollywood studio system. It was easy to lure the foreign stars with a king's ransom in salary and seduce the directors with lavish budgets, gleaming technology, and god-sent weather. Hollywood was a promised land, if not quite paved with gold then papered with hard currency dollars impervious to the runaway inflation of the Weimar Republic. Well before synchronous dialogue came to the screen, foreign accents rang out from what were not then called soundstages: Lubitsch's clipped German, Michael Curtiz's thick Hungarian, and Victor Seastrom's melodious Swedish. Ufa chafed at the poaching of its prime talent, but the studio executives could not begrudge artists the chance to perform in the main ring of the greatest picture show on earth.

Basically, though, the Hollywood-Berlin express worked to the mutual advantage of both sides of the hyphen. In 1932, George R. Canty, the Berlin-based trade commissioner for the U.S. Department of Commerce, lauded "the extraordinarily friendly relations of the industries of the two countries during the past 10 years."[9] The diplomatic niceties held more than a kernel of truth. Germany was a lucrative market to cultivate and exploit, or a business rival to co-opt and crush, certainly not a geopolitical threat, still less a moral dilemma.

"THE HITLER ANTI-JEW THING"

On January 30, 1933, Adolf Hitler ascended to the Reich Chancellorship of Germany, second in command only to the aged and addled President Paul von Hindenburg, a brittle relic of the Great War. For the conservative German nationalists trying to suffocate the wheezing Weimar Republic and muzzle the radical Nazis, the idea was to keep Hitler on a tight leash, close and contained. Within days, Hitler had outmaneuvered his hapless opposition and begun the ruthless consolidation of power that transformed a dysfunctional democracy into a gangster state.

Initially, Hollywood was optimistic. "New Hitler government is liable to present some strange anomalies for the film industry," *Variety* admitted in its first analysis of the new regime, but "Hitler's policy definitely calls for friendliness to America." The upbeat prognosis is a fair expression of the wishful thinking and purblind vision that befogged the minds of stateside filmmakers throughout the 1930s. "Hitler has always been careful to play politics in a way to keep pleasant official relations with the United States and his program as outlined calls for continuation and extension of this policy," insisted the trade weekly.[10]

Encouraging the complacency was the news that the nationalist leader Dr. Alfred Hugenberg, chief stockholder in Ufa, had become Minister of Agriculture and Economics in Hitler's cabinet. Hugenberg, a media mogul who made his fortune in munitions during the Great War, added Ufa to his portfolio in 1927. Though an ardent monarchist who employed the usual antisemitic rhetoric in his newspaper chain, Hugenberg tempered his prejudices with a keen business sense. As owner and operator of Ufa, he made no attempt to purge the studio of the talented and revenue-generating Jews on the payroll.

That policy changed. A media potentate with greater power than either Hugenberg or a Hollywood mogul seized the means of motion picture production and set about harnessing German cinema to the will of the triumphant Nazis—Dr. Paul Joseph Goebbels, the ringleader of the mob that had broken up the Berlin premiere of *All Quiet on the Western Front* in 1930.

If Hitler was the godhead of the Third Reich, Goebbels was his most identifiable minion. Clubfooted, scrawny, a man of the arts not action, Goebbels was the physical antithesis of a sculpted Nazi *übermensch*, but he made up in fanatical intensity what he lacked in body mass. A

The new regime: Adolf Hitler and the second most identifiable face of Nazi Germany, Minister of Popular Enlightenment and Propaganda, Joseph Goebbels, in 1933.

dedicated *alte Kampfer* (old fighter) of the Nazi movement and a certified Ph.D. in Romance literature, Goebbels had aspired to be a novelist before finding his true calling as a virtuoso of media manipulation, a grand conductor playing upon all organs of German art and culture "as upon a vast keyboard," to use his own metaphor.[11] Lifted by Goebbels' multimedia barrage, the Nazis soared to power on a wave of print, sound, and imagery that tapped in to the darkest catacombs of the German psyche. Alert to a threat that struck at the heart of their own livelihood, American journalists fixated on the self-styled composer of Nazi grand operas. A *Time* magazine cover boy in 1933, a headline name, and a newsreel close-up, Goebbels was second only to Hitler as the face of Nazi Germany in the media-saturated 1930s.

Like Lenin, who famously said that cinema was the most important of the arts for the Bolsheviks, Goebbels reserved a central place for movies in the totalitarian state. "We are convinced that the film is one of the most modern and far-reaching means for influencing the masses," he declared. "A government can therefore not possibly leave the film world to itself."[12]

Goebbels' official platform for the promulgation of Nazism across the media was the Reich Ministry of Popular Enlightenment and Propaganda, formally launched on March 13, 1933, with the branch in charge of cinema called the Reichsfilmkammer. In whatever tongue, *propaganda* had long been a dirty word sullied by the official lies purveyed on all sides during the Great War. Goebbels and the Nazis embraced the term without apology.

To enlighten the outside world, Goebbels articulated the Nazi theory of propaganda at two public lectures—an inaugural speech at the Hotel Kaiserhof on March 28, 1933, and a harangue delivered on February 16, 1934, before all elements of the Federal Film Corporation assembled in the Kroll Opera, the provisional meeting place of the Reichstag. Distilled, the philosophy boiled down to a combustible brew of aesthetics, politics, and eugenics.

Flaunting his literary credentials, Goebbels paid due lip service to the aura of art. "Nobody shall be allowed to develop commercial activities who is void of all artistic feelings," he decreed. "Film has no place for mere profit-makers." But if profit alone was not a sufficient motive, politics certainly was. "Motion pictures should be places of entertainment and pleasure, but at the same time they should not neglect their task of cultural influence," he instructed. Above all, German cinema "must be penetrated with German spirit and culture."[13]

Tracking back around again, Goebbels insisted that art, though a servant of politics, should not be a didactic snooze. "I don't expect every film to begin and end with Nazi parades," he joked. "Leave the parades to us. We understand more about it." Like any executive producer, he wanted patrons in the seats and eyes glued to the screen. "I am convinced that if a cinema theater here in Berlin would show a picture which would be a real national-socialist 'cruiser,'[b] this theater would be sold out for a long time."[14]

In ricocheting back and forth between art and ideology, Goebbels sent out wildly contradictory messages. In one breath he would expound on

---

[b] The "cruiser" reference was to Eisenstein's *Battleship Potemkin* (1925), sometimes billed as *The Cruiser Potemkin*, still alive in the German memory as the supreme cinematic expression of art in the service of politics. "Films that had made the deepest impression on [me] personally were *Potemkin*, a perfect artistic picture, although with a Bolshevist tendency; *Anna Karenina* [Frederic Zelnik, 1919], *Die Nibelungen* [Fritz Lang, 1924], and *Der Rebell* [Luis Trenker, 1932]," Goebbels elaborated. In his report on the speech to the U.S. Department of Commerce, George R. Canty pointed out that Goebbels was "probably unaware when he made this statement that all four of these [films] were turned out by Jews." (George R. Canty, Weekly Report No. 40, Apr. 1, 1933. Record Group 151, Records of the Bureau of Foreign and Domestic Commerce, National Archives, College Park, MD.)

the pure beauty of transcendent art, and in the next demand that all art be yoked inextricably to politics. German films must be brought "in still closer harmony with the spirit of [the] new young Germany," but they also must be aesthetically inspirational "because throughout the world they are regarded as the cultural product of National Socialism."[15] Over the next twelve years, Goebbels regularly pitched fits at the failure of Nazi filmmaking to rise to the level of Weimar glory or Hollywood quality.

Yet however muddled about the proper ratio of art to politics, the Nazi philosophy of film was, in one respect, clearheaded and single-minded. "The elimination of the Jews" from the work of cultural production in Germany was the prime directive. "Here and there that may lead to a human tragedy," Goebbels admitted. "But that is not apt to touch us since there were many human tragedies in the past 14 years which, however, did not affect the Jews but us."[16] On the Jewish question, Goebbels brooked no compromise.[17] Eugenics—not art, not politics—determined the course of Nazi cinema. "The German public's taste and psychology are not such as a Jewish director imagines them to be. In order to have a true picture of what the German people want and like, one must be German."

The official name for the policy was Aryanization—the purging of Jews from the economic and cultural life of Germany and their replacement with purebred Aryans, a crackpot racial category whose supreme incarnation was the mythic hero Siegfried in Fritz Lang's *The Nibelungen* (1924), a blood-spattered blond muscleman slaying dragons to the strains of a Richard Wagner score.

Even before Goebbels laid down the law, the Nazi rhetoric on race was being implemented by pumped-up S.A. thugs and zealous party bureaucrats. From Berlin radiating outward, the iron grip tightened over all aspects of film-related culture—artists and technicians, film content and style, trade periodicals and reviewer bylines, theater ownership and ticket buyers. Like the rest of the Reich, German cinema was to be *Judenfrei*— free of Jewish presence.

The elimination of Jews from the German film industry was sudden, ruthless, and comprehensive. By April 1933, the Reichsverband Deutscher Theaterbesitzer, the exhibitor consortium roughly equivalent to the Motion Picture Theater Owners of America, declared itself free of Jewish personnel.[18] The next month, the *Film–Kurier*, the motion picture trade daily that served as the German version of *Variety*, published by Alfred Weiner and his son Lucien Madelik-Weiner, both Jews, was reborn as a Reichsfilmkammer mouthpiece.[19] Across the lines of production, distribution, and exhibition, Nazis refused to deal with Jews, or Germans who dared to deal with Jews.

On July 1, 1933, a new law regulating the production and importation of motion pictures in Germany codified the antisemitic actions that had already been initiated by roving gangs of brownshirts.[20] "Adolf Hitler's Nazi plan prohibiting Jews from appearing or participating in German motion picture production finally became a law," read the forlorn dispatch in *Motion Picture Herald*. "The new law . . . not only excludes Jewish creative workers from any part in German production, but also prohibits American producers working in Germany from engaging Jews for films which they make in that country." By then, Dr. Hugenberg, the hoped-for "brake on Nazi radicalism," had been forced out of Hitler's cabinet.[21]

The most conspicuous casualty was the jewel of the German motion picture industry, the only production plant in the world that Hollywood respected, feared, and imitated. Within weeks, Ufa was hollowed out of its core talent—its artists, technicians, and office staff booted, sometimes literally, from the studio lot in Neubabelsberg. Toby Brenner, a Kansas City exhibitor on business in Berlin at the height of the purges, surveyed his German associates and tallied up the toll. Even before the official decree of July 1, Ufa had discharged 296 out of 310 Jews on the payroll.[22]

Among the first to be sacked was Erich Pommer, Ufa's longtime head of production and guiding visionary, then in charge of its topline production unit. Pommer was something of a unique case. Even Goebbels recognized him as an irreplaceable asset, at least for the short term, a hands-on executive whose abrupt departure would unravel the conveyer belt of production. Pommer was later told that "despite his race" he could return to work, under strict conditions, but, being in possession of a passport and an exit visa, he declined the offer and fled to Paris.[23] Pommer produced for Fox at the Joinville studios outside of the French capital, then went to London, and finally settled in Hollywood.

Another illustrious name despised by the new Germany was Max Reinhardt, the famed theatrical impresario and motion picture producer. "Professor Reinhardt (born Jew Goldman), ruled not long ago as High Priest of the Stage over no less than four Berlin theatres," gloated a Nazi mouthpiece after Reinhardt's ouster. "His worthless and soul-less art was passionately preached to a deluded German people by the Jew press."

The elimination of Jews from the work of cultural production: purged from Ufa and run out of Berlin, theatrical impresario Max Reinhardt signs a contract with Jack L. Warner to direct *A Midsummer Night's Dream* (1935). Producer Hal B. Wallis (*right*) looks on.

Reinhardt fled to Austria, which was not far enough away: in 1934, he escaped injury when a bomb exploded in his castle in Salzburg. He later found safe haven at Warner Bros.

The final holdouts from the ranks of big-name producers were the team of Arnold Pressburger and the Russian-born Dr. Gregor Rabinovitz, who managed to hang on until 1934. Pressburger escaped to Britain, Rabinovitz—described by *Variety*'s Cecelia Ager as "the very last non-Aryan permitted to function in the picture business under Hitler"—fled to Vienna, then France, and in 1936 to Hollywood, lured by a production deal at Universal.[24]

On the streets, the brownshirts gave daily reminders of fates worse than summary dismissal and exile. In Austria, the theatrical impresario Alfred Rotter and his wife were killed by Nazi thugs in a botched kidnap plot.[25] In Berlin, the German motion picture exhibitor David Oliver barely escaped with his life when his taxi was firebombed by brownshirts.[26]

Pommer, Reinhardt, Pressburger, Rabinovitz, and Rotter—all were brand-name businessmen of international stature whom the Hollywood moguls had haggled with and, in some cases, escorted around their studio backlots. Even in distant California, the news hit close to home.

Glibly at first, more grimly as the scale of the purges and seriousness of the stakes became apparent, the motion picture trade press tracked the ebb and flow of what *Variety* called "the Hitler anti-Jew thing."[27] "The Nazi regime has made a clean sweep and, by slow stages, has turned the entire stage and screen over to departmental functionaries of Hitlerdom," reported Wolfe Kaufman in June 1934, appalled at how quickly the heart had been cut out of Weimar cinema. "The last German Jew is out of the film business in Berlin." Kaufman was including himself. *Variety*'s veteran Berlin correspondent had fled home to file his report from the safety of New York.[28]

In Hollywood, the Nazi determination to sabotage a thriving industry in the midst of a worldwide economic meltdown baffled studio heads and tradewise journalists. Ufa manufactured one of the few German products bringing in a steady flow of hard currency from overseas. "Getting rid [of] or curbing [Jews] would about clean out half the Berlin film industry," *Variety* sputtered, making a lowball estimate. Surely, eventually, the Nazis would "minimize the anti-Jew thing" as a concession to economic reality.[29]

A few bottom-liners gloated that Berlin's loss would be Hollywood's gain. "With Jews out of German filming and the German film industry pretty well crippled, it ought to be a perfect moment for American product to walk in and clean up," figured *Variety*, getting over its astonishment to hear opportunity knocking.[30] Besides, "outside of the Jewish question the government has no especial quarrel with American filmers."[31]

But mainly the moguls and the trade reporters were more mystified than mercenary. Why would any sane businessman sack his best people and slash his own profit margins? "The entire German film industry is bordering on complete extinction as a result of the Nazi management," wrote the *Hollywood Reporter* in 1934. "What was once the outstanding production center of all Europe has now turned into a joke."[32] Not that anyone was laughing.

THE ARYANIZATION OF AMERICAN IMPORTS

Wherever motion pictures were made or marketed, censorship was the cost of doing business. Whether by government bureaucrats or self-appointed moral guardians, at the hands of state boards or ad hoc committees, under law or without portfolio, censoring cinema was a multinational pastime. The cuts were nation-specific; the practice was universal.

To sell its product overseas, Hollywood learned to navigate foreign shoals with sensitivities attuned to the quirks of national character. The British flinched at cruelty to animals, the French bristled at the slightest slight to Gallic honor, and Mexicans seethed at the sight of greasy banditos and spicy senoritas. "Dressing a Chinaman in the wrong hat brings official protests from the Imperial Government and hot tamales served as free lunch means the instant convening of the Mexican Congress in extra session," griped the *Film Daily* in 1934.[33] So much was lost in translation.

Prior to 1933, film censorship in Germany was of a piece—irksome, idiosyncratic, and costly—but only after the Nazis came to power did it become systematic, fixated, and bizarre. Under Goebbels, the Nazis established a strict new censorship regime that consolidated the scatter-shot dictates of provincial and city boards into a top-down bureaucracy. The move was part of a nationwide coordination of German culture in accord with the Nazi principle of *Gleichschaltung*—all circuits of the national grid firing in unity from a central command post.[34]

Under Nazi censorship, Hollywood films seeking play dates in Germany had to clear three hurdles. First, in a policy predating the Nazi era, a film needed to obtain an import permit under a strict "Kontingent" or quota arrangement limiting the total number of foreign films allowed into Germany. The Nazis added a second layer of review by requiring that a certificate issued by the Reich Ministry of Popular Enlightenment and Propaganda be obtained before the import permit could be granted. Third, the film then needed to pass the home censor, who scrutinized the contents for moral, political, and eugenic purity. At any of the three stages, a Hollywood film could be shut out or banned—denied entry in the first place under the quota restrictions, denied a certificate from the Reich Ministry of Popular Entertainment and Propaganda, or forbidden exhibition if failing to pass the third cut from the home censor. The film could also be censored and then cleared for exhibition in a version edited to Nazi specifications.

In many ways, the filter of Nazi censorship was business as usual. Like national censorship boards throughout Europe and Latin America, indeed across the United States, the Nazis banned scenes of communist agitation, social unrest, and immorality in word or image. In its aversion to civic upheaval and moral transgression, Nazi censorship was no more or less onerous than the edicts handed down by the Chicago Board of Censors or the Kansas State Board of Review. Goebbels' Reich Ministry of Popular Entertainment and Propaganda condemned Ernst Lubitsch's sly comedy of manners, *Design for Living* (1933), in language that might have been echoed by Victorian censor boards across America. "The film is not acceptable for new Germany because of the irony with which the establishment of marriage is treated," it decreed. "The fact that the story has been handled with humor and satire cannot conceal the fact that a laxity is created in the morals of the audience and that the human contacts and laws are played with in a frivolous manner which does not permit of conformity to the efforts towards protection of marriage vows and family life."[35] Prudish Nazis also blocked Fox's musical comedy *My Weakness* (1933) on the grounds that "the lace panties of the girls would contaminate the morals of new Germany."[36]

In one way, however, the Nazi eye on cinema was unique and unblinking. The new censorship regime forbade the importation of "any film in which Jewish characters appear or [that] presents a cheerful aspect of Jewish life." The sudden German aversion to all things Jewish was a wholly original and unsettling obstacle for a business whose executive ranks were dominated by American Jews of foreign origin and whose screen credits, Americanized or not, often denoted same.

Knowing the temperament of the new regime in Germany, no studio wasted time or money trying to obtain an import license for *The Cohens and the Kellys in Hollywood* (1932), but the Nazis' sensitivity to actors, characters, or plot points that smacked of Jewishness went well beyond vaudeville comics mouthing Yiddish-inflected malapropisms. MGM's *The Prizefighter and the Lady* (1933) was banned because the boxer was played by heavyweight champion Max Baer, who, though not a Jew, was widely thought to be so because he wore a Star of David on his boxing trunks. *The Rise of Catherine the Great* (1934), a British production released through United Artists, was banned because Viennese star Elisabeth Bergner, formerly the toast of the Berlin stage, was a known "Jewess." After the 1934 announcement that Max Reinhardt would direct *A Midsummer Night's Dream* (1935) for Warner Bros., and that the exiled showman would use the traditional score by Felix Mendelssohn, the project was banned preemptively a year before its release.[37] Having already been barred for the immorality of *Design for Living*, Ernst Lubitsch was again denied an import license for *The Merry Widow* (1934), this time on racial grounds.[38] Of course, the Lubitsch touch—the tactile signature of a German Jew from the Weimar Republic—made his films doubly noxious.

Still, since few Hollywood productions were totally free of a Jewish character lurking somewhere in the cast or credits, the ratio of Jewishness had to reach a critical mass before tripping the Nazi alarm. "Jews being in a picture don't get it banned, except in extreme cases," *Variety* pointed out. "With a percentage of the cast non-Jewish, film is okay, providing story is considered clean enough and not touched with political or Communistic tendencies."[39] So at least was the theory. Often, however, the offensive Jewish element was so far down on the list of screen credits as to be invisible to all but the Nazi eye. Paramount's *Give Us This Night* (1936) was rejected because the musical score was composed by Erich Korngold, a Viennese Jew.[40]

In whatever role, two imported Hollywood stars, both non-Jews, were toxic to the Nazi system: Marlene Dietrich, the blue angel of Ufa turned blonde Venus at Paramount, and Charles Chaplin, the comedian whose politics were as poisonous as his persona was blasphemous.

Though a picture of Aryan beauty, Dietrich was not a fair-haired model of *Kinder, Küche, und Kirche*, the Nazi motto relegating a woman's place to children, kitchen, and church. That Dietrich, the most famous German actress on the planet, was cavorting in the enemy camp enraged Nazi film theorists. "With all severity, we must take exception against the fact that an actress of German origin, who is also recognized in the whole world as German, continues to play the role of a hussy in all her pictures," read a statement rebuking her scandalous behavior in Paramount's *The Song of Songs* (1933).[41] When, on a three-month trip to Europe in 1933, Dietrich visited London and Paris but snubbed Berlin, the Nazis retaliated by banning *The Blue Angel* (1930) and *Blonde Venus* (1932).[c] "I have a long contract in Hollywood and I shall probably never return to make films in Germany," she announced, further unhinging the Nazi establishment.[42]

---

[c] Later, the German passion for a native daughter caused even the Nazis to relent. Frank Borzage's *Desire* (1936), from Paramount, produced by Ernst Lubitsch, was cleared for a German release and did huge business in Berlin, where it was released a week *before* its New York premiere. "Miss Dietrich was not liked by the Nazis for a while, but seems to be officially okay now," puzzled *Variety*. ("Dietrich Bows Ahead of N.Y.," *Variety*, May 13, 1936: 13.)

"A hussy in all her pictures": Marlene Dietrich, Germany's most famous defector to Hollywood, with Brian Aherne in Rouben Mamoulian's romantic melodrama, *The Song of Songs* (1933).

Not even Marlene Dietrich infuriated the Nazis as much as Charles Chaplin, who was ideologically, racially, and visually objectionable to the Third Reich. Born just four days apart in 1889, Hitler and Chaplin were pegged as cinematic doppelgängers as soon as the former achieved the fame of the latter. With matching physique, profile, and toothbrush moustache, the pair made for an irresistible Janus–face-off between jester and tyrant.

In 1933, Chaplin's name appeared on a Nazi list of "prominent non-Aryans," and, although not Jewish, he refused to deny it.[43] When Chaplin joked about shaving the Tramp's trademark moustache so his beloved alter ego would not be mistaken for Hitler, the Nazis took the bait. The "repellent yapping little Jew" who dared tweak the *führer*, frothed the *Film-Kurier*, was beneath the contempt of the butt of his joke. "The creator and leader of new Germany, the war veteran and staunch friend of

"A repellent yapping little Jew": Nazi nemesis Charles Chaplin in his anti-authoritarian comedy *Modern Times* (1936).

the new German film, stands much too high to even hear the barking of a dog from London's ghetto."[44]

Predictably, *Modern Times* (1936), Chaplin's long-gestating silent comedy defiantly released in the sound era, was rejected sight unseen. A spokesman for Goebbels stated that although United Artists had not submitted the film to the German censor, its banning was a foregone conclusion. "Nazi objection to *Modern Times* is based more on the convictions, firmly held by the authorities, that Chaplin is a Jew than on the film's supposed 'Marxist' tendencies," explained *Variety*.[45]

As the 1930s wore on, the list of films and personalities banned by the Nazis grew longer and more perplexing. "These certificates [from Goebbels' Reich Ministry] are now being refused one after another without reason being given except vague statements that the cast of the picture is not satisfactory, the story is silly, or unsuitable, etc.," complained Douglas

Miller, the acting commercial attaché at the U.S. Embassy in Berlin in 1936. "Our film representatives are referred from one official to another and can obtain very little in the way of definite refusals in writing; they are simply faced with a campaign of delay and evasion."[46]

The aversion to any trace of Jewishness in Hollywood cinema at least made sense, but the banning of *Charlie Chan at the Olympics* (1937) and the Dionne quintuplet films eluded rational explanation. Did the inscrutable Oriental detective sport too laconically with the Third Reich's gamesters? Did the hyperbolic fertility of the Canadian family set an impossible reproductive standard for the Fatherland's motherhood? Even Shirley Temple could be insufficiently wholesome for the Nazis, who banned *The Little Colonel* (1935), Fox's Dixiefied depiction of a Reconstructed South. In this case, though, the reason was plain enough: the "racial defilement" showcased in a hand-holding tap dance between little Shirley and the African American hoofer Bill "Bojangles" Robinson.[47]

Not suitable for the new Germany: Shirley Temple and Bill "Bojangles" Robinson show too much interracial harmony in *Just Around the Corner* (1938).

Like jazz music, that other racial pollutant from American popular culture, Hollywood expeditions into dark African rhythms and jungle locations were condemned with the Nazi epithet *entartete Kunst* (degenerate art). MGM's *Tarzan the Ape Man* (1932) was "perilous to Nazi theories" and RKO's *King Kong* (1933) was "nerve wracking and repugnant [to] German race instincts." Only after a lengthy appeal by RKO, and Nazi-editing of the beast's caressing of the blonde beauty, was *King Kong* cleared for exhibition.[48]

The Nazis also banned Hollywood films with no discernable *entartete* elements or Jewish influence on the grounds that someone in the cast, perhaps years previously, either in public or on screen, had done something somewhere deemed detrimental to German prestige. The practice fell under a broad, all-purpose category of "cultural reprisals" taken in response to perceived slights from Hollywood. "The reprisal policy may explain away the mystery about the banning from German screens of certain film stars who are clearly not amenable to the Nazi drive against non-Aryans," speculated the *Hollywood Reporter*, puzzling over why the likes of Fred Astaire, Ginger Rogers, Johnny Weissmuller, and Mae West were not agile, fit, or blonde enough for Nazi eyes.[49]

THE ARYANIZATION OF HOLLYWOOD'S PAYROLL

Hollywood films slated for exhibition in Germany might be cut, redubbed, or banned. People were not as easily removed from the picture. German and American alike, the personnel who manned the Berlin branch offices of the Hollywood studios were also subject to Nazi inspection. "Adolf Hitler's decree governing the personnel of the motion picture business in Germany literally means, 'Show me your grandmother and I'll tell you if you can work,'" read the gruff warning in *Motion Picture Herald* after the antisemitic decree issued on July 1, 1933. "Passport, birth certificate, and proof of religion of grandparents must be submitted for inspection to Mr. Hitler's 'brown shirts'—or else."[50] At the time, the "or else" still meant termination of employment only, but for the predominantly Jewish American executives back in Hollywood, the edict presented a delicate human resources problem.

In the 1920s, the major Hollywood studios had set up offices in Berlin to smooth the way for imports, supervise coproduction deals with

German studios, and, after the arrival of sound, oversee dubbing sessions for German versions of American films. The staff also kept an eye on Hollywood profits tied up in German banks—"frozen assets" that could only be spent in Germany or perhaps leveraged back home after paying exorbitant penalties and exchange rates. All the majors and most of the minors operated a Berlin office managed either by a Hollywood representative or a German citizen, with the office staff and traveling salesmen drawn from the locals. Universal, Paramount, and Warner Bros. also maintained ancillary offices in Düsseldorf and Frankfurt. MGM had by far the largest foothold with seven offices spread throughout Germany.

During the wide-open heyday of the Weimar Republic, a posting in Berlin was a plum assignment. The city throbbed with a vibrant nightlife that catered to outré sexual appetites, all better sampled with a strong dollar. Louise Brooks, one of the few actresses who reversed the Berlin-to-Hollywood trajectory to trade contract player status at Paramount for immortality in G. W. Pabst's *Pandora's Box* (1929) and *The Diary of a Lost Girl* (1929), testified that the lurid glitz later staged in *Cabaret* (1972) was not all musical fantasy. "Sex was the business of the town," she recalled wistfully. "At the Eden Hotel, where I lived in Berlin, the café bar was lined with the higher-priced trollops. The economy girls walked the street outside. On the corner stood the girls in boots, advertising flagellation. Actors' agents pimped for the ladies in luxury apartments in the Bavarian quarter. Race-track touts at the Hoppegarten arranged orgies for groups of sportsmen. The nightclub Eldorado displayed an enticing line of homosexuals dressed as women. At the Maly, there was a choice of feminine or collar-and-tie lesbians. Collective lust roared unashamed at the theater."[51]

After January 30, 1933, a tour in Berlin was combat duty. Tapped telephone calls, rifled mail, and, for Jews, the palpable threat of physical assault replaced floorshows and hookups. In 1934, looking out from his plush suite in the Adlon Hotel in Berlin, *Film Daily* publisher Jack Alicoate nervously watched the new Germany march by. "Before one could say Pilsner, a crack German detachment with colors flying and bands playing passes our window where formerly kings and princes stood. Followed shortly by a Nazi troop in full uniform. Makes one feel like a war correspondent."[52]

Officially, American Jews holding U.S. passports were a protected class, but to the roving bands of brownshirts, a Jew was a Jew. Soon after

Hitler seized power, disturbing reports filtered back to Hollywood about studio employees and visiting film folk being threatened, insulted, and worse. Nathaniel Wolff, co-owner of the Lyceum Theater in Rochester, New York, was kidnapped from a Berlin hotel, dragged to a nearby forest, and beaten senseless. When the American ambassador protested, the Hitler government apologized, blaming the incident on communist *agents provocateurs* dressed as brownshirts.[53]

The ad hoc thuggery was prologue to the first official outpouring of antisemitic fervor orchestrated by the new government. On April 1, 1933, the Nazis launched a violent, one-day boycott of Jewish businesses. Three weeks later, newsreel shots of shattered windows, antisemitic signage, and gleeful brownshirts cavorting through the streets of Berlin on trucks played in American theaters. "Deutsch! Wehrt Euch! Kauft nicht bei Juden!" read the placards. ("Germans! Defend Yourselves! Don't Buy from Jews!") Shot without sound, the newsreel imagery did not pick up the cries of "Juden heraus!" ("Jews out!") that filled the air.

The antisemitic slogan brayed on the streets was an imperative command not only for German Jews. "Every Jewish film man employed in all of the American film offices and branches in Germany will have to be removed," reported *Variety* in a boldfaced bulletin on April 18, 1933. "That's comprehensive and official, taking in all the companies and making not a single exception."[54]

A few weeks later, the managers of the Hollywood branch offices in Berlin were said to have "decided it was the wisest thing to flee the country."[55] The report was premature. Each of the studios responded according to its own business model and comfort level. For most, the German market, under whatever management, was too lucrative to abandon.

The German lineage of Carl Laemmle had long given Universal Pictures the coziest connections to Germany. Alone of the Hollywood majors, Universal maintained an ambitious production schedule in Germany. When Hitler came to power, the studio had two expensive projects in postproduction, the initial entries in a planned slate of sixteen coproductions: director-writer-star Luis Trenker's *The Rebel* (U.S. release, July 1933), a snowbound mountain film set during the Napoleonic wars; and *S.O.S. Iceberg* (U.S. release, September 1933), an adventure film, shot on location in Greenland, both overseen by Universal's ace foreign production manager Paul Kohner. Unwilling to write off the investments, the studio "played along" with the new regime until both films were in the can. Caught in the cultural lag, *S.O.S. Iceberg*, the last of the joint ventures between Hollywood and Berlin, collided with Nazi racial policy in the final weeks of production. After safeguarding the negative, valued at $450,000, under lock and key in Switzerland, director Tay Garnett took the non-Jewish members of the cast and crew to Berlin to complete shooting of the interiors. The Jews stayed in Switzerland.[56]

Garnett's gentile crew might have passed the Jews working for Universal in Berlin going in the opposite direction. Max Friedland, general European representative for the studio and a nephew of Carl Laemmle, fled to Switzerland, leaving the home office flatfooted. "We have not heard a word from Germany in over a week," said a Universal representative. "[The Nazis] are maintaining the strictest censorship possible." Friedland had good reason to be spooked: the Nazis had yanked him out of his bed early one morning and hauled him off to prison.[57] After five hours of incarceration, though by his own account no physical abuse, he was released. Friedland later used *Variety*'s well-connected Berlin correspondent, Heinrich Fraenkel, to put out a cover story. "Max Friedland [is] amused at Hollywood rumor that he escaped to Switzerland," reported Fraenkel. "Fact is, that he'd only been there for a short business trip. He's back at his desk as U's European boss."[58] Not for long: by year's end Friedland had set up headquarters in Paris with "a number of minor employees who found Naziland uncomfortable," including the trilingual Paul Kohner, an American citizen. (Friedland spoke only German.)[59] By July 1934, Universal had sold its assets and bolted from the homeland of its founder.[60]

Fox Film Corporation also had a long and congenial relationship with Germany. Besides importing high-profile Ufa directors such as F. W. Murnau and Ludwig Berger, the studio operated a German unit of Fox Movietone News, its top-of-the-line newsreel. Though Fox had been founded by William Fox, a Jew, its day-to-day operations were managed by Winfield Sheehan, a Roman Catholic, and its foreign arm by his brother Clayton. Yiddish not being quite the *lingua franca* at Fox as it was at the other studios, the company was tagged, in context, as the *goyishe* studio.

Fox's outpost in Berlin was headed by Henry W. Kahn, a Jew. In the run-up to the April 1 boycott, a rattled Kahn fled to Paris, straight into the unsympathetic arms of Clayton Sheehan, who happened to be in Europe on a tour of Fox's foreign branches. Sheehan ordered Kahn back to his desk "to face things out." To buck Kahn up, Sheehan escorted his reluctant underling to Berlin before himself heading back to New York. Soon realizing Kahn's position was untenable, management reversed itself and sent P. N. Brink, a former MGM executive in Paris and a non-Jew, to Berlin to replace him. Fox kept Kahn on the payroll, transferring him to Austria, but he left the studio the next summer after turning down an assignment in Calcutta.[61]

Paramount sent mixed signals. At first, the studio notified its 150 Berlin-based employees that it was closing up shop as of June 30, 1933. Given its "general financial headaches" (in the depth of the Great Depression, Paramount was on the brink of bankruptcy), the studio couldn't "afford to toy with a conflagration like Germany at a time like this."[62] Toy it did, however, being unwilling to walk away from any potential profit center. Paramount was fortunate in the lineage of its top Berlin employee, Gus Schaeffer, who was not Jewish. Though eager to return stateside, Schaeffer was ordered by the home office to stay put and mind the store. Meanwhile, the Jewish heads of Paramount's branch offices in Frankfurt and Düsseldorf were cashiered and replaced with racially acceptable management.

MGM, the self-styled Tiffany studio run by the rock-ribbed Republican Louis B. Mayer, had the biggest financial stake in Germany. Its man in Berlin was Frits Strengholt, a Dutchman and a non-Jew, who left for Holland when things got hot (you didn't have to be Jewish to feel uneasy in the new Germany) but returned when the situation calmed down—that is, when the first wave of Jew-purging violence had achieved the desired result.

Companies with less extensive holdings in Germany closed up shop quietly and arranged for their German business to be handled from other European capitals through German intermediaries. RKO claimed to be conducting business as usual, but transferred William Linsenmeier, its Jewish man in Berlin, out of the country. United Artists did likewise with Christopher Goldstein.[63] Armed with identification papers from trade commissioner George R. Canty, Dr. B. Lange of Columbia Pictures joined the exodus of studio branch managers who figured, as Canty put it, "that they could operate just as effectively [from Paris or London] as from Berlin (and with considerably more personal comfort)."[64]

Warner Bros. was a unique case, as it would be in most things concerning the Nazis in the 1930s. The head of the studio's branch office in Berlin was a British subject and a Jew named Phil Kaufman. What happened to Kaufman in the early days of the Third Reich rattled nerves throughout Hollywood—and earned the Nazis the undying enmity of his employers.

Kaufman's brush with Nazism was highlighted in a front-page article in *Variety* detailing Hollywood's travails under the new order. "Warner Brothers' Berlin representative, Phil Kaufman, is one of the few film men to get actual man-handling in Berlin," it reported. "His automobile stolen by Nazis, his house ransacked and himself beaten, despite the fact that he's British." *Variety* capped the account with an acid comment: "The Nazis later apologized to [Kaufman], explaining it was only a mistake. They thought he was two other fellows."[65]

Soon afterwards, Kaufman was said to be "scrambling to Paris for safety."[66] Warner Bros. executive Charles MacDonald denied the sense of urgency if not the departure. "What actually happened was that Kaufman was ordered to leave Berlin," said MacDonald. "He returned last Monday [April 25, 1933], however, and we expect he will remain there."[67] Kaufman, however, was not to remain in Berlin. He was quietly moved out of Germany and, based out of London, placed in charge of European operations.

The denouement to the Kaufman story may or may not have been written on the streets of Berlin, but that December, while in Stockholm, Kaufman suddenly collapsed and died. "Kaufman had been suffering from liver trouble for some years and was here [in Sweden] for treatment," reported *Daily Variety*, making no mention of the beating by brownshirts.[68] Back at Warner Bros., however, a suspicion soon hardened into gospel that Kaufman had been beaten to death by the Nazis. To the end of his days, studio head Jack L. Warner believed that Kaufman "had been murdered by Nazi killers in Berlin."[69]

In truth, with the Nazis controlling transatlantic telegraph and telephone lines, it was hard to separate rumor from fact. For weeks at a time, studios were in the dark about conditions on the ground. "We actually don't know what is going on," said an RKO executive in April 1933. "There has been no definite word from Germany in weeks."[70]

From his post in Berlin, trade commissioner George R. Canty was only slightly better positioned as he tried to figure out the Nazi policy on Hollywood's Jewish employees, whether American citizens or German nationals. Importuned by frazzled branch managers and staffers, he did his best to reassure and protect the business associates with whom, over the years, he had become friends. Canty's weekly reports to his superiors back at the Department of Commerce in Washington, D.C., trace a steady escalation from optimism, to alarm, and finally to disgust.

February 18, 1933: As regards the reported anti-Semitic plans of the Nazis, I doubt seriously that these will get down to any interference with American film managers, in case New York has any uneasiness on that score. Unquestionably, petty members of the party will raise questions now and then of embarrassment to foreign film managers of the Jewish faith, but I can not see that these will bother American trade interests so long as the managers in question are in good standing in the Spio.[d]

April 16, 1933: I have continued to advise all and sundry to keep cool in the way of waiting out the excitement surrounding the initiation of the movement [against the Jews]. That this counsel has been wise is probably proved by reports from our company managers that little by little they are receiving assurances of protection for many of their employees of the Jewish faith. I am still able to report that not one of our employees has been discharged because of the anti-Semitic feeling here. Although I believe a couple of our general managers, probably seeing the handwriting on the wall as regards the continued antipathy against Jewish salesmen, have of their own volition transferred as many of their employees as possible to foreign offices.

June 3, 1933: Although the film department of the Propaganda Ministry and the industry itself seem to be without competent head or tail and do not know in which direction they are going, the Ministry, nevertheless, is carrying out some of its promises. . . . First of all, they drove the best film experience they had right out of the market when they attacked the Jews so viciously at the outset of the boycott and now, while they are reported secretly to be trying to get some of them back, it is a question how much success they will have.

In Hollywood, the really old-timers—veterans of the patent wars from the dawn of cinema—remembered the rough-and-tumble days when burly Pinkerton guards attacked camera operators and disrupted

---

[d] "New York" referred to the headquarters of the Motion Picture Producers and Distributors of America. The Spio was the Spitzenorganization der Filmwirtschaft, the Film Industry Summit Organization, soon to be supplanted by the Reichsfilmkammer.

film shoots. By the early 1930s, studio executives preferred to fight their battles with lawyers. The hands-on brutality in Germany was difficult to believe and harder to fathom.

Regardless, the Nazi decrees were impossible to flout. The studios had two options—obey or pull up stakes. Warner Bros. was out by the end of 1933, the first of the majors to withdraw on principle, followed by United Artists, Universal, RKO, and Columbia. With the exception of Warner Bros., however, even the studios officially out of business in Germany maintained back-channel communications and intermediaries in country. Universal kept options open with a five-pictures-a-year deal with German distributors. United Artists conducted business through offices in Paris and London via the Bayerische Film Company in Munich. Moreover, if the Nazis offered to buy a Hollywood film outright, or to put up cash guarantees up front, the exiled studios—again, always excepting Warner Bros.—were willing to deal. Neither boycotts on one side nor blockades on the other were airtight: films had a way of slipping over the borders.[71]

Paramount, Fox, and MGM decided to stay open for business. The three holdouts "have too much coin tied up there [in Germany] and may be able to get some of it back by sticking," explained *Variety*. "They are loath to forget it and mark the sum down as a net loss."[72] To avoid the net loss meant acceding to Nazi hiring practices. "American companies are beginning to reorganize their Berlin business staffs to coincide with Nazi orders to get rid of Jewish help," *Variety* confirmed in May 1933. "For a very short time there was talk of not giving in, but most of the companies now feel it's the wisest course."[73]

Forced to fire their crack Jewish salesmen—on average, half of the payroll—the three studios scrambled to recruit a workforce without the proscribed bloodlines. An elaborate ethno-religious shell game ensued, as they moved Jewish American employees out of Germany and transferred non-Jews from other European capitals into Berlin to fill the slots. MGM issued a brusque order to its employees in Spain: brush up on your German. "American attitude on the matter is that American companies cannot afford to lose the German market at this time no matter what the inconvenience of the personnel shifts," shrugged *Variety*.[74]

As the studios shuffled their overseas personnel, the home offices were circumspect about their actions—in part, due to shame over their compliance with the antisemitic decrees, in part out of concern for their men on the ground.[75] "Claiming that they still have financial interests, property, and relatives in Germany, Jewish film folk here [in Hollywood] from that country refused to comment on the anti-Semitic campaign being waged by Hitler and the Nazis for fear of possible reprisals," *Variety* reported. "Writers, directors, and a producer who were approached claim that any statement ascribed to them might bring on physical violence to their families and property confiscations in Germany."[76] Fox's Clayton Sheehan commented that "it would be dangerous to say anything publicly which might react upon our workers over there. The moment anything is said in the public prints in this country it is cabled back to Germany by Nazi agents."[77]

After having obediently played musical chairs with their Jewish personnel overseas, the studios felt entitled to some consideration from the Nazis. "Attitude of Paramount, Metro and several other U.S. companies is that they have complied with race requirements of Nazi Germany insofar as their business staffs and offices in Germany are concerned and that they ought to be given a break on the films concerned," reported *Variety*.[78] The rough treatment of the imported films was the main concern. By the end of the year, the unimaginable had become standard business practice.

During the first wave of Nazi terror, the commentary from motion picture industry journalists and Hollywood producers reflects the natural befuddlement of cool businessmen up against hot-headed fanatics. With few exceptions, stateside professionals evinced an understandable obliviousness to the enormity of what was happening on the ground, still less what was on the horizon. Surely, the fever would eventually break and the sane, sober Germans would return to their senses. Before his own eyes were opened, trade representative Canty expressed the conventional wisdom, advising the studios to follow a "conservative course" with the expectation that "the unsettled state of things is bound to cool down [and return] to some degree of normalcy."[79] Until then, best to hunker down, make the best of a bad business, and ride out the storm.

2

HITLER, A "BLAH SHOW SUBJECT"

As reports of purges at Ufa and beatings in Berlin swirled though executive offices in New York and studio cafeterias in Hollywood, Col. Frederick L. Herron, foreign manager of the Motion Picture Producers and Distributors of America (MPPDA), left for Washington to consult with the State Department on "the Hitler activities in Germany so far as they affect [the] film business."[1] The effect of Nazism on the film business—the release of American pictures into Germany and the depiction of the new Germany in American cinema—was the overriding concern of Hollywood's corporate consortium. Jewish personnel in Germany were a fungible commodity.

Herron should have stayed in New York: no one knew anything for certain. The reliability of information from Nazi Germany was dubious and the flow of intelligence circuitous. On Hollywood matters, the official chain of communication began with trade representative George R. Canty in Berlin, who filed weekly reports and sent frequent cables to the Motion Picture Division of the Department of Commerce in Washington, D.C., whose director then funneled the information to Herron at MPPDA headquarters in New York. In turn, Herron kept Washington apprised of scuttlebutt from studio branch managers in Berlin and around Europe. The three-way back and forth can be traced in the staccato grammar of a cable sent in April 1933 from Washington to the MPPDA:

REPLY TO CABLE SENT CANTY QUOTE CONFIDENT CONDI-
TIONS UNALARMING BUT PROBABLE NECESSITY CERTAIN

PERSONNEL READJUSTMENTS TALK SHEEHAN WHO KNOWS
STORY WROTE HERRON TODAY

Translation: Canty assumes that the Jewish employees of the Hollywood studios in Germany will have to be fired or transferred. Fox's foreign manager, Clayton Sheehan, recently in Berlin and now back in New York, should be spoken to directly for a firsthand account. Colonel Herron will be kept in the loop.[2]

Formed in 1922, the MPPDA served as the political arm of the economic cartel that was the classical Hollywood studio system. To front for the oligopoly, the moguls selected a man of impeccable credentials, unimpeachable probity, and high-level contacts on Capitol Hill and Wall Street—Will H. Hays from Sullivan, Indiana: Republican Party kingmaker, former Postmaster General for President Warren G. Harding, and a nondrinking, nonsmoking elder of the Presbyterian Church. At the helm until 1945, Hays led the industry from rough-and-tumble adolescence to prosperous maturity. As Hollywood's public face, the slight, imperturbable Hoosier—dubbed "the Czar of Movieland"—soon found the MPPDA remade in his name. Inside and outside the industry, it was better known as the Hays office.

The Hays office was also the common signifier for the corset of Hollywood censorship, but here the billing was false. The man who tied that knot was a stern Irish Catholic named Joseph I. Breen, whose background in diplomacy (as a consular officer during the Great War) and public relations (as media maestro for the Eucharist Congress held in Chicago in 1926) proved almost as useful as his religious pedigree (as a prominent Catholic layman and regular contributor to topline Catholic journals). In 1931, Hays summoned Breen to Hollywood to run interference with Catholics aghast over Hollywood's post-talkie lurch into vice and violence. By December 1933, the gregarious workaholic had wrangled control of the Studio Relations Committee, the nominal enforcer of the Production Code. The Production Code was Hollywood's moral guidebook, a catechism of Catholic bylaws written by Father Daniel A. Lord, a multitalented Jesuit priest from the archdiocese of St. Louis, and Martin J. Quigley, editor-publisher of *Motion Picture Herald*, an influential weekly for independent exhibitors. The Code had been adopted by the moguls in 1930 and then promptly ignored.

Breen steered Hollywood back onto the straight and narrow. On July 15, 1934, he formally took over the new agency created to give teeth to the

The front man and the mogul: Will H. Hays (*left*), president of the Motion Picture Producers and Distributors of America, presents Paramount Pictures founder Adolph Zukor with a commemorative autograph album during a celebration of the studio's twenty-fifth anniversary, July 1, 1937.

Code and established with Breen in mind as enforcer in chief: the Production Code Administration (PCA), an in-house arm of the MPPDA. In matters pertaining to motion picture morality, Breen was not quite omnipotent, but from 1934 until his retirement in 1954 he was more potent than anyone else in town. Around Hollywood, the office, whose formal name was the Production Code Administration, and that the public knew as the Hays office, was named after the man whose iron hand signaled stop or go for the machinery of motion picture production: the Breen office. A film that received a Code seal, the emblem of his inspection, was said to have been "breened."

Officially, Breen's purview was limited to screen morality while Hays governed the political and economic precincts of the industry. In practice, however, the spheres of influence overlapped and the pair worked in harmony.

Hays and Breen were especially in tune in a desire to keep Hollywood far away from the rocky shoals of political conflict. The Hays office and the Breen office shared an acute aversion to ideological controversies or partisan disputes of any stripe.[a] For characters in a Hollywood film to squabble over politics in front of moviegoers—Democrat or Republican, American or German—was bad for business all around.

Unfortunately, the binding text of the Code, a document fixated on morality, offered little guidance on domestic politics or foreign policy. Though eloquent on the moral duty of filmmakers toward the young and innocent, insistent on the sanctity of Christian American civilization, and meticulous about what should be neither seen nor heard on the Hollywood screen, it was mute on the stance of a democratic art toward a totalitarian nation. The pertinent phrase in the document, under a section devoted to "National Feelings," simply read:

> *The history, institutions, prominent people, and citizenry of all nations shall be represented fairly.*

As interpreted by Breen and Hays, the vague injunction codified a see-no-evil, speak-no-evil, hear-no-evil policy toward any regime on the planet, especially if the nation in question offered a lucrative market for Hollywood imports. Under the Code, the transformation of the Weimar Republic into the Third Reich was Germany's business.

Thus, though privately worried that the erratic behavior of the Nazis might disrupt the course of commerce, the Hays office maintained a stoic demeanor in public. Even as Jewish American employees of the studios were roughed up and forced to flee Germany, the MPPDA insisted that "these men left the country willingly and have since returned to work there."[3] The trade between Hollywood and Berlin, said a spokesman, was "a matter of strictly individual action by the major companies" rather than a matter of collective MPPDA policy. "Haysian officials and others in the trade recently have heard rumblings over the possibility that strict regulation and censorship based largely on racial prejudice might prompt one or more of the majors to abandon German distribution," *Variety* reported in 1936, but whatever Hollywood decided, New

---

[a] Henceforth, "the Hays office" will refer to the MPPDA and its Board of Directors based in New York and "the Breen office" will refer to the enforcers of the Production Code based in Hollywood.

York washed its hands of the matter. "Feeling with Haysians currently is that the entire matter is one that should be handled directly by each company."[4] On matters related to Nazism, the official position of the MPPDA was to deny the existence of an official position. If Universal and Warner Bros. decided to withdraw from Nazi Germany, fine; if Paramount, Fox, and MGM decided to stay, fine also.

However, the MPPDA's laissez-faire attitude toward the studios' business dealings with the Nazis did not extend to the production of films dealing with the Nazis. On the Hollywood screen, Germany was not to be slighted, the Nazis were not to be criticized, and Hitler was not to be mentioned. The official policy deflected pitches, discouraged projects, and relegated anti-Nazi sentiments to the margins of American cinema.

Between 1933 and 1939, a dedicated American moviegoer whose only source of foreign news was the Hollywood feature film knew only a world of exotic adventure, courtly romance, and scenic locales. Scarcely a glimpse of Italy in Ethiopia, Spain in flames, or Germany on the march penetrated the blackout. Even mild jests and veiled allusions were scratched from scripts and clipped from prints. In MGM's *Dancing Lady* (1933), Jerry Howard of the comedy trio Howard, Fine, and Howard, an early incarnation of the Three Stooges, was shown working on a jigsaw puzzle until he finally supplies the missing piece. Mugging a queasy expression, he exclaims: "I've been working on this for five weeks and look what I finally got—Hitler!" To which comedian Ted Healy responds, "What did you expect—Santa Claus?" The reference to Santa Claus was left in the final film, but the punch line about Hitler was cut.[5] More conspicuous by his absence than Santa Claus, Hitler was the missing piece in Hollywood's cast of characters in the 1930s.

With the Hollywood studios on the sidelines, the fight against Hitler and Nazism in American cinema was taken up by films so little circulated as to barely register on the cultural radar, then or since: the offbeat documentary, the low-budget independent feature, and the odd foreign import. Looking over the minimal returns and paucity of projects in the pipeline, *Variety* pronounced Hitler "a blah show subject," and puzzled over the anomaly of a charismatic headline maker who failed to translate into box office gold. "Theory that a hot news subject is sure-fire theatrical material seems to be negated by the Hitler matter," the paper concluded in late 1933. "Thus far no one's been able to sell a Hitler item as entertainment."[6]

With no commercial incentive and plenty of official disincentive, Hitler was ignored by the Hollywood screen even as he redrew the map of Europe. Stirrings of anti-Nazism were squelched before the cameras rolled or exiled to the fringes of a subaltern independent market. Projects about Hitler and Nazis went unmade or came to the screen so ill-made as to be dead on arrival.

THE DISAPPEARANCE OF JEWS *QUA* JEWS

Nearly as conspicuous as the absence of Nazis was the disappearance of Jews. After 1933, the cinematic spotlight on Jewish *schmaltz* and *shtick* went dark. The German market was the first reason: why showcase an ethnicity sure to get the film banned from import? The strict enforcement of the Code after July 15, 1934, was the second reason. The injunction to represent the history, institutions, and prominent people of all nations fairly meant that the broad stereotypes that branded a stock character as Jewish tended to be eliminated or softened. Commerce and censorship colluded to erase Hollywood's most prominent ethnic group from the Hollywood screen.

Though never a major current in Hollywood cinema, Judeo-centric scenarios were a modest undertow in silent-screen melodrama and Jewish entertainers a major wave in the comic mode of the early talkies. With so many Jews in the business and so many avid moviegoers in New York, it was only natural that Jews occur more frequently on screen than in the national census. The lilt of Yiddish comedy routines (what the trade press called "Hebe humor") enlivened the early sound cinema, especially in the rich tributary of ethnic hybrids marrying the children of Israel and Ireland: *Kosher Kitty Kelly* (1926), *Abie's Irish Rose* (1928), and the long-running series *The Cohens and the Kellys* (1926–1933). Occasionally a Jewish-themed melodrama warranted feature-length treatment, *The Jazz Singer* (1927) being the loudest shout-out. But no canny businessman builds a mass entertainment around 3 percent of his consumer base. However prominent Jews might be in Hollywood, on the Hollywood screen they left lighter footprints. Throughout the 1930s, Jewish stars continued to reign as big, though usually Anglicized, names on the motion picture marquee (Edward G. Robinson, Paul Muni, Paulette Goddard, Melvyn Douglas—formerly Emmanuel Goldenberg, Meshilem

Meier Weisenfreund, Pauline Marion Goddard Levy, and Melvyn Edouard
Hesselberg, respectively), but in the narratives proper, Jews *qua* Jews
were scarce.

Nonetheless, in the immediate aftermath of January 1933, a minor
tributary of feature films—too small in number to constitute a cycle
much less a genre—served as allegories by default on Nazi antisemitism.
Of the four films released on American screens, only one came from
a major Hollywood studio; two were imported from Great Britain; and
one was a domestic production in a foreign language. Nettlesome controversy and tepid box office dampened the prospects for further ventures in
Judeo-themed cinema for the balance of the decade.

The highest-profile of the quartet was *The House of Rothschild* (1934),
a prestige bio-pic of the Jewish banking family starring British actor
George Arliss, a thespian famed for his theatrical turns as Great Men
from the pantheon of European history. "Policy of following the headlines in writing film material will be carried out in *Rothschild*," *Variety*
noticed, connecting the dots across time when 20th Century Pictures
announced plans for the film. "Story of the international banking family
in its present form deals in part with the persecution of the Jews in Germany around the period of 1850."[7] After the studio received letters pro-
testing a story deemed "too Semitic" for its portrayal of the Jewish family
as more or less human, producer Darryl F. Zanuck and George Arliss
vetted the script for undue pro-Jewish slants, confirmed its evenhandedness, and resolved "to make no further alterations in the story which is
based on fact."[8]

Directed by Alfred Werker, adapted by Nunnally Johnson from the
stage play by George Hembert Westley, and showcasing the versatile Arliss playing both patriarch Mayer and son Nathan, *The House of Rothschild*
was a handsomely mounted period piece that hardly needed to strain to
make explicit what was so strongly implicit. Over two generations, the
Rothschilds are snubbed and insulted even as they reshape European
commerce and bankroll the British Empire. The origins of the international banking system having limited box office appeal, a good deal of the
family tree is traced via the star-crossed romance between the beautiful
Julie Rothschild (Loretta Young) and the dashing Captain Fitzroy (Robert
Young), a Christian. "In sequences that have a definite modern parallel, the Jew is scorned and the romance between Julie and gentile Captain Fitzroy is thwarted," observed *Motion Picture Herald*, also alert to the

geopolitical reverberations, before passing along a word to the wise exhibitor. "Don't succumb to the temptation of even whispering propaganda. Rather sell *The House of Rothschild* with dignity, in which enthusiasm is untempered." That is, keep mum about the pro-Jewish slant.[9]

Pro-Jewish *The House of Rothschild* was. Herded with his wife and five sons into the Jew Street ghetto of eighteenth-century Frankfurt, old man Rothschild is an honest but penny-pinching merchant who dons the mask of the conniving Jew when corrupt German tax collectors barge into his home. A generation later, operating from five European capitals, his sons are the first family of European finance, with Nathan now head of the house. Nattily dressed, urbane, and socially connected, Nathan is every inch the complete modern banker. Unlike his father, he never has to touch filthy lucre, much less bite a coin to test it for counterfeit metal. He rules the London stock exchange through his genius at math and his insight into human psychology.

But where the British respect and honor Rothschild—he is on a first-name basis with the Duke of Wellington—his ethnic stock on the Continent is not so high. Rothschild's economic acumen earns him the undying enmity of a German antisemite whose campaign of "lies and propaganda" incites pogroms throughout Germany. As nineteenth-century brownshirts run riot through the ghetto, Nathan thinks twice about betrothing his beloved daughter to Anglo-Christian society. "Go into the Jewish quarter of any town in Prussia today and you'll see lying dead Julie's people killed by your people, but for one crime—that they were Jewish!" he scolds his would-be son-in-law.

The House of Rothschild was a capital-A picture sold on pageantry and the appeal of its top-billed star Arliss (nothing if not ecumenical in his historical role playing, the actor had already won an Oscar for *Disraeli* [1929] and followed up his turn as Mayer and Nathan Rothschild with *Cardinal Richelieu* [1935]). The film opened to huge business and rave reviews and earned a Best Picture nomination from the Academy of Motion Picture Arts and Sciences. Admired though it was, however, *The House of Rothschild* left no descendents. Throughout the 1930s, its familial Judeo-centricity remained an anomaly in Hollywood's monolithically Christian neighborhoods.

A pair of films from Great Britain, both starring Conrad Veidt, the somnambulist in the German Expressionist classic *The Cabinet of Dr. Caligari* (1920), now an exile from Nazi Germany living in London,

Allegorical anti-Nazism: ethnic chameleon George Arliss as patriarch Mayer Rothschild (*top*), counting up his coins, and as Nathan Rothschild, threatened by nineteenth-century brownshirts in 20th Century Pictures' *The House of Rothschild* (1934), a sympathetic biopic of the European banking dynasty.

received chillier receptions. Veidt plays the title Jew in two incendiary projects with deep roots in European antisemitism, each tale trafficking in medieval myths and libels. The English productions stumbled into the American marketplace unaware that two nations speaking the same language might not share the same response to Jewish-themed material.

Directed by Maurice Elvey and based on E. Temple Thurston's play (which itself was based on Eugene Sue's book and Gustave Doré's painting of the same name), *The Wandering Jew* (1933; U.S. release January 1935) featured Veidt as the nomadic scapegoat for his accursed race. After spitting at Christ on the day of His Crucifixion, the haughty Matathias (Veidt) is condemned to wander through time, immortal and damned. He is a randy knight during the First Crusade in 1150; an avaricious merchant in Palermo, Sicily, in 1290; and a beloved physician in Seville, Spain, in 1560, during the Spanish Inquisition.

In the last incarnation, as a healer of the poor and outcast, Matathias performs penance for his insult to Christ and the narcissism of his past lives. When a prostitute in his care falls in love with him ("I love you as Mary Magdalene loved Him," she confesses), his transformation from sinner to saint is nearly complete, awaiting only his martyrdom at the hands of the Spanish Inquisition. An offhand remark ("It would be hard with Christ to know His own if He came back again," he says of the bloated clerics overseeing the reign of terror) is enough to seal his fate. Dragged before the Inquisition, he refuses to deny his Jewish faith, but by then his religious roots are a technicality. The Wandering Jew has become Christlike in his suffering and Christian in his acceptance of the divinity of the messiah he once spat upon. Tied to a stake in a crucifix-like posture, he awaits burning alive—but Christ reveals Himself and delivers Matathias not to death but to eternal life. The Jew has wandered straight into the grace of Christian salvation.

A lavish production, especially by the impecunious standards of British cinema, *The Wandering Jew* was imported in 1935 by Loew's Inc., MGM's parent company, and slated for release during Yom Kippur for promotional tie-ins. That was a miscalculation. Though the film oozes at least as much anti-Catholicism as antisemitism, an opening act featuring a lecherous Jew spitting on Christ was not a gesture calculated to foster interfaith comity. Also, in 1935, the word "Jew" on a theater marquee was enough to make its referents wince at a description that was also spat out as an insult. Alarmed at the provocation, Hollywood Jews maneuvered behind the scenes to suppress the film. Knowing where the levers of power were located, they launched a full-court press on the Breen office.

"Friday last, I received a formal, dignified protest from a local group of Jewish women against the picture entitled *The Wandering Jew*," Breen wrote Hays. "The protest was made on the grounds that the picture was a libelous attack upon the Jews, and, generally, very offensive." No sooner had the women's delegation left his office than Breen received a phone call from George Cohen, from the law firm of Loeb, Walker, and Loeb, who wanted Breen to know that "a number of his Jewish friends had spoken to him about this picture and urged him to use his influence with us to have the picture very critically examined before it received our approval." Later that same day, Breen was on the receiving end of yet another protest call from a concerned Jew, this time from screenwriter Al Cohn, who as scenarist for *The Jazz Singer* and *The Cohens and the Kellys* films, claimed a proprietary interest. "Al tells me that there was considerable apprehension about this particular picture at the local meeting of some sort of anti-defamation league," Breen reported.

Importuned by a Jewish women's group, a Jewish lawyer, and a Jewish screenwriter all in one day, Breen contacted the New York office, where the British import would have been vetted, to find out what was up. To his relief, he learned that the film was never formally submitted for a Production Code seal. Breen asked Hays to make sure that Vincent G. Hart, head of the New York branch of the PCA, exercise great care in handling the case should the film be submitted. "I know that you want no approval given on a picture that libels any race of people," he told Hays, speaking for them both.[10]

Meanwhile, in New York, protests by the Anti-Defamation League of the B'nai B'rith forced Loew's head Nicholas M. Schenck—who was initially enthusiastic about the picture and had signed a deal to distribute it—to renege on the contract. The company also withdrew its planned application for a Code seal, thus saving Vincent Hart the trouble of a tough call. Originally slated to open at the 5,400-seat Capitol Theatre in New York, it was demoted to the 875-seat Criterion, where it played to enthusiastic crowds for five weeks.[11] Clearly, American Jews were of two minds about the film, reading it more as an attack on Christian anti-semitism than a regurgitation of old slurs against the Jews. However, influential voices in the trade press and American Jewry—sometimes overlapping categories—were uneasy about the whole affair: the title, the spitting, the avarice. "It's not entertainment. It's not enlightenment. It's not even propaganda, one way or the other—it's just disturbing," commented *Variety*, troubled at "the reopening of ancient racial wounds."[12]

The trigger word in the title of *The Jew Suss* (1934), the other British-made meditation on the plight of European Jewry, was expunged for the American market. Based on Lion Feuchtwanger's novel *Jew Suss*, directed by Lothar Mendes, and masked by a tactical relabeling for the American marketplace, *Power* (1934)—as it was rechristened—hit an even heavier wave of resistance.

In the Duchy of Württemberg in eighteenth-century Germany, up-from-the-ghetto hustler Reb Joseph Suss-Oppenheimer (Veidt again) insinuates his way into the royal court. He sinks so low that he is willing to pimp his sweetheart to the lecherous Duke, but when he tries the same trick with his beautiful teenage daughter, she plunges off a roof rather than surrender her virtue. Heartsick and bent on revenge, Suss confronts the Duke, who dies of a stroke. Put on trial for murder, the defiant Suss boasts that no tree will be high enough to hang him. Born again to the faith of his fathers, he also refuses to reject his Jewish heritage even though he is revealed to have been born of a Christian mother. In the harrowing finale, the Jew Suss is hanged from a steel cage hoisted high over the public square, as snow falls and the crowd roars.

For many observers, the inflammatory content—a conniving Jew in Germany executed to the delight of a howling mob—overpowered the aesthetic virtues or box office potential. "This is not entertainment; it is a medium by which the basest passions are appealed to," seethed Pete Harrison, editor and publisher of *Harrison's Reports*, a weekly newsletter for motion picture exhibitors. Harrison was appalled by every aspect of the "abhorrent" production, which he found offensive in equal measure to Jews ("because of the slur it casts on their race") and Christians ("because of the sensationalism and tyrannical character" of the Christian protagonists). "Unsuitable for any decent person—Class C," he decreed, giving the film his own personal "condemned" rating. "I am making a personal appeal to every exhibitor in the land not to show this picture. In addition to the fact that it is not entertaining, this is not the time to show anything that arouses racial prejudice."[13]

After *Power* opened at Radio City Music Hall, the Loew's circuit, which had agreed to distribute the film, got cold feet. To salvage its commercial prospects, A. P. Waxman, the stateside press agent for British imports, arranged a private screening for a pair of very influential Jewish leaders—Albert Einstein, who went on record praising the film, and Rabbi Stephen S. Wise, the era's most prominent spokesman for liberal Judaism, who devoted a sermon to the film on his radio broadcast. Loew's reconsidered and distributed the film, but despite the blurbs from the professor and the rabbi, *Power* flopped.[14]

The fourth film was not in either British or American English. *Die Vandernder Yid* (*The Wandering Jew*, 1933), a Yiddish-language variation on the Temple-Sure-Doré theme, uses Nazi Germany as a backdrop for a history of antisemitism that stretches from the captivity in Babylonia, the carnage of the Crusades, and the torments of the Spanish Inquisition, on through the pogroms of Czarist Russia, and into the wilderness that is now Nazi Germany. Directed by George Roland; written by Jacob Mestel, already a multi-hyphenate talent in Yiddish theater and later its historian; and starring Jacob Ben-Ami, a heartthrob of the Yiddish stage, it has the distinction of being the first American, though not Hollywood, attack on Nazi Germany in a feature film.

A brilliant painter, Great War veteran, loyal German, and esteemed professor at the Berlin Academy of Art, Arthur Levi (Ben-Ami) enjoys all the perquisites of assimilation in Weimar Germany, including a beautiful blonde gentile fiancée, until the Nazis raise "the New German Racial Question." Suddenly, the Berlin Academy refuses to hang his painting, brownshirts shout "Juden!" outside his home, and his shiksa girlfriend bails. Newsreel footage of the Nazi book burnings staged in Berlin on May 10, 1933, is stitched into the melodrama, the flames of the fires reflecting on Levi's face.

Rather than see his masterpiece consigned to the flames (a full-length portrait of his deceased father as Jehovah, also entitled "The Wandering Jew"), Professor Levi prepares to destroy it himself—whereupon the portrait comes to life. To put the present troubles in perspective, the patriarch guides the son through the bitter history of the Jewish people, a tour through time illustrated with copious footage from silent-era costume dramas. The lesson concludes on the note of uplift offered by the Zionist movement launched by Theodore Herzl. Just as Moses and Herzl led oppressed Jews to the promised land, a new prophet will arise to lead the chosen people out of Germany. The Nazis may burn Jewish literature, "but they can never extinguish the Eternal Spirit" of the Jewish people.

The first American, though not English-language, anti-Nazi feature film: Natalie Browning, Jacob Ben-Ami, and Ben Adler in George Roland's Yiddish-language production, *Die Vandernder Yid* (1933). (Courtesy of the National Center for Jewish Film)

The prospects for *Die Vandernder Yid* with its target audience seemed propitious. "This film is definitely of the nature of propaganda aimed intensely at the current anti-Semitic activity carried on by the Hitler government in Germany," commented *Motion Picture Herald*. "As such, in theaters which may count upon a reasonably large Jewish attendance, the exhibitor has something to sell here."[15] *Variety*'s Wolfe Kaufman concurred: "First of the anti-Hitler pictures, there ought to be a market for it."[16] Yet static camerawork, histrionic acting, and glacial pacing doomed *Die Vandernder Yid* even among that percentage of the demographic likely to lend a box office mandate to anti-Nazi cinema. Booked for a four-week run at the Cameo, the arthouse venue of choice in New York for politically tinged ethnic fare, and publicized as the first film to dare "a vigorous denunciation of Hitlerism," it barely survived two weeks before management pulled the plug.[17]

THE UNMAKING OF *THE MAD DOG OF EUROPE*

In 1933, Sam Jaffe, a low-powered Hollywood producer, and Herman J. Mankiewicz, the high-living Hollywood screenwriter, shopped around a project entitled *The Mad Dog of Europe*. It seemed like a surefire high concept: first out of the gate, inspired by headline material, and precast with a magnetic villain. Yet perhaps no film—or non-film—better illustrates the Hollywood aversion to anti-Nazi cinema in the 1930s than the long-gestating, never-realized scenario caught in a 1930s version of development hell. As Hitler consolidated power and remade Germany, conquered new territory and pushed Europe to the abyss, the project stumbled and sputtered, hit false starts, raised expectations, dashed hopes, and, finally, curled up and died.

Not to be confused with the well-known character actor of the same name, producer-turned-agent Sam Jaffe began his career at Paramount as a production manager under the legendary producer B. P. Schulberg. Jaffe was well connected: Schulberg was married to Jaffe's sister, Adeline Jaffe Schulberg, who was in her own right a powerful talent agent and activist for progressive causes. In 1932, after a blowup with director Josef von Sternberg on the set of *Blonde Venus* (1932), Jaffe resigned from Paramount and moved down a notch on the studio hierarchy to RKO, where he scored with *Diplomaniacs* (1933), a hit comedy starring the manic duo Bert Wheeler and Robert Woolsey.[18]

In July 1933, Jaffe left RKO to devote full energies to *The Mad Dog of Europe*, which was to be his first venture into independent production. In a blatant bid for ecumenical outreach, the project was described as "an anti-Hitler film of the sacrifice of Jews and Catholics."[19] Declared Jaffe: "With the exception of certain essential newsreel matter, I am planning to make this picture in Hollywood with Hollywood personalities and labor." In full-page ads in the trade press, he trumpeted his opus-to-be as "an anti-Hitler subject depicting the intolerance and bigotry resulting in the persecution of the Jews and Catholics in a Central European nation and the world catastrophe involved." Shooting was scheduled to begin on August 23, 1933.[20]

The Motion Picture Producers and Distributors of America had other plans. Unofficially but unmistakably, Jaffe was told to back off.

Jaffe decided not to buck the power brokers whose goodwill he depended upon. That September, after only a short summer vacation away from the studio treadmill, he joined Columbia Pictures in a general executive capacity working directly under studio kingpin Harry Cohn.[21] Finding the irascible Cohn unbearable, Jaffe shifted career paths. Joining his sister's talent agency, and ultimately taking it over, he spent the balance of his work life as one of Hollywood's most successful agents.

By October 1933, the project had come into the hands of Al Rosen, who planned to reverse Jaffe's career trajectory: he was an agent eager to move into motion picture production. In his commitment to *The Mad Dog of Europe*, Rosen would prove to be made of sterner stuff than Jaffe.

Under the shingle March of Time Productions, Inc., Rosen set up shop at Tiffany Pictures, a Poverty Row shop specializing in one- and two-reelers, and announced that *The Mad Dog of Europe* would begin shooting on November 1, 1933. He described the screenplay as being "based on the Hitler career, cinematizing the lives in Germany from 1914 to 1933, of a Jewish [and] a Catholic family. Film's nucleus [is] 7,000 feet [of newsreel footage] taken in Germany in the past decade, [and] smuggled from the country."[22] Rosen aimed at a "states rights market," which in industry parlance meant exhibitors without formal contractual affiliations with the major studios. To generate buzz, he flashed around a picture of a Hitler lookalike hired "to portray the heavy" in his forthcoming production. Apparently, the actor was a dead ringer for the original. "He isn't being invited to any social functions," deadpanned the *Hollywood Reporter*.[23]

Again, official Hollywood moved in. Frederick W. Beetson, secretary-treasurer of the Association of Motion Picture Producers, tried to dissuade Rosen from undertaking the project—first by jawboning then by strong-arming.[b] On October 15, 1933, Beetson met with Rosen and urged him, for the sake of the German market (and presumably with no pun intended) "to let sleeping dogs lie." Rosen waved a bundle of supportive letters from religious organizations in Beetson's face. MPPDA or not, he vowed to bring the project to the screen.[24]

Fed up, Rosen went public with the MPPDA's intimidation tactics. According to Rosen's account of his meeting with Beetson, he was ordered outright to shut down production. Having already invested

---

[b] Although administratively distinct from the MPPDA, the Association of Motion Picture Producers (AMPP) was effectively the West Coast adjunct of the cartel. In 1933 the president was Louis B. Mayer, MGM chief; the first vice president was Jack L. Warner, head of production at Warner Bros.; and the second vice president was Winfield R. Sheehan, head of production at Fox.

thousands of dollars in the project, Rosen did what any independent producer would do: he sued. Alleging "malicious interference with contracts and conspiracy," he asked for $1,022,200 in damages—$7,200 for money expended, $15,000 for incurred obligations, and $1,000,000 in punitive damages.[25] Rosen claimed that the MPPDA told him it would "be to his best interests not to" produce *The Mad Dog of Europe* and that, if he persisted, "the association would do everything in its power to prevent him."[26] The suit went nowhere.

Scared away by the MPPDA and Rosen's uncertain financing, potential artistic collaborators backed off. Herman Mankiewicz asked Rosen to take his name off the script; B-movie director Phil Rosen (no relation to the would-be producer), whose name had been attached to the project, also dropped out. "They tell me I am dealing with a controversial subject, but I don't call it that," said Rosen. "There have been plays and pictures before based on the crime of oppression and social bigotry, so why not again?"[27] Nonetheless, with the antipathy of the MPPDA common knowledge around town, securing financing and A-list talent in Hollywood was hopeless.

The undeterrable Rosen traveled to New York to solicit funding from Jewish leaders. No luck.[28] He then trolled for seed money in Paris, where he reportedly "picked up several thousand feet of stock shots and some atrocity stuff from Germany" but failed to secure financing.[29]

In February 1934, back in Hollywood, Rosen put up a good front for potential investors. He announced the start of production with Lowell Sherman slated to direct and Lynn Root signed on as screenwriter. (Root was unknown at the time, but Sherman was a major coup, a hot commodity after helming the smash-hit Mae West vehicle *She Done Him Wrong* [1933].) He sent out word that Sam Rosoff, the wealthy New York subway builder, had put an "unlimited bankroll" at his disposal, the MPPDA be damned.[30] He took out trade press ads declaring that *The Mad Dog of Europe* would "shortly go into production."[31]

Over the next months, Rosen kept up the charade that the project was a done deal by announcing the acquisition of ten thousand feet (approximately 110 minutes) of authentic sound pictures "showing Hitler in action, and also giving unusual views of how the Jews have been treated." With such compelling newsreel footage, Rosen confided, all he really needed to do to make a surefire thriller was to "shoot sufficient added stuff to carry a story." If he was unable to cobble together a drama as timely as the day's headlines, he planned to reedit the newsreel footage into a feature-length documentary. Either way, the shooting of the dramatic sequences would begin within a month.[32] Really, the cameras would start rolling any day now.

To show he meant business, Rosen submitted his proposal for *The Mad Dog of Europe* to the Production Code Administration. Bound by its own rules, the Breen office had no option but to vet the project. In the process, it formulated a policy that shaped Hollywood's attitude to anti-Nazi cinema for the rest of the decade. The film and the guidelines were debated at the highest levels of the industry—meaning the Breen office in Hollywood and the MPPDA's board in New York.

The consensus and "*un*official judgment" of the motion picture industry was laid out by Breen in a widely circulated memo that set a

The men of the Breen office in November 1934: Production Code Administration chief Joseph I. Breen (*first row, center*); his right-hand man Geoffrey Shurlock and, on Breen's left, Dr. James Wingate, former head of the Studio Relations Committee. *Standing left to right*: staffers Douglas Mackinnon, Karl Lischka, Islen Auster, Arthur Houghton, and John McHugh Stuart.

precedent not limited to the case at hand: "such a picture should not be produced." The Breen office was not issuing an official prohibition; it was offering a word to the wise in the form of an advisory opinion. Of course, around Hollywood, in dealing with the Breen office, an official prohibition and an "unofficial judgment" was a distinction without a difference.

Breen knew Rosen—and any other producer contemplating an anti-Nazi scenario—deserved more than an imperious thumbs down. Patiently, a bit defensively, he explained:

> This general and unofficial opinion is based pretty generally upon the thought that such a picture is an out-and-out propaganda picture and, while it might serve a good purpose from a propaganda angle, it might likewise establish a bad precedent. The purpose of the screen, primarily, *is to entertain* and *not to propagandize*. To launch such a picture might result in a kind of two-edged sword, with the screen being used for propaganda purposes not so worthy, possibly, as that suggested by The Mad Dog of Europe idea.

The likelihood that American Hitlerites would seek a Code seal for a pro-Nazi film was remote, but Breen was covering all the bases. Interestingly, the PCA head let slip that he himself considered the project "worthy" of purpose. As ever, though, his internal barometer was sensitive to the possibility of domestic blowback:

> Then, too, it is to be remembered that there is strong pro-German and anti-Semitic feeling in this country, and, while those who are likely to approve of an anti-Hitler picture may think well of such an enterprise, they should keep in mind that millions of Americans might think otherwise.

After all, Breen need not remind a man whose surname was Rosen that

> Because of the large number of Jews active in the motion picture industry in this country, the charge is certain to be made that the Jews, as a class, are behind an anti-Hitler picture and using the entertainment screen for their own personal propaganda purposes. The entire industry, because of this, is likely to be indicted for the action of a mere handful.

With this in mind, "thinking people" within the industry believed that "*The Mad Dog of Europe* should *not* be made, despite the fact that it may appear at first sight to be a worthwhile enterprise." Breen closed with a clincher: "It is certain to be inflammatory and might result in a boomerang."[33] Of course, the "thinking people" within the industry were Breen's immediate superiors on the MPPDA's board in New York—the policymakers and moneymen, Jew and non-Jew alike, who thought it best to let sleeping dogs lie.

At that juncture, even the tenacious Rosen was shut down. Throughout the 1930s, he tried repeatedly to get the project off the ground—at Paramount, at RKO, at Columbia—with different scripts, but always with the same incendiary title and identifiable tyrant. In 1936 he attempted an end run around the Breen office by soliciting the official blessings of the State Department. The State Department alerted the MPPDA, where foreign manager Col. Frederick L. Herron fielded the call. "Confidentially, the State Department tells me that they have had a letter from our old friend Rosen of *The Mad Dog of Europe* fame, stating that he wants to make a picture built around a Jewish girl and a German boy with [a] world war background," Herron informed Breen. He asked Breen to dig up the old memo "quietly" and "as soon as possible, in confidence" copy it to New York for Herron to pass on to the State Department.[34]

Like Hollywood, Washington wanted nothing to do with *The Mad Dog of Europe*.

"WHAT ABOUT THE JEWS, YOUR EXCELLENCY?": CORNELIUS VANDERBILT JR.'S *HITLER'S REIGN OF TERROR* (1934)

In the 1920s and 1930s, when the motion picture camera was still a novel invention and exotic peoples in remote regions had yet to be captured on film, a few young men with the requisite moxie and money assumed the guise of intrepid newsreel photographers. Working freelance or on spec, the amateur shutterbugs roamed the world and cranked away in the days when the Eyemo camera—a durable, handheld 35mm camera marketed by Bell & Howell with an eye to the newsreel market—was still a luxury item. Newsmen without portfolio, they practiced a kind of journalistic *noblesse oblige*—traveling far and wide, often in first-class cabins, but sometimes enduring severe hardships and courting real danger.

One of the most energetic of the breed was Cornelius Vanderbilt Jr., scion of the nineteenth-century robber barons. Though born with the most silver of spoons in his mouth, Vanderbilt looked upon his plutocratic kith and kin as a tribe of "dull, uninteresting, hopelessly mediocre people."[35] Resolving to break free from the ballrooms of the mundane superrich, he enlisted as a private in the Great War and tried to live down his blue-chip name. Deployed as a message carrier, he motored between battlefronts, dodged artillery shells, and nearly perished in a gas attack. Mustered out, disgusted by the effete New York social scene, he migrated to California, founded a newspaper, went bust, returned to New York, and lived in a flat that became party central for the intoxicated fops and flappers of a metropolis in full Jazz Age swing. He also used his contacts to interview some of the most inaccessible newsmakers of the age—Al Capone, Joseph Stalin, Benito Mussolini, Pope Pius XI, and, on the historic evening of March 5, 1933, his biggest catch, Adolf Hitler.

Earlier that year, operating out of plush quarters in Paris, Vanderbilt had set about stalking his quarry. Registering as a journalist, he toured European capitals, and with two French cameramen went to Vienna

The plutocrat as journalist: Cornelius Vanderbilt Jr. (*right*) with producer-director Cecil B. DeMille in Hollywood in the 1920s.

to cover mass meetings and political demonstrations.[36] In Berlin, he interviewed the former Crown Prince of Germany and, in Holland, the prince's father, Kaiser Wilhelm. Getting within range of the present leader of Germany was far more difficult than gaining an audience with the former rulers. "Strange, isn't it," Vanderbilt remarked to the Crown Prince, "that you Hohenzollerns are so much easier to see than Hitler?"

Vanderbilt persisted and on the evening of March 5, 1933, the day of the Reichstag elections that gave the Nazis a parliamentary plurality, he obtained an audience, of sorts, with Hitler. The vaunted interview actually consisted of little more than a few shouted exchanges as Hitler prepared to go on stage at the Sports Palace in Berlin to speak to throngs of hysterical Nazis marshaled to greet their new, democratically validated Reich Chancellor. "Tell the Americans that life moves forward, always forward, irrevocably forward," said Hitler, gesturing to the rapturous multitudes awaiting his entrance. "Tell them that Adolf Hitler is the Man of the Hour, not because he has been appointed Chancellor by Hindenburg, but because *no one else could have been appointed Chancellor instead.* . . . Tell them that he was sent by the Almighty to a nation that had been threatened with disintegration and loss of honor for fifteen long years."

As Hitler strode into the spotlight, Vanderbilt yelled out a final question. "And what about the Jews, Your Excellency?"

Hitler shrugged off the impertinence. "My people are waiting for me!" he snapped. "You hear that song? You hear those drums? See this man here [Dr. Ernst "Putzi" Hanfstaengl, Hitler's Harvard-educated foreign press chief]. He will tell you about the Jews and all the other things that worry America. Good-bye, sir." Hitler then marched on stage to deliver his speech.

A few weeks later, still trying to arrange a sit-down interview, Vanderbilt spoke by telephone with Hanfstaengl, whom Vanderbilt described as Hitler's "Man Friday." Seeing dollar signs in Vanderbilt's name, Hanfstaengl attempted a shakedown, asking $5,000 for an exclusive session with Hitler. Vanderbilt slammed down the phone.[37]

On May 24, 1933, after having made "a number of documentary shots of Jewish refugees" and writing "on the Jewish problem in Germany," Vanderbilt sailed for New York with the footage.[38] Word of Vanderbilt's scoop and motion picture plans preceded him. "The Hitler storm will gather when Cornelius Vanderbilt's picture of Nazi oppression of the Jews is released in this country," predicted *Motion Picture Daily.* However, unlike the putting down of *The Mad Dog of Europe*, the MPPDA made no effort to block Vanderbilt's production.[39] Vanderbilt, after all, was not a Hollywood regular. Doubtless too his patrician roots and personal connections made him less susceptible to pressure than cash-poor Hollywood Jews like Sam Jaffe and Al Rosen.

Not that Vanderbilt—the family black sheep—was flush. He had to take financing where he could find it. Shut out by the major studios, Vanderbilt cobbled together a deal with two independent producer-distributors—Joseph Seiden, who specialized in Yiddish-language cinema, and Samuel Cummins, who would later hit the jackpot as the stateside distributor of *Ecstasy* (1933), the Czech-German import featuring a quite naked young actress later christened Hedy Lamarr.

Directed by Mike Mindlin, a hired gun fresh off the sexploitation flick *This Nude World* (1933), and edited by Vanderbilt and Edwin C. Hill, a veteran NBC newsman known as "the Globe Trotter," *Hitler's Reign of Terror* was a 65-minute mélange of stock newsreel footage, ragged reenactments, and original material shot by Vanderbilt. "At last before your eyes actual uncensored scenes of Hitler's reign of terror!" shrieked exclamation-pointed, all-capitals copy blazing across the trailers for the film. "Ripping aside the curtain on history's most shocking episode and exposing the Nazi menace in America!" A virtually unseen curiosity in its time, and certainly since, the film has seen its quirky status grow as its availability over the years hovered somewhere between scarce and nonexistent.

Hitler's Reign of Terror opens with newsreel footage of Samuel Seabury, the crusading New York judge; Rabbi Stephen S. Wise, the voice of liberal Judaism in 1930s America; novelist Fannie Hurst, author of the tearjerking novels *Back Street* (1931) and *Imitation of Life* (1933); and Edward Neary, head of the American Legion, all denouncing Nazism during a rally at Madison Square Garden in 1933. Both Vanderbilt and Hill appear in the film as themselves, Hill assuming on-screen commentator duties and Vanderbilt playing the dauntless American reporter. In a framing device, Hill reads a statement on Nazism, illustrated with newsreel footage of torchlight parades and book burnings, and dispatches Vanderbilt to go forth and investigate, spawning more newsreel footage of ecstatic crowds, antisemitic signage, book burnings, and still more torchlight parades. Already, the images of frenzy and fire have become visual shorthand for the Nazi fever.

Back in America, Vanderbilt reenacts for Hill a fanciful embellishment unmentioned in his magazine articles and memoir. Claiming the film was stolen from him, he demonstrates how he managed to save several reels of raw footage by taping the film cans to the bottom of his car during a border inspection.

The brief interview with Hitler is reenacted by Vanderbilt, microphone in hand, confronting a Hitler impersonator. Thrusting the mike into the face of the faux *führer*, Vanderbilt repeats the question he dared to ask Hitler at his moment of triumph. "And what about the Jews, Your Excellency?"

After the face-off between Vanderbilt and Hitler, padding abounds: newsreel footage of the Great War, reenactments of Vanderbilt's interviews with Crown Prince Louis Ferdinand and the Kaiser, and an authentic interview, for whatever reason, with Helen Keller. A sampling of speeches from the Madison Square Garden rally, including excerpts from Undersecretary of State Raymond Moley and Congressman Samuel Dickstein (D-NY), fills out the balance of the running time. Narrator Hill closes with a summary of Nazi history till now—and a warning for the future.

Premiering on April 30, 1934, at the Mayfair, an independent theater on Broadway, and guaranteed a warm reception from an island dense with anti-Nazi Jews, *Hitler's Reign of Terror* gave the house the biggest single opening day in its history, surpassing the receipts of the previous record holder, another hair-raising tale from a strange land, big-game hunter Frank Buck's *Bring 'Em Back Alive* (1932). On the lookout for trouble, police stood outside the theater, but no disturbances were reported.[40]

The Production Code Administration was still a couple of months away from formal operation—July 15, 1934, was the official opening day—so *Hitler's Reign of Terror* never received an inspection from the Breen office. Nonetheless, officials of the MPPDA kept a wary eye on the film. Roy Norr, who worked for the MPPDA in public relations, was dispatched from the New York office to attend the opening day at the Mayfair and report back to MPPDA trouble-shooter Maurice McKenzie. According to Norr, the film "included only a few original 'reproductions' of alleged interviews had by Mr. Cornelius Vanderbilt, Jr. with the Kaiser, Mr. Hitler, and others. A general statement on the screen covered the fact that such interviews were 'reproductions' and it was obvious that the actors took the parts of the Kaiser, Hitler, and others in certain scenes."

A series of frame enlargements from Cornelius Vanderbilt Jr.'s *Hitler's Reign of Terror* (1934): Vanderbilt reenacts his interview with Hitler (*top*), discusses his exploits with collaborator Edwin C. Hill, (*middle*), and, in an authentic scene, walks among the brownshirts in Nazi Germany (Courtesy of the Cinémathèque Royale de Belgique)

As to what industry policy should be toward Vanderbilt's exposé, Norr was open-minded. "The fact that it is a propaganda picture does not make it necessarily unsuitable for the screen," he wrote McKenzie. "There is no more reason why a theater owner may not take a given side on a public question than why a newspaper publisher should not adopt a definite policy one way or another re Hitlerism." True, *Hitler's Reign of Terror* portrayed Hitler and Nazism in a manner likely to bring about ill will toward Germany, but "the film certainly does not go beyond responsible newspaper reports and actual happenings published." Norr concluded his remarks with impeccable logic: "A government cannot be insulted by the depiction of its own acts."[41]

An official of the U.S. government thought otherwise. "The film serves no good purpose," wrote George R. Canty from Germany, responding to inquiries from the Department of Commerce after protests from the German ambassador in Washington. On this matter of film policy at least, Canty agreed with the Nazis. "The German government has, in my opinion, heretofore been very arbitrary for one reason or another in its treatment of American films, but in this case, I am inclined to sympathize with the viewpoint of the German ambassador."[42]

Censors across America were also inclined to sympathize with the German viewpoint. Though the MPPDA put up no hurdles, *Hitler's Reign of Terror* was banned and cut by state and city censor boards reluctant to offend Nazi sensibilities. The New York State Censor Board denied the film a license, a decision that usually shut down exhibition throughout the state. Billing the docudrama as a news film, the Mayfair played it anyway and producer Samuel Cummins threatened a court fight if the board tried to block the screening.[43] The board blinked and backed off.

In Chicago, after the film had cleared the Chicago Board of Censors, the local Nazi consul, who claimed the footage was faked and shot in New York, successfully persuaded the police commissioner and mayor to halt screenings. Cummins denied the charges, sued the consul for slander, and filed a writ demanding a halt to the injunction. The film was eventually released, but only after being slashed to ribbons by the reeducated censor board, which demanded fourteen cuts and a title change to the less judgmental *Hitler's Reign.*

Under whatever name, *Hitler's Reign of Terror* needed all the controversy it could muster. Even critics sympathetic to Vanderbilt's good intentions cringed at the clunky pacing, blustering narration, and slipshod technique. "The word for this one is 'fiasco,'" decreed *Variety.*[44] "This picture adds nothing to the knowledge of Nazism that is not already known," frowned *Film Daily.*[45]

The peripatetic Vanderbilt was undaunted. Returning to Germany, he claimed to have obtained exclusive pictures of Nazi riots in Berlin and Munich during the bloody purge of the S.A. and the murder of its leader Ernst Rohm in June 1934. Smuggling the footage out to London, he announced plans to recut the new footage into an updated version of *Hitler's Reign of Terror*.[46]

The revised release never came to fruition, perhaps because the original fared so poorly. In San Francisco, a local German delegation somehow persuaded the police to arrest Herman Cohen, owner-manager of the Strand Theater, for booking the film. After bailing himself out, Cohen secured an injunction against further police actions and, no fool, set about milking his arrest for publicity value. "Come and see why the Nazi element had the manager arrested for showing *Hitler's Reign of Terror!*" urged ads in the San Francisco papers. Yet not even curiosity about a cause worth going to jail over could drum up business: the film flopped—and promptly vanished.[47]

THE STORY OF A HOLLYWOOD GIRL IN NAZILAND: *I WAS A CAPTIVE OF NAZI GERMANY* (1936)

On August 10, 1934, Isobel Lillian Steele, a pretty, 23-year-old American music student, was arrested in Berlin on suspicion of espionage. Hauled into Alexanderplatz Prison for interrogation, she was later transferred to Moabit Prison, already notorious as a Gestapo house of torture. Above her cell door was painted a white cross, the mark for a condemned inmate.

Canadian-born but a naturalized American citizen raised in Hollywood, Steele had come to Germany in June 1931 to study violin. Virtually stranded in Berlin when the exchange rate for the U.S. dollar cratered, she made ends meet by freelance magazine work and radio commentary. Being young, attractive, and artistic, she spent few evenings alone, partaking of the wide-open Weimar nightlife and, not being Jewish, missing few beats when the Nazis pushed decadent entertainment options underground.

Sometime in early 1934, Steele became infatuated with a dashing Polish aristocrat and well-known spy-about-town, Baron Ulrich von Sosnosky, a captain in the Polish military. To loosen lips and facilitate compromising positions, it was his business and pleasure to host hedonistic parties attended by film actresses, aristocrats, high-ranking Nazi officials, and fun-loving expatriates like Isobel Steele. Miss Steele, however, was not the only woman who had fallen under the spell of the enchanting captain. Also smitten were the Baroness Benita von Berg and Frau Renate von Natzmer, two beautiful secretaries in the offices of the Reichswehr, the regular German army. Both women were passing secret military documents to Sosnosky.

A Weimar-style libertine and foreign agent as colorful as Baron Sosnosky could not operate for long in the new Germany. On February 28, 1934, a squad of Gestapo officers converged on his opulent Berlin apartment and broke up the party. Along with the captain and his female retinue, some fifty guests were rousted from the parlor and taken into custody—sobbing noblewomen in evening gowns, screen actresses, and Nazi officials not privy to word of the bust.

Fortunately for Steele, who flitted on the fringes of Baron Sosnosky's social circle and espionage ring, she happened to be home on deadline that fateful night. Getting word of her near miss, however, the good daughter of Hollywood knew immediately what to do: turn the story of the charismatic Polish nobleman and his elegant Mata Haris into a motion picture scenario. "It wasn't an anti-Nazi film," she later insisted. "It was merely a story of the most romantic man I can recall."[48]

The Nazis suspected more subversive motives. Informed of Steele's on-spec screenwriting and indiscreet opinions of the Nazi regime ("I did not approve of the persecution of the Jews. I believed in the freedom of the press. I told my friends these things. And from that grew the whole monstrous affair of lies and rumors on which the Nazis sent me to prison."), the Gestapo barged into her apartment, confiscated the manuscript, and arrested her.[49]

In Alexanderplatz and Moabit prisons, Steele endured four months of harsh questioning, spartan conditions, and threats of execution. Outside the gates, meanwhile, her plight ballooned into a major diplomatic incident. That December, through the efforts of the American ambassador to Germany, William E. Dodd, and the intervention of Sen. William E. Borah (R-ID), she was released, shunted by train up to Hamburg, escorted on board the U.S. liner *President Harding,* and deported.

Steele's German coconspirators were not so lucky. Employing the traditional means of execution for traitors to the German state, the Nazis beheaded the two Reichswehr secretaries seduced by Captain Sosnosky. Captain Sosnosky's own neck was saved by an exchange of spies between Germany and Poland.

When Steele's ship docked in New York, a phalanx of reporters and newsreel cameramen waited at the pier. A reporter for the *New York Daily News*, which had paid $1,000 for the exclusive rights to her story while Steele was en route, tried to keep his prize catch quiet, but the newsreel boys were not taking no for an answer. "We don't care what she says," snarled a cameraman, "as long as she talks about something while we get fifty more feet of film." Steele relented, but gave away no juicy details. "It was no fun," she said. "If you are seeking pleasure, I would advise you to look elsewhere."[50] The *Daily News* then took possession of its exclusive, spiriting Steele away to a downtown hotel where she dictated her account. Under headlines like "One Hundred Days of Hitler Horror," her story was serialized in newspapers across the nation.

Back in Hollywood, Steele started work on a prison memoir, lectured to women's clubs, and—of course—shopped the story around to the studios. Predictably, the major studios passed. Constrained by the MPPDA and the Breen office, Hollywood balked at bankrolling any project liable to roil relations with Germany, upset her American fifth column, or validate the screen as a soapbox for political speech. However, a wily independent producer saw the makings of a marketable film in Steele's tale of intrigue, imprisonment, and anti-Nazism.

Alfred T. Mannon was a former president and treasurer of Republic Studios, a decidedly second-tier nonmajor studio, and an independent producer of long experience. In 1935 he partnered with Steele to form Malvina Pictures Corporation, Malvina being the name of a stuffed doll Steele clung to for comfort in her cell. Mannon decided to build the film version around two clever exploitation angles. Steele's story would be called *I Was a Captive of Nazi Germany*, echoing the first-person desperation of Warner Bros.' well-remembered exposé of another prison society, *I Am a Fugitive from a Chain Gang* (1932). To further underscore the she-was-there melodrama, and sensing star power in the photogenic ex-captive, he cast Miss Steele as herself in the title role.

In early 1936, production commenced—whereupon, almost immediately, the German Consul in Los Angeles, Dr. Georg Gyssling, demanded that the MPPDA intervene to stop the project. Gyssling was Hitler's man in Hollywood. A career diplomat and former winter Olympian, he joined the Nazi Party in the 1920s and in 1933 was rewarded with the plum assignment of Vice-Consul in charge of the German Consulate in Los Angeles.

▬
The redeemed captive: former
prisoner of the Nazis
Isobel Steele waves to reporters
upon her arrival in New York,
December 26, 1934.

No sooner had Gyssling submitted his credentials than he began to hector the studios about alleged anti-German tendencies in their production schedule. He lodged a protest with Columbia Pictures against *Below the Sea* (1933) on the grounds the seafaring adventure story was "highly detrimental to German prestige" because "the crook of the story is a German submarine commander, who is represented in a most hideous way and furthermore whose acting is not at all based on established facts."[51] Hearing that 20th Century-Fox's Great War espionage thriller *The Lancer Spy* (1937) would show scenes of "drunken German Army officers, who beat each other and molest women," he warned that such an insult to German honor "may lead to serious difficulties which should be avoided in mutual interests."[52] The leverage he applied was always the same: that if the studio persisted in the project at hand, said company would be refused permission to bring its films into Germany and the entire slate of Hollywood imports might be caught in the backwash.

When the MPPDA pleaded no jurisdiction over Mannon's independent venture, Gyssling sent Steele a threatening letter on consulate

Deutsches Konsulat
(GERMAN CONSULATE)
117 WEST NINTH STREET
ROOM 817
Los Angeles, Calif.
TEL. VAndike 5865

Miss Isobel Steele,
6118 Glen Holly,
Hollywood, Calif.

Bei Beantwortung bitte folgendes
Aktenzeichen anzugeben:
In Answering Please Refer To:

Film 1028.

Dear Miss Stele:

As you might be interested in it with regard
to your participation in the making of a film allegedly
dealing with certain experiences of yours in Germany,
I beg to send you herewith copy of § 15 of the German
decree concerning the showing of foreign films published
in the "Deutscher Reichsanzeiger" of June 28th, 1932.

Truly yours,

(Dr. Georg Gyssling)
GERMAN CONSUL.

"Detrimental to German prestige": reproduction of a letter from Los Angeles–based Nazi consul Georg Gyssling threatening Isobel Steele and the makers of *I Was a Captive of Nazi Germany* (1936).

stationery. An exposé "allegedly dealing with certain experiences of yours in Germany" having come to his attention, he warned her against the production of a film "detrimental to German prestige." Gyssling also summoned German members of the cast, many of whom were German citizens, to a meeting at the consulate to deliver the threat in person.[53]

Mannon and Steele could afford to shrug off the pressure. As a one-off production company, Malvina Pictures had nothing to fear from a boycott by Germany. By July 1936, Gyssling notwithstanding, *I Was a Captive of Nazi Germany* was wrapped and booked for a New York premiere at the Globe.

At this juncture, Mannon did something unusual: he submitted the film to the Breen office for a Production Code seal. In this, the producer departed from the standard application procedure, which was to submit early screen treatments and the final screenplay before the commencement of actual shooting. The process of preproduction revision was the most cost-effective way of doing censorship, far less expensive than altering a finished film. It was in fact a central rationale for Hollywood's system of in-house censorship.

Breen informed Mannon of what he already knew: that Dr. Gyssling had objected to "the [possible] approval by the PCA [of] your picture . . . on the grounds that it does not fairly represent the German Government and its people." Breen quoted chapter and verse to Mannon. "If such a protest can be sustained, we would have to reject your picture as a violation of the Production Code which directs that 'the history, institutions, prominent people and citizenry of other nations shall be represented fairly.'"

A tad disingenuously, Breen then tried to sidestep the diplomatic minefield by reminding Mannon that the length of time required for the proper adjudication of so serious a matter might delay the film's release to the detriment of its commercial prospects. Perhaps, he suggested, Mannon might want to withdraw his application for a Code seal?[54]

Mannon was not about to let Breen off the hook so easily. An old Hollywood hand, he knew that a Code seal was the essential transit visa into the prime theatrical venues, motion picture palaces and neighborhood Bijous alike, contractually obligated to exhibit only cinema approved by the PCA. Without the coveted imprimatur, *I Was a Captive of Nazi Germany* would be consigned to a limited number of second-rate venues.

Responding with a firmness unusual for an independent producer, Mannon insisted on a fair hearing. "I am informed by competent authority that the German Consul exceeds his authority when he protests to your organization about the subject matter of pictures or the conduct of private individuals or films in connection with a picture to be exhibited in the United States," he told Breen. In this, he was technically correct, but politically obtuse: foreign consuls, Nazi or not, wielded considerable influence on the MPPDA by threatening to block Hollywood imports from their homelands.

From Mannon's vantage, withdrawing *I Was a Captive of Nazi Germany* would also be an admission that Gyssling's charges had merit, that the picture—which neither the consul nor any other German had yet seen—was an unfair representation of Germany. Mannon asserted that, on the contrary, "I was particularly careful not to depict political incidents that did not actually happen and have supported Miss Steele's personal knowledge of these incidents with headlines from the *New York Times* and other back numbers of newspapers. In fact, the inserts in the picture are actual photographs of back numbers of newspapers." Mannon had strived to portray the German citizenry as "wholesome people" and to cast no aspersions on the character of "prominent people." Moreover:

> If the present regime in Germany did not win its popularity by inspir-
> ing the youth of Germany, if there was no Boycott of the Jews, if the
> Blood Purge and the burning of the books did not happen, if Minister of
> Propaganda Herr Goebbels did not suppress Herr Von Papen's speech
> on the necessity of a free speech,[c] if Isobel Steele was not arrested and
> charged with high treason [and] espionage and held for four months in
> solitary confinement at the Alexander Platz and Moabit prison in Ber-
> lin, subjected to rigid cross-examination and deported without trial only
> after the United States Department of State demanded that she be given
> an immediate trial or freed, then the picture is unfair to the German
> Government.

Under the circumstances, Mannon saw no reason why Gyssling "should
endeavor to suppress a re-enactment of actual photographs of these
scenes." Therefore—and here he tossed the ball back into Breen's court—
"I must urgently insist that the picture be given your code approval
or refusal."[55]

Mannon's demand for due process ignited a buzz of activity in the
upper ranks of official Hollywood. The MPPDA and the Breen office
could discourage the major studios from bankrolling an anti-Nazi project, or browbeat an underfinanced independent into backing off, but
Mannon confronted the association with a fait accompli—a finished film,
in the can, ready for PCA examination. Hemmed in by its own ground
rules, the Breen office was compelled to review the film, grant or deny it
a Code seal, and, if denied, state the reasons in plain English.

Like any bureaucrat faced with a decision above his pay grade, Breen
passed the buck upstairs. He informed Hays that after discussion with
B. B. Kahane, president of RKO, and Emanuel Cohen from Paramount
Pictures, the decision should be a "matter of industry policy" and as such
"the Board of Directors in New York [should make] the decision as to
whether or not this picture should be approved."[56] Breen would serve as
messenger boy.

---

[c] On June 17, 1934, at the University of Marburg, Franz von Papen, former Chancellor in the Weimar Republic then serving as Vice-Chancellor under Hitler, delivered a bold speech calling for the
restoration of democratic principles and an end to brownshirt terrorism. The "Blood Purge" is a
reference to Hitler's purge of elements of the S.A. and other opponents on June 29–July 2, 1934, an
orgy of political murder known to history as the "Night of the Long Knives."

Having gotten his marching orders from above, and his Irish up by Gyssling's meddling, Breen delivered the news with a straight face. Backpedaling, he assured Mannon that far from caving in to pressure from Gyssling, he had merely had Mannon's best commercial interests at heart. His suggestion that Mannon withdraw his application for a Code seal "was prompted by a desire on our part not to delay the release of your picture. The official protest filed with us by the Consul for Germany at Los Angeles, could not, we feel, be passed over lightly." After that defensive feint, however, Breen abruptly informed Mannon: "Attached hereto we are sending you our formal Certificate of Approval, No. 2526." Just like that, though with a caveat:

> In this connection, I want to make it clear that this formal approval by the Production Code Administration does not carry with it an endorsement of the authenticity of the facts set forth in your picture. It must not be understood that in approving your picture, the Production Code Administration approves the picture's content in any way. The judgment of the approval is based solely upon the picture's technical conformity to the Production Code.

Mannon had scored a major victory. He had forced the Breen office to concede *fair* treatment of a foreign nation did not mean *sympathetic* treatment. He also created an opening for anti-Nazi cinema that any of the major studios might have slipped through—had they been so inclined.

On August 1, 1936, *I Was a Captive of Nazi Germany* opened at the Globe on Broadway in New York, but without the Code seal in its title credits.[57] (Breen's approval had come too late to redesign the title credits even had Mannon been willing to pony up for the postproduction costs.) Whether fearing Nazi retribution or professional embarrassment, the actors and offscreen talent, with the exception of Steele, went unbilled.

Drawn from Steele's serialized narrative, *I Was a Captive of Nazi Germany* suffers from the limitations of the lead actress (whatever her talents as a musician, Steele is no thespian) and the constraints of budget (neither the décor of the Berlin apartments nor the Nazi prisons could pass for the originals). Its interest lies in its unique status as the only anti-Nazi feature film produced in America and granted a Code seal before 1939.

A written prologue sets the stage:

The TRUTH is often stranger than fiction.
Isobel Steele's experiences in Nazi Germany in 1934 astounded the world when her book was first published.[d]

Now it has been possible to reenact the whole sequence of events so that the world can see, what hitherto, it has only been able to read.

The chief character in this amazing drama is reenacted by Isobel Steele herself and in order to safeguard the welfare of the other members of the cast their names are not disclosed.

A newsreel montage and a voice-over narration survey the disintegration of Weimar Germany and the rise of Nazism, exculpating the old regime and excoriating the new. The naïve but honorable President Paul von Hindenburg is forced to grant Hitler the Reich Chancellorship "to purify the Aryan strain," whereupon "Hitler's anti-Semitism gained by leaps and bounds."

After the crisp history lesson, the voice-over makes an unusual invitation. "Let us meet someone who actually witnessed the political drama—an American girl who stood [on the] sidelines and was by August 1934 caught in the whirlpool of this sweeping revolution. I take pleasure in introducing Miss Isobel Steele."

Sitting in a plush apartment, Steele is dressed to the nines—black gloves, sleek dress, draped in mink.

"How do you do?" she says pleasantly.

After some small talk, the voice inquires, "Tell me, did you like making this picture?"

"Very much. Although the prison scenes depressed me. Hollywood has a way of making things realistic."

In a bombastic timbre borrowed from Westbrook Van Voorhis' pronouncements for the *March of Time* series, the voice-over resumes the thumbnail history of Nazi Germany. The "greatest outburst of political prejudice modern history has recorded" finds its logical expression in the subjugation of the Jews, the deification of Hitler, and the chill pervading everyday life. "Jewish persecution began at once. It is estimated that over 90,000 were thrown into prison and concentration camps, while 70,000 leaving homes and possessions fled in poverty." Over newsreel footage of

---

[d] No book was published.

the Nazi book burning of May 10, 1933, book jackets with Jewish bylines are superimposed on the pyre. Overdubbed in German-accented English, "the diminutive but fiery" Dr. Paul Joseph Goebbels rants before the bonfire. Inserts of Steele watching the spectacle among a crowd of Germans, the glow of the flames flickering on her face, are an eerie reminder that she was, in fact, an eyewitness to this history.

The reenactment proper begins with Steele meeting a German film producer at a suitable locale: a dubbing session for the German-language version of an American motion picture. Doing the voice-over work is the actress who will draw her into the web of Baron Sosnosky.

Though the broad currents of Nazi history pass in review (the murder of S.A. leader Ernst Rohm on June 30, 1934, is reenacted with a Hitler impersonator), the off-to-the-side details of life in the new Germany are more arresting to the eye. A sign on a Berlin taxi bears the slogan "Ich faber kein Juden!" ("I carry no Jews"). A brownshirt looks forward to his new assignment as a paid informer. "My days of enforcing Jewish boycotts and fighting communists are about over," he gloats. Fanatical worship of the *führer* energizes the true believers and terrorizes ordinary Germans into submission.

After the Gestapo arrests Baron Sosnosky and his female spy ring, a German producer approaches Steele to write an insider's account of the sensational case. "I know nothing about writing scenarios," she blurts out with unwitting self-reflexivity.

When Steele is arrested by the Gestapo, a character destined for a long life in Hollywood cinema—the sinister Nazi villain—makes his screen debut. "Crying will not help you here, Fräulein," sneers Steele's interrogator, jolting awake the comatose melodrama. "Up until the time she is nabbed by the secret police, this feature appeared to be dying on its feet," noted *Variety*. "Once she is under the stern hands of the Nazi authorities, it perks up appreciably. Prison scenes are fairly realistic and Miss Steele's acting improves in her new environment."[58]

Before too much duress, the intervention of "the brilliant Idaho statesman" Senator Borah secures Steele's release. The final shot of Steele, now safe on native shores, taps into deep wellsprings of American mythology: the redeemed captive—smiling, her hair blowing in the sea breeze—stands on the deck of a ship in New York Harbor with the Statue of Liberty standing firm in the background. The American girl is no longer tormented by brutal savages.

"Hollywood has a way of making things realistic": a lobby card advertising Isobel
Steele's real-life story.

Watching *I Was a Captive of Nazi Germany* on a warm summer evening in 1936, William Weaver of *Motion Picture Herald* witnessed the
kind of rowdy outbursts that always made exhibitors nervous about films
that stirred up emotions besides yuks or tears. During a prison sequence,
when German slogans on a cell wall were translated by the narrator as an
anti-Nazi slogan ("for every man imprisoned by Hitler a hundred more
were at liberty to oppose him"), "abrupt applause, and not necessarily
planted, broke out, followed by a guttural 'Heil Hitler' en solo."[59] Newsreel shots of Hitler also "received a mild salvo of Bronx cheers."[60]

After the promising debut in New York, however, *I Was a Captive of
Nazi Germany* endured the stunted distribution prospects of an orphan
film lacking the support system of a parent studio. Not until April 20,
1937, did Mannon secure a booking in Los Angeles. Playing up the local
angle, the film was ballyhooed as "the story of a Hollywood girl in Naziland," an innocent abroad whose head was "always in the shadow of the

beheading ax." Skittish newspaper ads deleted the party and place from the advertising, truncating the title to *I Was a Captive*.

Critical response to Isobel Steele's season in hell ranged from tepid to contemptuous. As with *Hitler's Reign of Terror*, reviewers felt duty bound to pan a work whose good intentions were no compensation for its dreadful artistry. "A blundering anti-Nazi propaganda film . . . crudely produced and performed," cringed Frank S. Nugent at the *New York Times*. "There is too much need of a righteous denunciation of stupid despotism, bigotry, and narrow nationalism to entrust the attack to amateurs."[61]

No doubt—but the professionals were missing in action. American moviegoers seeking insight into Hitler and Nazi Germany had to look elsewhere on the film program.

3

THE NAZIS IN THE NEWSREELS

"One of these days there is quite liable to be a mild riot in this house over Hitler. Two factions are definitely shaping up in the Embassy audience. There was a contest to a draw Saturday between applauders and booers. The din reached a deafening climax. It was just the opposite at the Luxer which, through Pathé, was daring enouh to semi-close Hitler. Only manifestation there was subdued hissing."[1]

The ear- and-eyewitness report on the vox populi reaction to Hitler's screen image was filed by Tom Waller, *Variety*'s man on the newsreel beat. Throughout the 1930s, week in and week out, Waller or his colleagues Roy Chartier, Mike Wear, or Robert Landry, promethean screen watchers all, attended the shows at the two newsreel theaters located in midtown Manhattan, the Embassy Theater and the Trans-Lux. As exquisitely attuned to the vibrations in the air as the news on screen, they commented not only on the contents of the clips but the reactions of the audience. Their observations comprise a kind of ethnographer's field notes on the folkways of an exotic tribe of moviegoers, a community of news-hungry spectators whose tastes were uncommercial and whose opinions went unmuffled.

The Embassy Newsreel Theater, located at Broadway and 46th in Times Square, and the Trans-Lux (nicknamed "the Luxer"), located at Broadway and 49th, granted top billing to what elsewhere was the appetizer on the motion picture menu.[a] In metropolitan palaces and neigh-

---

[a] The flagship theaters for both operations were located in midtown Manhattan, but the Embassy and the Trans-Lux each maintained franchises in other locations. The Trans-Lux had branches at Madison and 60th St. in Manhattan and in Brooklyn, and the Embassy had three additional

borhood theaters, the newsreel was typically screened at the top of what exhibitors called "the balanced program"—the full-course motion picture diet that also included a cartoon, a short subject, and a feature-length attraction. In the newsreel theater, the side dish was the entrée.

The newsreel had been a standard item in the motion picture lineup since 1906, when the French company Pathé pioneered a weekly news issue. By the early sound era, and for most of the classical Hollywood era, five commercial newsreels, each with a name-brand studio distributor, divided up the market in approximately 16,500 theaters: Fox Movietone News, Paramount News, Universal Newsreel, RKO-Pathé News, and MGM's Hearst-Metrotone News (renamed the News of the Day in 1936). Like the big-city dailies, they jostled for pride of place and scrambled to scoop the competition. Trademark segments and announcers ("spielers" in trade jargon) also imprinted the identity of the individual brands. In 1930, Universal inaugurated the use of an offscreen narrator with the hiring of staccato-voiced radio sportscaster Graham McNamee.[b] Edwin C. Hill spoke for Hearst-Metrotone News until 1936 when NBC radio announcer Jean Paul King assumed duties behind the microphone. Fox Movietone employed the most prestigious of all the vocal hosts, the famed journalist and radio commentator Lowell Thomas.

The friendly newsreel commentator, boasted Universal Newsreel, "adds that human touch that gives life and fire to the events as they flash on screen." Perhaps, but the "commentator" title was largely honorific: wary of offending any moviegoer's ear, the spielers kept their opinions to themselves. "Illuminating comments, especially when voiced by erudite students of affairs, are bound to prove interesting to millions of persons, but the foundation of a newsreel will always be its pictures," lectured the *Film Daily*. "There is just one danger in the situation, and that is the possibility of overdoing the editorializing and moralizing aspects."[2] There

---

branches in Manhattan and one in downtown Newark. In 1938 the showcase Trans-Lux ("the deluxer of the species") moved 400 feet south down Broadway to the former site of Churchill's Restaurant. In New York and elsewhere, newsreel theaters tended to be located in or around train stations so passengers with time to kill could pop in for a quick viewing. In 1938, *Variety* estimated there were only ten extant newsreel houses in the country, eight in and around New York, one in Boston, and one in Philadelphia.

[b] Universal Newsreel footage dominates present-day archival documentaries because its library is in the public domain, readily accessible from the National Archives and Records Administration in College Park, Maryland, and more importantly, free. Motion picture memory is thus filtered by what the Universal cameraman caught in his lens.

The Embassy Newsreel Theater, the flagship venue for New York City news junkies in the 1930s, and its midtown rival, the Trans-Lux. (Photofest/Courtesy of the Michael R. Miller Collection, Theatre Historical Society)

was little danger of that. When it came to editorializing, the newsreels were cautious to a fault.

Originally, the Embassy built its program around clips from Fox Movietone and Hearst-Metrotone, while the Trans-Lux culled from Universal, Pathé, and Paramount. Over time, however, and despite the risk of duplicate programs, the rival houses each drew on material from all five companies. The newsreels clips were supplemented by documentary short subjects and sundry screen novelties, such as sing-alongs, comedy shorts, or cartoons. Again, over time, both houses cut down on the kid-friendly ephemera for a news- and documentary-centric program that clocked in at around 50 minutes.

The newsreel companies used the high-profile New York houses to showcase their best footage and headline scoops prior to shipping the reels out of town. The Trans-Lux tended to have a shorter program, more generously sweetened with novelty shorts, color travelogues, and cartoons; the Embassy was the preferred forum for spectators who wanted their news served straight. In March 1933, already heeding the war clouds overseas, it adopted "a policy of more internationally significant news."[3]

The Embassy opened on November 2, 1929, not an auspicious debut date, the week of the worst news of the decade, the stock market crash. Still, the 600-seat house was an instant hit, drawing in 7,000 patrons a day with eleven shows beginning at 10:00 a.m. and running until midnight. Signs plastered in the front lobby and barkers shouting the headlines roped in passersby. "Hear with your own ears the actual sound of the assassin's shot exactly as it happened!" yelled the shills for the Embassy's premiere program, highlighting Fox Movietone's exclusive sound pictures of an attempted assassination of Italy's Crown Prince Umberto. Admission was a reasonable 25 cents. "Everyone ought to be able to pay two bits to pass an hour away," figured the good-natured Phil M. Daily, the eponymous columnist for the *Film Daily*.[4]

The newsreel theater attracted a select, or rather self-selected, audience. Even by the standards of the classical Hollywood moviegoer—by all accounts a loquacious spectator given to audible expressions of approval or disgust—newsreel audiences were notoriously mouthy and unruly. Many came not just to watch the news but to vent at the newsmakers: the motion picture theater as town hall meeting. "Taking newsreel theaters as an example, where world-renowned personalities and events are shown, hisses, catcalls, stamping of feet, booing and applause are intermingled by conglomerate audiences who have fixed opinions on the subject matter thrown on screen," *Variety* noted in 1938.[5] Irving Hoffman, the *Hollywood Reporter*'s envoy in New York, agreed that "newsreel audiences take the palm as being the most demonstrative of all theater patrons." In 1937, watching the first reports of Japanese depredations in China, Hoffman harkened to a fiercely partisan outburst at the Embassy. "The shots of raped Nanking, for instance, inspire hisses from all parts of the house, and when a Japanese aviator is shot to earth, the house rocks with applause."[6]

The demographic makeup of the newsreel audience—who were these avid jeerers and cheerers?—is a matter of guesswork, but the core clientele was what today would be called opinion makers or news junkies— a breed apart who, compared to the average rung of motion picture fandom, tended to be more politically minded, better educated, and (this being midtown Manhattan in the 1930s) disproportionately Jewish. Newsreel audiences, wrote a bemused Jane Cobb, the gal-about-town columnist for the *New York Times*, "are recognized as being more intelligent than the average, and even if there were no other reason for attending, one would go to a newsreel theater for the pleasure of feeling smug."[7] The Embassy catered to a more obstreperous, foreign-born, and left-wing crowd, a claque known to applaud if a close-up of Joseph Stalin flashed on screen. When the Trans-Lux screened a 35-minute propaganda film from Moscow entitled *Soviets on Parade* (1933), Tom Waller interpreted the addition as a naked bid to tempt some of the rowdy "Communist attendees" away from their usual haven at the Embassy.[8]

The crowd of regulars rubbed shoulders with a more casual cohort lured by a screeching headline or simply the need to kill time between appointments or train departures. In 1930, *Variety*'s publisher-editor Sime Silverman lauded the newsreel aficionados, upmarket intelligentsia and downtown ramblers alike, with an affectionate homage. "The Embassy draws the strollers along Broadway, the impatient date makers, the train waiters, the time-killers, and after those the untold thousands who think the newsreel is the best single feature, now that it is in sound, ever devised in the film industry." The experiment in screen journalism, said Silverman, was "drawing the best, the class, and the intellectuals of New York into its seats each and every week."[9] Less romantically, a reporter for *Exhibitors Herald-World* sized up the Embassy crowd as "what can only be called a constantly changing hard-boiled audience."[10]

From a bookkeeping perspective, the profit margin of the newsreels was always slim, more shades of red than black. "The amount of actual labor and talent put in to making our newsreels is incredible and yet for all of that, the newsreel is the least productive of actual profits of any short subject series on the market," reported *Film Daily* in 1934. Yet as prestige makers and flag wavers for their corporate parents in Hollywood, the twice-weekly issues recouped in respect what they lost in cash. "It is a fair assertion that not less than half of the whole status and repute of the motion picture is based on what an intelligent public thinks of newsreels and topical shorts," declared *Motion Picture Herald* editor Terry Ramsaye, himself a former newsreel editor, who maintained a proprietary interest in the medium throughout the 1930s.[11] Fiscally sound or not, the newsreel was "second in importance on every screen," asserted the *Film Daily*, surpassed only by the featured attraction in popularity and status. "The ordinary theatergoer doesn't care a whoop what newsreel is included on the program, just so long as one is on the bill."[12]

Trafficking in the real world news of the day, the newsreel stood apart from the animated shenanigans of the cartoon, the exotic realms of the travelogue shorts, and the escapist lure of the feature film. Though surely entertaining—the issues were packed with sports coverage, human interest stories, and antic silliness—the newsreel also informed and confronted audiences with the raw stuff of political upheaval, war, crime, natural disasters, and man-made horror. Even if the news was rehashed and well known by the time it unspooled on screen, the format was a rough cinematic approximation of the headlines typeset on the pages of the daily paper. Its unique purview gave the newsreel special prerogatives, especially when up against the bane of motion picture existence—censorship.

Throughout the 1930s, and well beyond, motion pictures were exhibited at the pleasure of a nationwide honeycomb of state and municipal censor boards. In 1915 the United States Supreme Court had ruled that the medium was "a business pure and simple" and as such was not protected by the guarantees given the print press under the First Amendment of the U.S. Constitution. Nothing prohibited city, state, or (by logical extension) the federal government from setting up a censorship board to clip and ban films according to the standards of the community or the whims of the membership.

Nonetheless, even in the pre–First Amendment era for the motion picture medium, the newsreels enjoyed a greater degree of freedom from censorship than the rest of the Hollywood lineup. A kind of penumbra effect emanating from the freedom accorded the print press shielded the news-on-film medium from the narrow-eyed scrutiny bedeviling the rest of the program. Unlike the feature films and short subjects on the motion picture bill—indeed, unlike the cartoons—the newsreels were exempt from oversight by the Production Code Administration, the in-house agency that from July 1934 onward precensored all Hollywood product. Occasionally, when the newsreels issued a short subject on a news event of special interest, the company would request a courtesy review from the PCA. In 1937, when Universal Newsreel, purely for form's sake, asked for a Code seal for its short subject on the sinking of the *Panay*, the U.S. naval vessel attacked by Japanese warplanes on the Yangtze River in China, *Variety* noted that Will Hays and his outfit gave newsreels a wide berth. "[The] understood Haysian attitude is that all matter in [the *Panay*] short is newsreel material, and as such would be approved with little or no change since [the] MPPDA never has attempted to change newsreel material."[13]

Like the MPPDA, state and city censorship boards usually exempted newsreels from the frame-by-frame scrutiny applied to the Hollywood feature films—but not always. Clips of civic unrest, political activism, or criminal lawlessness tended to rouse censors to scissor material that might give insurrectionist ideas to audiences beaten down by the Great Depression. However, on those occasions when the newsreels did run afoul of state oversight, the deletions and bannings sparked more controversy than the censorship routinely applied to the rest of the program. Newsreel cameramen could still be pushed around and roughed up, their film confiscated and their cameras busted, with an impunity that the print press would neither abide nor be subjected to, but when rogue cops or hired goons attacked newsreel cameramen, their allies in the print press hit back. After a barrage of editorial denunciations, local censorship boards tended to withdraw their original demands and approve on second thought what they had banned on first look.

Yet despite the greater leeway accorded the newsreels as journalistic entities, they were more lapdogs than watchdogs, seldom straying outside the comfort zone of consensus opinion. The pressures of commerce, the threat of legal action, and the risk of official clampdown kept newsreel editors from challenging shibboleths, bucking authority, or defying convention. The controversies the newsreels generated were seldom political, in a partisan sense, a result of defiant editors taking a fearless stand on the divisive issues of the day. Almost always, the dustups were over matters of taste and decorum—showing the bullet-riddled body of Pretty Boy Floyd in a ditch or the corpse of John Dillinger laid out on a slab.

Under a concept called "voluntary restraint," the newsreel editors heeded an internal barometer as to what was most conducive to the mood of good cheer necessary for a moviegoer to digest the forthcoming contents of the balanced program. Both the MPPDA and the state censorship boards were "convinced that the principal guardianship of what should be cut or left in, from the great mass of material that is photographed, should rest with newsreel editors," *Variety* reported in 1937, noting approvingly that the "newsreelers know when to lay off."[14] The newsreels did not need to be censored because they censored themselves.

"THE SWASTIKA MAN"

In 1932 the veteran newsreel cameraman Charles Peden observed that "the Kaiser, the Pope, and Stalin are the only public personages in the world who have not been personally interviewed by the sound newsreel."[15] When Peden penned his wish list, the obvious omission had not yet walked onto the world stage, a public personage who, had he agreed to sit for a face-to-face interview before a sound newsreel, might have qualified for the scoop of the century.

The aloof disdain of Adolf Hitler was in distinct contrast to the accommodating availability of his fascist precursor. Ever since seizing power in 1922, Italian dictator Benito Mussolini had been only too happy to preen for the American cameras and, with the advent of synchronous dialogue, to rush before the microphones so his voice might be heard. By 1931 the Italian dictator was so ubiquitous a camera hog that the "popular impression [was] that there isn't a program released that doesn't contain Il Duce or some reference to him," joked Tom Waller. At the end of that year, a trade press survey ranked Mussolini with President Herbert Hoover, British Prime Minister Ramsay MacDonald, and New York Mayor Jimmy Walker in an elite quartet of "the world's greatest newsreel stars." Hitler rated not a single mention.[16]

The first glimpse of Hitler in the American newsreels is hard to pinpoint with any precision, but by 1931 he was appearing in a handful of clips, flashing by quickly, usually paired with Mussolini, the predecessor dictator who was then seen as the senior partner in European fascism.[c] "What a lot of fans have been thinking for a long time is being cracked by Graham McNamee this week," Waller reported in his review of a Universal Newsreel issue in November 1931. "He likens Hitler's personal pose to Mussolini."[17] Later that year, Paramount scored a vivid clip of Hitler in an automobile, "wearing a hackenkreuz [swastika], receiving an ovation from his followers."[18]

To most Americans, foreign news with a political edge was a distant buzz on the mental periphery, a distraction from the more urgent news of the Great Depression (another blight given scant coverage by the chronically upbeat newsreels). Even for the curious moviegoer, news from afar was badly dated by the time it unspooled on screen, generally taking two weeks or more from European filming to New York screening. The newsreels preferred to showcase the splendor of European royalty on parade rather than obscure political leaders with esoteric gripes having little relevance for an American audience. In 1932 most news-minded Americans were more interested in their own presidential election and the end of Prohibition than the internecine squabbles of the Weimar Republic.

Still, 1932 was Hitler's breakout year in the American newsreels, the year the violent and historic presidential election in Germany received extensive international news coverage and, in America, modest notice in the newsreels. In the run-up to the election, the newsreels featured images of Hindenburg and Hitler campaigning, including the now famous shots of Hitler deplaning on landing fields, images that document his pioneering use of the airplane for campaign stops while valorizing a forward-looking leader in step with advanced technology. "Welcome clips," remarked Waller, hinting at the general paucity of footage,

---

[c] The first newsreel image of Hitler, animated in the motion picture medium, is a shot from 1919, caught by chance. It shows an obscure civilian among a crowd at Garmisch station, greeting a Frei Korps unit returning from crushing a communist uprising in Munich. Like an apparition, a well-dressed man leans out from the crowd and the camera catches a full body, head-to-toe portrait of an instantly recognizable figure. The shot is freeze-framed in "The Unchained Camera" episode of *Cinema Europe* (1995), the six-part BBC documentary series. The first headlined clip of Hitler noted in the synopsis sheets of Universal Newsreel occurs in the issue of May 5, 1932, reporting the results of the German elections: "Hitler Gets Big Vote but Fails to Nab Prussian Power."

"in view of the wide publicity given the event in the [newspaper] dailies."
In a report on the results of the election, which Hindenburg won but in
which Hitler gained ground and momentum, Waller spotted a fresh face
on the Embassy screen and recorded the response from the crowd:

> Embassy Saturday [April 15, 1932] got more audience reaction on this
> one clip than it has on others in weeks. References to Hitler were met
> with fan hisses and applause. The single mention of the new German
> president [Hindenburg], however, did not get a division of opinion. That
> the matinee audience was well interspersed with Germans was also evi-
> denced by the understanding of Hitler's speech.[19]

German-speaking Jews, up from the Lower East Side, and German-
speaking nationalists, down from the heavily German district of Yorkville, met in midtown to check out the momentous news from the home
country—and to vent their opinions at the screen.

By the end of the year, Hitler was a recognizable face, though not yet a
star presence, in the American newsreels. "Paramount titles a clip showing Hitler in a crowd, as he has been seen numbers of times, as signify-
ing he is headed for an audience with Hindenburg," Waller commented
in December 1932. "When the flash is repeated, it is after the Hindenburg conference. All of which means nothing to an American audience.
For all the fans over here know, the subject might have had Hitler going
to and returning from a saloon."[20] The remark indicates first that Hitler was becoming an increasingly common sight, and second that the
images were unspooled with little context or coherence.

Yet even without a flowchart explaining Weimar politics, American
audiences seem to have been able to spot one of the great villains of history. Unlike Mussolini, a blowhard whose strutting often inspired deri-
sive cackles, Hitler radiated a pictorially ominous presence. In the frothy
newsreel lineup, he was a serious splash of cold water. Most Americans
watched warily, and some hissed. A few applauded or shouted "Heil!" No
one seems to have snickered.

In mid-February 1933, the first newsreel clips reporting Hitler's ascension to Reich Chancellor on January 30 reached New York. "There was
scattered applause for Hitler in the Luxer," reported Waller, manning his
usual post at the Saturday matinee screenings. "Embassy reaction was
mixed with marked hisses added."[21]

In any newsreel report, the image that sparked the most vociferous reaction from viewers was a close-up shot of the newsmaker. A huge square portrait looming over audiences in crisp, 35mm celluloid, it was the signal to hiss, cheer, jeer, burst into applause, or let loose with a plosive "Bronx cheer." After his solo flight across the Atlantic in 1927, a close-up of Charles Lindbergh spurred spontaneous cheers and applause for years afterwards. FDR's smiling visage also inspired partisan hoorays or, more rarely, hissing. In Hitler's case, a close-up—typically a worshipful low-angle shot filmed by Nazi crews—infuriated the anti-Nazis and delighted his stateside claque. "Hitler audience reactions are back stronger than ever at the Embassy," Waller reported in May 1933. "Hitler at Berlin's May Day was the signal for a storm of boos and applause."[22]

So Pavlovian was the revulsion or rapture incited by a close-up of Hitler that newsreel editors—responding to complaints from nervous exhibitors—often deleted his picture rather than agitate audiences. "The key city deluxers either eliminated or played down Hitler's newsreel clips as a means to obviate disturbances which had asserted themselves with the flashing of the Nazi leader's pictures," *Variety* reported

The signal to heil or hiss: a newsreel shot of Adolf Hitler, 1933.

in March 1933. "Newsreel editors are all dodging Hitler close-ups."[23] Other tradewise observers also noticed the conspicuous absence in the newsreels of the headline maker in the newspapers. "In many instances scenes depicting Hitler operations have been cut out of the newsreels," *Motion Picture Herald* pointed out in 1933. "Thus far Universal is the only company which has eliminated Nazi scenes. It was understood that Paramount, Pathé, Fox Movietone, and Hearst-Metrotone were considering similar moves."[24]

In stitching together segments on Nazi Germany, the newsreel editors had to balance their service to two masters. In order to maintain the flow of German motion picture footage, they were compelled to show some clips provided by or filmed under the approval of the Reichsfilmkammer. Yet they were also leery of angering the anti-Nazi contingent in their consumer base. "Hitler is proving an admittedly ticklish subject for the newsreels," Waller noted in March 1933, commenting on clips of a tribute to German dead in the Great War. "The editors are obviously exerting all caution not to offend an important trade in Germany and at the same time not to arouse the ire of portions of American audiences." *Variety*'s eagle-eyed correspondent noticed an interesting trend. "But Herr Hitler is not getting the close-ups that were his just a few months ago," continued Waller. "It seemed that efforts had been made to 'bury' him in the current subject."[25]

Caught between vitriol from one side and a defiant "Heil!" from the other, newsreel editors thought long and hard about projecting the face of Adolf Hitler. Not that so prominent a profile could always be edited out of the story. The funeral of President Hindenburg, held in Germany on August 7, 1934, with Hitler delivering the funeral oration, reached American screens about ten days later. "Some of the reel editors frowned upon including the Hitler eulogy, evidently figuring the swastika man would spoil the solemnity of the occasion with some American audiences," observed Waller. "In the Embassy, however, the usual hissing was not in evidence during the generous running time Pathé allowed Hitler."[26] Presumably the anti-Hitler contingent was constrained by respect for the ritual.

Calibrating the frequency of Hitler's appearance in the newsreels and gauging the audience reaction is made more difficult by the fact that newsreel editors did not have the final say over what was actually projected in individual theaters. In the days when projection booths came equipped with flatbed editing tables, house managers were able to reedit newsreel programs at the site of exhibition, trimming the contents to fit personal prejudice or community standards. Thus, even when newsreel editors in New York opted to include shots of Hitler, local theater managers might slice out his picture. "Following repeated complaints to the newsreel companies about the continual insertion of Nazi propaganda, without results, exhibs are taking matters into their own hands in eliminating all Nazi clips prior to theater showings," *Daily Variety* reported in September 1933. "Both major and independent circuits have officially instructed managers to delete any and all shots of Hitler and the Nazis from the newsreels."[27] In New York, the Rialto Theater was also said to be "scissoring everything about Hitler."[28]

In an atmosphere fraught with tension and invective, vocal outbursts sometimes boiled over into scuffles and fisticuffs in the theater. The first recorded instance of an actual brawl incited by Hitler's image on screen occurred at New York's Acme Theater on May 9, 1933. A showcase for Soviet imports and pro-communist foreign films, the Acme had booked Slatan Dudow's *Whither Germany?* (1932), a German-made paean to the proletariat in which the workers of the world united around parades, anthems, and agitprop theater, followed by a coda—recently added— denouncing Hitler and the Nazis. When a lone member of the audience, who should have known better, heckled the screen, he was jumped on and pummeled by the regulars.[29]

In the early days of the Third Reich, getting word of a Hitler-centric newsreel clip, claques of pro-Nazis infiltrated the left-leaning crowd at the Embassy to demonstrate solidarity. "For once Hitler got a rousing reception, one which drowned all hisses, in the Embassy," reported a surprised Waller in July 1933. "It was a Saturday matinee and the house was well filled when Fox-Hearst dared the first close-up of the Chancellor in action which it has projected for months."[30] To discourage trouble, the Embassy stationed private security guards and burly ushers in the back of the house.

Even with an influx of pro-Nazi *agents provocateurs*, the mood of the newsreel crowds in New York was predominately, and soon monolithically, anti-Nazi. "In the old days every time Hitler was mentioned there was a rough combination of hisses and applause," noted Waller. "Last Saturday afternoon [March 10, 1934], the reaction was negative, although the house crew was mustered in the back expecting trouble." That afternoon spectators watched two sides of the Nazi story—first, coverage of a Nazi festivity in Germany, and then a lengthy clip from Pathé reporting on a huge anti-Nazi rally in Madison Square Garden held three days earlier, featuring former New York governor Al Smith, New York Mayor Fiorello La Guardia, and Rabbi Stephen S. Wise.[31]

Soon the anti-Nazi crowds not only outdrew but physically intimidated the smattering of pro-Nazis. By the end of 1935, not a single voice dared shout a defiant "Heil!" "When Hitler comes into focus on the occasion of celebrating Germany's 100th anniversary of railroads, it's a cue for plenty of hisses and no applause," observed Roy Chartier, not displeased.[32] The next year, a Fox Movietone report on the Berlin Olympics showed a brief excerpt from Hitler's opening speech. "Embassy audiences got the opportunity for vocal partisanship," noted *Variety*, "first, of course, when Hitler is pictured." That "of course" is the parenthetical giveaway of a permanent shift in the temperature of the room.[33]

Even so, outside of news-hungry New York, the newsreel rule on Hitler was the less seen of him the better. "Hitler is taboo, or nearly so, on most American screens," *Life* observed as late as 1938. "Because of a notion that audiences do not wish to be aroused, newsreels seldom include his picture."[34]

But if the core anti-Hitler clientele out-shouted and ultimately silenced the pockets of pro-Hitler sentiment, both sides were drowned out by expressions of the consensus attitude toward the convulsions wrought by the Third Reich. In 1935, during a Pathé report on Nazi Germany, the spieler commented that "the American people look to Roosevelt to keep them out of the mess." The isolationist sentiment "drew heaps of applause," noted Roy Chartier, the like-minded reporter in attendance.[35] The silent majority of newsreel audiences neither hissed nor heiled—just hoped that the face of the swastika man would be kept at a safe distance.

"NAZIGANDA"

While the decision to show a close-up of Hitler was a matter of editorial judgment, newsreel cameramen faced a more practical problem in covering the Third Reich—getting the pictures. Independent, uncensored footage of the Nazis in the 1930s was nearly impossible to obtain. Though never camera-shy and always cinema-centric, the Nazis preferred to pose for their own cameras and insisted on calling the shots. Unless willing to wear Nazi blinders, the American newsreel companies were shut out.

Fox, Paramount, and Hearst represented the American newsreel companies in Germany and operated under the stringent supervision and constant surveillance of the Reich Ministry of Popular Enlightenment and Propaganda. Nothing could be filmed in Germany without special permission, often from Joseph Goebbels personally. American cameramen who took off their lens caps without the necessary paperwork quickly learned an oft-barked German imperative: *streng verboten*, strongly forbidden.

Nazi Party events were, of course, strictly monitored and the footage censored before export. To secure permission to film, the newsreels were also required to screen "at least some shots which are of propaganda value for Germany."[36] The written intertitles and sound synchronization of pictures shot in Germany were not to be altered for stateside consumption. To ensure compliance, German agents in America monitored newsreel screenings.

For the American newsreel editors in New York, covering Nazi Germany was a journalistic dilemma that devolved into a devil's bargain: either ignore the charismatic personalities, dazzling pageantry, and military mobilization of Nazi Germany altogether, which meant ignoring the most momentous and photogenic story in the world, or screen Nazi-approved or -provided footage, which then invited accusations of complicity with the regime. The trade press coined a special term for the Nazi-aggrandizing footage channeled to the newsreels via the Reichsfilmkammer: "naziganda."

Fox Movietone and Paramount News seemed to be especially compliant conduits for naziganda. Both studios had well-established newsreel branches in Germany that served not only as a base for foreign news stories but as a kind of money-laundering operation. As arms of their studio parents, the newsreel offices in Germany offered a roundabout way for the companies to spend "blocked currency"—box office profits earned from their films playing in Germany but prevented from leaving the country. Studios could spend the restricted funds on the production of the newsreels in Germany, export the footage, and then profit off the sales accrued outside of Germany—a circuitous accounting path and not exactly a windfall profit, but better than letting the money sit in a Nazi bank.

In particular, Fox Movietone, which maintained the biggest operation in Germany, was thought to be an uncritical conveyer belt for Joseph Goebbels. "Rumors are flying about town [New York] that certain newsreels are giving the Hitler regime favorable treatment in the newsreels blanketing the United States," the *Hollywood Reporter* revealed, without naming the culprits.[37] Not as circumspect, *Variety* fingered the accused. "Consistent use of Hitler propaganda scenes in Fox Movietone Newsreel is beginning to revive previously scouted report of a deal between one of the American reels and the Hitler crowd for propagandizing Hitlerism," it confided in September 1933. "Fox Movietone, some time ago, officially denied such a deal."[38] Even so, whether a quid pro quo or a nod and a wink, Fox enjoyed closer proximity to Nazi bigwigs than the competition. "Fox treks to Germany for Goering and Hitler stuff," read a survey of the only Nazi news item on an Embassy program from 1936.[39]

Undeniably, the official footage from Nazi Germany made for chilling viewing. What critic Susan Sontag later dubbed "fascinating fascism"— the hypnotic allure of the pageantry and iconography of Nazism on screen—was first experienced by a generation of moviegoers for whom it was the spellbinding news of the day, not grainy archival footage. "Nazi kid army taking the pledge is a massive subject, showing blocks of youngsters as far as the camera eye could see, taking the arm up gyration," observed Tom Waller in 1933, impressed and a bit rattled. One can almost hear his low whistle of amazement at the robotic synchronization of the precision drill.[40]

Two exceptions to the Nazi monopoly on newsreel coverage bequeathed an infinitely serviceable cache of raw footage to the newsreel library—motion picture images of the nationwide German boycott of Jewish goods held on April 1, 1933, and the cinemagenic book burnings presided over by Goebbels in Berlin on May 10, 1933. Emblematic even at the time, screened forever after as visual synecdoche for the conflagrations ignited by the Third Reich, the antisemitic signage and street scuffles from the boycotts and the flames from the book bonfire distilled into a few feet of film the race hatred and thought control of the Nazi regime.

Touted by the Nazi propaganda machine with the expectation of international support, the boycott of Jewish goods was billed as a righteous response to the calls made by Jews around the world, and especially in the United States, for boycotts of Nazi goods after Hitler's ascension to power. "If the incitement in foreign countries stops, then the boycott will stop," Goebbels wrote in his diary, blaming "the international atrocities propaganda" for slurring the Nazis.[41] Paramount News captured moving-camera shots of brownshirts marauding in trucks, street scuffles, and full-frame close-ups of a skull and crossbones on a shop window and signs reading "Deutsche! Kauft nicht bei Juden!" ("Germans! Don't buy from Jews!"). "First definite screen news of the German boycott was credited to Paramount," reported Waller two weeks later. "A talking reporter interpreted posted signs and editorialized about the situation while the crowd was shown milling about Berlin."[42] In Germany the boycott was something of a bust, but the American newsreels captured images that would forever after conjure the first stirrings of the Nazis in power.

Also ballyhooed in advance by the Nazis, the book burning was a major media event, in fact a pioneering "pseudo event" because so photogenic a spectacle would not have been staged had the cameras not been present to record it. "High toward the sky will reach tongues of vicious flame on May 10 as 62 German institutions of so-called higher education consign to the flames, under Nazi direction, any books which might in the slightest degree be construed as of Jewish origin," announced a preview of the coming attraction in *Motion Picture Herald*.[43] The night-for-night photography of brownshirts silhouetted against the flames, tossing volume after volume into the pyre, rendered a nightmarish *Walpurgisnacht* with the temperature set at Fahrenheit 451.

The scene in Berlin was the center stage, with Goebbels himself presiding over the incineration. Three weeks later, when the images of the bonfire in Berlin hit newsreel theaters in New York, the scene was "greeted in silence at the Luxer while the Embassy mobs hiss it mildly."[44] Rewound as library stock in year-end roundups of the news from Nazi Germany, the tableau was a picture-perfect snapshot of the mob frenzy of Nazism and a taste of the firestorm to come. The scene was also stitched into or reenacted in feature-length films such as *Die Vandernder Yid* (1933), *Are We Civilized?* (1934), *I Was a Captive of Nazi Germany* (1936), and *The Mortal Storm* (1940).

With the exception of the boycott and the bonfire, the early years of the Third Reich, as recorded by the newsreels, were a distant glimmer on the horizon. In April 1937, the popular monthly magazine *Scribner's* asked the five newsreel companies to choose their six best newsreel moments, the scoops each outfit was proudest of. Of the thirty stories selected, only one tracked the rise of fascism in Europe: Paramount's selection of the

Foreshadowing the conflagration to come: a newsreel shot of the instantly iconic book burning in Berlin, May 10, 1933.

Nazi book burning in Germany. The choices underscored both the paucity of footage and the profile of the story.[45]

The ubiquity of World War II–era documentaries and the huge cache of archival footage that has emerged since 1945 can deceive the modern viewer into thinking that film of the Nazis was as vivid and plentiful in the 1930s as it is today. With only the newsreels before their eyes, American moviegoers had far less in their sights.

4

THE HOLLYWOOD ANTI-NAZI LEAGUE

On the evening of April 26, 1936, in the swank dining room of the Victor Hugo Café in Hollywood, a mixed congregation of Jews, Catholics, and Popular Fronters paid upwards of $100 a plate to hear Prince Hubertus zu Löwenstein deliver a lecture entitled "Hitler's War on Civilization." A blueblood exile from Nazism, Prince Löwenstein had fled Germany one step ahead of a Gestapo hit squad. On a lecture tour of America to raise funds and consciousness, the Old World aristocrat was guaranteed a friendly reception from the local version of royalty.

As if drawn to the searchlights of a gala premiere, an A-list lineup of screen stars and studio power brokers converged to hear the fearless Catholic intellectual decry an ongoing terror and prophesy a future nightmare. "Reservations for the Lowenstein dinner-lecture avalanched the headquarters at late hour last night," reported *Daily Variety*. "Many of the picture executives placed orders on a wholesale scale asking for tables of 12 and upwards."[1] Putting aside doctrinal differences and personal animosities, the town's Irish Catholic elite (director John Ford, producer Winfield Sheehan, screenwriter Marc Connolly, Production Code head Joseph I. Breen, actors Pat O' Brien and James Cagney, and, on the dais serving as honorary chairman, the Most Rev. John J. Cantwell, Bishop of Los Angeles) and a phalanx of name-brand Jewish moguls (Jack L. Warner, David O. Selznick, Irving Thalberg, and B. P. Schulberg) broke bread with a cadre of brazenly leftist artist-activists (including the organizers of the soiree, the agnostic wits Dorothy Parker and Donald Ogden Stewart, late of the Algonquin Round Table, currently prowling the gilded cage of the screenwriters stable).[2] Dr. A. H. Giannini, founder of the Bank of America, was treasurer for the event. The diversity of the turnout testified to the consensus coalescing in Hollywood—that Nazism was not a distant menace but a clear and present danger, a realization that was not to dawn on the rest of America until the very eve of World War II.

The Nazis, said Löwenstein, had annihilated all that was good in German culture. "Everything that had made for the glory of Germany has been destroyed in the past three years," he told the gathering. "The best actors and artists have been expelled. Approximately 1100 scholars and scientists have had to leave, only because they believed in the freedom of art, of thought, and of religion." Jews were forbidden to buy milk for their children, and Catholics were jailed for keeping the faith. The jackboot crushing the Jews and the Catholics, he predicted, was but a preview of oppressions to come.[3]

Also speaking that night were Otto Katz, a communist agent operating in Hollywood under the *nom de guerre* Rudolf Breda; the actor Fredric March, winner of the Academy Award for Best Actor for *Dr. Jekyll and Mr. Hyde* (1932); Bishop Cantwell; and screenwriter Stewart, who served as master of ceremonies. All urged a united front against Hitler. "We must organize to fight the Nazi invasion before Americans lose their constitutional liberties," warned Stewart.[4]

The next week a blind item in *Variety*'s gossipy "Inside Stuff" column (doubtless fed to the paper by Stewart or Parker) flattered the diners with reports of just how far the voices in the Victor Hugo Café had echoed. In hush-hush tones devoid of definite articles, the trade paper confided:

> Info around Hollywood studios is that Adolf Hitler is perturbed over tenor of speeches delivered at dinner to Prince zu Lowenstein of Bavaria in film colony a week ago, and that ban against American films into Germany may be ordered in retaliation. Undercover word that has reached various lots is that Hitler regime has been given transcript of the speeches and that drastic action may be expected. Major producing-distributing organizations are little disturbed, as under present German setup prohibiting money being taken out of country, American films are getting little or nothing as is.[5]

Actually, Hitler was busy presiding over the festivities attendant to the Reich's annual labor celebration, a massive propaganda bash staged

The catalyst for the Hollywood Anti-Nazi League: the Catholic nobleman and fearless anti-Nazi activist Hubertus zu Löwenstein and his wife Princess Helga Maria, arriving in New York for a lecture tour in 1938.

under the slogan "let's enjoy life and make merry," but the notion that in distant Berlin the all-powerful *führer* was piqued by a Hollywood confab must have delighted the organizers.

A hot ticket for stouthearted antifascists, the banquet for Prince Löwenstein was the first ripple in a wave of anti-Nazi activism that swept Hollywood in the late 1930s—a movement spearheaded by the Hollywood Anti-Nazi League for the Defense of American Democracy. From 1936 to 1939, the Hollywood Anti-Nazi League (HANL) galvanized a stellar cast of mediagenic artists and media-savvy activists to oppose the rise of fascism overseas and advance the cause of social justice at home. Distinguished by star power in the ranks and proximity to the industrial plants of the major studios, HANL was a classic, if uniquely glamorous and auspiciously located, Popular Front group born of the Great Depression.

The Popular Front was the umbrella name for a broad coalition of New Deal Democrats, liberals without portfolio, socialists, and party-line communists, the last doing most of the drudge work of street-level organizing and office management. Bound together by a shared hatred of

Nazism, it was an alliance of convenience made by strange bedfellows, a shotgun marriage of reformers and revolutionaries. Like dozens of other groups marching under the banner of anti-Nazism in the 1930s, HANL also agitated for the causes that warmed the hearts of a generation of militant men and women "of the Left," as the phrase went: labor solidarity, civil rights, and, the best of all the good fights of the 1930s, the Loyalist side in the Spanish Civil War.

The actions initiated by HANL took a multitude of forms. Exercising skills honed during the bitter fights to organize below-the-line workers on the studio soundstages and the underpaid "schmucks with Underwoods" who banded together in the Screen Writers Guild in 1933, members pamphleteered, picketed, delivered lectures, mounted plays, staged screenings, collected funds, and proselytized at private parties and huge rallies. They published full-page advertisements in the trade press and tacked manifestos to studio bulletin boards. The publication of a newsletter, at first irregularly as the *Anti-Nazi News*, which later became *News of the World*, and then biweekly under the title *Hollywood Now*, spread the word and bucked up the faithful. Through the facilities of KFWB, the house radio station owned and operated by Warner Bros., HANL transmitted ideologically laced satire and strident exhortation to living rooms throughout Southern California. Blending high-society diversions, educational outreach, and street-level activism, the group aspired to be what it eventually became—the hectoring conscience of the motion picture industry on all matters pertaining to Nazism.

Of course, the logical means of production for HANL to seize was the one that employed its membership. Covertly at first, more boldly as the Nazis gobbled up territory and war clouds gathered, the members of the group conspired to inject anti-Nazi sentiments into Hollywood cinema. Given the political conservatism of the Motion Picture Producers and Distributors of America and the moral policing of its censorship arm, the Production Code Administration, the Hollywood studio system proved the hardest medium to crack.

Not least, HANL pioneered the celebrity-centric, pseudo-eventful tactics that have since become commonplace for progressive causes that grip the social conscience of famous entertainers: the deployment of star power to publicize and validate a political agenda, with the body of the celebrity dangled as bait. While flashbulbs popped and cameras whirred, HANL stage-managed events where stars presided over rallies, orated from the podium, pled for donations, and signed petitions. If near enough to a famous face, a placard or slogan might avoid being cropped from a syndicated wirephoto.

In its heyday, HANL attracted a remarkably broad coalition of donors, volunteers, and signatories: not just the usual Popular Front spectrum of FDR New Dealers and Communist Party minions, but also a solid core of conservative Catholics and Jewish businessmen. All had good reason to oppose Nazism, a triple threat to ethnicity, religion, and trade. In 1937, at a celebration marking HANL's year anniversary—a dinner, dance, and musical-variety show held in the proletarian digs of the Fiesta Room of the Ambassador Hotel—card-carriers and fellow travelers rubbed elbows with devout communicants and cutthroat capitalists. Though its membership roster peaked at around 4,200, HANL exerted an influence far beyond its formal subscription list.[a] Its rise, dominion, and fall offer a case study in the merging of media and politics, celebrity status and social activism, and the ultimately irreconcilable marriage between starry-eyed liberalism and hard-nosed communism in the 1930s.

"UNHEIL HITLER!"

The credit line for the idea that grew into the Hollywood Anti-Nazi League was shared by a mismatched pair of high-priced screenwriters, Donald Ogden Stewart and Dorothy Parker. He was a natural charmer, she a shy neurotic. Both spent the 1930s dividing their creative energies between art and activism, churning out screenplays for the studios and working pro bono for the Popular Front. Stewart was better paid; Parker made better copy.

Born in 1894 in Columbus, Ohio, the son of a judge, Donald Ogden Stewart was a blue-blooded red who saw no contradiction in living the good life while plotting the overthrow of his fellow plutocrats. Well-born and

---

[a] In October 1939, HANL filed a statement with the U.S. Post Office stating that the group had 4,206 subscribers to *Hollywood Now*. Since subscriptions came with membership, the number seems a reliable index. The figure probably signaled the high-water mark for membership. Although hundreds of liberals bolted the group after the shock of the Hitler-Stalin Pact in August 1939, their names would still have been on the subscription list until year's end. The vast majority of members (3,981) resided in California, with 3,717 living in Los Angeles. Publicly, HANL tended to round its membership upwards to 5,000. (Hollywood Anti-Nazi League, FBI File: 36–37)

well-liked enough to be tapped as a member of Yale's elite Skull and Bones Society, he deviated from his class trajectory sometime in 1936 to become a member of another secret society, the Communist Party. "Nor did I shed my new dinner jacket and distribute the pieces among the deserving poor," he later recalled. "I saw no reason to stop dancing and enjoying the play of life."[6] Having written or collaborated on the screenplays for the posh MGM hits *Dinner at Eight* (1933) and *The Barretts of Wimpole St.* (1934), and, even while chief executive officer of HANL, burnishing his credentials with frothy soufflés such as *The Prisoner of Zenda* (1937), *Marie Antoinette* (1938), and *Holiday* (1938), Stewart boasted the kind of gold-plated screen credits that made the moguls overlook his pink politics.

By the time Dorothy Parker—née Rothschild—rented her byline to the movies, she was already famous for her whiplash wit and languid dissipation. Parker first came to Hollywood (a place where, she couldn't resist saying, "the streets are paved with Goldwyn") in the early sound era, during the great migration of New York wordsmiths drawn by the promise of $2,000-a-week salaries for remedial dialogue.[7] In 1933 she married the actor Alan Campbell, and the couple accepted a contract with Paramount to collaborate on screenplays; their most notable shared credit was *A Star*

The blue-blooded red: screenwriter Donald Ogden Stewart, cofounder of the Hollywood Anti-Nazi League, with his wife and comrade-in-arms, Ella Winter, 1939.

Is Born (1937), a close-to-home melodrama about a wife whose artistic talent outshines her husband's. A Jazz Age avatar staggering uncertainly into the harsh glare of the 1930s, she was destined to be remembered as much for the *bon mots* she uttered as for the words she put to paper. Too quotable for her own good, she used the smart-mouthed dame persona as both a shield for her social anxieties and a weapon in her tireless political activism.

Writers with a social conscience and a taste for the high life, Parker and Stewart made an effective tag-team, with the gregarious Stewart assuming duties in the spotlight and the anxiety-ridden Parker closing the deals for donations and commitments one-on-one. Before the dinner at the Victor Hugo, the pair hosted a cocktail party for Löwenstein at Parker and Campbell's house on Canyon Drive in Beverly Hills. It was there, over drinks, that the idea for a permanent Hollywood-based anti-Nazi action group took shape.

The notion had been bandied about in Hollywood for some time. In New York, the well-funded and well-connected Non-Sectarian Anti-Nazi League to Champion Human Rights had been operating since 1933 under the dynamic leadership of lawyer Samuel Untermyer. A more

Artists as activists: screenwriter-wit Dorothy Parker and her husband, screenwriter Alan Campbell, returning from a trip to war-ravaged Spain, October 22, 1937.

direct spur to action—namely, orders from on high—came in 1935, when the Comintern, the Moscow-based bureau tasked with coordinating the activities of Communist Parties worldwide, sent out word to party appa-ratchiks to cooperate with socialists, liberals, and other left-wing groups in a broad-based "popular front" against fascism.

Over cocktails at the Campbell-Parkers', at the Löwenstein dinner, and in the glow of victory the next morning, the dream of a local anti-Nazi group coalesced into a practical plan of action. The congenial, energetic, and high-profile Stewart was the natural choice for president; he modestly claimed to be merely a figurehead, but he was always a hands-on manager. On June 8, 1936, the group was formally incorporated as the Hollywood League Against Nazism; on September 28, 1936, it became the Holly-wood Anti-Nazi League for the Defense of American Democracy.[8]

Behind the scenes and out of the headlines, a crucial catalyst was Otto Katz, a communist agent who played more parts than any of the actors he circulated among at the Victor Hugo Café. It was he who handled the details for Löwenstein's visit to Hollywood and he who revolutionized left-wing fund-raising by introducing Moscow agendas to Hollywood checkbooks. Silky smooth and coolly mysterious, Katz had been a well-known actor in both the experimental theater and street politics of Wei-mar Berlin. He first came to America in 1935 to raise money for the anti-Nazi German underground.

By the time Katz hit Hollywood, he had perfected a line of patter that was a siren call to a community who knew mystery, danger, and espio-nage only from screenplays. Theodore Draper, the historian of Ameri-can communism who observed Katz work his magic, described him as "the international Communist huckster par excellence." Before Katz had his entrepreneurial brainstorm, recalled Draper, "the American Communists had never thought of the movie capital as a party mint." Katz was proud to have corrected the oversight. "Columbus discovered America," he bragged, "and I discovered Hollywood."[9] (Katz had the con man's knack of being different things to different people: on the night of Prince Löwenstein's talk, Stewart recalled that Katz delivered a commu-nist spiel that so outraged Bishop Cantwell that His Excellency bolted the dais. Löwenstein recalled that, on the contrary, Katz charmed the bishop by genuflecting and solemnly kissing his ring.) "Katz 'sold' communism to the wealthy Hollywood magnates by working on their bad social con-sciences until they were cringing with contrition," observed a bemused

Prince Löwenstein years later. "The complete religious and metaphysical desert in the minds of many in the motion picture colony made [his] game easier."[10]

HANL's first anti-Nazi initiative was a suitably literary gesture, a protest against an article by William Stidger in *Liberty* magazine posing the counterintuitive question "Hitler Planning to Be Kind to the Jews?" Answering in the negative, the group dictated an angry telegram to the editor:

> WE PROTEST THE INSIDIOUS PRO NAZI PROPAGANDA CONTAINED IN YOUR CURRENT ISSUE ENTITLED HITLER PLANNING TO BE KIND TO JEWS STOP THE RECORD OF HITLERS BROKEN PROMISES INDICATES THE COMPLETE UNTRUTH OF THE IMPLICATIONS MADE BY YOUR WILLIAM STIDGER STOP THERE CAN BE NO COMPROMISE WITH THE AMERICAN PRINCIPLES OF RELIGIOUS AND POLITICAL FREEDOM (SIGNED) HOLLYWOOD LEAGUE AGAINST NAZISM[b]

The name of the League had not yet congealed, but the signatories represented some of the core ·activists: Stewart and Parker; screenwriter Edwin Justus Mayer, a yeoman member of the Screen Writers Guild and emphatically no relation to Louis B.; the actress Gloria Stuart; Charles J. Katz, a prominent labor attorney active in progressive causes; playwright Samson Raphaelson, author of *The Jazz Singer* (1927); director Frank Tuttle, best known for guiding radio stars like Bing Crosby and Jack Benny through lighthearted musical comedies at Paramount; the husband-and-wife team of screenwriter Herbert J. Biberman and actress Gale Sondergaard, Hollywood's premiere Communist Party power couple of the 1930s; the gravel-voiced character actor Lionel Stander; Parker's husband, screenwriter Alan Campbell; the vaudeville and radio performers Ray Mayer and Edith Evans; screenwriters Viola Brothers Shore, Arthur

---

[b] HANL's characterization of the article was unfair to Stidger, a skeptical reporter who merely recounted an interview with Nazi ambassador at large Joachim von Ribbentrop. Stidger told Ribbentrop that "the United States could never befriend Germany with Jewish atrocities going on" and that the only way to win American friendship was "to see to it that the Jewish persecutions were modified." Ribbentrop solemnly assured Stidger that "the two or three leaders in the Jewish persecutions would lose their power in the Reich. I could count on that definitely."

Sheekman, and Hy Kraft; and writer Felice Paramore.[11] A chastened *Liberty* printed the protest telegram in its next issue and published an article attacking Hitler soon afterward.

On July 24, 1936, the group held its first public coming-out party at the Wilshire Ebell Theater in midtown Los Angeles. Some 500 artist-activists gathered to hear Prince Löwenstein, back for a return engagement, and his wife, the Princess Helga Maria. The meeting was presided over by producer Lester Cowan, a founding member of the Academy of Motion Picture Arts and Sciences, who joked about Hitler's recent categorization of the Japanese as "honorary Aryans." The radio and screen star Eddie Cantor decried the distribution of hate-mongering Nazi propaganda smuggled stateside and repeated a comment he made to the press when asked about the banning of his films in Nazi Germany. "I'm glad it happened because I don't want to make people laugh that make people cry." The Löwensteins recounted their brushes with death in the new Germany and sounded the alarm for America. Fredric March introduced the Prince; Gloria Stuart introduced the Princess.[12]

Buoyed by the enthusiastic turnout, the League moved on to bigger things—protesting American participation in the 1936 Berlin Olympics, exposing subversive pro-Nazi outfits such as the Silver Shirts and the German American Bund, and, on October 20, 1936, inaugurating its house organ, the *Anti-Nazi News: A Journal in Defense of American Democracy* (first headline: "Hollywood Fights Nazism"). The paper's main beat was the activism of its readership: the lectures, rallies, exhibits, and shows mounted to expose the Nazi threat at home and abroad.

Being the only place in Hollywood where writers called the shots, HANL often made its political points through public rhetoric and literary discourse. It wallowed in talk, telegramming, sloganeering, speechifying, writing, the circulation of petitions, the passing of resolutions, and the issuing of manifestos. A gabfest tailor-made for the group was the motion picture session of the Western Writers Congress, held in San Francisco on November 15, 1936. Convened to ponder the problem of "the writer in relation to contemporary social problems," the writers workshop-cum-political rally saw Hollywood's highly paid screenwriters rubbing elbows with hardscrabble scribblers lucky to get piecework from the Writers' Project of the Works Progress Administration. The writers' trade not being a classless society, disgruntled scriveners from the floor railed at the pampered Hollywood bourgeoisie as "fascistic, infantile, and anti-social" and attacked guns-for-hire like Stewart and Parker as "literary prostitutes engaged in passing the buck." For once beating Parker to a punchline, Stewart—a richly rewarded screenwriter who still considered himself underpaid—snapped back, "Passing what buck and to whom?" Parker tried to mollify the crowd by insisting that "whether or not the public got more honest pictures there was no question of the Hollywood writers ever quitting fighting for them."[13]

The most popular living-room medium of the day provided the loudest megaphone for HANL rhetoric. On November 16, 1936, the group set up a committee—chaired by radio personality Alfred Leonard and including Lester Cowan, set designer Harry J. Zutto, and songwriter Jay Gorney—to penetrate the radio airwaves. "Hitler and his head propagandist Goebbels . . . are adepts at the use of radio in their efforts to fool all the people all the time," HANL reasoned. "We will try to beat them at their own game. We will try to prove that facts can be just as colorful as fraud and fiction over the air."[14]

HANL turned to the radio dial "to reach those circles of American society which are most directly exposed to PRO-NAZI PROPAGANDA and who—on the other hand—can not be reached by the primarily intellectual appeal of the printed word." Given the susceptibility of the bovine masses to Nazi trickery, "all efforts to counter-act the influence of Nazi-propaganda or to make people immune against it must have a dual purpose: first, to gain the individual's sympathy for what he is about to learn and second, to present the material in a way which reaches his or her personal interest and at the same time supplies the necessary facts to sustain the first emotional reaction."[15] Ironically, or not, HANL's radio propagandists embraced the same "hypodermic needle" theory of mass communications propounded by Joseph Goebbels: inject the message into mass consciousness through repetition, simplicity, and raw emotion.

Debuting on February 20, 1937, and transmitted over KFWB every Saturday evening from 7:30 to 8:00, HANL's "professionally planned and produced program" of anti-Nazi agitprop took possession of a small piece of the dial, "radiating from the Hollywood broadcast towers of KFWB into hundreds of thousands of homes, enlightening, educating, warning." Donald Ogden Stewart served as moderator-host for the premiere episode, a series of dramatic monologues from a diverse range of Americans united in their opposition to Hitler: projectionist Don Thomas Freiling spoke for the American Catholic; the African American actor-activist

Jay Moss for the American Negro; screenwriter Viola Brothers Shore for the American woman; and the exiled author Erich Rix for the German anti-Nazi. A regular segment featured a pair of popular characters created by Stewart and transplanted to the Reich, "Mr. and Mrs. Haddock in Germany," played by Ray and Edith Mayer. HANL's sympathetic patrons at Warner Bros. also made the facilities of KFWB available for screenwriter Hy Kraft to put an anti-Nazi spin to the news of the day, Thursdays from 9:15 to 9:30 p.m. PST.

Making the agitprop easier to digest was the peppy tonic of commercial radio-speak. "So remember Saturdays 7:30 to 8:00, a good day, a good hour, and the best possible cause—the cause of genuine democracy against its one real enemy, Nazi fascism," chirped the advertising. "Tune in on the liveliest trend of the times. We'll be with you at 95 on the dial, 7:30 on the clock, every Saturday—and our slogan is 'Unheil Hitler!'"[16]

Besides spreading the anti-Nazi word, the radio shows were a boon to recruitment. "Have you noticed all those new faces around Hollywood Anti-Nazi League meetings lately?" asked *Hollywood Now.* "They are there largely because of the League's radio programs, which are bringing in more new members than any other series the League has ever offered."[17]

On the morning of April 16, 1937, HANL awoke to the first concrete evidence that its agitation had struck a nerve—the trashing and burglarizing of its offices at 6912 Hollywood Blvd. "It is apparent, as a result of this latest indication of Nazi vandalism, that the followers of Adolf Hitler are desperately trying to cover their activities in our country," reported *Hollywood Now,* trying not to sound too thrilled about the publicity windfall. "It becomes increasingly necessary, therefore, to intensify the work—of anti Nazis toward ridding the American scene of the evil influence of these swastika-branded anti-democratic leaders and their vandal gangs."[18]

The local police did not leap into action to run the perpetrators to ground. Captain J. J. Jones of the Hollywood Detective Bureau refused to fret over what he considered an intramural squabble. "You are a political organization," Jones told HANL, "and if another political organization doesn't like you—so what?"[19]

Six months later, no thanks to Captain Jones, the culprit was caught, and he had a familiar Hollywood surname—Leopold McLaglen, brother of the actor Victor McLaglen, winner of the Academy Award for Best

Actor in John Ford's *The Informer* (1935).[c] McLaglen was arrested in connection with an extortion plot targeting millionaire socialite Philip M. Chancellor, who had employed him as his jujitsu instructor. According to court testimony by Chancellor's "chauffeur-secretary," McLaglen had vandalized the offices at the behest of Chancellor and then tried to blackmail Chancellor with the threat of exposure. Asked on the stand if he had anything to do with the crime, McLaglen toyed with his monocle, looked at his shoes, and played coy. "Well, now, I want you to understand, anything I did against anyone was at the direction of Mr. Chancellor."[20] In lieu of jail time, McLaglen was deported to England. Brother Victor paid for the boat ticket.[21]

The trashing of its headquarters only accelerated the forward momentum of the group—confirming its influence, increasing its membership. In April 1938, HANL moved to more commodious quarters at 6513 Hollywood Blvd., a suite of four rooms "where the multiplying activities of the League will be carried on with greater efficiency."[22] On June 4, 1938, when HANL marked its second anniversary, the news was all upbeat. "Launched by scarcely more than a dozen Hollywood artists, it has had a phenomenal growth," boasted a self-promotion. "Its membership is now at its highest point—5000 men and women united in a movement to stop Nazism and protect American democracy. The activities of the League have been manifold—a constant stream of meetings, rallies, radio broadcasts, benefits, educational campaigns."[23]

The talent on stage and the executives sitting at the tables during HANL's banquets and benefit performances confirmed the group's status as the premier political action committee in Hollywood, a wired network of insiders, membership in which conferred social cachet and political influence. To commemorate the second anniversary, KFWB provided airtime for a special program featuring Parker, Campbell, and other HANL

---

[c] *Hollywood Now* described Leopold McLaglen as the "fascist minded Britisher and brother of troop-commanding film-actor Victor McLaglen." Though Victor specialized in playing hard-drinking soldiers in films directed by Raoul Walsh and John Ford, the reference was not to McLaglen's screen persona but to his offscreen role as the leader of a paramilitary band of horsemen called the Light Horse Troops. "Sure, we're organized to fight," said McLaglen. "We consider an enemy anything opposed to the American idea, whether it's an enemy outside or inside these borders. If that includes Communists in this country, why, we're organized to fight them too." ("Exhibitors and Public Protesting McLaglen's 'Army' in Hollywood," *Motion Picture Herald*, Nov. 28, 1936: 30.)

Every Thursday, 9:15 p. m.
LISTEN IN — KFWB
"Voice of the League"
Important Speakers
(Watch daily newspapers for any change in time)

NEWS OF THE WORLD
A Journal in Defense of American Democracy
VOL. II—NO. 1   HOLLYWOOD, CALIFORNIA, NOVEMBER 19, 1937   5 CENTS

Every Saturday, 7:45 p. m.
LISTEN IN — KFWB
"Dots and Dashes"
The news made real
(Watch daily newspapers for any change in time)

Burglary of Anti-Nazi League bobs up in Leo McLaglen case

Accuser Chancellor

He hired McLaglen . . . to investigate — what?

Under two flags . . .

Accused McLaglen

Faces accuser in court on 'shakedown' charge

McLaglen said he did it on orders from rich boss, charges witness in court

"He (Leopold McLaglen) said Chancellor caused him to burglarize the Hollywood Anti-Nazi League . . . and that he (McLaglen) would expose him (Chancellor) in every newspaper in the country. . ."

This testimony, given by Stanley M. Glinn, chauffeur secretary to millionaire socialite Phillip M. Chancellor, was only one of the lightning flashes through the murky atmosphere filled with allegations of blackmail, perjury, espionage, and Nazi machinations, in Municipal Judge Oda Faulconer's court yesterday.

Occasion was the preliminary hearing of Leopold, Fascist-minded Britisher and brother of troop-commanding, film-actor Victor McLaglen.

McLAGLEN MUST STAND TRIAL

Leopold is now out on bail again, faced with an order to stand trial in Superior Court, Dept. 41, on December 6, handed down yesterday afternoon after Judge Oda Faulconer had heard testimony on examination and cross-examination from multi-millionaire Chancellor, chauffeur Glinn, and a sheriff's officer.

Shakedown attempt to the tune of $20,000, was the essence of the charge against hulking McLaglen, chief state's witness against him stout Chancellor, admittedly the man who employed McLaglen to investigate "subversive activities" and other subjects not made clear. McLaglen attempted to extort the sum from him, Chancellor charged, when fired last September after working at a monthly salary of $250 all through 1937.

The hearing abounded in murky insinuations of Nazi affiliations an l operations; "intelligence" (espionage) that was turned over by Chancellor, himself a naval reserve officer, to the U. S. Naval Intelligence authorities in San Pedro and San Diego; and hints of dynamite being held in reserve for use at the trial itself.

Q. AND A.

Asked point blank after the hearing whether he had anything to do with the burglary of the Anti-Nazi League office (Monday night, April 13, between 8 and 10 p. m.), Leopold McLaglen toyed with his shell-rimmed monocle, looked at his be-spatted shoes and answered: "Well now, I want you to understand that anything I did against anyone was at the direction of Mr. Chancellor . . ."

His attorney, ex-Judge Harry F. Sewell, was more positive in denial. He stated, in substance: "Mr. McLaglen did not do it or other things he is charged with, but Mr. Chancellor wanted him to do it."

McLaglen, testimony revealed, was in the employ of Chancellor during the periods when he attempted violently to disrupt a public meeting at the Hollywood Chamber of Commerce (see issue of NOW for May 1, story entitled "Coast Nazi Leader Heads Hoodlum Gang").

(Continued on Page 8)

League envoys check on angles of "bomb plot"

Closely following incomplete radio and newspaper stories of a "bomb plot" against prominent Hollywood personalities, a committee representing the executive board of the Hollywood Anti-Nazi League today interviewed District Attorney Buron Fitts to check on information received by the Hollywood Anti-Nazi League that the "bomb list" had included members of the executive board as well as motion picture producers who have and have had no connection whatsoever with the League.

The District Attorney denied that the list, whose contents he stated he knew, included any of the League executive board members.

He described the list as the work of "a small group of bums." Only the lack of any overt act in furtherance of the "bomb plot" plan, prevented him from instituting taking legal action against all the framers of the document, he said.

In the case of one man involved in drawing up the list, charges have already been brought on another basis, and trial is pending, he said.

Information received from other sources by the Hollywood Anti-Nazi League supports the belief that the "bomb plot" incident—first revealed in his last Sunday night's broadcast by "sees-all, knows-all" Walter Winchell—is traceable to the small, as yet uninfluential, but highly virulent circle known here as followers of William Dudley Pelley, Silver Shirt "Fuehrer."

Pelley, in the East, is clearly disturbed. A long, worried article in his special bulletin "Scourge of Cords," has just reached Pelley-ites here and elsewhere. It complains of the "direct-actionists" in the organization who "did too much, and too soon, too loud, and tossed at it wrong."

Pelley's past connections with Nazi agents have long since been exposed. His present policy of pro-Hitler propaganda bristles from every page of his publications, especially "LIBERATION" which purports to show 'latest inside developments of battle vs. Jewish radicalism in U. S.'

"The directionists blistered me for following a do-nothing policy" . . . writes Pelley . . . "inasmuch as I did not favor the silly sabotage of our adversaries as individuals." On the contrary, Pelley says a

Part of a company who gathered not long ago to celebrate the "ordination" of Bishop Bell, Hollywood cleric, by (self) appointment. The home No. was 6814 Cahuenga Terrace.

THE LITTLE BISHOP is on the left, front row.

A favorite text of the Bishop is the Jew-baiter's gospel, "Protocols of the Elders of Zion." He and McLaglen used to work together, exchange information, and plan to make America safe for Aryans, at a profit.

Now they have fallen out.

BIG LEO McLAGLEN is on the right, front row.

Incidentally, among those gathered under the Swastika in this picture, in the group which studied anti-Semitic forgeries, is Frank Gompert, member of the County Sheriff's force.

few lines later, "I see the Silver Legion as . . . (an) organization made up of Enlightened Christian reservists who shall act AS A FORCEFUL VIGILANTE UNIT against Jewish Reds . . . (Italics ours) . . . hastening to add, of course, "if the latter attempt to rule insolently and openly. . ."

However in the meantime, "Pending a more violent form of revolution by its adversaries (Silver Legionists) do not conduct themselves in any flamboyant or unseemly manner to create unfriendly sentiment against them from an ignorant or still-hoodwinked public."

So the Silver Legion busy elsewhere are to take warning from the Hollywood bombshell and avoid the business of framing bomb lists —that may reach the public ears and eyes—and stick to this business of trying to make contact with men of wealth and influence who can finance Fascism.

Two prominent local Pelley-ites, Henry Allen and Kenneth Alexander, conferred with Nazi Consul Killinger, here recently.

D. A. PLEDGES ACTION IF POSSIBLE ON PLOTS

A statement given to the Anti-Nazi League delegation by District Attorney Fitts pledges:

"If such a plot (against persons of Jewish faith in this city) does exist, or develops, this office will utilize every resource at its command to promptly break up such a movement.

"It is inconceivable that, in an enlightened country like the U. S. —where religious freedom has been the very backbone of the country's history—that such a movement could or would be tolerated."

The D. A. further stated he believed the law governing conspiracy could be more broadly interpreted, so that drilling, even with fake arms, might be construed as action; able if existence of an underlying plot to prepare for unlawful action against any person or group of persons, could be established.

HERE'S HOW the office of the Hollywood Anti-Nazi League looked after the burglary last April . . .

AND NOW the affair is again a matter of public record . . .

ACCORDING to Stanley M. Glinn, testifying at the preliminary hearing of the Leo McLaglen case, McLaglen threatened to reveal he (McL) had committed the burglary under orders from Phillip M. Chancellor, who hired him to bring in highly confidential reports on this and that.

MORE DIRT will certainly be dished out with all the abandon of a Mack Sennett pie-slinging session, when the McLaglen case comes up in Superior Court next month. Chancellor and Glinn are chief witnesses for the state.

CHARGES against McLaglen are quadruple: (1) bribing witnesses, (2) soliciting commission of a crime, (Section 653F), (3) attempted extortion, (4) preparing false evidence.

stalwarts. "There can be no doubt that the League is more active than any other local organization in opposition to the doctrines and persecutive practices of power-crazed European dictators and in its stand against the spread of these Nazi principles in democratic America," wrote Ivan Spear in the trade weekly *Box Office*. "In fact, it is doubtful that there is another organization anywhere in the nation which can point to a more impressive record of activity."[24]

President Roosevelt, if not Hitler, was taking notice of HANL's New Deal–friendly work. On October 19, 1938, Harold L. Ickes, FDR's Secretary of the Interior, arrived in Hollywood to speak at a mass meeting in the Shrine Auditorium, sponsored by HANL, the Hollywood Council for Democracy, and the Motion Picture Democratic Committee (left-wing Hollywood shared the Popular Front penchant for generating like-minded political groups with overlapping memberships). Before the main event, Ickes was honored at a luncheon at Twentieth Century-Fox. Flanked by Fox's Darryl F. Zanuck and MGM's Louis B. Mayer, FDR's emissary played to the crowd with a fervent defense of freedom of speech and screen. "There are two industries in the U.S. that every day and every night must work for, stand for, and fight for our liberties," Ickes declared. "They are the movie industry and the newspapers. Once we let anyone dictate to the newspapers or the film industry what they can or can't do, we are licked."[25]

At the Shrine Auditorium that night, speaking on "The Crisis of Democracy," Ickes singled out the members of the motion picture industry for their fight against the "spirit of intolerance and oppression that is now a threatening storm on the far horizon." As Hollywood's liberal elite beamed, the audience adopted a resolution calling upon FDR to lift the embargo against Loyalist Spain and to convene "a genuine peace conference to plan for collective defense of democracy throughout the world." Afterward, Donald Ogden Stewart called the evening "one of the happiest and proudest moments in the Hollywood liberal movement."[26]

But if conferences, rallies, and radio shows kept the ranks busy and made everyone feel good, HANL could not boast of a single motion picture that bore, undeniably, the imprint of anti-Nazism. Screenwriter and HANL fixture John Bright resigned himself to the fact that while "Hollywood is not a factory for Fascism," as long as the public demanded films that "dilute and distort life, Hollywood will continue to do just that."[27] Bright was speaking from personal experience: with his partner Robert Trasker he had spent the last year laboring on barely-above-B-picture froth such as *Here Comes Trouble* (1936) and *Girl of the Ozarks* (1936). From the evidence on screen, the "Hollywood" in the Hollywood Anti-Nazi League stood only for the location of the office. Unable to harness the power of the Hollywood feature film, the group concentrated on what powered the entertainment machine—the motion picture star.

THE POLITICS OF CELEBRITY

The body of the Hollywood star had first been drafted into national service during the Great War. Attracting crowds, selling war bonds, and lending legitimacy to the crusade against the bloodthirsty Kaiser and the bestial Hun, the celestial trio of Charles Chaplin, Douglas Fairbanks, and Mary Pickford marched at the head of the martial parade orchestrated by the Committee for Public Information, the first federal propaganda agency in American history. In film clips, the Little Tramp bonked the Kaiser on the noggin with a wooden mallet and Doug and Little Mary, America's heartthrob and America's sweetheart, implored moviegoers, in intertitles, to enlist in the great crusade Over There.

Yet except for shilling for the War to End All Wars, the Hollywood star was too valuable a commodity to squander on idealistic ventures with no return on investment. Republicans and Democrats—for that matter, Ku Klux Klansman and communists—all went to the movies. To alienate any portion of the moviegoing public, no matter how small or eccentric, was to shorten the line at the ticket window. The controversial issues and *causes célèbres* of the 1920s—immigration restriction, labor strikes, the execution of the anarchists Sacco and Vanzetti—were disputed without Hollywood stars manning the picket lines. It was as if the silent screen had muted the exercise of free speech.

Of course, celebrity endorsement of commercial products had been an ancillary gold mine since the first screen face was recognizable from a billboard. Also, a heartfelt solicitation for a charitable cause made from the stage or in a newsreel clip was an unassailable way to trade on stardom. The March of Dimes, the campaign founded in 1938 to eradicate the blight of polio, presided over by its most famous victim, FDR, attracted perhaps the biggest cast of entertainers performing gratis on the side of the angels. HANL stalwart Eddie Cantor coined the name for the charity, a pun on the popular screen magazine, the *March of Time*.

Aside from charities, however, studio moguls and matinee idols alike minded their show business.[28] Stars were clothes horses who did not wear their politics on their sleeves. As far as the public and the fan magazines knew, not a thought occupied their pretty little heads.[d]

It took the crisis of the Great Depression and the charisma of FDR to push Hollywood out of the wings and onto the political stage. In 1932, publicly and vocally, motion picture stars, top-rank directors, screenwriters, and even studio executives enlisted in the Democratic campaign, including the biggest name of all, the multimedia superstar Will Rogers. If not the first, Rogers was the most prominent of the famous entertainers who ventured from humanitarian causes into political waters. The beloved cowboy-philosopher was unique, however, a partisan commentator who somehow managed to rise above partisanship, whose disarming manner took the edge off his contempt for Herbert Hoover and his advocacy for FDR's New Deal programs. "I'm not a member of any organized political party," he famously cracked. "I'm a Democrat."

In Hollywood, Rogers was not alone. On September 24, 1932, a stellar lineup of Democrat-minded motion picture personnel took over the Olympic Stadium in Los Angeles for a huge pageant, electoral parade, and sports show that drew some 65,000 people to what was both a fund-raiser for the Motion Picture Relief Fund and a pep rally for FDR. Winfield Sheehan of Fox and Jack Warner of Warner Bros. handled the arrangements, with Will Rogers and actor Conrad Nagel on hand to host the event. FDR spoke about his own motion picture experience—in the newsreels—and praised the industry for its generosity to so many worthy causes, leaving his own unspoken. Never before, joked Will Rogers, had so many people paid to see a politician. Hollywood's minority Republican caucus—Louis B. Mayer and David O. Selznick—stayed away.[29]

Motion picture artists were also caught up in the rampant politicization of the arts in the 1930s, a polemicist streak crystallized by the social realist movements in literature and the arise-and-sing-alongs presented on the

---

[d] The most notable exception to the political neutrality was an act of economic self-preservation. In 1934, the major studios intervened on the side of Republican candidate Frank Meriam in his race for California governor against the Democrat Upton Sinclair, the socialist who threatened a state takeover of the Hollywood studios. To defeat Sinclair and preserve their fiefdoms, the moguls poured money, resources, and fake newsreels into the race—but that, to their minds, was business not politics.

New York stage. Incubated by the Group Theatre in New York, an ensemble of fourth-wall-breaking artist-activists founded in 1935, and the Federal Theatre Project, a New Deal make-work program for indigent players, a generation of playwrights and thespians acted out a Popular Front platform before live audiences. After performing in productions that blended the adrenaline rush of putting on a show with the righteous fervor of consciousness-raising, little wonder that many in the cast took their lines to heart and recited the dialogue off stage. When the actors moved west from New York, they brought along more than their elocution and stagecraft.

Locally too, Hollywood actors were finding it hard to keep the destitution beyond the studio gates at bay. In 1936 a bitter strike by lettuce workers in the Salinas Valley in central California attracted the sympathetic support of a wide circle of actors from across the political spectrum (James Cagney, Eddie Cantor, Gary Cooper, and Fredric March) who each donated $1,000 to a cause that most might have seen more as a charitable contribution than a blow for labor solidarity. "Performers and others who contributed in collection to help sufferers from [the] Salinas lettuce strike are plenty burned up because [a] section of [the] press is trying to tag them as red contributors," reported *Daily Variety*. "Real dope is that the contributors gave their dough to feed hungry little children and women whose fathers and husbands are unable to buy food or provide shelter because of the strike."[30]

The *Daily Worker*, the official newspaper of the Communist Party USA, noticed the sensibility turnabout and welcomed the new recruits to the ranks. Hollywood communists "will find immediate support in the dynamic progressive movement that has developed on the West Coast, where great numbers of progressives are currently rousing mass sentiment for aid to Spain and China and organizing all liberals into a solid front against Fascism at home and abroad," wrote the party organ, before blowing the cover of one of its front groups. "The Hollywood Anti-Nazi League, for example, in its fight for democracy and peace, has stirred the imagination of the West Coast progressives." Not that the working-man's paper of record was going soft on capitalism. Elsewhere, of course, "the motion picture industry reflects the vicious anti-democratic offensive being conducted by finance capital in every part of the world today."[31]

The Hollywood Anti-Nazi League encouraged and exploited the rising political consciousness of the indigenous star power. In casting actors as activists, it was a farsighted pioneer.

Neither puppets nor poseurs, the first stars to stick their necks out and risk career suicide tended to know whereof they spoke. Having worked and hung out with the playwrights and theater directors energized by the ethos of art-for-Marx's-sake, actors such as Melvyn Douglas, Fredric March, Gale Sondergaard, and John Garfield did not have to read their lines from a script. Before his popular radio show went live over the airwaves, Eddie Cantor warmed up the studio audience with anti-Nazi patter.[32] United Artists founder and silent screen superstar Mary Pickford found her voice in broadsides against Nazism—calling on the nation's women to back a strong national defense program, denouncing Hitler as "mad as a March hare" and predicting, "When he finishes with the Jews he will turn to the Catholic Church, then to the Protestants" and finally "to the country that has the most gold."[33]

Then as now, the attraction of rich and beautiful artists to a doctrine of wealth redistribution in a classless society inspired a good deal of psycho-rumination. Did a profession whose practitioners channeled vicarious emotions feel the pain of the poor and dispossessed with special intensity? Had the emotional internalization of the Stanislavsky method wrought a permanent change of heart? Or was it something as simple as guilt for making so much money for so little labor in so bleak an economy?

Perhaps the best explanation for the affinity of motion picture artists—actors and screenwriters especially—to an ideology counter to their economic self-interest was the respectful hearing accorded them by the Communist Party USA. In Leninist doctrine, the artist stood among the vanguard elite, a cadre whose shining example would lead the benighted proletariat into the dawn of revolutionary enlightenment. In the eyes of the Hollywood moguls, actors and writers were hired hands and piecework drones, given their lines to speak and assignments to write, patted on the head if obedient, kicked in the ribs if recalcitrant. The communists and the Popular Front were starstruck, but not like the fans who swooned over the covers of fan magazines. The artist was the antenna of the revolutionary race—so much the better if he or she was a magnet for publicity and a donor with deep pockets.

In the 1930s, seeing stars selling something besides cosmetics, cigarettes, or themselves was a novel sight. "Actors are entertainers who make their living from the public, and I don't think the public is interested in their political, racial, or religious affiliation," harrumphed gossip columnist

Hedda Hopper, a reliable mouthpiece for studio opinion.[34] Drunken scuffles, moral turpitude, and temper tantrums were familiar foibles that the
studio's publicity departments had long experience covering up by greas-
ing the palms of the local cops and newshounds. Stars who sought out
publicity for ambulances for Spain and boycotts of Nazi goods were a
new kind of problem children. "The names of 26 Hollywood movie stars,
directors, and screenwriters, which usually appear only in bright lights
and on movie house billboards, have been painted across the sides of
two new ambulances soon to be shipped to Loyalist Spain," crowed the
Daily Worker.[35]

For the studios that underwrote the careers of the stars and expected
a steady return on the investment, the off-the-reservation performances
were not just novel but troubling. "Following urgent requests from their
foreign departments, major companies will take action soon to prevent
players from taking part in political movements, and lending use of their
names to campaigns on which national and international opinion is
divided," the *Hollywood Reporter* announced in 1937. "Open anti-Nazi and
anti-fascist stand of Hollywood stars has caused box office losses to their
companies, not only in Germany and Italy, but in other countries, where
these political principles are bitter issues. Since Hollywood depends on
foreign territory for 40 percent of its grosses, the 'isms' publicly praised
or denounced by film personalities may reach the point of bringing serious loss." To contain the damage, the studios threatened to insert political clauses into the contracts of uppity actors "similar to the morality
clauses now in most deals." Said one executive: "The players are under
contract to us and as such must obey us."[36]

Reporters from the trade press tended to agree with the studio bosses
that the contract player was an indentured servant. "The Hollywood stars
who are so earnest—and so public—in their sympathies for anti-Nazism,
anti-fascism and other antis, are doing more harm to themselves than
good to the causes they sponsor," insisted columnist Frank Pope in the
Hollywood Reporter. "How long will it be before the unpopularity which
they certainly will gather, in some countries, will begin to affect their
screen standing and, later perhaps, their salaries?" The prudent course
was to shut up and count their blessings. "The private opinions and
beliefs held by picture players are their own and no one has the right to
say that they shall not hold such opinions," conceded Pope. "But when
they make those opinions public, to the detriment of their own screen

value and therefore, to the detriment of the company that employs them, that is something else again. In such cases, we believe, the industry has the right to object."[37] Like the antique furniture and period costumes stored in the studio warehouses, the star was company property, part of the inventory.

Actors were not simply ventriloquist's dummies, responded the Motion Picture Artists Committee, another glitzy Popular Front group composed exclusively of movie personnel but basically an offshoot of HANL. Neither the studio front office nor the trade press had any right to restrict "the exercise by Hollywood stars of their constitutional right of free speech, because of the possible effect [on motion picture box office] in countries where free speech is denied." The committee scoffed at a mentality so devoted to commerce it was repulsed by altruism. "It may be that the act of signing one's name to an ambulance in order to send medical supplies to relieve the agony of Spanish men, women, and children is 'bad' publicity—whereas the endorsement of a new kind of lipstick or the 'reported engagement' to a famous 'socialite' is a blessing greatly to be desired."[38]

Whether tagged as useful idiots or ingrates, actors who got the left-wing religion made inviting targets for cynics and red-baiters. Wags delighted in jeering at (variously) the "champagne Communists," "swimming pool reds," "white tie and tail anti-Nazi movement," and "cocktail party activists" who linked arms with the scruffy proletariat to croon a chorus of the "Internationale" before being chauffeured back to the mansion in Beverly Hills. Dunces at best, traitors at worst, the slogan-spouting stars were pretty boys and girls who got fat off the fruits of capitalist America and then bit the hand that fed them. It was one thing for stagehands or electricians to cozy up to the communists, but flush screenwriters and pampered stars?

Beneath the smirks, darker insinuations were muttered: that Hollywood's political naïfs were being jerked around by Soviet puppeteers. "While we would not for an instant question the sincerity of the members of the anti-Nazi league and of the Motion Picture Artists Committee, there is always the possibility that, somewhere in the background, are clever manipulators who are exploiting the Hollywood names for the value they bring to a cause," suggested Frank Pope.[39] That the actor might be pulling his or her own strings was a notion too absurd to contemplate.

For HANL, the publicity windfalls and $1,000 checks compensated for the snickers and slanders. Besides, life as a Hollywood anti-Nazi wasn't all Marxist study groups and Soviet newsreels, what with annual summer dances at the Hillcrest Country Club, swimming parties and picnics at the Malibu beach house of the high-powered agent Mrs. Adeline Jaffe Schulberg, and black-tie fund-raisers at the most fashionable place to eat and be seen—Chasen's. Whether attending the West Coast premiere of the Broadway hit *Pins and Needles* (1937), a musical revue sponsored by organized labor (sample lyric: "If a radical idea / gives you nervous diarrhea / call it un-American"), or cheering on Joris Ivens's *The Spanish Earth* (1937), a documentary paean to the Loyalist side in the Spanish Civil War, the membership was ready to man the barricades with a night out on the town in the service of uplifting left-wing entertainment.[40]

"White tie and tail activism": the husband-and-wife team of screenwriter Herbert J. Biberman and actress Gale Sondergaard, animating members of the Hollywood Anti-Nazi League, at the premiere of Warner Bros.' *The Life of Emile Zola* (1937) at the Carthay Circle Theatre in Los Angeles, September 9, 1937. "She's wearing a novel jacket of black monkey fur, with long velvet gloves, and muff of the fur," noted the original International News Photo caption.

The local anti-Nazi ensemble was also—in good Hollywood-musical fashion—ready to pitch in and put on a show. In 1938 the Motion Picture Artists Committee mounted a madcap "political cabaret" called *Sticks and Stones*, a series of sketches and blackouts "more or less on the racy and raucous side," with a deep talent pool of performers (John Garfield, Gale Sondergaard, Milton Berle) and composers (Marc Blitzstein, Ira Gershwin, Johnny Green, Yip Harburg). At $5 a head, "a varied assortment of sophisticates, intellectuals, intelligentsia, and just plain Hollywood folk" laughed at twenty-three rapid-fire sketches lampooning fascism at home and overseas.[41] A smash hit—in political-theater terms—the show also generated a pop anthem of sorts, "It Can Happen Over There, But It Can't Happen Here."

Not least, and even without the garnish of political relevance, HANL laid out a sumptuous intellectual feast for its membership. In tandem with the Associated Film Audiences, yet another film-minded Popular Front group, it sponsored talks from industry notables. A series of eight lectures on "How Motion Pictures Are Made" served to tighten solidarity while providing a congenial forum for career networking. The program featured a stellar cast of experts, including actor-director Irving Pichel on "The History of Motion Picture Production," exiled German director Fritz Lang on "The Influence of Foreign Theater and Technique," screenwriter Viola Brothers Shore on "The Screen's Interpretation of Controversial Subjects," Donald Ogden Stewart on "Censorship," and Walter Wanger, who would know, on "The Troubles of a Producer."[42]

As the 1930s wore on and the menace from Nazism grew more palpable, HANL felt the wind at its back. The rallies got bigger, the soirees more glamorous, and the rush to sit on the dais more competitive. On November 18, 1938, in the wake of Kristallnacht (the Reich-wide wave of antisemitic violence launched on November 9–10) over 3,500 motion picture industry personnel packed a mass "Quarantine Hitler" rally at Philharmonic Auditorium in Los Angeles. Actor John Garfield, director Frank Capra, and Donald Ogden Stewart made impassioned speeches against the pogrom. Bringing the crowd to its feet, Garfield called for a militant campaign to fight "the rising wave of intolerance both in this country and abroad." Supportive messages were read from exiled German author Thomas Mann, who said that America must be the "strong unswerving protectress of the good and the godlike in man," and actress Joan Crawford, who "would have considered it an honor to have been present" had not her busy shooting schedule detained her.[43] The crowd unanimously voted to send a telegram, signed by dozens of prominent Hollywood personalities, urging President Roosevelt to "quarantine the aggressor nations."[44]

The League needed all the celebrity firepower it could muster. With the conspicuous exception of the left-leaning trade weekly *Box Office*, the mainstream press, both trade and civilian, often buried or ignored HANL's activities. The Los Angeles newspapers—always eager to cover gala premieres and stars hobnobbing in nightclubs—found HANL news unfit to print. "Certainly the most bigoted editor, and even laymen, must have recognized the news value of such a gathering," wrote Ivan Spear, of the mysterious silence that greeted the massive, star-studded "Quarantine Hitler" rally. "The metropolitan press completely ignored the assemblage—both before and after."[45] The only attention from another trade press source came in the form of a lecture. "Sincere but mistaken zeal," responded *Variety*, editorially, fretting over the siphoning off of even the smallest percentage of pro-German or anti-interventionist moviegoers. "There has been enough talk, enough protest meetings, enough name calling in the press and on the air" and "further concerted agitation can bring on the alienation of the sympathy of this country."[46]

In fact, HANL was earning the sympathy rather than the alienation of most of the country. By late 1938, anti-Nazism was far more popular than pro-Nazism, and by saying so, noted the Motion Picture Artists Committee, "the stars are identifying themselves with the great mass of the American people and the democratic peoples throughout the world."[47]

Shortly after the Shrine Auditorium rally, some sixty members of the Hollywood Anti-Nazi League met at the home of Edward G. Robinson to plan further action. The meeting was presided over by Melvyn Douglas, and the marquee names in attendance gave proof of the group's wiring into Hollywood's brightest star voltage: actors Bette Davis, Fred Astaire, Ginger Rogers, Paul Muni, Miriam Hopkins, and Robert Montgomery; directors John Ford and Anatole Litvak; producers Jack L. Warner and Walter Wanger; and, the *éminence grise*, Carl Laemmle. The gathering outlined a petition for an embargo of German goods. Douglas emphasized the "spontaneous" grassroots origins of the idea. "The President cannot order an embargo because this is not a dictatorship. He has done all he can in the matter." Public opinion, insisted Douglas, was the real force.[48]

The meeting resulted in HANL's most elaborate star-studded publicity-political stunt—the Declaration of Democratic Independence, modeled after the American original. "On July 4, 1776, the people of this country determined to submit no longer to an implacable despot," read the preamble to HANL's version. "Today, a new tyranny has arisen to challenge democracy's heritage. The leaders of Nazi Germany openly threaten national security, defy international decency, and proclaim the end of the democratic world." Adopting the Jeffersonian cadences of the original, the document lists a long train of abuses:

> Hitler and his Nazi dictatorship have attacked the religions of the world and substituted paganism in their stead.
> They have abolished freedom of speech, press, and assemblage, imposing their will upon 75,000,000 people and preparing a similar imposition of will upon all mankind.
> They have brought chaos and disunity into sovereign nations and then seized and dismembered them.
> They have degraded women to the function of producing soldiers.

Though the undersigned did not pledge their lives, fortunes, and sacred honor, the petition ends with a call that "all economic connections between the people of the United States and Germany be totally severed until such time as Germany is willing to re-enter the family of nations in accordance with the humane principles of international law and universal freedom."[49]

On December 21, 1938, a roster of marquee names dubbed "the Committee of 56" staged a photogenic signing of the petition, "fifty-six" being the number of the signers of the original Declaration of Independence. Seventeen stars and artists posed for the cameras in a variety of different configurations, among them such famous faces as Melvyn Douglas, Henry Fonda, Myrna Loy, Groucho Marx, Paul Muni, Claude Rains, Edward G. Robinson, James Cagney, and Gale Sondergaard. The first HANL-sponsored pseudo-event to be covered by the newsreels, the signing was featured in Fox Movietone, Universal Newsreel, and MGM's News of the Day. Timed with the release of the newsreels, copies of the document were circulated in fifty-six sections of the United States.[50] The ever-supportive *Box Office* lauded the Declaration of Democratic Independence as "a milestone in the progress of Hollywood liberalism" and

"A milestone in the progress of Hollywood liberalism": representatives from the star-studded "Committee of 56" sign the Declaration of Democratic Independence, December 21, 1938. *From left to right, standing:* Claude Rains, Paul Muni, Edward G. Robinson, Arthur Hornblow Jr., Helen Gahagan, John Garfield, Gloria Stuart, James Cagney, Groucho Marx, Aline MacMahon, Henry Fonda, Gale Sondergaard. *Sitting:* Myrna Loy, Melvyn Douglas, and Carl Laemmle. (Courtesy Getty Images)

"perhaps the strongest document ever made public by any group identified with the industry."[51]

Being experts in the politics of celebrity, HANL's leadership understood that the publicity machine hummed along on either alternate or direct currents. The flip side of fame was notoriety. The best use of the body of the celebrity for political reeducation was inspired by the appearance in Hollywood of two stars from the enemy camp—one a true son of Fascist Italy, the other a good daughter of Nazi Germany. In October 1937, Vittorio Mussolini, the son of the Italian dictator, came to town to finalize a coproduction deal with producer Hal Roach. In November 1938 the Nazi filmmaker Leni Riefenstahl arrived to publicize *Olympia* (1938), her marathon documentary of the 1936 Berlin Olympics. The HANL-orchestrated protests against "Il Duce Jr." and "Hitler's honey" showed that revulsion could be just as ideologically potent as attraction.

5

MUSSOLINI JR. GOES HOLLYWOOD

arold Eugene Roach, known around town and above the title as Hal, was there, in Hollywood, at the creation. A founding father of the motion picture industry and name-brand producer since 1916, the former muleskinner, prospector, trucker, movie extra, and gag writer was presiding kingpin of the Hal Roach Studios, the Culver City funhouse from which he mined the golden vein of slapstick screen comedy. With his friendly rival Mack Sennett, another Irish American *macher* among the Jewish American moguls, he churned out hundreds of picaresque one-and-two reelers crammed with cartwheeling flivvers, spritzing seltzer bottles, and aerodynamic custard pies.

In 1919, Roach put a pair of black-framed glasses on a pallid Chaplin imitator named Harold Lloyd and helped create, dollar for dollar, the most bankable marquee attraction of the 1920s. That same year, he corralled Will Rogers, the rope-twirling superstar of the vaudeville stage, for a hitch in motion pictures that somehow transferred the cowboy's free-ranging wit into the silent medium. He also teamed a brilliant pantomime artist from British music hall theater and a rotund bit player to create the immortal ectomorph-endomorph duo of Laurel and Hardy.

Unlike Sennett, a talent tethered to the madcap chaos of the silent screen, or Harold Lloyd, a go-getter too enmeshed in the discredited Jazz Age to prosper in the Great Depression, Roach not only survived the transition to sound but thrived after the sonic boom. Without missing a beat, he guided Laurel and Hardy into verbal byplay and secured first-place prominence for his second-billed two-reelers on the motion picture program.

Roach's trademark franchise and cash cow was his "Our Gang" short subjects, a monthly series featuring a multiethnic stock company of ragamuffin moppets whose membership was recast whenever puberty threatened to adulterate the kid stuff. Launched in 1920, it was the oldest continuous production unit in Hollywood.[1] It was also his ticket to a lucrative long-term deal with MGM, the Tiffany studio, which in 1925 contracted to distribute the shorts.

By the mid-1930s, Roach's child labor was working like a well-oiled machine. Built around the antics of cherubic everyman Spanky, cow-licked soprano Alfalfa, cutie-pie heartbreaker Darla, and saucer-eyed, coal-black Buckwheat, his litter of pint-sized scamps inhabited a prelapsarian world uncontaminated by grown-up worries and bigotries. "As spry a troupe of youngsters as ever gathered under the Klieg lights," bragged the taglines, accurate for once. By then, the underage ensemble had undergone four complete turnovers, with Pete the Pup, at six years in harness, the longest-serving gang member.

The Irish American *macher*: producer Hal Roach in his office with an iteration of his "Our Gang" ensemble in 1933. The children (*left to right*): Carl "Alfalfa" Switzer, Bobby "Wheezer" Hutchins, Darla Hood, George "Spanky" McFarland, and Matthew "Stymie" Beard. (Courtesy of the Collections of the Margaret Herrick Library)

In 1937 Roach was at the top of his game. He was bathing in the glow of an Academy Award for Best Short, *Bored of Education* (1936), a ten-minute "Our Gang" charmer, and his first A-feature hit, the supernatural screwball comedy *Topper* (1937). "When a studio steeped in tradition of more than 20 years standing for turning out custard-pie cantatas and prat-fall fantasies suddenly goes dignified, severs all connections with the past, and brings in a picture of the caliber of *Topper*, that studio and the people connected with it bear watching," noted an impressed Billy Wilkerson at the *Hollywood Reporter.*[2] Also impressed, MGM sweetened Roach's deal for the production of twelve "Our Gang" shorts per year and agreed to launch Laurel and Hardy into top-drawer feature-length attractions.

Flush with cultural cachet and reserve capital, Roach aspired to graduate not only from shorts to features but from mini-mogul to industry titan. On August 7, 1937, the stocky, debonair entrepreneur sauntered up the gangplank of the Italian luxury liner the *S.S. Rex*, bound for Genoa, Italy, and sailed into the treacherous shoals of international finance and big-power geopolitics. Undeterred by or just plain oblivious of the minefield he was cruising into, Roach planned to negotiate a coproduction deal that would link his name with a marquee performer not known for his comic timing—Benito Mussolini.

The Italian dictator had been Italy's iron-fisted, vainglorious ruler since 1922, stepping into the international spotlight with a personality so charismatic and an agenda so transformative he brought new words into the American vocabulary—*fascist*, for the ideology; *blackshirt*, for his paramilitary followers; and *Il Duce* ("The Leader"), for himself. A shameless camera hog and publicity hound, Mussolini posed frequently for the American newsreels and, upon the arrival of sound, obediently recited English to secure face time on screen, his eyes scanning cue cards held just out of frame. A feature-length documentary entitled *Mussolini Speaks* (1933) further inflated his outsized presence on the American screen. Narrated by Lowell Thomas, the laudatory biopic toyed with the notion that Italian-style fascism might be just the thing to solve the American economic crisis. Bald as a cueball, arms folded across his chest, chin out and head bobbing, Mussolini on screen was a made-to-caricature personification of the puffed-up dictator with imperial delusions—until 1935, when the brutal invasion of primitive Ethiopia by the mechanized forces of Italy transformed his persona from strutting buffoon to ruthless warmonger.

Like his partner in Germany, Mussolini fancied himself a patron of the newest of the arts. He inspected foreign films as censor-in-chief and meddled with the scripts and casting decisions of Italian-made feature films. His most enduring cinematic legacy was architectural. Inspired by an earlier line of Caesars, he oversaw the design and construction of a modern Colosseum—Cinecittà, a massive 120-acre motion picture plant built on the outskirts of Rome. Boasting nine soundstages linked by six miles of macadamized roads flanked by towering pine trees, the "Roman Hollywood" was a monument to his grandiose ambitions and a testament to the central role of cinema in the totalitarian playbook.[3]

The first American producer to set his sights on Cinecittà was, ironically enough, Walter Wanger, Hollywood's most urbane and unabashed liberal. In 1936, while in London on business, Wanger flew to Rome to meet with Mussolini and angle for a bilateral alliance. Encouraged by the discussion, Wanger formed an outfit known as Société Anonyme Cinematografie Italiano Walter Wanger, with Henry Fonda and Sylvia Sydney slated to star in the first joint venture.[4] Spellbound by his glimpse of the Fascist future, Wanger hailed the glory that was Mussolini's Italy. "A new Europe is definitely emerging" and "youth is at the helm," he enthused to Cecelia Ager, *Variety*'s lady reporter, who passed along Wanger's musings about a woefully misunderstood nation. "Italy has been hurt that we have an unfair attitude toward Fascism, that we don't understand that Italy wants to help the Ethiopians, that the Ethiopians welcomed the Italian armies and went over gladly to their side," said Wanger, spouting the Fascist line on the African carnage. "We only hear the other side of the picture over here." Provincial folks in Hollywood would do well to think more globally. "Our America-made pictures will have to be less nationalistic, in order to interest the foreign market," he advised.[5] As late as July 1937, even as Roach was edging him out, Wanger insisted that his deal with Mussolini was "more alive than ever," that transatlantic coproduction was a marvelous way to "help to cement friendly relations between film leaders in Italy and the United States."[6] The deal fell apart when Warner Bros., Wanger's unlikely partner in the scheme, balked and pulled the plug.

With the field clear, Roach moved in. Upon arriving in Italy, he was ushered into the presence of the self-styled "Iron Man of Europe," an audience that held little fear for a man who had gone nose to nose with MGM chieftain Louis B. Mayer. Being an old Hollywood hand, Roach also knew how to puff up an inflated ego. He tapped into both the dictator's aspirations as a motion picture impresario and his paternal affections with an irresistible proposition: he would go into business with Mussolini's 20-year-old son, Vittorio, in a company called RAM, an acronym combining Roach's and Mussolini's initials. The senior man would be the junior partner, the young Vittorio would be president.

Born in 1916, Vittorio was Mussolini's second son, and a decorated veteran of the Ethiopian invasion, where he had flown bombing and strafing missions. Besides lineage, Vittorio's qualifications as a Hollywood mogul included his irregular byline as the screen columnist for his father's paper, *Il Popolo d'Italia*, published in Milan, and his contributions to the Italian film magazine *Cinema*. As a film critic, he hewed to the Fascist line and slammed the Hollywood studio system for its lack of virility and surplus of feminine flesh. In contrast to most of his countrymen, he expressed the fervent hope "never again to see the ears of Clark Gable, or Dietrich's legs, or Garbo's feet, or Joan Crawford's mouth, or Katharine Hepburn's nose, or Luise Rainer's eyes, or Goldwyn's and Ziegfeld's ballet girls."[7]

The younger Mussolini listed another literary achievement among his credits. In 1936 he had published a memoir of his service as a pilot in the Ethiopian campaign entitled *Voli Sulle Ambe*, known in America as *Wings Over Ambe*. In purple prose whose bloody hue was not lost in translation, he exulted over the joys of low-altitude bombardment and the pyromaniacal rush gained from incinerating straw-hutted villages. Modern warfare, he rhapsodized, was "the most beautiful and complete of all sports."[8]

Being groomed for bigger things, Vittorio was appointed assistant director on Goffredo Alessandrini's aerial melodrama *Luciano Serra, Pilot*, released in 1938. "If he shows any talent, he will be packed off to Hollywood with his new bride to study American technique," *Variety* reported. "Idea is to train Vittorio as a sort of Will Hays for the Italian cinema and get Americans interested in playing ball with the Big Boy's favorite son."[9] On April 21, 1937, while his father beamed and Fascist dignitaries stood at attention, Vittorio presided over the elaborate ceremonies marking the opening of Cinecittà.[10]

The son was thus a natural conduit for the Hollywood producer to insinuate his way into the father's graces. Roach left his audience with Mussolini with a coproduction deal in his pocket and an anecdote too juicy not to repeat. According to Roach, during his pitch meeting with

Mussolini, neither the cost overruns at Cinecittà nor the punctuality of the Italian rail system preoccupied the dictator's mind. A devoted fan of Laurel and Hardy, he was distraught over the reported breakup of Roach's perennially squabbling duo. Regretfully, Roach confided that the news was true. Already depressed by setbacks on the diplomatic front, Mussolini blurted out, "and just at a time like this, I learn that my very good friends have quarreled!"[11] Surely, Vittorio and Hal would prove more amicable partners.[a]

On September 16, 1937, with his young ward in tow, Roach boarded the *S.S. Rex* for the return trip to America. No sooner had the ship lifted anchor than Roach spied a familiar figure strolling the decks—Charles C. Pettijohn, general counsel for the Motion Picture Producers and Distributors of America. Happily met, the trio sunbathed, shuffleboarded, and dined together on the voyage home. They also posed for pictures fore and aft, a cozy scrapbook that gave the impression the MPPDA was also on board for the RAM deal. Moreover, while still at sea, Roach moderated a radio show broadcast over a nationwide hookup in which Pettijohn interviewed Mussolini.

Back in America, news of the Roach-Rome axis and wirephotos of the smiling threesome had preceded the *Rex*. On the morning of September 23, 1937, when the ship docked in New York Harbor, a horde of reporters, photographers, and newsreel cameramen waited at the pier to document the merger of Italian Fascism and Hollywood filmmaking.

To duck the flashbulbs, the trio boarded a Coast Guard cutter and raced for shore, leaving the howling press corps in their wake. "It was a beautiful day for sailing up the Hudson yesterday but 50 reporters, newsreel men, and photographers didn't seem to enjoy it," groused a stranded reporter.[12] The journalists were not the only pesky greeters best avoided. Popular Front protesters, with the communists in the vanguard, had organized a shore party of placard-waving demonstrators. As soon as the tug hit dry land, Roach and Mussolini were rushed away under police guard to the Ritz Tower Hotel, a getaway arranged by the State Department at the behest of the MPPDA.[13] By then, sensing the impolitic blowback, Pettijohn had ditched the pair en route and gone his own way.

---

[a] Mussolini need not have fretted. Roach coaxed Laurel and Hardy into reuniting the next month.

■

Happily met (*left to right*):
Charles C. Pettijohn,
general counsel for the
Motion Picture
Producers and Distributors
of America, Vittorio Mussolini,
and Hal Roach aboard the
S.S. Rex during their voyage
to New York from Italy,
September 1938.

That afternoon, at a boisterous, good-humored press conference, Roach and Vittorio made nice to the sulking journalists. Ebullient about the coproduction deal, he praised his partners, pater and fils. "I think [Mussolini] is the only square politician I've ever seen," he said, describing himself as "100% sold on Premiere Mussolini and what he has done for the rich and poor of that country." The son was a chip off the old block. "Vittorio Mussolini is here on a holiday as far as the kid is concerned," Roach said, and immediately contradicted himself. "He's going into the picture business and I'm going in with him." Modestly, the Hollywood veteran pledged to be but a kindly mentor to the tyro producer. "I'm in sort of an advisory capacity," he insisted. "Mussolini wants his son to go in to business. Vittorio decided on the film business and I'm sort of a chaperon for him."[14]

Despite the smiles all around, a sense of buyer's remorse already hung in the air. Pressed by skeptical journalists, Roach vehemently denied that Fascist propaganda would infect the two planned coproductions at Cinecittà, film versions of *The Passion Play* and the opera *Rigoletto*.[15] The epics were to be "filmed with Italian voices and beauty, but with American

"Il Duce Jr.": 20-year-old Vittorio Mussolini (*far right*) meets the press at a convivial news conference at the Ritz Tower Hotel in New York, September 23, 1937.

screen technique."[16] Getting into the cross-cultural spirit, Roach dangled the tantalizing prospect that the RAM *Rigoletto* would be a parody featuring a reunited Laurel and Hardy.[17] Amid the clamor, he also made a nervous request. "Please don't mention MGM in this deal," Roach pleaded. "MGM doesn't want to be mentioned and, if you do, not only will this company be sore but Italy as well."[18] Nicholas M. Schenck, president of Loew's, MGM's parent company, was not happy about being linked to Fascist Italy and had told Roach as much when he landed in New York.[19]

Like MGM, the MPPDA also sought to keep the RAM pact at arm's length. The home office in New York denied any official involvement with the transaction, insisting the MPPDA had "absolutely nothing to do with the Roach-Mussolini company," and that the pictures of Pettijohn, Roach, and Mussolini on the high seas were occasioned by the mere happenstance of Mr. Pettijohn having "met the party aboard the *S.S. Rex* while returning to New York."[20]

Immediately after the New York press conference, Mussolini and Roach headed out to Newark and boarded a TWA flight to Hollywood, the former aviator opting for the speed and novelty of a transcontinental flight when most motion picture executives still preferred the comfort and safety of a first-class berth on the Twentieth Century Limited.

When the pair touched down at the Union Air Terminal in Burbank the next day, the press was waiting on the tarmac. Vittorio strode to the radio and newsreel microphones and ventured a few comments calculated to endear himself to the natives. "Well, here I am in California. I have just arrived in this beautiful country," he said in tentative but well-pronounced English. "It seems like my Italy. I think California is very beautiful. I know I will enjoy Hollywood."[21] He was then whisked to Roach's mansion in Beverly Hills, where the police had already set up mounted guards and arranged a three-man, round-the-clock security detail to stand watch throughout Mussolini's visit.[22]

Over the next few days, Mussolini toured soundstages, met with local politicians, and smiled for the cameras. At the Hal Roach Studios, he was trotted out for a full-dress press conference. Asked whether his father was disturbed by press reports of "communistic demonstrations" in New York, Vittorio chuckled and replied through his interpreter that his father had "much more important things to worry about than me."[23] Before leaving the Roach plant, he posed for pictures with studio technicians and the "Our Gang" kids.[24] Later at Twentieth Century-Fox, he met with Darryl F. Zanuck for a photo op with a far more valuable child property, Shirley Temple.

On the balmy evening of September 28, Roach and his wife Margaret hosted an extravagant dinner and dance party in honor of their guest. The celebration would commemorate two joyous dates: Vittorio's twenty-first birthday and the Roach's twenty-first wedding anniversary.

Roach spared no expense for the lavish blowout, a swellegant soiree that shimmered with all the glitter of Hollywood's Golden Age. "Undoubtedly this was typical of the party you readers all would like to attend," teased syndicated columnist Ed Sullivan, regaling the hoi polloi with a peek at the high life. "Champagne, celebrities, commotion, cops, crowds, cakes, cliques, cars, carriages, carnival capers, chagrin, complications." Under billowing tents set up over the mansion's grounds, 300 tuxedoed and begowned guests ("the *crème de la crème* of the celluloid industry") nibbled on cosmopolitan delicacies spread out over four buffet tables. Each table dished out an ethnic cuisine matched to a Central Casting character actor, dressed in festive native costume: Chinese bit player Chester Gan for the Chinese menu, Spanish singer Stelita for the Spanish dishes, Italian character actor Paul Procasi for the Italian food, and, presiding over the table for Southern-style home cooking, playing a servant once again, the African American actress Hattie McDaniel.[25]

Two orchestras—one Hawaiian, one Algerian—took turns serenading the stars, who moved to the music on a makeshift dance floor that was usually a tennis court. Flashing a red carnation in his lapel, Vittorio cut a dashing figure, twirling with the Roaches' daughter Margaret, an aspiring actress whose *nom de screen* was Diane Rochelle. MPPDA president Will H. Hays honored the fete with a rare night out, but, of course, the abstemious Presbyterian declined the champagne. Among the swarm of guests, a stargazer could spot Cary Grant, Bette Davis, Spencer Tracy, Fred Astaire, and the gorgeous Constance Bennett, swanning by on her way back from the buffet tables "in black satin with skull cap featuring a large black ostrich feather." The hawk-eyed reporter for *Daily Variety* also noticed a dolled-up Dolores Del Rio, attired "in a black dress with a hem bordered with silver fox to match her cape and black velvet bag with silver fox pom pom," conversing in Italian with a smitten Vittorio.[26] "He has a grand sense of humor, he's very modest and thoughtful, and dances divinely," cooed Del Rio.[27]

Outside the privileged perimeter, however, the atmosphere was not so bubbly. Fearing more than gate-crashing autograph seekers, a tense squad of L.A.'s finest enforced a tight security check for the shindig. "Uniformed cops halted you at the sidewalk, checked your name against the list in their hands, before you were allowed to proceed into the house and out past the lighted swimming pool to the tennis courts," reported Ed Sullivan. "At the close of the party, outside as you left, cops examined you closely and accompanied you to your car." For the giddy Isabel Sheldon, the society reporter for the *Los Angeles Times*, nothing could dim the splendor of an evening that was "one of the most brilliant social events of the season."[28]

Not everyone in Hollywood thought the open-air bash at the Roaches' was the hottest ticket in town. While motion picture royalty broke bread and clinked glasses with the Fascist prince, a cadre of lesser-known names was determined to spoil the party. Understanding that notoriety

Before the morning after (*right to left*): Hal Roach, his daughter Margaret, guest of honor Vittorio Mussolini, Roach's wife Margaret, and his son Hal Roach, Jr., at the swank Hollywood party celebrating Mussolini's twenty-first birthday and the Roaches' twenty-first wedding anniversary, September 28, 1937.

could be as useful as fame in furthering a cause, the Hollywood Anti-Nazi League mobilized to make Mussolini an object lesson. Mussolini's "presence here is not an occasion for celebration or social fetes," lectured the League from its preferred platform, a full-page ad in the trade press. "Those who welcome him are opening their arms to a friend of Hitler and an enemy of democracy."[29] Dancing cheek to cheek with the boy prince the group dubbed "Mussolini Jr." blemished the face of the entire movie colony.

Mussolini being technically a Fascist not a Nazi, the Motion Picture Artists Committee (MPAC) took point position from the Hollywood Anti-Nazi League, but the byline on the protest ads and handbills hardly mattered: membership in the two groups overlapped promiscuously. Full-page ads in *Daily Variety* and the *Hollywood Reporter* denounced Mussolini, Roach, and the knaves who associated with them. "Hollywood is on record throughout the country as having welcomed Signor Vittorio

Mussolini with open arms," read the copy. "We feel that Hollywood does not deserve this reputation."[b]

By 1937, Italy's war crimes in Ethiopia were a moot point and the African nation a lost cause. Moreover, it was a battlefield out of the sphere of Soviet interest. Mussolini's arrival in Hollywood provided a consciousness- and fund-raising opportunity for a crusade closer to the heart of the Popular Front. As the Spanish Civil War raged into its second bloody year, some 40,000 Italian troops were fighting alongside Franco's Rebels on land, sea, and air. "We can best show the world what Hollywood really does feel about Vittorio Mussolini by helping to bind the wounds of innocent victims of Signor Mussolini's favorite sport," HANL urged. An already iconic photograph of a dead child—a dead white child, from Spain, not a black child from Ethiopia—stared out from the ads and leaflets. The pang of a guilty conscience could be soothed by donating truckloads of medical supplies to the Loyalist cause in Spain.[30]

At some point in the time between the acceptance of Roach's party invitation and the publication of protest ads from MPAC and HANL, the cultural zeitgeist around town had shifted a decimal point to the left. The stars who had dined and danced with Mussolini at Roach's tennis court-ballroom awoke the next morning to discover that their big night out had left an unexpected hangover. According to *Variety*, the partygoers "resented the printing of their names as guests, especially when they learned that correspondents were now pasting the list in a convenient place [on studio bulletin boards] as a sort of blacklist." In a business built on personal relationships and mutual back-scratching, mixing with the wrong crowd could have crippling career consequences. Seemingly overnight, the social pressure applied by HANL exerted a greater force than a potential job with Hal Roach. "Town is seething over the young warrior's visit, and even those who were invited to Hal Roach's party, which merged young Vittorio's 21st birthday party and Roach's 21st wedding anniversary, were sore at the producer for putting them on the spot."[31]

Nor was the intramural Hollywood squabble over Roach-Mussolini merely a local news story. The war between the stars was avidly stoked by the national media. "It is a story inferentially revealed—a tale of 'snubs'

---

[b] Also listed among the guests at Roach's party for Vittorio Mussolini was Donald Ogden Stewart, president of the Hollywood Anti-Nazi League, attending either out of curiosity or in keeping with the screenwriter's credo of never turning down a free meal.

and 'cold shoulders' by some of the swankiest cinema stars who, it would seem, were not of one mind with Il Duce's son as to Fascism, war, etc.," reported the *New York Daily Mirror*.[32]

The hard-news headlines from overseas ratcheted up the controversy. While the younger Mussolini was dancing with the stars in Hollywood, his father was meeting with Hitler in Munich. As the international press held its collective breath, the two dictators presided over a huge military jamboree strengthening the ties of the Rome-Berlin axis. The Associated Press report on the meeting paused to note that affairs of state did not totally consume a father worried that his son might be the target of anti-Fascist demonstrations. "Mussolini is keeping a watchful eye on the movements of his son, Vittorio, who is in Hollywood to learn something of motion picture production."[33]

Red Kahn, the respected columnist for *Motion Picture Daily*, noted the sinister parallelism in the headlines. "Mussolini and Hitler in Germany, giving the world a renewed case of the ague," he scowled. "Vittorio and Hal in Hollywood, giving the American film industry what ought to be a sweating bee of its own." To Kahn, the coproduction deal between Mussolini and Roach was a "reckless lark" that boded ill all around. "No one individual has the right to consort with such a danger for his industry. Yet this is what Roach, unthinkingly or otherwise, has done. He has turned Metro nervous. He is seemingly unaware of the damage he may do to his own product in this market. He has aroused and angered the sensibilities of many liberal-minded men in the business. He has brought over a Mussolini, a product of a freedom destroying despot."[34]

A shaken Roach dialed the long-distance operator and called Kahn in New York to respond to what Kahn later characterized as the ugly "vibrations of a number of thinking men in this industry, Jew and Gentile alike, to an arrangement by a prominent American producer with the son of the founder of Fascism and the current consort of the founder and chief trumpeter of Nazism."

Aghast at the printed venom and personal shunning, Roach portrayed himself as an agent of constructive engagement. "I never made a move in Europe on this matter at any time without the advice and cooperation of some of the most prominent Jews there who told me I was doing the finest thing ever done in their estimation [by] tying up [Mussolini's] son and taking the boy back to Hollywood." While trying to explain, Roach only dug himself in deeper. "Particularly I did this on the advice of one of the most prominent Jews abroad" —here Kahn inserted a parenthetical assurance that the name of said prominent Jew would be furnished off the record upon request—"who thought it would do more good for the situation concerning Jews over there than anything that possibly could be done."[c]

Roach blundered on. "After all, if a lot of people would get a little closer to this situation and understand that there are hundreds of thousands of Jewish refugees now in Italy under the protection of that government, they would stop taking cracks at a guy who is in a position to talk to the guy who is a friend of the worst enemy a Jew ever had." The envoy without portfolio imagined a situation in which, perhaps over dinner with Mussolini, "maybe I can suggest to him that Hitler is not going quite right about things and maybe Mussolini will write Hitler a note and tell him so."

Roach's diplomatic initiative on behalf of the Jews failed to mollify the Popular Fronters, who smelled blood and pressed their advantage. The *Hollywood Reporter* measured the chill in the air. "Feeling runs so high in some quarters regarding the present visit of young Mussolini, Hal Roach had best keep him off some of the major studio stages as he may be embarrassed by the actions of some of the top stars should he visit their sets."[35] The extras were no more cordial than the top stars. Watching pictures of Mussolini and Roach in the newsreels, Hollywood audiences hissed.

A star bigger than any on the studio rosters delivered the most stinging rebuke. On October 5, 1937, speaking in Chicago, President Roosevelt called for a "quarantine" against the "aggressor nations" that threatened the peace of the world. "The present reign of international lawlessness," he proclaimed, "has reached a stage where the very foundations of civilization are threatened." FDR named no names but he didn't have to: Germany, Italy, and Japan were the aggressor nations cruelly sacrificing innocent people "to a greed for power and supremacy which is devoid of all sense of justice and humane consideration."[36] Roach suddenly found himself not only on the wrong side of Hollywood but of Washington as well. Just two weeks earlier, when the RAM deal was announced, it was seen as a coup. *Box Office* had praised Roach as "the man who beat all

---

[c] Any savvy industry insider could read between the lines of Kahn's coy aside: the reference was to Ludwig "Lawdy" Lawrence, MGM's European manager, based in Paris.

other American producers to the draw and made a deal with Italian interests for production at Cinema City near Rome."[37] Now he was the town
pariah. Walter Wanger must have thanked his lucky stars.

Scorched by the press criticism and personal invective, Roach scrambled to untangle himself from the alliance. "Ever since his arrival in
Hollywood with Vittorio Mussolini, Roach has been in a dilemma as a
result of the plainly evinced antagonism which immediately sprang up
in the picture colony for having associated himself with the Italian premiere's son," explained *Daily Variety*. "As the adverse pressure got stronger locally, with reluctance and positive refusal in some instances of
important people in the biz to fraternize socially with the young Italian
visitor, Roach began to figure out what would be most expedient."[38]

What was most expedient was to cut his losses. No more the kindly
mentor, Roach hustled Vittorio out of town, unceremoniously bum-
rushing "the kid" on a plane up to San Francisco under the name "W. J.
Willis." Columnist Ed Sullivan waved a snide farewell. "Vittorio Mussolini leaves Hollywood suffering from frostbite," he gloated.[39]

To save face, the Italians told a different story. Taking umbrage at FDR's
Chicago speech, Mussolini senior had telephoned his son that same night,
ordering him back home, under the pretense that the insulted prince was
leaving Hollywood, in high dudgeon, on his own accord.

No one was buying the cover story. Smirking between the lines, *Variety* knew whom to credit for the abrupt departure. "A concerted drive
of the [Hollywood] Anti-Nazi League against his presence in town made
Vittorio Mussolini's Hollywood visit too much for the 21-year-old boy to
support in a style to which diplomacy is accustomed." While progressives celebrated their "moral victory," Roach was "incommunicado at his
home nursing Public Headache No. 1."[40]

In the person of the son of the bald dictator, the Hollywood Anti-Nazi
League had taken its first scalp. "I went over [to the Italian film industry]
on the wrong premise, and got in by mistake," a whiplashed Roach sputtered afterwards.[41] Looking back over the fiasco, *Daily Variety* tallied up
the cost in social capital and hard cash with a snarky headline. "Mussolini Deal Off: Duce's Son Chilled by Reception." As for his host: "Roach
Out 12 Grand." He got off cheap.[42]

6

THE SPANISH CIVIL WAR
IN HOLLYWOOD

In March 1938, as Nazi troops stormed into Austria, Will H. Hays, president of the Motion Picture Producers and Distributors of America, issued his annual report, a corporate press release that, along with the usual unctuous blather, hinted that even the imperturbable Hoosier hearkened to the clack of goosesteps in Europe. "In a period in which propaganda has largely reduced the artistic and entertainment validity of the screen in many other countries, it is pleasant to report that American motion pictures continue to be free from any but the highest possible entertainment purpose," he intoned. "The industry has resisted and must continue to resist the lure of propaganda in the sinister sense persistently urged upon it by extremist groups." Barely pausing for breath, Hays recited the Hollywood mantra. "Propaganda disguised as entertainment" had no place on the American screen.[1]

The first line of defense against the lure of propaganda in the sinister—that is, overtly political—sense was the Production Code Administration, whose vigilance was typified by the narrow eye cast by regulator-in-chief Joseph I. Breen on a screen treatment entitled *Personal History*. Based on a best-selling memoir by *New York Herald Tribune* foreign correspondent Vincent Sheean and submitted for vetting in 1938 by independent producer and outspoken liberal Walter Wanger, the project dared to broach two headline happenings on the European continent—the Spanish Civil War and the Nazi persecution of the Jews. Breen predicted "enormous difficulties from the standpoint of political censorship, both here and abroad" because the scenario "raises, and takes sides in, such controversial racial, political, and religious questions as the civil war in Spain, and the treatment of Jews in Germany." Smelling "a definite flavor of pro-Loyalist propaganda in the Spanish war sequences, and of pro-Jewish and anti-Nazi propaganda, in the sequences laid in Germany," Breen suggested a wall-to-wall fumigation. "Such a flavor, it seems to us, will inevitably cause you enormous difficulties, when you come to release the picture."[2]

Heeding the caution lights, Wanger shelved *Personal History*. "Although this book has had a terrific sale and is widely read, it is going to take the work of magicians or soothsayers to get it to the screen," he groused.[3] Breen did not issue a definitive thumbs-down; he simply signaled his displeasure, which was usually sufficient to change a producer's mind.

Nonetheless, despite the best efforts of the executive ranks of the MPPDA and the regulators at the Breen office, "propaganda disguised as entertainment" was burrowing into Hollywood cinema. *Personal History* may not have made the cut, but the Spanish Civil War was too close to the hearts of Hollywood's Popular Front not to infuse screenplays and inspire finished films. Besides, Spain was already a motion picture attraction of sorts—the first of the twentieth-century wars to be covered in all its street-level carnage and battlefield brutality by the newsreels.

The Spanish Civil War erupted on July 1936, when forces in North Africa led by Gen. Francisco Franco rebelled against the duly elected Popular Front coalition governing the Republic of Spain, and raged on until May 1939, when Franco's triumphant Rebels (also known as the Insurgents) finally routed the fractious Republicans (also known as the Loyalists due to their fidelity to the elected government). A clash of political and religious temperaments as well as armies, the conflict pitted the aristocracy, the military, and the Catholic Church against liberal democrats, socialists, anarchists, and communists; Nazi Germany and Fascist Italy backed the Rebels; the Soviet Union and communist parties from around the world supported the Republicans. Each side poured supplies, advisors, and warriors into the cauldron. Recruits from far beyond the borders of Spain marched in to fight a war that was at once civil and symbolic. The fate of Spain itself might have been an afterthought.

Perceived then, and portrayed ever since, as a dress rehearsal for the main event on the horizon, the Spanish Civil War played out as foreshadowing even at the time. "This squalid brawl in a distant city is more important than might appear at first sight," warned George Orwell in his 1938 war memoir *Homage to Catalonia*, speaking not only of the battle for the besieged city of Barcelona. When Barcelona, and more, was lost, he returned to London and wandered around Trafalgar Square, filled with dread and dismay. As Spain smoldered in ruins, the bobbies, the pedestrians, and the passengers on the double-decker buses were "all sleeping the deep, deep sleep of England, from which I sometimes fear that we shall never wake till we are jerked out of it by the roar of bombs."[4]

The backfire from the Spanish Civil War was also cinematic. For the first time in motion picture history, the sights and sounds of mechanized warfare on European soil were captured by newsreel cameras. In terms of sheer visceral impact, the spectacle beggared the mock-heroics of the Hollywood feature film. Unlike the geographically distant and racially alien vistas of Ethiopia, invaded and conquered by Mussolini in 1935, or China, terrain for Japanese aggression since 1931, Spain was a blood relative on the map of Europe. The full-court press of the modern media of the day—wire service reporting, photography, radio broadcasts, and sound newsreels—brought the slaughter home to civilians who might be heartsick, horrified, and, if planted safely in a theater seat, perhaps a little thrilled.

Nonetheless, in any gallery of the visual arts documenting the Spanish Civil War, the motion picture medium warrants minimal wall space. From a century drenched in bloody images of war, Spain bequeathed two indelible tableaux, both of them stationary—Picasso's mural *Guernica*, the wall-sized painting depicting the surreal horror of aerial bombardment on a civilian population, first displayed at the Spanish pavilion at the World's Fair in Paris in 1937; and Robert Capa's *Falling Soldier*, a photograph of a Loyalist militiaman freeze-framed at the moment of death, published in *Life* magazine on July 12, 1937. The art of cinema left behind no pictures of comparable resonance.

The poor finish was not for lack of effort by a dedicated cadre of motion-picture-minded artists, activists, and journalists. In 1937, galvanized by the threat to the cause of Spain, and encouraged by the work of a resourceful band of radical filmmakers (notably the social realist wallop of photographer Paul Strand's *Redes* [*The Wave*, 1936], a homage to a fisherman's strike in Mexico, and *The World Today*, a *March of Time*-like screen magazine that covered news the *March of Time* deemed unfit to screen), a group of seventy-five writers and filmmakers banded together to form Frontier Films, a production company dedicated to repudiating "the notion that independent films of valid social import cannot be produced in this country." If the city whose name was synonymous with the movies refused to engage "the subject matter that needs to be dramatized in America's most popular medium," then the pioneers of Frontier Films ("a group of forward looking professional scenarists, directors, dramatists, and cameramen") would assume the responsibility of harnessing "the most popular medium of entertainment." Only then could films be created "that truthfully reflect the life and drama of contemporary America." The like-minded Popular Front media review *New Theatre and Film* praised the outfit as "a step of incomparable importance to be welcomed and supported by all who resent the distortion of American life by the products of Hollywood."[5] Less credulous, *Variety*'s brief notice about the self-styled "Group Theatre of motion pictures" dedicated to "expressing an 'enlightened' social and economic philosophy" described the agenda as "frankly propaganda."[6]

Along with Frontier Films, natural allies such as the Hollywood Anti-Nazi League, the Motion Picture Artists Committee, and the Theatre Arts Committee worked to create an American home front for Republican Spain, with many of the artist-activists holding dual, triple, or quadruple memberships in the various wings of the movement. They raised money for medical supplies; recruited volunteers for the Abraham Lincoln Brigade, the American unit mustered to fight for the Spanish Republic; and worked to end the boycott of goods and guns mandated by the Embargo Act of 1937, the noninterference directive passed by an isolationist U.S. Congress in thrall to a powerful Catholic lobby. "I have been in Spain and I have seen what the people of that democracy, the people who elected that democracy, are doing there to protect it," wrote Dorothy Parker in *Hollywood Now*, with no witticisms or smirks. "I don't know when that war will end—but I know how it will. Democracy—and therefore civilization—is not going to be wiped out there."[7] In 1937, overcome by emotion while speaking to reporters upon her return from Spain, Parker wept.

The cause that brought the decade's most quotable cynic to tears was taken to heart throughout the ranks of left-leaning Hollywood. Stars wrote checks, spoke at rallies, and signed their names to ambulances slated for shipment to the Republicans. "Joan Crawford is the sweetheart of democratic Spain," boasted *Hollywood Now*, in fan magazine mode, gushing over the activism of MGM's screen queen. "On the arrival of the famous Hollywood ambulance in Spain, the sight of Joan's name inscribed on its side caused more comment than the other names."[8] Even Errol Flynn, Warner Bros.' swashbuckling action star and an actor not known for political idealism, traveled to Spain in 1937 to file reports as "a sort of war correspondent." (When Flynn was erroneously reported to have been wounded in Madrid, a panicked Jack L. Warner ordered the star of his stable back to safety.) "Professional Hollywood has been in a flutter over the European political situation for several years," *Variety* noted in 1938. "Some of the leading stars and writers have participated at open forums and as contributors to warring factions in Spain. Latter is a Hollywood *cause célèbre*, and Hollywood hostesses long ago forbade mention of Spain at Hollywood dinner tables."[9]

Dinner parties were not the only gatherings broken up by the Spanish Civil War. The death match between Catholics and communists in Spain created fissures in the Popular Front alliance between Catholics and progressives in Hollywood. For the Catholic actors, writers, and directors

A Hollywood *cause célèbre*: actresses Luise Rainer (*left*) and Gale Sondergaard (*right*) host a cocktail party for dancer Angna Enters (*center*), in Hollywood for a recital sponsored by the Motion Picture Artists Committee on behalf of the Loyalists in the Spanish Civil War, November 16, 1937.

who attended Sunday mass at the Church of the Good Shepherd in Beverly Hills, rallying to the anticlerical Republicans backed by Joseph Stalin qualified as matter for confession. On May 28, 1937, in a meeting in Shrine Auditorium, twelve Popular Front organizations, banding together as the North American Committee to Aid Spanish Democracy, held a rally to raise funds for the Republican cause. The usual Hollywood suspects came out in force, not only to support Republican Spain but to sign on to a resolution, drawn up by the screenwriter Herbert J. Biberman, a zealous communist foot soldier, expressing outrage over "being called Communists, reds, and other names." *Variety*'s report on the meeting included a telling comment. "Many Catholics in the picture biz gave the resolution their moral support, but said they couldn't join the blast at this time."[10]

Even without all of the Catholics on board—and many, including actor James Cagney and director John Ford broke with their church on this matter of faith—Hollywood's Popular Front maneuvered to get their medium into the fight. As the Spanish Civil War raged, its stateside reserves fought their own war to bring the battle to American screens.

"CENSORED PAP!" WALTER WANGER'S *BLOCKADE* (1938)

In late 1936, Twentieth Century-Fox chieftain Darryl F. Zanuck was mulling a motion picture project called *The Siege of the Alcazar*, to be supervised by H. R. Knickerbocker, the foreign-affairs correspondent for the Hearst newspaper syndicate, a media outlet notorious in Popular Front circles as a shill for the rebellion led by General Franco. Alcazar, a historical citadel and military academy in Toledo, was seized, defended, and ultimately won by Rebel forces in a dramatic siege that lasted from July through September 1936, a military action that was either a demonstration of "stoical bravery and deathless chivalry" or the invasion of a mercenary army made up of "Moors, the riff-raff of the foreign legion, Nazis, and Italians." Paramount and Fox Movietone crews on site captured riveting footage of the siege and the defense of the fortress, the dynamiting of the fortress by the Loyalists, and the exodus of the defenders after Franco's forces relieved the garrison.[11]

Getting word of the proposed film, anti-Fascist activists flooded Fox with angry protests. From London, the critic-screenwriter-producer Ivor

Montagu, an upper-crust communist whose auteur network stretched from Sergei Eisenstein to Alfred Hitchcock, composed an "open letter to Darryl F. Zanuck" laced with invective and threats. If "you are thinking of telling, not a true story, but a fairy version of this tale—then, Mr. Zanuck, let me whisper just this little warning in your ear: there are men and women and children in every corner of the world, Mr. Zanuck, who will remember it, Mr. Zanuck, as long as they remember the real heroes of the Alcazar. And one day, Mr. Zanuck, you might come to regret it."[12]

Under siege himself, Zanuck scrapped the project.[13] The battleground of Spain, it seemed, was a real-world location no more suitable for Hollywood than Italy or Germany.

Unlike Nazi Germany and Fascist Italy, however, the legally elected and diplomatically credentialed Republican government of Spain voiced no objections to motion pictures about the Spanish Civil War, at least those with the correct sympathies. The objections to Hollywood's depictions of the Spanish Civil War came closer to home, from the MPPDA, which, as ever, was against politically inclined motion pictures on general principles and especially politically inclined motion pictures that leaned leftward. Yet without a diplomatic protest from a foreign embassy to provide cover and justification, the MPPDA might frown but it could not forbid. As a result, two Hollywood films brought the war in Spain closer to American screens than either the Fascism in Italy or the Nazism in Germany. One was a modestly budgeted and little noticed programmer that tilted mildly toward the Rebels; the other was a prestigious and high-profile A-picture that stood staunchly with the Republicans.

Paramount's *The Last Train from Madrid* (1937) was first out of the gate. In late 1936, early on in the production process, anti-Fascist groups were reported to be "keenly interested" in the project. Paramount, said *Variety*, "has always been regarded as the least offensive, to the antis' way of thinking, in both its newsreels and feature productions of all the major filmers."[14] Perhaps some of the sympathy for the victims of Rebel bombing seen in the newsreels might seep into the studio's feature film.

To assure otherwise, the Breen office pruned the early versions of the script with its customary care. John Hammell, Paramount's in-house liaison with the Breen office, was advised to take great pains "not to inject any material into your picture which might be offensive to either of the sides now fighting in Spain." Breen tagged two sequences for deletion: in one, a Loyalist soldier's foot stomps on a hand holding a crucifix; in the other, Loyalist soldiers stage a mass execution of Rebel prisoners of war.[15] Playing an even hand in its commitment to bland neutrality, the Breen office judged the depiction of the Loyalists as anti-Catholic war criminals no more acceptable than the depiction of the Rebels as heroic crusaders for Christian civilization.

On April 6, 1937, *Variety* announced that "after long deliberation, the Hays office has finally okayed the script for Paramount's *The Last Train from Madrid.*"[16] Using his standard phrasing, Breen informed Hays that Paramount "has exercised great care to avoid taking sides."[17]

Doubtless *The Last Train from Madrid* passed muster with relative ease because the plot leaned—not egregiously but perceptibly—toward the Rebels, or at least the atmosphere was not suffused with the romance of Spanish Republicanism swirling through the Popular Front. Directed by James Hogan, a high-yield studio journeyman, and written by Louis Stevens and Robert Wyler, the film was conceived as a hybrid of *Grand Hotel* (1932) and *Shanghai Express* (1932), with the Spanish Civil War providing background scenery and plot motivation. While artillery shells rumble offscreen, a cross-section of humanity scrambles to escape the war-torn city, trading lives and virtue for a ticket out of the combat zone.

A pre-credit crawl scrolling over newsreel footage of the fighting in Spain takes pains, as per Breen's suggestion, to stress the impartiality of the forthcoming "account of fictional characters caught in beleaguered Madrid, fired with one common desire—Escape." In Paramount's version of the Spanish Civil War, no one is fired with a militant fervor either to defend or overthrow the Republic. "We neither uphold nor condemn either faction of the Spanish conflict," a title crawl insists. "This is a story of people—not of causes."

The people's stories criss-cross promiscuously. Two old army friends, one a Republican (Anthony Quinn), the other a Rebel (Gilbert Roland), are in love with the same woman (Dorothy Lamour); a chatterbox American newspaperman (Lew Ayres) is hijacked by a female Republican soldier (Olympe Bradna) whose romantic yearnings sweep aside her military training; a Republican soldier (Robert Cummings) deserts because he can no longer serve on a firing squad; a Baroness (Karen Morley) will literally kill to get her ticket out. In the film's climactic sequence, set at the Madrid train station, the loose threads are sewn together—the fortunate riders take their precious berths, the luckless are left on the platform or arrested. In the curtain-closer, Hollywood makes love not war. Cozy

Below the radar of the Popular Front: American newspaperman (Lew Ayres) and a Loyalist soldier (Olympe Bradna) in Paramount's *The Last Train from Madrid* (1937), set during the Spanish Civil War.

and cuddly in a compartment in the last train from Madrid, the male lead and female ingénue embrace for the sign-off clinch.

As a talking point in the partisan debate over Spain, *The Last Train from Madrid* performed little service to either side. Like so many interwar films with a war backdrop, it keeps a tone amorphously antiwar and blithely oblivious of the stakes in this particular war. Still, the geographical and historical specificity of the story—this is Spain at war, the setting is Madrid, the refuge is Valencia, the dreaded front is Cardoza—meant that the stern military command structure controlling movement out of Madrid can only represent the Republican forces, though perhaps only a well-informed partisan of either side would discern the contestants from all the background noise.

War being hell all around, neither Rebel nor Loyalist is conspicuously noble or morally culpable. Authentic Paramount newsreel footage is interspliced into the drama, showing scenes of civilians scattering in the streets and cradling infants, victims who can only be innocent Republican civilians attacked by Nazi war planes in league with the Rebels. Yet the Republicans also have blood on their hands. When a Republican colonel orders the execution of Rebel political prisoners, his subordinate is shocked. "Their only crime was to differ with us," he objects. "In revolution, that's treason," snaps a true believer. In the end, the film does not so much take an evenhanded approach to the war in Spain as shrug its shoulders. The larger meaning of the Spanish Civil War is immaterial; only the interpersonal conflicts matter. Friendship is a cause "greater than patriotism," says the Republican officer who throws away his cause, his career, and his life for a blood brother. "It keeps carefully away from the political issues," the *Hollywood Reporter* noted with relief.[18] "Strictly uncolored melodrama," was the verdict from the disappointed Popular Front.[19]

Lacking big stars, lavish budget, and an overt political agenda, *The Last Train from Madrid* slipped under the radar. A film with a loftier pedigree and a double-edged title would be credited with—and blamed for—running Hollywood's long-standing embargo against "propaganda disguised as entertainment."

Blockade was the brainchild of producer, pundit, and *bon vivant* Walter Wanger. In class if not ethnic roots, Wanger was a Hollywood anomaly: born to privilege, Ivy League educated, and unabashedly liberal. The son of a wealthy San Francisco clothing manufacturer who came west with the great wave of German Jewish migration in the mid-nineteenth century, Wanger enjoyed the perquisites of a patrician upbringing and a Dartmouth education. (The family's original name was Feuchwanger, and Wanger was related to Lion Feuchtwanger, author of *The Jew Suss*.) It was at Dartmouth that an encounter with the theater department derailed a planned career in the diplomatic service. In 1918, after a hitch in the U.S. Army Signal Corps during the Great War, Wanger signed on with Famous Players-Lasky and quickly moved up the ranks with the company that became Paramount Pictures.

In 1928, Wanger left Paramount, first for Columbia, and then MGM, where he hit his stride with the edgy political satire *Washington Merry-Go-Round* (1932) and the lavish costume drama *Queen Christina* (1933), the pairing being an apt expression of his dueling political and commercial sensibilities. In 1937 he signed a distribution deal with United Artists and went fully independent. A frequent commentator on the motion picture industry at public forums, in magazine articles, and on radio, Wanger was a press darling inevitably referred to as "urbane" and "erudite," adjectives seldom applied to his fellow producers. Though considered a bit high-hat by Hollywood standards, he was also deemed capable of checking "his brains and aesthetic taste at the studio gates," which was meant as a compliment.[20] Even as Wanger was guiding *Blockade* through the Breen office, the "canny showman instinct" of a producer prominent enough to have his name not just above but in the title was on display in *Walter Wanger's Vogues of 1938* (1937), a garish Technicolor fashion parade worlds away from rag-tag, war-torn Spain.[21]

Blockade meandered through preproduction for over a year, the shifting titles of the many early drafts of the screenplay a sign of its troubled gestation: *Castles in Spain, The Loves of Jeanne Ney, The River Is Blue, The Adventuress, The Rising Tide.* "*Castles in Spain* (Wanger) is the first picture to use the Spanish Revolution as a background," Breen informed Hays in February 1937 when the project first appeared on his desk. "The studio has taken great pains not to take sides in the matter."[22]

Hollywood's urbane, progressive independent: Walter Wanger with fiancée Joan Bennett at the banquet for the Academy Awards ceremony at the Biltmore Hotel in Los Angeles, March 10, 1938.

Actually, Breen had taken great pains to see that the studio would not take sides. Knowing Wanger had lobbed a grenade in his lap, he personally shepherded the project through the Code's bureaucracy, assisted by his number two man Geoffrey Shurlock and Code staffer E. R. O'Neil. "Any material involved with, or played against, the background of the present Civil War in Spain, is, in our judgment, highly dangerous, at the present time, from a practical standpoint, as well as [regards] distribution in Europe," Breen told Wanger after looking at thirty pages of the first script, a collaboration between Clifford Odets, author of the ur-Popular Front play *Waiting for Lefty* (1935), and Lewis Milestone, director of *All Quiet on the Western Front* (1930) and member of the Hollywood Anti-Nazi League. "I take it that your plan is to steer a middle course and to play no 'favorites' in the present Civil War in Spain," Breen queried, or suggested to, Wanger. Even so, "grave danger" awaited any picture "played against the background of the Spanish Civil War." Merely to pinpoint the location was a risky gambit that would "be pretty generally booted about in Europe by those governments which may be 'for' or 'against' the parties engaged in the war."[23]

A year later, with Spain still in flames, a second continuity draft by John Howard Lawson, now titled *The River Is Blue*, finally cleared both the moral and political hurdles put up by the Breen office. A playwright and screenwriter who had come West from Broadway in 1931, Lawson was the Communist Party's commissar in Hollywood, a committed Stalinist tasked with whipping the freer literary spirits into the party line. Still, Lawson knew enough to keep his Marxism in check and to shade the picture with enough Catholic devotion from the Spanish peasantry to mute the pro-Loyalist coloring.

Breen judged the Lawson rewrite "reasonably free from danger from the standpoint of political censorship," but warned Wanger "not to identify, at any time, the uniforms of the soldiers shown throughout the story" and to scrupulously avoid "'taking sides' in the present unfortunate Spanish Civil War." The PCA chief underscored that last point: "It is imperative that you do not, at any time, identify any of the warring factions."[24] Of course, along the corridors of the Breen office, the staff was wise to Wanger. "This is a story of the present Spanish Civil War, in which neither of the warring factions are identified," stated E. R. O'Neil in an internal memo.[25]

Uniform distortion: Henry Fonda (backframe, with Madeleine Carroll to his left) and Leo Carrillo (second in line) in *Blockade* (1938), Walter Wanger's compromised depiction of the Spanish Civil War.

Besides military outfits, Breen insisted on further obfuscations to prevent viewers from connecting the dots. "You should assure yourselves that none of the *incidents*, or *locations*, in your story could possibly be tied in with the actual events that have occurred, or are occurring in Spain," he instructed.[26] Not that Breen's fixation on military uniforms blinded him to other fashion risks. "The statue of the nude nymph should not be too pointedly 'nude,'" he warned, before dispatching two staffers to the set to eyeball the risqué statuary.[27]

Satisfied that both the war and the wardrobe in *Blockade* were sufficiently opaque, Breen took off for Rome, to receive an honor that recognized his service as Defender of the Faith in a pagan realm: a Knighthood of St. Gregory, a coveted papal decoration for Catholic laymen, personally bestowed by Pope Pius XI.

Meanwhile, Wanger's plans to bring aid and comfort to the Spanish Republic leaked out to precincts far beyond Hollywood. The more optimistic members of the Popular Front in America dared hope that a cinematic indictment of Fascist depredations in Spain might arouse Americans to petition Congress to repeal the Embargo Act and to intervene on the side of Spanish democracy. With no other marquee attraction to hold to its bosom, stateside partisans of the Spanish Republic invested great emotional resources in *Blockade*.

According to Wanger, the enemy's forces were also monitoring his shooting schedule. Suspicious Spanish-looking strangers skulked outside the studio gates and trespassed onto the premises. Wanger complained to Secretary of State Cordell Hull that "spies" or other "mysterious persons" had infiltrated the lot during filming.[28] "The fact that I have dared to use a civil war now going on in Europe as the background for a motion picture really caused all the discussion," he told a radio audience. "I think that you will agree with me that I would be an unworthy American if I gave up my dramatic subject for fear it might offend some foreign nation." He vowed to soldier on.

Wanger was as good as his word. To direct, he hired William Dieterle who, as a German Jewish refugee from Nazi Germany, possessed firsthand experience with the subject matter. Ironically, Henry Fonda, the top-draw star of the anti-Fascist *Blockade*, was originally slated to adorn the premiere production for the Société Anonyme Cinematografie Italiano Walter Wanger, Wanger's ill-considered flirtation with Italian dictator Benito Mussolini for a coproduction deal at Cinecittà. He also tapped novelist James M. Cain to punch up Lawson's preachy dialogue. (At the time, screen adaptations of Cain's own pulpy novels were themselves under blockade by the Breen office, a prohibition not lifted until *Double Indemnity* [1944].)

Set in spring 1936, *Blockade* opens in a landscape of rolling hills and fertile fields. This is a pastoral nation at peace, idyllic, Edenic, basking in the natural light of a friendly sun. Flute-playing shepherd Luis (scenery-chewing character actor Leo Carrillo) dotes on his flock while the gentle farmer Marco (Henry Fonda) waxes eloquent on the good earth. "The secret of life is in the ground," he tells his companion, rubbing the dirt reverently in his hands. "Man must learn that secret and use it wisely. People have wasted the richness of the soil."

The action moves from the agrarian fetishism of a Soviet five-year plan into a patented Hollywood "meet cute." Norma, a beautiful, mysterious antiques dealer (Madeleine Carroll), zooms by in her roadster and crashes into Marco's cart. After the symbolic collision of nineteenth- and twentieth-century horsepower, the oxen are hooked up to the battered vehicle and the couple is pulled slowly to the sleepy port town of Castelmare. He recites Byron, she gives him a flower.

The distant thunder of artillery blasts Spain out of paradise and interrupts the budding romance. As shells rain down, the terrified peasants of the valley flee in panic until Marco steadies their nerves and fires their patriotism. "This valley—it belongs to us!" he shouts. "Turn back and fight!" Morphing into a cohesive military unit, the peasants shoulder their weapons, take up defensive positions, and repulse the invading rebels.

Marco is rewarded with a medal for valor, the rank of lieutenant, and an assignment as a counterintelligence officer. "Spies and traitors are spreading false rumors, sending out information, betraying every move we make," explains his commandant. "Our greatest danger is from the enemies among our own people. We must find them and clean them out!" Marco is soon papering home-front walls with signs reading: "WARNING! DO NOT DISCUSS MILITARY MATTERS WITH STRANGERS. BEWARE OF SPIES."

Lawson's screenplay is of the same mind. As the plot lurches forward, the trope of enemy infiltration is writ in capital letters. *Blockade* is not a combat film, a political screed, or a melodrama of lovers caught in the crossfire of war, but an espionage thriller in which the main threat is not the army across the battlefield but the spies behind the lines. "I have agents all over the country," boasts a Germanic advisor to a treasonous military officer. "Every soldier in this place is one of my men." Mirroring the fratricidal infighting that helped doom the real Republican forces, and perhaps already preparing a fallback, stab-in-the-back explanation for the looming defeat of the Republican forces the next year, Lawson's screenplay imagines a nest of spies on the home front and traitors at the highest levels of military authority. The phrase is not used in the dialogue, but fifth columnists are everywhere.[a]

Despite the traitors in the ranks, a relief ship bringing aid to the starving and sickly civilians breaks through the blockade. Peasants give

---

[a] Soon to be common parlance, the term *fifth columnist* derived from a comment attributed to the Rebel commander Gen. Emilio Mola during the battle for Madrid in 1936. Mola claimed to have four columns of troops surrounding the city and a "fifth column" within the city ready to join the attack. The phrase is the singular contribution to English vernacular from the Spanish Civil War.

thanks at the altar, children cheer, and babies drink milk. Yet Marco feels no sense of victory. Tormented by the plight of his people and enraged at an uncaring world, he delivers an impassioned speech that was as close as Hollywood's Popular Front ever came to launching a full-throated anti-Fascist broadside via American cinema during the 1930s.

Beginning in plaintive bewilderment, the peroration builds to a crescendo of righteous anger, the camera moving in for a close-up of Marco and then pivoting so his eyes look straight into the lens, beseeching the spectator.

> Marco: Our country's been turned into a battlefield. There's no safety for old people and children. Women can't keep their families safe in their houses. They can't be safe in their own fields. Churches, schools, and hospitals are targets.

By now, this is no longer Marco speaking, but a screenwriter, a director, and a producer going eye-to-eye with moviegoers in a rare instance of direct address in classical Hollywood cinema.

> Marco: It's not war—war's between soldiers! It's murder—murder of innocent people. There's no sense to it. The world can stop it! Where's the conscience of the world?

The question hangs in the air as the film fades to black and the credits roll.

Blockade was given a send-off commensurate with the hopes riding with it. On June 3, 1938, at the Village Theatre in the tony Los Angeles district of Westwood, the film premiered to a packed house of pumped-up Popular Fronters. Arriving late, Wanger could find no seat at the standing-room-only screening and had to sit on the floor of the foyer, a good vantage from which to appreciate the rapturous reception his production engendered in its target demographic. "The audience cheered it to the echo, rising to its feet as a close-up of Fonda thundered direct to the audience the final line: Where is the conscience of the world?" reported the delighted critic for the *Daily Worker*, who had wangled a ticket.[29]

Not all moviegoers were to cheer so wildly. Despite Wanger's disclaimers, the Code's cleansing, and an advertising campaign that obscured the allegory ("Tense, unforgettable drama—compelling, youthful romance—

"Where's the conscience of the world?" Norma (Madeleine Carroll) and Marco (Henry Fonda) sift through the ruins of what can only be Spain in *Blockade* (1938).

welded into magnificent entertainment!"), *Blockade* was received by friend and foe alike as a brief in defense of the Soviet-backed Loyalists. On that, the Catholics and the communists agreed. Audiences "not sympathetic to the Red Cause in the Spanish Revolution will not be pleased with *Blockade*," said a displeased notice in *Motion Picture Herald*, in synch with the house ethos. "Although somewhat cloudy and besmoked, [the film] will have satisfactions in abundance for the Left Wing."[30]

Cloudy allegory or not, the Left Wing did indeed pronounce itself abundantly satisfied. Whatever its compromises, "*Blockade* cannot be regarded as impartial," insisted *Hollywood Now*. "The world will understand, as it sees *Blockade*, that the film is arguing the cause of the Loyalists. . . . It's so emotionally stirring that if only a collection could be taken after every performance, enough money would be handed in for us to buy up Franco outright and send him as a present to Hitler."[31] Agreed the *Daily Worker*: "It makes the position of the Spanish people so clear that the naming of names is superfluous. Coupled with today's headlines, there can be no question as to the meaning of the film."[32]

American Catholics certainly got the message. Having assumed Hollywood was a wholly owned and operated theological subsidiary, they were astonished to discover so heretical a deviation. The Catholics at the Breen office may have been mollified by Wanger's compromises, but the Catholics in the pews were livid. "The Trojan horse is dragged within the walls!" cried the *Catholic News.* "It is a plea for peace, but peace at the Reds' price!"[33] What for the Popular Front was a dress rehearsal for the inevitable clash between Fascism and democracy was for Catholics a chapter in the long twilight struggle between Holy Mother the Church and godless Bolshevism. Little wonder that *Blockade* incited the most acrimonious case of doctrinal difference among movie-minded Catholics in the history of the Breen office.[34]

The shock troops for Catholic action against Hollywood were commanded by the National Legion of Decency. Formed in 1934, the Legion was far and away the most formidable and feared of all the private groups monitoring motion picture morality. Its mission was to assure Hollywood's fidelity to the Production Code, a document that was, after all, a fair summation of Roman Catholic doctrine, having been written by a Jesuit priest, Daniel A. Lord of St. Louis, and Martin J. Quigley, the devoutly Catholic editor of *Motion Picture Herald.*

The Legion put the screws to Hollywood in two ways—first, through its trademark "Legion pledge," in which Catholics raised their right hand to God and promised, on pain of sin, not to attend immoral movies; and second, by a letter-grade system that judged films by the light of Catholic teaching: Class A-1 (Unobjectionable for General Patronage), Class A-2 (Unobjectionable for Adults), and Class C (Condemned). The C was the mark of Cain, a brand that forbade Catholics from attending the blaspheming film without risk to their immortal soul. Catholics recited the Legion pledge at Sunday masses, at parochial school assemblies, and at Knights of Columbus and Ladies Sodality gatherings. The grades were printed in Catholic newspapers, distributed in parish newsletters, and read out from the pulpit by priests. Practically speaking, American Catholics exerted prior censorship over Hollywood cinema in two ways—through the in-house self-regulation of the Catholic-minded Breen office and through the *ex officio* pressures of the Legion. The two-pronged pincer movement gave American Catholics a virtual veto power over motion picture content throughout the classical studio era.

After 1934, with the antics of Mae West securely corseted and the tommy-gunfire of the gangsters muzzled by the enforcement of the Code, the watchful eye of the Legion fell increasingly on any glimmer of communist influence in Hollywood cinema. No less than smut peddlers, "those who would make motion pictures an agency for the dissemination of the false, the atheistic, and immoral doctrines repeatedly condemned by all accepted moral teachers" needed to be exposed and opposed. "Films which portray, approvingly, concepts rooted in philosophies attacking the Christian moral order and the supernatural destiny of man serve not to ennoble but, rather to debase humanity and, as such, these films are an affront to right thinking men and women," declared the Most Reverend John T. McNicholas, archbishop of Cincinnati, in a statement on behalf of the Legion in 1938. "The Legion of Decency, with every resource at its command, shall challenge any program using the popular theatre screen to exploit such insidious doctrines."[35]

Blockade seemed to fit the archbishop's bill of particulars, but, like the Breen office, the Legion was unable to condemn *Blockade* on moral grounds. Also like the Breen office, it was unwilling to admit that a political agenda skewed its letter grades. Caught between religious loyalties and intellectual dishonesty, reluctant either to pass the film or flunk it, the Legion judges devised a "Special Classification" category for *Blockade*, appending an explanation warning that "many people will regard this picture as containing foreign political propaganda in favor of one side in the present unfortunate struggle in Spain."[36]

For less literal-minded Catholics, neither the Breen office nor the Legion of Decency properly understood the transcendent values in play. Not constrained by the Code contract or the Legion's letter grades, Catholic newspapers and fraternal organizations met the enemy head-on when *Blockade* premiered at Radio City Music Hall in New York. "Let the Reds, the anti-Christian forces, those who like to poison the wells, patronize United Artists and Radio City," seethed Patrick Scanlon, the editor of the *Brooklyn Tablet*, taking aim at Wanger's distributor and the venue across the bridge. "They do not want our support or our presence and they shall not have it."[37] The Knights of Columbus fired off a telegram to Will Hays decrying the "historically false and intellectually dishonest" portrait of the Spanish Civil War smuggled into the nation's theaters "under pretense of entertainment."[38] More effective than the prose was the action on the street. The Knights manned picket lines in front of theaters daring to book *Blockade,* a tactic that terrified exhibitors. Rare was the Catholic moviegoer who would cross *that* picket line.

From the other side, the Hollywood Anti-Nazi League and the Motion Picture Artists Committee rallied their overlapping memberships against the "Fascist boycotts" and "reactionary censorship" afflicting *Blockade.*[39] Hollywood's Popular Front understood that the argument was about more than a single film daring to wade into the political turmoil surrounding the Spanish Civil War. As left-wing standard-bearer the *Nation* put it, the attacks on *Blockade* were "fundamentally an attack not so much on an inferentially pro-Loyalist film as on the whole idea of making films on serious social and political themes."[40] Frank S. Nugent, film critic for the *New York Times,* was of the same mind. "Considering the customary insipidity of our pictures, we think the public would be grateful now and then for one with the power to stir indignation and controversy. We argue about books, plays, speeches, essays and editorials. A rousing fight over a movie should be a treat."[41]

With no rooting interest in *Blockade* except their own, exhibitors gauged what the local market would bear. Very much wanting Catholic business, the Loew's chain purchased an ad in the *Brooklyn Tablet* replying to editor Scanlon's blast. "We leased this picture without feeling that it might be out of harmony with our policy of presenting only sheer non-propaganda entertainment," Loew's insisted by way of apology.[42] By contrast, in San Francisco, the 1,200-seat United Artists Theatre wore its politics and studio pride on its advertising sleeve. "Censor be hanged!" screamed the copy. "The only Hollywood studio that dared make this picture!"[43]

No fool, Wanger tried to ride the publicity wave. Fueling the headlines to heat up a tepid melodrama, he declared that *Blockade* was imbued with the deeply American message "that ruthless bombing of noncombatants, no matter which government does it, is something that is horrible and should not be tolerated."[44] Whatever the Catholics felt and whatever the cost, he would not be intimidated. "I'm going to release this Spanish picture, as is, and if it's banned in Europe, I'll have to take my loss."[45]

The response that mattered most—the box office tally—was not encouraging. Buoyed by sympathetic reviews ("the loudest explosion of praise in years!" bragged Wanger's ads) and patronage from every stalwart Popular Fronter in New York, *Blockade* enjoyed a good first week at Radio City Music Hall, but faded thereafter. "It is too depressing, too heart-rending to be classified as entertainment," Pete Harrison told exhibitors. "It may arouse the spectators, but it will leave them restless and unhappy, and, in the face of conditions today, it seems that such a picture is not what the masses want. Enough is said in newsreels and shown in newsreels to enlighten those who are interested in what is going on in Spain." Worse: "The romance is in the end left hanging in the air."[46] Wanger and Lawson's "preachment against war" sounded like a sure thing, *Variety* lectured after the limp returns came in, but "they learned too late that John Public dishes out coin for its entertainment rather than for sermonizing."[47]

Back from Rome, the newly dubbed papal knight Breen, who had managed to duck the controversy during his absence, put things in perspective. "While I was in Europe on vacation the boys approved a picture called *Blockade*," he wrote his friend Father Lord, the Jesuit priest and Production Code coauthor. "Shortly after it was released, the Knights of Columbus set up a howl, charging that it was 'communist propaganda.'" To that, Breen observed, "there seems to be considerable differences of opinion. . . . I myself have seen the picture twice, and I do not believe that the charge made by the Knights is a fair one, and I am confident that there was no intent to propagandize. I have also heard from a large number of Catholics, many of them priests, who write and ask, 'What is all the shouting about?'"[48] To Breen, *Blockade* was nothing special. "The fact is that it is an ordinary spy picture of a kind that has been done many times before."[49] Of course, Breen and his staff had worked overtime to make certain *Blockade* would be nothing *but* an ordinary spy picture.

For that, the MPPDA was duly appreciative. "I want to say bravo to you for what you did about *Blockade*," Arthur E. DeBra, research director for the MPPDA, wrote Breen, after the firestorm had died down and the film was safely out of the headlines.[50] Soon, Spain too was a lost cause and the hopes for politically minded cinema from Hollywood nearly as defeated.

In a rueful postmortem written for *Liberty* magazine, Wanger reflected on his tangle with international politics and internecine Catholicism. Touting his capitalist credentials ("I believe in bigger, wetter swimming pools and more polo ponies"), he assailed the double standard applied to political speech when it happened to be expressed on celluloid. "Just because it has a timely setting *and is a film*, it is regarded as radical! The uniforms worn were confused in order to establish that the picture didn't take sides. Yet each side called it propaganda for the other side!" Fed up,

Wanger spat out a two-word description for Hollywood's craven product line: "Censored pap!"[51] In his heart, he must have known the epithet applied to *Blockade*.

LOYALIST RED SCREEN PROPAGANDA

Shut down by the MPPDA and the Breen office, Hollywood cinema depicted but two veiled versions of the Spanish Civil War. Independent cinema, however, a subterranean current that either snubbed a Production Code seal or was refused one, might intervene directly into the conflict. Spurred mainly by the Spanish Civil War, the second half of the 1930s witnessed the creation of a homegrown variation on the ideologically laced cinema that its practitioners in the Soviet Union called agit-prop—the deployment of the motion picture medium to inspire militant action, the very impulse that Will H. Hays and Joseph I. Breen worked overtime to suppress. A spate of partisan manifestoes on film aspired to do in documentary what Hollywood refused to do in fiction.

The newsreel coverage of the Spanish Civil War laid the groundwork and provided much of the raw material for the documentary cinema of the 1930s. The images of war that began to flow out of Spain after the outbreak of hostilities in July 1936 projected a new order of raw intensity and visual explicitness. Though the worst of the carnage was self-censored by a medium whose editors well knew the limits of audience tolerance, the pictures of combat brought home by the mobile sound camera jarred moviegoers heretofore sheltered from blood and brutality. Most unsettling was the sight of dead and wounded civilians—women and children—in a total war where neither side placed noncombatants off limits. Vistas of ruined cities, tearful mothers, traumatized children, wailing babies, and corpses littering streets shocked spectators whose notions of cinematic war were shaped by the sanitized images—whether from the battlefield or the studio lots—of the Great War.

The aesthetics of combat photography emphasized the rupture. Breaking with the steady line of sight and privileged perspectives that defined the "invisible style" of classical Hollywood cinema, the jagged angles and jiggly motions of the camera seemed a visual correlative for the frantic zigzagging of frightened civilians scattering for shelter while the streets exploded around them. So much newsreel photography of the 1930s is static and monotonous, a drowsy slide show of plodding parades and droning speeches. The combat photography from the Spanish Civil War was fast-moving, explosive, and horrifying.

For newsreel cameramen—closer to the action—the war was a trial by fire. "Up until even a year ago, I'd say, the average newsreel cameraman, as regards his war experience with a tripod, was just a rookie in a class with a shavetail on West Point graduation day," figured Paramount News cameraman John Dored, reporting from Madrid in the early days of the war. A former White Russian, Dored had earned his stripes covering the Russian Civil War and by the time he reached Spain had become a seasoned veteran. "During the past year, the Italo-Ethiopian matter [Fascist Italy's brutal invasion of primitive Ethiopia in 1935] gave many of the newsreel boys an opportunity for post-graduate courses which brought them within sound range of rifles and exploding bombs. Now this Spanish trouble is ripening them for anything that may happen." A confirmed adrenaline junkie, Dored sounded eager about the prospect of better and bigger battles to come. "Be it a European fracas or a catastrophe involving the entire world, American cameramen will be numbered among the most competent."[52]

On the home front, American audiences were more solemn before the first sounds and sights of modern war in the newsreels. "Spanish unpleasantness is just as grim and bloodthirsty as in previous weeks," reported *Variety*'s Robert Landry from a seat at the Embassy Newsreel Theater. "Fascist reinforcements arriving at the Alcazar reveal Toledo as a shambles and the survivors scarred and suffering. Paramount unspools some excellent stuff. Its boasts of escaping censorship seems plausible on the evidence." In a flash, though, the solemnity turned to anger. "Embassy audience roundly hissed General Franco, adding his mugg to the gallery of hootables."[53] Landry's description—both the impact of the imagery and the Loyalist sympathies of the audience—seems a fair reading of the crowd: terror before the up-close exposure to combat carnage, pity for the civilian victims, and fury at Franco.

Yet viewed from the comfort of a seat at the Embassy, the vicarious encounter with danger might also induce a tingle of excitement. The newsreels certainly ballyhooed the cinematic rush of their thrilling war coverage over its educational value. "American newsreels are hungry for Spanish revolutionary stuff, but so far none is obtainable," wrote *Daily Variety* in July 1936, noting how tough the censorship and ground conditions were.

"'Too tough'—eh?" taunted the ads heralding a scoop by Fox Movietone News the next month. "Now on the world's screens! *Exclusive* and sensational pictures of Spain's revolt filmed under fire by Movietone News."[54]

"Under fire" was the operative phrase. The peril of the cameraman—struggling to keep focus and framing, ducking for cover, running for dear life—was imbedded in every shot of combat action. For him, the danger was not vicarious. "Reading between the information sheets coming through to all newsreel headquarters in New York with the film from Spain, there is evidence that every time a crew ventures out to make pictures the men's lives are ventured also," noted an impressed report from *Motion Picture Herald*. "Stray bullets are commonplace when a nation is torn by civil strife, and hot-headed commanders, sullen in defeat or flushed with triumph, are wont to regard cameramen as enemy spies or as persons on whom to vent spleen or newly acquired power."[55] Spectators did not have to read between the lines to feel the death defiance in the camerawork: the sickening proximity to combat fatalities, the narrow escapes from bullets and shelling, and the shell-shocked perspective from behind the lens.

Besides mortal danger, a more familiar problem bedeviled the newsreel coverage from Spain. "In Spain today the censor problem—it's hardly a problem," said Paramount's intrepid Dored. "It's almost a catastrophe."[56] Battlefield commanders—who regarded newsreel cameramen as distracting annoyances and possibly security risks—confiscated cameras and destroyed exposed film. The New York offices felt lucky "if 25% of the negative which their staffs are exposing in Spain escapes seizure or mutilation."[57] To smuggle out the footage, crafty newsreel men hid the film cans in their coats and bribed troops to look the other way.

By common consent, the Republican side showcased itself to better advantage in the newsreels than Franco's rebel forces—either by providing the newsreel outfits ready-to-screen footage or by guiding American cameramen through the battlefields and street fights. "Spain is treated by Pathé and Paramount with the horror and human stupidity of the whole mess again made manifest," reported Robert Landry in March 1937, not really bothering to conceal his own loyalties. "Here is emotional heart-tug that has not failed to excite sympathy, applause, and hisses for the past six months or longer in the newsreels."[58]

Some of the loudest hissing was aimed at one of the messengers: Hearst-Metrotone News. The newspaper chain owned by William Randolph

Hearst tilted brazenly toward General Franco and the rebels. Though the newsreel arm of the mogul's media empire covered the war more evenhandedly, the reel was held guilty by association. At theaters around Popular Front strongholds, sympathizers for Republican Spain booed, hissed, and catcalled at first sight of the Hearst logo, less because of any slant in the newsreel itself than because of the name on the title card. "Mr. Hearst's newsreel has in fact, and conspicuously, never been for him a medium of personal expression or concerned with purveying his editorial policies," insisted Terry Ramsaye at *Motion Picture Herald.* "His newsreel has been marked by its neutrality and general conformity to the conventions of newsreel production."[59] Of course, from a Popular Front standpoint, neutrality was the moral equivalent of lending aid and comfort to the enemy.

Hearst-Metrotone News was distributed by MGM through the Loew's chain, and neither company wanted any audience agitation under its imprint. In November 1936 the reel changed its name and logo to News of the Day and underscored the rebranding by replacing longtime commentator Edwin C. Hill with NBC radio announcer Jean Paul King, a voice with no prior Hearst callback. Undeceived by the switch, Popular Front moviegoers continued to hiss. "These uprisings and expressions came from Communists and committed leftists," muttered Ramsaye.[60]

Cathartic though it might be, hissing at a Hearst newsreel contributed nothing to the Republican cause on screen. To truly get in the fight, supporters of Spain needed to seize the means of motion picture production, not simply jeer or applaud at what the Hollywood-backed newsreels happened to unspool. No matter how heart-tugging the footage, its full potential as pro-Republican propaganda could only come with the directional guidance of a partisan narration (anathema to the newsreels) and a broader documentary canvas (anathema to the exhibitor locked in to tight running times for each item in the balanced program). With a confidence born of revolutionary fervor, Popular Front filmmakers took matters into their own hands.

In 1936 the Dutch filmmaker Joris Ivens voiced the do-it-yourself credo of the radical filmmakers of the 1930s. Having looked around Hollywood and seen nothing to encourage a revolution from within, he declared, "the days of merely cursing or deploring Hollywood are over."[61] Quit griping and get into the action, he told his filmmaking comrades. Drawing on the raw footage culled from the commercial newsreels, and the talents of cameraman-activists on site who shouldered their cameras as weapons of war, the Popular Front sponsored or produced a slate of shorts and feature films that gave the Republican cause a visible place on the motion picture marquee—or at least on the marquees not affiliated with the major Hollywood studios. Edited for maximum punch, sweetened with music tracks, and given exhortative voice-overs, the films sought both to buck up the faithful and to mobilize recruits for the beleaguered Republic. With running times averaging twenty to thirty minutes, the shorts would have fit snugly into the top of a balanced program had a studio-affiliated theater been a viable outlet for exhibition.

Cobbling together newsreel footage and just-above-amateur footage by filmmakers at the front, the shorts were earnest, emotional, and makeshift endeavors. Entries included *Madrid Document* (1937), a chronicle of the resistance of the Republican defenders of the capital; *America's Lafayettes* (1938), a homage to the volunteers of the Abraham Lincoln Brigade; *Behind the Lines in Spain* (1938), a British import by Ivor Montagu; and *The Will of the People* (1939), a survey of the resistance in Barcelona. By far, the two best-known and widely circulated of the group were a matched pair focused on the care of the sick and wounded, *Heart of Spain* (1937) and *Return to Life* (1938).[62]

Both *Heart of Spain* and *Return to Life* were the work of Herbert Kline, editor of *New Theatre and Film*, the Popular Front must-read monthly. A dedicated partisan of the Republic and, at the time, a totally inexperienced filmmaker, Kline itched to trade his typewriter for more direct action. In December 1936, disgusted by the political backbiting at the magazine, he resigned his post and headed for the Spanish battlefield. Soon he was in the thick of the fight for Madrid "with Franco's forces 150 yards away" and "scattered exchanges of rifle, machine gun, and artillery fire exploding nearby," as he later recalled. Kline was doing radio broadcasts for the Republicans when the Hungarian photographer Geza Karpathi approached him to write a script for a documentary chronicling the medical work of Dr. Norman Bethune, a Canadian doctor and founder of the Hispano-Canadian Blood Transfusion Institute, an outfit dedicated to tending Republic soldiers and civilians. Bethune had developed a new technique for preserving blood. Kline and Karpathi were such novices at the craft that neither knew how to load a 16mm Eyemo: they brought it to a camera store, pretended it was broken, and watched carefully as the owner inserted the film in the sprockets.[63]

Kline and Karpathi were quick studies. Dr. Bethune was featured front and center as a dedicated caregiver ministering to frightfully wounded heroes, emerging as a motion picture hero in the tradition of the self-sacrificing physicians who labored for the good of humanity in the medicinal melodramas Hollywood favored in the 1930s. Taking the raw footage back to New York, the pair entrusted the final cut to the more experienced hands at Frontier Films. Pegged to the story of a mother and her wounded son, it was edited into an inspirational tale of the role of medicine in the fight against Fascism.

Encouraged, Kline and Frontier Films undertook a follow-up, *Return to Life*, a like-minded documentary on the medical mission in Spain. Working with the French photographer Henri Cartier and expert cameraman Jacques Lemare, Kline shot in Madrid and then edited the film in Paris, where it was released under the title *Victorie de la Vie*, before being Americanized by Frontier Films with a commentary by Ben

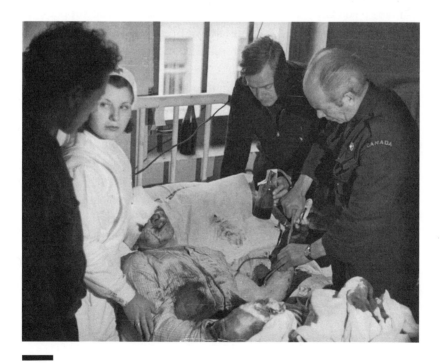

Medicinal melodrama: a scene from Herbert Kline and Geza Karpathi's pro-Loyalist short *Heart of Spain* (1937). (Courtesy of Robert D. Farber University Archives and Special Collections, Brandeis University)

Maddow and a new soundtrack.[64] Of course, the focus on medical aid and the treatment of the wounded was calculated to tug at the heartstrings and disarm critics of Popular Front interventionism. *Return to Life* was billed as "the moving and poignant story of the work done by the International Medical Aid in connection with the plight of refugee children and the wounded soldiers who hope to fight again for the life of Spanish Democracy."[65] Few Americans could begrudge ambulances and medical supplies—as opposed to guns and ammunition—to a besieged civilian population.

Yet no matter how wide the net cast by the Spanish Civil War shorts, they received scant commercial exhibition. Documentaries, especially documentaries with a left-wing slant, played in a few New York independent houses specializing in foreign and political fare, and in arthouse sure-seaters in limited engagements. They also circulated in 16mm at political clubs and in Popular Front gatherings to raise money and fortify the faithful. Celluloid rallying points, the shorts were ritual occasions for comradely solidarity and fund-raising, mainly for medical supplies, as when the Friends of the Abraham Lincoln Brigade used *America's Lafayettes* to raise money for volunteers wounded in Spain.

To spread word of the good fight, the idealists of the Popular Front were not averse to borrowing a page from Hollywood's ad-pub hucksters. The Spanish Civil War shorts were the unlikely objects of studio-style publicity stunts, endorsements, and gimmicks. To draw attention to *Heart of Spain*, the Motion Picture Artists Committee outfitted two special ambulances for a coast-to-coast tour in conjunction with screenings of the film.

Glitzier screenings and fund-raisers were also built around the shorts. At the Roosevelt Hotel in Hollywood, the Motion Picture Artists Committee sponsored a fund-raising screening of *Heart of Spain* with co-director Geza Karpathi speaking before the film and actress Nancy Carroll and director Irving Pichel asking for funds in filmed appeals. Screenwriter Herbert J. Biberman and the tireless Donald Ogden Stewart chaired the proceeding.[66] For the world premiere of *Return of Life*, the film division of the Theatre Arts Committee commandeered the Grand Ballroom of the Waldorf-Astoria Hotel in New York.

The shorts could count on sympathetic reviews from *Hollywood Now*, the *Daily Worker*, and other organs of the Popular Front. *America's Lafayettes* was "a fine documentary showing everyday scenes of life in the Brigade, in the trenches, going in and out of the lines, with close-ups of Spanish heroes who are dead today."[67] *Return to Life* was awash "in humorous and touching scenes [of] front line battles, the care of the wounded, their convalescence in American hospitals, and their return to life and the battlefield once more."[68] *The Will of the People* was a powerful tale "of the heroic perseverance of the Spanish people in their efforts to fight off Fascist domination."[69] No reviewer with a Popular Front mast-head dared pan an anthem to the cause.

By definition, however, shorts were second-class cinematic formats. Attention, prestige, and money for the Republican cause could only come with the expansion of the agitprop to feature length. To promote the shorts to the top of the marquee, a group of high-profile writers—John Dos Passos, Lillian Hellman, Ernest Hemingway, Archibald MacLeish, Clifford Odets, and Herman Shumlin—organized themselves into Con-temporary Historians, Inc., to bankroll that most commercially unre-warding of motion picture genres, the political documentary.

The first of the feature-length pro-Loyalist documentaries was *Spain in Flames*, released in February 1937 by Amkino, the distributor for Soviet cinema in the United States. A program note dedicated the film "to the heroism of those who today are giving their lives that Spain may be free," but the provenance of the production was obscure: no cred-its were included in the original release, and the only identifiable per-sonalities on screen were Fernando de los Rios, Spanish ambassador to the United States, who spoke in a prologue introduction, and Dolo-res Ibárruri, the female firebrand known as La Pasionaria, the face of revolutionary Spain, who delivered a stirring call to arms. Amkino failed to respond to trade press inquiries about the identity of the narrators. Possessing better contacts in left-wing film circles, the *Nation* revealed that the editing was done in the United States under the sponsorship of the North American Committee to Aid Spanish Democracy and the narration was written by novelist John Dos Passos and poet Archibald MacLeish. Dos Passos recited the narration and the actual editing was done by Helen von Dongen, an unheralded worker bee for Frontier Films.[70] Its 63-minute running time took dead aim at a target audience *Variety* sized up as "the communistically-minded fans, the laboring ele-ment, and the Spaniards."[71]

Spain in Flames sutured together two distinct parts, the first enti-tled "The Fight for Freedom," filmed by Spanish Loyalists, the second entitled "No Pasaran" ("They Shall Not Pass"), filmed by Soviet camera-men in Spain.

The first section reviewed the harsh feudal history of Spain before its deliverance by the Republicans in 1935. The reign, oppression, and overthrow of King Alphonso, the medieval pomp of a tyrannical priest-hood, and the strutting pageantry of an oppressive army pass in news-reel review. Never resigned to the overthrow of their lordly power, the aristocracy, the church, and the military collude in Franco's coup d'état. As illustrated maps show the strategic designs of Italy and Germany in Spain, the narration asserts that without outside aid from the Nazis and the Fascists the rebellion would have folded overnight. To beat back the onslaught from the foreign Fascists, "Spain needs men of military expe-rience to officer its armies."

The second section records the arrival of a Soviet relief ship at the port of Alicante, one revolutionary socialist republic extending the hand of fellowship to another. Spanish workers surround the ship, raising their hands in the "clenched fist" salute of communist solidarity. Under the able command of José Diaz, leader of the Spanish Communist Party, the 5th Battalion trains and turns raw recruits—young boys and old men—into soldiers. In a big finish, La Pasionaria urges the defenders onward.[72]

Spain in Flames premiered at the Cameo Theatre, located on 42nd Street in New York, "where Union Square, the Red Square of Moscow, and Times Square overlap on one corner," sniped *Motion Picture Her-ald*.[73] Truth be told, the Cameo worked hard to live up to its subversive reputation. For 25 cents for daytime matinees and 40 cents for evening shows, a typical program bill at the Popular Front hangout consisted of the "only complete newsreels!" of the May Day parade in Moscow ("the greatest military demonstration in Soviet history"); the latest in Soviet news ("industry-arts-culture-education, etc."); and *With the Lincoln Bat-talion in Spain* (1938).[74] During screenings of *Spain in Flames*, reported the *Herald*'s reviewer, who doubtless sat on his hands, "applause for scenes of Loyalist heroism was counterpointed by booing and hiss-ing of Sig. Mussolini and Herr Hitler when their faces appeared upon the screen."[75]

Fully understanding that a box office mandate was the only measure that mattered to exhibitors, the Popular Front rallied around its first fea-ture-length fusillade at Franco. "Let us rally the widest possible support in favor of a real anti-fascist film," the *Daily Worker* urged. "With proper support today *Spain in Flames* can be held another week at the Cameo Theatre. If there is a big turnout in the next few days, dozens of neighborhood theaters will be influenced to show it. And if it can obtain mass support in New York and elsewhere, it will make all the more possible the production of more films from the point of view of the audience."[76] *New Theatre and Film* was equally emphatic. "Must be seen," it ordered. [77]

Actually, it was the next film that had to be seen. The sole documentary classic to emerge from the motion picture activism inspired by the Spanish Civil War, and by far the highest profile of the cinematic calls to arms for the Republican cause, was *The Spanish Earth* (1937), directed by Joris Ivens, practicing what he preached; scored by Marc Blitzstein, the Popular Front's favorite soundtrack composer; and written and narrated by Ernest Hemingway, the avatar of terse masculine prose. The cinematic, musical, and literary pedigrees guaranteed coverage in the press and playdates at the sure-seaters. The quality of the film guaranteed its place in the history of documentary cinema.

A documentary precursor and companion piece to *Blockade* (Wanger's Hollywood film, released a year after *The Spanish Earth*, also bows before the revolutionary spirit of the peasant stock), Ivens' contribution to the Republican cause was financed by donations from prominent writers and Hollywood luminaries with deep pockets. The fund-raising campaign was overseen by Archibald MacLeish, who, with John Dos Passos and the playwright-screenwriter Lillian Hellman, sketched out the original scenario. All felt that "no more effective defense against fascist propaganda in this country could be raised" than "to have made in Spain and distributed in America a documentary film giving the background of the Civil War and the true facts of its development."[78]

In January 1937, Ivens went to Spain ("at the very real risk of his neck" as MacLeish put it) to yoke documentary cinema to the Republican cause. He was accompanied for part of the filming by Hemingway, who was reporting on the war as a special correspondent for the *New York Times* and who, self-deprecatingly for once, cast himself as mere "grip" on the crew. Besides adding to the luster of his own legend and gaining material for *For Whom the Bell Tolls*, his novel of the war published in 1940, Hemingway's dispatches served as a prepublicity tease for the film. "I had gone with Joris Ivens to film infantry and tanks in action, operating behind infantry and filming the tanks as they ground like ships up the steep hills and deployed into action," he wrote in a report datelined

Madrid. The novelist-journalist painted a vivid portrait of combat photography under the gun:

> All night the heaviest Insurgent artillery, mortar, and machine gun
> fire seemed close enough to be outside the window. At 5:40 A.M. the
> machine guns were hammering so that sleep was impossible. Ivens
> came in to the room and we decided to wake up the sound-sleeping John
> Ferno, film operator, and Henry Gorrell, United Press correspondent,
> and start out on foot.

While Republican forces "in the gray, olive studded, broken hills of the
Morata de Tajuna sector" shelled an enemy stronghold, Ivens, Hemingway, and Ferno scrambled for good vantage on the action:

> We decided to set up the big telephoto camera. Ferno had gone back to
> find a healthier position and he chose the third floor of a ruined house.
> There, in the shade of a balcony, with the camera camouflaged with the
> old clothes found in the house, we worked all afternoon and watched
> the battle.

Hemingway confirmed MacLeish's comment about the very real risk to
Ivens' neck. "Just as we were congratulating ourselves on having such
a splendid observation post out of the reach of danger a bullet smacked
against a corner of a brick wall beside Ivens's head."[79]

In May 1937, Ivens returned to New York for postproduction work.
With editor Helen von Dongen, he labored feverishly to complete the
film, under pressure not from a studio deadline but the deteriorating position of the Republican forces in Spain. At the suggestion of
Archibald MacLeish, the radio star Orson Welles was brought on board
to narrate the film in his mellifluous baritone, but Ivens ultimately preferred the unvarnished timbre of Hemingway. By July 1937, with editing
and Hemingway's narration wrapped, *The Spanish Earth* was ready for its
rollout. Ivens estimated the total cost at $18,000—a pittance.[80]

The Spanish Earth pits Republican civilization against Rebel savagery,
with the opening images seeming to presage an Iberian version of a glacial Soviet homage to the sturdy Russian folk. Peasant women sweep village streets and men knead bread, scenes that might have been shot in
the Middle Ages were it not for the Republican propaganda posters hang-

At the very real risk of their necks: Joris Ivens, with camera, and Ernest Hemingway to his right, on location filming *The Spanish Earth* (1937). (Courtesy of European Foundation, Joris Ivens)

ing in backframe. No element of Republican life is too mundane for reverence, including baked goods. "It is good bread, stamped with the union label," says Hemingway, as the loaves, imprinted with the UGT acronym (Unión General de Trabajadores, the General Union of Workers), are delivered from a bakery. Republicans live not by bread alone, however. Despite the turmoil of war, they preserve the treasures of Spanish civilization from the rapacious Rebel bombing and rescue from the rubble ancient portraits, religious icons, and first editions of *Don Quixote*.

Fortunately, the Soviet-style social realism gives way to a more poetic portrait of the face of war. Eschewing the hallucinatory surrealism of Picasso's *Guernica* for the stark photorealism of 35mm, Ivens lingers over the aftermath of aerial bombardment on the civilian population, namely corpses on the street—a gruesome tableau of adults and children alike. Though mainly out of camera range, the perpetrators of the war crimes—Fascist Italy and Nazi Germany no less than Franco's Rebels—are featured players. "I can't read German either," snarls Hemingway, as the camera looks over the wreckage of a downed plane with made-in-Germany mark-ings. As further evidence, the camera pans—not without satisfaction—the corpses of Italian fighters. "Without the aid of Germany and Italy, the revolt would have ended six weeks after it began," says Hemingway.

Though the politically unsophisticated viewer would not learn that the Soviet Union intervened on the side of the Republicans or that Spanish communists were in the vanguard of the battle, clued-in Popular Front-ers could read the signs. Communists leaders are valorized with close-ups and extended selections from their radio speeches, while the charis-matic La Pasionaria is framed for movie-star treatment.

On the evening of July 7, 1937, Ivens and Hemingway debuted *The Spanish Earth* to the most exclusive of preview audiences—a private screening at the White House. The gesture was classic FDR, showing sympathy for the Republican cause, shoring up his left wing, and not lift-ing a finger for tangible help. After a sumptuous dinner, the director and writer screened the film for the president, his wife Eleanor, and a small party of guests. Impressed with FDR's "expert appreciation" of cinema aesthetics, Ivens reported that the president admired the "fine continu-ity" of the film. FDR was also said to be annoyed by a less attentive mem-ber of the audience who "disturbed him during the screening."[81]

The next week, Hemingway and Ivens arrived in Hollywood to unveil *The Spanish Earth* to its donor base. A crowd of 200 specially invited guests attended a swank screening in the ballroom of the Ambassador Hotel. An even more exclusive group got a sneak preview at the home of actor Fredric March, where fifteen members of the audience donated $1,000 each.[82]

On the night of July 16, 1937, at the Philharmonic Auditorium in Los Angeles, the rollout for *The Spanish Earth* continued with a Popular Front version of a gala Hollywood premiere. Politically-culturally speaking, it was the hottest ticket of the year and the auditorium was packed. With admission priced at 25 cents to $1.10, the film grossed $2,000 with an additional $2,500 taken in by donations. "At least 2500 persons were turned away and the place was a madhouse of congestion," blurbed Frank Scully in *Variety*. "The picture seems sure to make an army of con-verts for the Loyalist cause."[83]

In truth, the converted were more like a platoon whose members had already enlisted for the duration. *The Spanish Earth* faced the familiar problems—limited bookings and sparse audiences. Like the rest of the

Spanish Civil War documentaries, it was less a recruiting device for new converts than a ritual exhibition for true believers. "Ivens pushed his camera into the thickest part of the fight, and came out with enough footage to satisfy the exacting tastes of the 'art cinema' customers," observed *Box Office*, the most sympathetic of the trade weeklies to the Republican cause, all too aware of the narrow market niche for the documentary. It urged exhibitors to link up with "labor unions, farmer's cooperatives, peace societies, etc." likely to "canvass their membership by mail in behalf of the film."[84]

Critical reaction fell along predictable fault lines. "It is humanly impossible for any warm-blooded man or woman to sit through the film without feeling a burning need now, here, at once, this very minute, to do something to support the epic, Homeric battle of the Spanish people for the right to live like human beings," proclaimed the choked-up notice in the *Daily Worker*.[85] Nonetheless, warm-blooded American Catholics remained unmoved and unconverted. "There is not a scene in the entire film of a desecrated church, a butchered nun, or a murdered priest," complained *Motion Picture Herald*. "Reference is made to the foreign support given to the rebel forces by Germany and Italy. However, there are some soldiers in the Loyalist ranks who look suspiciously non-Iberian."[86]

Short and feature-length alike, the Spanish Civil War documentaries faced opposition on another front. American censor boards harassed the pro-Republican programming with special fervor. Lacking the protection of a Code shield, the films were blocked by city and state boards, especially in regions inhabited by a solid bloc of registered Catholic voters. The Chicago Board of Censors took one look at *Spain in Flames* and cut every reference to the Nazi interventions in Spain. The Ohio Board of Film Censors banned it outright for exuding "harmful effects," explaining that "it was not in accord with the policy of neutrality adopted by this country to allow exhibition of a film which takes one side or another in a civil war in another nation."[87]

The state of Pennsylvania went to great lengths to enforce cinematic neutrality.[88] In Philadelphia, as 300 people waited in line to see *Spain in Flames*, an agent for the Pennsylvania State Board of Censors walked in with a constable, arrested the theater manager and his secretary, and shut down the screening.[89] "Pure communist propaganda, dressed up as a plea for democracy," decreed Pennsylvania governor George Earle.[90]

The filmmakers fought back with lawyers and won the case in state court. "*Spain in Flames* is a film containing current and timely news and thus is not within provision of censor law," ruled Judge Louis E. Levinthal. "The pictorial part of the film is certainly news and the current events of today are the history of tomorrow." The judge further held that the soundtrack, narration, and titles were also protected news and hence not subject to the censorship laws.[91]

Undeterred by the judicial clearance of *Spain in Flames,* the Pennsylvania State Board of Censors next banned *The Spanish Earth.* The board was chaired by Mrs. A. Mitchell Palmer, a woman not predisposed to give communist-backed motion pictures a fair viewing: she was the widow of the United States attorney general under Woodrow Wilson, the overseer of the notorious "Palmer raids" that rounded up and deported anarchists and communists in 1919–20. Mrs. Palmer called *The Spanish Earth* "horribly gruesome and not proper for general release." The Prometheus Pictures Company, the film's New York–based distributor, counterargued that the film was "moral and proper" and the board's action was "arbitrary and discriminatory."[92]

Surprisingly, before the case could go to court, Pennsylvania's Governor Earle overruled Mrs. Palmer and the state board—and his own earlier policy on *Spain in Flames.* Although he regretted that the United States was becoming "a dumping ground for propaganda pictures which attempt to sell the American people the doctrines of Communism, Fascism, and Nazism," he had concluded, on second thought, that "showing the horrors of war" was "a good lesson for us Americans."[93] Lest partisans of Republican Spain be too gladdened by his change of heart, the governor warned about a flip side to freedom of the screen. "I await with interest the time when Herr Hitler sends us a picture glorifying Nazism. Will there be the same clamor about freedom for alien propaganda as there is now?"[94]

Despite censor hassles, *The Spanish Earth* was an arthouse hit screened in 300 theaters in the United States. American moviegoers "are awakening their appetites for documentary cinema," said Ivens. "I think that such pictures will bring more persons to theaters. Documentary films should find a niche between newsreels and entertainment." Encouraged, Ivens and the same network of supporters (MacLeish, Dorothy Parker, Lillian Hellman, Ernest Hemingway) produced a documentary in another theater of war, *The 400,000,000* (1939), a six-reel chronicle of the Sino-Japanese War.[95]

In the end, the legacy of the Spanish Civil War documentaries was more significant cinematically than militarily. The experience taught a dedicated cadre of filmmakers that it was possible to produce and market a non-Hollywood product line; it schooled a generation of activists in the art of documentary filmmaking; and it added the motion picture camera to the list of weapons to be taken up in the good fight. The cliché that the winners get to write the history was disproved by the Spanish Civil War: the losers won the propaganda battle, in film, as in the other arts—a victory that was scant consolation.[96]

7

FOREIGN IMPORTS

"That new picture that Amkino has looks interesting," speculated the pseudonymous Phil M. Daily, the chatty columnist for the *Film Daily*. "Titled *Der Kampf*, produced in Russia by German refugees, . . . it shows the events leading to the rise of Hitler, including the Reichstag fire,[a] the Leipzig trial of Dimitroff, with actual shots . . . view of the concentration camps . . . and of how cells were formed by the Communists and [how] underground work continued."[1]

Sure enough, *Der Kampf* (1936) sounded interesting, but access to a foreign film, especially an anti-Nazi German-language film from the Soviet Union, was severely limited in America during the 1930s, even to that thin slice of the demographic undeterred by didactic melodrama, threadbare production values, and semi-legible subtitles. At fault was a pair of familiar culprints—the Motion Picture Producers and Distributors of America and its enforcement arm, the Production Code Administration.

The key initial in the MPPDA acronym stood for America: the association existed to maintain the domestic monopoly and global hegemony

---

[a] On the night of February 27, 1933, the Reichstag, the German parliament, went up in flames, torched by a Dutch anarchist named Marinus van der Lubbe. The Nazis blamed the fire on a communist conspiracy and used the incident as a pretext for outlawing the German communist party. The Bulgarian communist Georgi Dimitroff, head of the Communist International in Berlin, and three fellow communists were tried in Leipzig and Berlin for the crime. During the sensational trial, Dimitroff's impassioned oratory secured their acquittal from a judiciary not yet fully Nazified. In 1934, Dimitroff was deported to the USSR (Union of Soviet Socialist Republics), where he was greeted as a national hero. Van der Lubbe was convicted and beheaded.

of the national cinema. In addition to his Presbyterian probity, MPPDA president Will H. Hays was chosen by the moguls for his connections to power brokers in Washington and Wall Street. The office that bore his name sought to restrict the import of foreign cinema while flooding the overseas market with product beyond the budget and skill set of non-American craftsmen.

In assuring that the balance of payments worked to Hollywood's advantage, the PCA played a vital role. The Code seal was the essential transit visa for entry into America's showpiece motion picture venues—the big-city emporiums that generated momentum for major attractions and the thousands of small-town neighborhood theaters ("nabes") contractually obligated to play only films stamped with the Code seal of approval. Conveniently, foreign permissiveness about flesh, language, and ideology—immodest French décolletage, salacious British quips, or seditious Soviet agitprop—affronted provincial American tastes nearly as much as the competition alarmed the MPPDA. While patrolling the moral universe mapped out by the Code, PCA chieftain Joseph I. Breen also helped maintain a quarantine on foreign cinema.

Breen's opposite number at the New York office of the PCA was, from 1934 to 1937, Vincent G. Hart, a New York attorney who had worked at Fox before becoming a legal advisor for the Hays office, and thence to censorship duties. Serving in the same office was Dr. James Wingate, former head of the New York State Censor Commission, who had been recruited by the MPPDA in 1932 to head the Studio Relations Committee in Hollywood, the weak-kneed predecessor of the PCA. A feckless enforcer incapable of going nose-to-nose with the moguls, Wingate was edged out by Breen in December 1933 and shunted off to the New York office. In 1937, Francis S. Harmon, a lawyer, journalist, and former national executive secretary of the YMCA, took charge of the East Coast office to add heft to a position that was seeing more controversial action on the import front. Hart and Harmon inspected foreign imports from a berth closer to the port of entry, always keeping in close touch via telegram or telephone with Breen on policy matters and tough calls. As a well-known Protestant layman, Harmon also provided a dollop of theological balance to the monolithic Catholicism of the Code's inner sanctum.

Harmon, however, was not the only agent looking over foreign films. Just as Dr. Georg Gyssling, the Nazi consul in Los Angeles, kept tabs on the Hollywood studio system, German consular officers across America monitored the content, exhibition, and impact of foreign films critical of the Third Reich. Unable to sell pro-Nazi cinema, the Nazis could at least try to block the circulation of anti-Nazi cinema. When *Der Kampf*, billed as an answer to Hitler's programmatic memoir *Mein Kampf*, was booked in St. Louis, the local German consul Reinhold Freytag wrote city Mayor Bernard Dickmann to demand the cancellation of a film that was "communist propaganda for creating hatred against anything German." The mayor obliged.[2]

"Hollywood keeps discreetly away from controversial pictures," *Variety* noted approvingly in 1938, complaining that "such controversial pictures that do deal with world events, their causes and effects, may be considered good box office for the arty theaters which cater to special audiences who are always on the lookout for pictures that are in [tune] with their thoughts on questions of a social and political nature."[3] With theaters in liege to Hollywood out of the game, the "arty theaters"—also called "arties," "arty cinema parlors," and " 'art' houses"—were the only places in town for moviegoers bent on contributing their entertainment dollars to the anti-Nazi cause.[b] As a result, some of the fiercest conflicts over Nazism on screen in the 1930s took place away from the main stage of American cinema, on the fringes, around films that did not even speak the native language.

"GERMAN TONGUE TALKERS"

Before January 30, 1933, German cinema was far and away the most popular alternative to the domestic product in American theaters. Though the revenue was chump change compared to the receipts raked in from Hollywood fare screened in the plush first-run houses, German cinema had carved out a solid niche market in the big cities and in German enclaves in the Midwest.[4] "Profits derived from these films are much larger than generally believed," noted George R. Canty, trade commissioner for the

---

[b] The "arty" monikers express both the tangential nature and condescending attitude on the part of mainstream Hollywood toward the venues for foreign cinema with avowedly artistic ambitions. As early as the 1920s, the trade press noticed the emergence of venues it also referred to as "art" houses, but only in the postwar era would the category lose both the snickering diminutives and the quotation marks.

U.S. Department of Commerce, in 1932.[5] That same year, 67 of the 141 foreign imports released in the United States were made in Germany, a tally that surpassed even the imports from the Anglophone British.[6]

About 200 theaters specialized in what the trade press dubbed "German tongue talkers," with twenty of the venues operating in New York City alone, most clustered in the Yorkville district in upper Manhattan, a concentration of German Americans of both Jewish and non-Jewish lineage.[7] Whatever the location, almost all the outlets for foreign films were in theaters seating 600 or fewer, often known as "sure-seaters" because of their corner on a small but reliable market. Though a *succès d'estime* would cross over to an emergent arthouse crowd of urban intellectuals, the core audience for German cinema was German-speaking Jews, estimated to account for 65 to 70 percent of the consumer base.[8]

The optimal commercial fate for a German import was achieved by Leontine Sagan's *Maedchen in Uniform* (1931), a rough Weimar gem that marked the crest of the German wave in the early-sound, pre-Nazi era. Released stateside in September 1932 and imported by veteran foreign-film distributors John Krimsky and Gifford Cochran, the distaff *bildungsroman* was buoyed by word of mouth insinuating lesbian shenanigans in a girls' boarding school and perhaps a glimpse of maedchen *out* of uniform. Like so much late Weimar cinema, Sagan's tightly corseted melodrama seems to flash forward to the Third Reich: the school is built around brutal authoritarianism and spartan living, a claustrophobic milieu seething with the hormonal energy of repressed adolescence. The film garnered full-throated critical praise and landed on many of the year's Ten Best lists. "It is vastly different from the run-of-cargo Hollywood diet," confirmed the *New York American*, spotlighting the lure of the exotic.[9]

Maedchen in Uniform was the last of the crossover hits from the Weimar era. After Hitler was appointed Reich Chancellor, American moviegoers fled German cinema as if propelled out the doors by Nazi stink bombs. "The sudden hostile Hitler attitude is being reflected pronto at the box office of the German talkers in this country by several of the sure-seaters switching to French product or resuming American subsequent run bookings," *Variety* reported less than two months into Hitler's reign.[10] The number of theaters specializing in German imports plummeted to single digits—three in New York, one in Boston, and a few scattered around the Midwest. As Nazi antisemitism flared, stateside exhibitors of German cinema looked out over rows of empty seats.[11] They changed marquee fare or went belly up.

So acute was the revulsion to the Nazi brand that slates of imported German films that had been produced *before* Hitler came to power, but which were already in the distribution pipeline, found themselves judged guilty by linguistic association. Importers Cochran and Krimsky pleaded, to no avail, that the lately chic *Maedchen in Uniform* showed "the failure of institutions and governments founded on the militaristic regime which Chancellor Hitler is said to be trying to restore."[12] No matter: any echo of the German tongue grated on American ears. In 1934, just making its way to the American marketplace, Fritz Lang's creepy thriller *M* (1931) was also caught in the cultural lag. At the Mayfair, a landmark sure-seater in New York, the management was forced to withdraw the German-language version of *M* and substitute the English dubbed version when irate customers asked for refunds "after listening to a few minutes of German dialog."[13] (Lang was getting shut down on both ends: in Germany, the Nazis banned his *The Testament of Dr. Mabuse* [1933] as "communistic.")[14]

One production conceived in the late Weimar era earned its antipathy with a postproduction gesture of solidarity with the successor regime. Tay Garnett and Arnold Fanck's spectacular Arctic adventure film *S.O.S. Iceberg* (1933), the last of the big German American coproductions, starred Leni Riefenstahl, still an outdoorsy actress, and Maj. Ernst Udet, the famed Great War flying ace, as intrepid polar pilots. It was Major Udet, not the future Nazi auteur, who undermined the film's box office while on a promotional tour in America by brandishing a swastika in Hollywood and Chicago.[15]

Predictably, nabes in Jewish districts were most sensitive to the stain of German origin. In the Jewish enclave of Brighton Beach, New York, the Tuxedo Theater canceled its booking of Erich Washneck's *Zwei Menschen* (1931), a faithfully bleak version of Peter Voss's novel, "in protest of Hitler's anti-Semitic outrages." In red typeface, the printed program for the theater declared: "All German films will be boycotted at this theater until Hitlerites cease their brutalities against the Jews." Other former fans of German cinema made common cause with the Jewish moviegoers in Brighton Beach. *Variety* pointed out that "a goodly portion of the German American population is figured as being in sympathy with Jewish feelings on the matter and are also laying off the German product."[16]

American Jews in the motion picture business warned that any boycott of German imports would only rebound to the grief of their kinsmen overseas. Arthur Ziehm, general manager of the World's Trade Exchange and a prominent importer of German cinema, reminded boycotters that "by far the larger percentage of German producers, scenario writers, directors, and artists are Jews" and therefore a boycott would "injure the Jews of Germany more than it would affect the Hitlerites."[17] But few Jewish Americans could watch German cinema without seeing Hitler's face in every frame.

A defiant exception to the embargo against Nazi cinema was the Yorkville Theatre located at 96th Street and Third Avenue in upper Manhattan, a no longer sure-seater notorious as a showcase for Nazi releases. In 1933 the newly refurbished, 550-seat Yorkville opened its doors as an unlikely business proposition "run by two Jewish boys in an Irish neighborhood and showing straight German films," joshed Wolfe Kaufman, *Variety*'s former Berlin correspondent, now keeping an eye on Nazi film culture from his desk in New York. The Jewish boys were independent exhibitors Joe Scheinman and Al Schiebar, and the "Irish neighborhood" was a reference to the fact that despite its name, the Yorkville was situated on the outer periphery of German hegemony in New York. It's "tough enough to sell German pictures right in the thick of the German nabes these days without trying to peddle them in [a] spot that's composed of about 60% Irish and almost all the rest of them Jews," puzzled Kaufman.[18]

The Yorkville hoped to draw crowds with a provocative line of counterprogramming. Catering to the estimated 40,000 Nazi sympathizers in and about the city, Scheinman and Schiebar booked what they thought the market would bear. In May 1934, almost a year after its Berlin premiere, *S.A.-Mann Brand* bowed at the Yorkville. Tagged as the first "100% Nazi propaganda film to get a public showing in the United States," the original version included newsreel shots of Hitler and antisemitic slurs in the dialogue ("Juda verrecke!" meaning "Perish Jewry!"), phrases deleted by domestic censors. "Pure propaganda for the Nazis," declared the *Film Daily*. "Anti-Semitic stuff is avoided."[19]

S.A.-Mann Brand tanked, as did a follow-up, *Hitlerjunge Quex* (1934), the story of a youth, raised in a family of perfidious communists, who converts to clean living with the Hitler youth. By then, even the venue notorious as "America's only Nazi film house" balked at raising its arm

The first "100% Nazi propaganda film" to play stateside: the titular storm trooper (Heinz Klingenberg) shares a tender moment with his mother (Elise Aulinger) in the Nazi import *S.A.-Mann Brand* (1933), booked by the Yorkville Theatre in New York in 1934.

directly to Hitler. Released under the title *Our Flags Lead Us Forward* to avoid the onus of the surname, *Hitlerjunge Quex* was publicized with nary an inkling of its Nazi sympathies.[20] To expose the subterfuge, a sly anti-Nazi activist handed out handbills in front of the theater outing the owners as Jews, thereby alienating two core audiences: Jews, who refused to patronize a theater showing Nazi cinema, and Nazis, who refused to patronize a theater owned by Jews.[21]

With the German logo repellent in the American marketplace, the Nazis tried cloaking devices. A 20-minute Ufa short entitled *A Trip Through Germany* (1935) attempted to smuggle in Nazi propaganda in the guise of a travelogue. Celebrating the conjoined spirit of old and new Germany in a guided tour of the landscape and architecture, it mixed pastoral scenes of *gemütlich* peasantry with the vibrant energy of a swastika-bedecked nation. "Unsuited to general audiences," *Variety* cautioned exhibitors. "What little entertainment value it might hold is nullified by the bald propaganda for Hitler and the Nazi rule that is its prime purpose." Snuck into the program at the Embassy Newsreel Theater, the film was greeted with stony silence.[22]

The Nazis also sought to infiltrate the American market under the cover of a different foreign language. In 1937, Ufa released the French-language production *Amphitryon* (1935) without the studio logo or other telltale indicators of national origin. Based on the racy play by Jean Giraudoux and directed by Reinhold Schuenzel at the Ufa plant in Neubabelsberg, the film was a sophisticated comedy of manners, human and divine, drawn from the Greek legend of a priapic Zeus attempting to seduce the virtuous Alceme. Booked unknowingly by the 55th Street Playhouse in New York, the imposter was exposed by the most vocal of the anti-Nazi groups in America in the 1930s, the Non-Sectarian Anti-Nazi League to Champion Human Rights (NSANL).

Based in New York and founded by Samuel Untermyer, a high-powered lawyer and tireless Zionist, NSANL boasted a core membership of 10,000 activists and maintained branches throughout the country. Though less glamorous than the Hollywood Anti-Nazi League, the New York outfit was better connected to the American mainstream through a network of churches, synagogues, and community centers. The group forged links with the American Federation of Labor, listed New York mayor Fiorello H. La Guardia on its board of directors, and claimed access to some 2,000,000 sympathetic Americans. Its monthly *Anti Nazi Economic Bulletin* tracked imported Nazi goods and coordinated boycotts.[23]

As sites for anti-Nazi consciousness-raising, motion picture theaters offered ideal targets of opportunity. The double signage of a picket line under a theater marquee drew newspaper photographers—and traumatized theater owners. As Nazi attempts at cinematic subterfuge became subtler, NSANL launched regular campaigns of exposure and retaliation. "Although in the past the League has successfully invoked the boycott against Nazi-made films, a more emphatic movement has become necessary because German film interests are releasing pictures through subsidiaries in other countries, often concealing the real Nazi ownership," the group declared.[24]

NSANL meant business. On November 13, 1936, it summoned stateside distributors and exhibitors of foreign films to a meeting at its New York headquarters and delivered an ultimatum: stop playing Nazi films or face boycotts and picket lines. The League then force-fed its guests a resolution that none refused to swallow. To wit: "We will not exhibit or release any film unless the same bears upon its face a title descriptive of the country of production of the film and, where the information is available, the producer thereof." The cross-dressing *Amphitryon,* the film that had spurred the League to action, was peremptorily canceled by the 55th Street Playhouse.[25] Six months later, hoping that memories had faded, the Belmont, an off-Broadway theater, tried to revive the picture for a two-week run. After a week of picketing by the Joint Boycott Committee of the American Jewish Congress and the Jewish Labor Committee, the house bowed to popular demand. "The film," reported a pleased notice in *Box Office,* "is headed for oblivion, as far as another attempt at a New York showing is concerned."[26]

Foreign film distributors—decidedly small fry in the scheme of the motion picture marketplace—grumbled that NSANL's anger was selective. What about Loew's, MGM's corporate parent, which was distributing *Olympic Ski Champions* (1936) and *Sports on Ice* (1936), a pair of short films about the winter Olympics in the Bavarian Alps shot by Nazi filmmakers? Both shorts also boasted commentary by the laconic Pete Smith, the voice of MGM's popular series of specialty short subjects.

Taking the point, NSANL telegrammed Nicholas M. Schenck, president of Loew's. "We understand the Pete Smith shorts on the Olympic Games were produced by the Nazi German Government and sold to your organization for exclusive distribution," the League informed Schenk. "As we boycott all German goods and services sold in this country, we should be interested in a statement by you in this regard before we take definitive action against your organization and theaters booking these shorts throughout the country." MGM responded with the immediate withdrawal of the two films—but only in New York, the hub of anti-Nazi activism.[27]

Stymied by boycotts and bad films, Nazi attempts to penetrate the American motion picture market hit an ever-hardening wall after 1933.[28] Though the Nazis offered the films to exhibitors on an advantageous rental agreement (a straight percentage basis, with no minimum cash guarantees), outside of the handful of houses in Yorkville and German enclaves in the Midwest, exhibitors shunned the titles on principle or to avoid negative publicity. Even at the venues that played German fare, the flashpoint signs of Nazi origin were nowhere in sight. The Ufa logo disappeared from the title cards, and Hitlerite imagery—swastikas, eagles, and the face of the man himself—vanished from theater fronts. Tellingly too, overtly antisemitic and pro-Nazi productions stayed in Germany. Historical pageants and musicals set far away from the Third Reich were the designated representatives of German cinema abroad.[29]

A typical entry was the nondescript *Der Katzensteg* (1938), a costume drama set during Napoleon's invasion of Prussia, which played at the Casino in New York. "Title is meaningless and best so," commented *Variety*, unable to figure out why the film was called *The Catwalk* in German. "It won't drive away anti-Nazis."[30] Nor would it drive in non-Germans: like many of the German films that managed to secure a stateside play-date, *Der Katzensteg* was screened without English subtitles. Why waste money on translating, subtitling, and duping special prints for a nonexistent crossover audience? "Without [sub]titles, it is a hopeless jumble of words for any but those hep to the Nazi jive," complained *Variety*'s long-suffering critic on the German beat, referring to the lingo not the message in a by-the-numbers juvenile comedy-drama called *Jugend von Heute* (1938).[31]

No sign of a swastika: a still from the *Der Katzensteg* (1938), a costume drama taking place during the Napoleonic wars and typical of the fare imported into the United States from Nazi Germany between 1933 and 1939.

Given the business and the locality, the odds were good that a Jewish-owned operation would be counted among the few remaining distributors of German films in New York. The irony did not go unremarked. "The Germans in Germany don't mind Jewish help in trying to scrape some money out of the U.S.; that kind of money is still money to them, not distasteful or tainted," commented a bitter Wolfe Kaufman. He also suspected a more direct financial subvention by the Nazis in the form of under-the-table bribes to American exhibitors. "The German government helps behind the scenes, apparently, since no money was asked for to speak of," Kaufman noted of one arrangement.[32]

In 1939 the U.S. government levied a 25 percent duty against German imports, a move that had little impact on the total number of German films playing in America. "The films are essentially German propaganda," said an industry insider. "The Nazi government will see to it that they continue to be shown here regardless of the cost." Observing that German exchanges were "not experiencing any difficulty in bringing over pictures," *Box Office* tallied the number of German imports that year at a respectable fifty-five.[33]

Bringing in paying audiences, however, was another matter. The number of German films clearing American customs may have held steady, but the baseline figure was no gauge of the number of German films that received commercial playdates or made a profit. In 1935, Wolfe Kaufman crunched the numbers and explained how things worked. "German imports still lead imports numerically," he conceded, but that "means very little." Getting a film past customs was not the same as getting it in circulation. "More than half of the films brought in and shown were played in only one or two houses. They were modest cheap indies brought in by desperate two-penny exhibs on straight percentage"—that is, with no minimal rental guarantee. "If [there was] any profit, the German producers got paid off in percentages; if not, no one much cared." Scoffed Kaufman: "If they made coffee money, that was something." What the Germans got out of the arrangement was a continued foothold in "a once profitable market that might yet reopen. And the German government, of course, approves for propaganda purposes."[34]

The German films that filtered into America in the 1930s played almost exclusively to a small clique of German speakers either in sympathy with or agnostic about the nation of origin—with no way to tell who in the crowd were ardent pro-Nazis and who just wanted to hear the native tongue in a period piece. Of the fifty-five German imports registered in

1938, *Variety* reviewed only seventeen from playdates at two Yorkville theaters, the Garden and the Casino. *Harrison's Reports*, the exhibitor's trade sheet, reviewed none. If any of the films had a discernibly Nazi agenda, the reviews did not mention it. "For what negligible market there is in the U.S. for Naziland-made pics, *Eva* [1938] will offer more than recent importations," *Variety* remarked of an above-par romantic comedy.[35]

The negligible market for "Naziland-made pics" was not due solely, or even mainly, to boycotts and protests from NSANL. Subtitled or not, the poor quality of the films spoke for itself. Having himself been hounded out of Germany, Wolfe Kaufman was entitled to gloat. "The Third Reich is finding it harder to make films without talent than it had suspected," he snickered.[36] For most American moviegoers, staying clear of Nazi cinema was simply a matter of taste.

ANTI-NAZISM IN THE ARTY THEATERS

With anti-Nazi sentiment strong enough to shut down German cinema in America, an avid market for anti-Nazi cinema might seem to have been ripe for exploitation. Such was not the case. American moviegoers shunned the Nazi imprint and the German tongue, but outside of a small coterie of cinephiles with Popular Front affinities, anti-Nazism on screen was also a losing proposition. Foreign cinema with an anti-Nazi plotline or subtext, usually from the Soviet Union, trickled in to New York City and usually dried up there.

As with German imports in the pre-Hitler 1930s, the venues that welcomed anti-Nazi cinema were the independent "arty theaters," a circuit of small metropolitan venues that in the postwar era would be dubbed art houses. Occasionally, if a foreign film gained a high enough profile through aesthetic quality (Jean Renoir's elegant *Grand Illusion* [1938]) or prurient interest (Gustav Machety's scandalous *Ecstasy* [1933]), it might secure a booking in independent theaters that normally avoided subtitled fare. In 1939, *Motion Picture Herald* estimated that the highest possible number of bookings for a foreign picture—a category exempting the Anglophone British imports—was 3,500, with most imports receiving between 200 and 400 playdates.

By then too, exhibitors were tracking a bellwether shift in the demographic profile of foreign moviegoers—the replacement of linguistic allegiance by artistic taste. "The appeal of foreign pictures is to the American intelligentsia rather than to individual language groups," asserted *Motion Picture Herald, intelligentsia* being a code word for highbrow types with left-wing leanings.[37] For the Popular Front filmgoer, purchasing a ticket to an anti-Nazi film was the moral equivalent of donating money to the anti-Nazi cause. Patronage meant a comradely night out on the town— applauding on cue, bonding in the lobby, and spreading the news by word of mouth.

The cinematic solidarity was all the stronger when the foreign films that assailed Nazi Germany were exported by its totalitarian rival. Of all the nations with the industrial wherewithal to manufacture world-class (or would-be world-class) cinema, the Soviet Union alone invested major resources in anti-Nazi productions. To the Nazis, international Bolshevism was a threat second only to world Jewry, to which it was invariably linked, and the Bolsheviks returned the loathing in kind. Joseph Stalin, like Hitler a confirmed film buff, personally annotated screenplays and reserved for cinema an honored place as an instrument of the revolution. Ironically, the citadel of anticapitalism held a virtual monopoly on anti-Nazi cinema. In the 1930s, no one else was competing.

The passage of Soviet films into America was arranged by Amkino Corporation, the designated distributor for motion pictures made in the USSR. Formed in 1926 and run by Soviet officials based in New York, Amkino funneled the most commercially viable of Soviet cinema into America to spread the revolutionary word and accrue hard currency. First, Dmitry Vassiliev and, after 1934, Vladimir I. Verlinsky, loyal apparatchiks both, landed the choice stateside assignment of president of Amkino, operating always under the watchful eye of Soyuzkino, the film branch of the Soviet government. Fittingly, the outfit's breakout venture into the U.S. market was the most momentous of all Soviet imports, Sergei Eisenstein's *Battleship Potemkin* (1925). In 1938, after Verlinsky was called back to Moscow, and figuring an American face provided a better front, Nicola Napoli, a reliable New York-born communist and Amkino's longtime treasurer, became de facto overseer of the marketing of Soviet film culture in America.[c]

---

[c] In 1940, after the implosion of the Popular Front, Amkino dissolved itself and reincorporated as Artkino Pictures, the trade name "Amkino" linking "America" and *kino*, the Russian word for cinema, now being out of favor with Moscow's foreign policy. Artkino took over where Amkino left off, with Nicola Napoli (who had always handled the English-language paperwork) formally appointed president. ("Art Kino, Russe Outlet," *Variety*, Aug. 7, 1940: 12.)

Amkino handled the American release of two to three dozen Soviet imports a year. Few circulated outside of a select number of sure-seaters patronized by coteries of dedicated communist filmgoers. Fewer still rose to the level of a *Variety* or *New York Times* review. Yet for the fan base, the arty cinema parlors in and around midtown New York (the 55th Street Playhouse, the Acme, the Waldorf, and the Cameo) offered a welcome relief from Hollywood false consciousness and an imaginative link with the future that was the Soviet Union. The 600-seat Cameo, with its wide aisles, marble lobby, and black-walnut foyer, was especially beloved. If the Embassy Newsreel Theater was the hot spot in town for Manhattan-based news junkies, the Cameo was the mecca for devotees of red-starred foreign cinema. The Cameo was run by the kingpin exhibitor of Soviet cinema in the United States, Matty Radin, sometimes referred to in the press as "Tovarich Matty Radin" ("Tovarich" being Russian for "comrade"). In 1932, while introducing the American premiere of Sergei Yutkevich's *Golden Mountains* (1931), a Soviet-made paean to a factory strike in prerevolutionary Russia, the most famous name in Soviet cinema bestowed his personal blessing on the venue. Finding a warmer home at the theater than in the Hollywood studio system, Sergei Eisenstein[d] praised the "the good work that the Cameo is doing in bringing communism to Times Square."[38]

To the extent the films became known to the average rung of moviegoers, Amkino could thank the public relations work performed by anticommunist censors across America. Sometimes abetted by local police chiefs with ideological vendettas, city and state censor boards sliced and banned Soviet-made films with a zeal reserved for no other national cinema, especially when the Soviet imports called for workers of the world to unite against Nazism. Technically, Nazi Germany was a "friendly nation": attacks on it were deemed a controversial intervention in American foreign policy. Censors claimed to be scrupulously neutral in ferreting out propaganda from foreign shores, but the messages from Moscow always received closer scrutiny than the messages from London, Paris, or, for that matter, Berlin.

The anti-Nazi Soviet films that made headway in the American marketplace were a select group. Gustav von Wangenheim's aforementioned

---

[d] Eisenstein was stateside at the invitation of Paramount Pictures, which figured to exploit the talents of the Russian as profitably as it had exploited the talents of the Germans. The arrangement did not work out.

Der Kampf (1936) was the first to edge into awareness. Half Jewish and all communist, von Wangenheim had fled Nazi Germany for the shelter of Moscow, where he had no trouble assembling a German-speaking cast of seasoned actors among the growing refugee community. *Der Kampf* was a patented coming-of-communist-age story (a callow youth who prefers sports to dialectics ultimately sees the light) told against the background of the Reichstag fire and the heroism of the unjustly accused communist Georgi Dimitroff.

A dedicated Popular Front filmgoer might also have patronized *The Oppenheim Family* (1939), directed by Grigori Roshal and based on a novel by Lion Feuchtwanger, author of *The Jew Suss*. It weaves together the tale of a Jewish family in Berlin persecuted by the Nazis (the young son is driven to suicide by the racial theories of his Nazi professor) and the resistance of the unyielding German communist underground. The film was praised by up-and-coming *New York Times* film critic Bosley Crowther for its portrait of brutishly Neanderthal storm troopers, its "authentic flavor of uniformed mobocracy," and (in a slap at Hollywood timidity before the likes of Dr. Georg Gyssling) its fearlessness in naming Nazi names "with a fine Soviet disregard for consular protests."[39]

Also gaining some traction in the American marketplace, mainly on the strength of an exploitable English-language title, was *Concentration Camp* (1939). Directed by Aleksandr Macheret, the Soviet version of a Warner Bros. prison movie went behind the gates of the Nazi penal system for an *exposé* that even at the time seemed too mild. Nazi guards try to break the spirit of communist inmates, to no avail. Outside the camps, undaunted communist workers stage a strike in an airplane factory, rejecting Nazi militarism for people's solidarity. In all the anti-Nazi Soviet films, ruthless Nazi repression only inspires the indefatigable communist party to redouble its efforts.

Besides the rampant message-mongering endemic to the species, bad subtitling, choppy editing, and technical flaws limited the crossover appeal of Soviet cinema. Placed beside Hollywood's flashy formalwear, the pallid fare from the USSR looked drab and frumpy. "Photography ranges from topflight to sloppy, badly lighted scenes," complained *Variety* of *Concentration Camp*. "English titles are n.g. [not good]."[40] The trade paper found nothing good at all to say about *The Oppenheim Family*, a film pockmarked with flaws "of the sort that Hollywood solved years ago." It lambasted the pacing ("the picture takes 97 minutes to put over an idea that Hollywood could punch home in half the footage"), the cardboard-cutout Nazi bad guys ("The Soviets seemingly cannot admit that a villain may look otherwise than villainous"), and even the gams of the leading lady ("the otherwise attractive ingénue G. L. Minovitskaya [has] the thickest ankles that ever distracted an audience's attention").[41] Prone to clunky plotting and hectoring speechifying, the Soviet style was long on dialectics and short on thrills. *New York Times* critic Frank S. Nugent's dry comment on *Der Kampf* summed up the reactions of moviegoers who might be sympathetic to the message but impatient with the packaging. "If the propaganda film is to be a telling instrument against Hitler, it must be used with the icy precision of a surgeon's scalpel, not as a butcher's cleaver."[42]

As if made to Nugent's order, a Soviet film whose plot actually wielded a surgeon's scalpel would break out beyond its loyal communist fan base to become an authentic hit, at least by "arty house" standards. Far and away the best known and most widely circulated of the anti-Nazi films from the USSR, *Professor Mamlock* (1938) was the story of a noble but naive surgeon consumed by the flames of Nazi Germany a-borning. Based on a play by Friedrich Wolf, an exiled German communist playwright, and codirected by Herbert Rappaport, an Austrian-born émigré and former assistant to G. W. Pabst, and Soviet filmmaker Adolph Minkin, the film peddled a presold product. Stalwart Popular Fronters would have known Wolf's play from stage productions by the Federal Theatre Project in New York in 1937 and in Hollywood (in Yiddish) in 1938. As the first explicit anti-Nazi production mounted by the controversial New Deal agency, the stage version of *Professor Mamlock* put flocks of anti-Nazi activists in theater seats. Among communist moviegoers, the motion picture version—from Leningrad not Hollywood—was highly anticipated.[43]

Professor Mamlock opens not on January 30, 1933, the day Hitler became chancellor, but on February 27, 1933, the day, as all Soviets and well-versed Popular Fronters would know, of the burning of the Reichstag, the German parliament building, an act blamed on a conspiracy by the Bulgarian communist agitator Georgi Dimitroff and three comrades. Since the action is set during the run-up to the critical Reichstag elections on March 5, 1933, the vote that gave the Nazis their electoral plurality, the communists are still an active, above-ground political party street fighting against the brownshirts in the name of the true proletariat. After its defeat at the polls, the ruthlessly suppressed but unbowed party apparatus is forced underground to continue the battle.

In reviewing the tumult of the early days of the Third Reich, *Professor Mamlock* is part history lesson and part blueprint for revolutionary action, but the spine of the story is spiritual, a parable of political conversion, communist style. Professor Mamlock (played by Semyon Mezhinsky, an Honored Artist of the Soviet Republic) is a loyal German, an enlightened humanist, and a decorated veteran of the Great War. His brilliance as a surgeon is matched only by his saintly bedside manner. He takes no money from the poor; he comforts crippled children; he keeps long hours. Beloved by his patients, revered by his staff, the kindly old caregiver floats above the upheaval on the streets, oblivious of the world unraveling around him, keeping his gaze fixed on the bacteria under his microscope lens. As if to lend immune protection from the material world, a white surgical gown covers his body, a vestment symbolizing his purity.

Alas, the good doctor is a political naïf in the new Germany, befogged in a false consciousness that estranges him from his wiser son, Rolf (Olge Zhakov), a muscular medical student whose real vocation is fomenting revolution. The two butt heads when the apolitical professor refuses to abide Rolf's agitation under his roof. "What business have you with politics?" asks the father of his firebrand son. "Isn't Pasteur and Koch sufficient for you? Science alone will change mankind." "No," retorts Rolf. "Pasteur, Koch, Marx, and Lenin!"

The professor soon learns the truth of his son's words. The burning of the Reichstag ("we won't allow communists and Jews to undermine our nation!" screams a radio announcer) accelerates the Nazis' persecution of political enemies and racial minorities. The jackboot comes down hardest on the communists, who, though chased underground, continue to work for the cause—meeting in cafes, passing information, and circulating anti-Hitler leaflets.

No longer a refuge from street politics, Professor Mamlock's hospital also falls under Nazi control. A Nazi doctor, long jealous of Mamlock and now drunk with power, sets about purging his rival, ordering Mamlock, in the middle of surgery, to stop practicing medicine. "What the Jew Mamlock does any of you can do!" he barks to the stunned operating team.

Directors Rappaport and Minkin then perform a neat operation of their own. Outside the hospital, German citizens mill in the streets, distracted by a hubbub of activity just out of sight. The crowd parts to reveal the cause of the commotion: Professor Mamlock, paraded through the street by brownshirts, the word "Jude" scrawled in big black letters across the front of his white surgical gown. It is a haunting image of ignorance defacing wisdom, of a lion of a man set upon by jackals.

Shattered, Mamlock staggers home. Brushing past his horrified wife, he locks himself in his study. From his desk drawer, he takes out a pistol—a gift bestowed on him for courage at the battle of Verdun during the Great War—and begins to write a letter.

Back at the hospital, irony ensues: a big-shot Nazi requires immediate life-saving surgery. Only the Jew Mamlock can perform the necessary procedure. When the Nazis come to implore Mamlock to return, he is still at his desk contemplating suicide, but true to his Hippocratic oath, he agrees to perform the operation. Slowly, he stands up to reveal his desecrated gown, still branded "Jude." No, he tells his visitors, he does not want to change his clothes.

Reunited with his loyal medical staff, the professor saves the Nazi's life. The gesture is futile. The hospital still must be "liberated from this Jew Mamlock." Distraught beyond consolation, Mamlock walks in a daze

▬ "A surgeon's scalpel": Semyon Mezhinsky as the kindly Jewish doctor in the Soviet anti-Nazi film *Professor Mamlock* (1938), based on the play by Friedrich Wolf.

down the hospital corridor. From offscreen, a shot rings out. Mamlock's body is found slumped on the floor, but the old man is not dead.

During Mamlock's torment, a parallel track of action charts the exploits of the underground communist cell, led by Rolf, still working heroically under the noses of the Nazis. Several sequences play as instructional vignettes for revolutionaries in training: how to hide and distribute anti-Nazi leaflets and (Hollywood's influence being felt even in Leningrad) how to mount an exciting rescue operation.

The plotlines and the ideological currents converge when Rolf, risking all, sneaks into the hospital and goes to the professor's bedside. Father and son are reconciled. The old man has seen the light. Pasteur and Koch must be yoked to Marx and Lenin.

Discovered and pursued, Rolf flees, making good his escape when his love interest kills his Nazi nemesis. In the confusion, Mamlock leaves his bed and walks to a balcony overlooking the city street outside. Heedless of the soldiers assembling below, he delivers a scathing anti-Nazi speech to the gathering crowd. "Now I understand what you're all about," he shouts to the Nazis. While proclaiming his German patriotism, he curses the Nazis for the torture, tears, and blood they have brought to the nation. Mamlock's denunciation ends when a Nazi machine gunner cuts him down midsentence. From the crowd, a voice yells "Murderers!"

The coda shows Rolf—still free, still fighting—at an underground cell meeting, exhorting his brave comrades. He clenches his fist in the arm-upright gesture of the Red Front, the universal sign of communist solidarity. If a Hollywood film ends with a romantic clinch, a Soviet film ends with a clenched fist.

Professor Mamlock was stirring stuff, and not just for communists. The stiffness of Soviet agitprop was softened with human touches and comic relief and enlivened with well-paced action sequences shot in the streets of Leningrad. The music track (the rousing theme was by Y. Kochrov and M. Timofeyev) and the sound design (the click-clack steps of the brown-shirts on pavement) came in for special praise from critics.

From a non-Stalinist perspective, however, *Professor Mamlock* was not without ideological difficulties. The party-line valorization of the German working class makes the Nazis seem more like an invading army than an expression of popular will. In the elaborate underground network operating around Berlin, seemingly every German except those in brown shirts embraces the communist cause. Just where did all those marchers at the Nuremberg rallies come from? According to *Professor Mamlock*, and contrary to the Nazi slogan, the German *Volk* are not one with the *Reich* and the *Führer*.

The addled class dynamics were clouded over by a coincidence of historical timing. Premiering on November 7, 1938, on home turf at the Cameo Theatre, *Professor Mamlock* lived up to the hoariest cliché of adpub taglines: as timely as today's headlines. By grim serendipity, the stateside release coincided with the surge of nationwide revulsion over Kristallnacht, the antisemitic orgy of destruction that erupted throughout the greater Reich two days later. "It is Hitler who is conducting a grisly promotion campaign across the world's press, driving home the film's call for unity with each terrifying headline," proclaimed the *Daily Worker*, the broadsheet of the Communist Party USA. "Audiences coming from the Cameo walk the short half-block to Times Square and look up at the electric news bulletins banding the Times Building and feel no transition from the mood of the picture." For once too the Cameo was packed with crowds made up of more than the true-believing regulars. Thrilled to support a film that was not just preaching to the converted, the *Daily Worker* figured that "a large percentage of the nightly audience at the Cameo have never before witnessed a Soviet screenplay." Mamlock's hospital-bed conversion and his defiant speech from the balcony seldom failed to inspire cheers and applause.[44]

Having endured years of stilted agitprop and inept melodrama, critics from across the Popular Front relished the chance to trumpet a film that combined righteous politics and—finally—impressive artistry. The *New York Times* praised a "great picture," and the *New York World-Telegram* lauded "a fierce and shattering indictment of Nazi terrorism." Even the Hollywood trade press amplified the buzz. "Strong anti-Nazi propaganda dished up with entertainment elements which carry a load of visual sock," said the *Hollywood Reporter*. "Gruesome flashes of whippings, mass murders, and various prosecutions leave a lasting memory."[45] It was no surprise that in a year-end survey of the year's best movies, the *Daily Worker* hailed *Professor Mamlock* as "the most significant picture of the year," but the National Board of Review also ranked it as one of the best foreign films of the year.[46]

Seizing the momentum, Nicola Napoli, Amkino's hands-on manager, made a bid to cross over into the American mainstream by doing something the Soviet importer had never done before. Amkino applied for a Code seal for *Professor Mamlock*.

As usual, the Breen office was ahead of the curve. Unbeknownst to Amkino, Francis Harmon, head of the East Coast branch of the Production Code Administration, had already checked out the film with the paying customers at the Cameo. "The film is a powerful anti-Nazi story with some incidental boosts for Communism," Harmon informed Will Hays in a carefully worded memo copied to Breen on the coast. "In our opinion it conforms to the Code section which provides that 'the history, institutions, prominent people and citizenry of other nations shall be represented *fairly*.'" Elaborating, Harmon set off in quotes the distinction that, since *I Was a Captive of Nazi Germany* (1936), had guided PCA policy toward anti-Nazi cinema:

> This section does not state that the people and other nations must always be portrayed sympathetically. It says "fairly" and in our judgment the scenes portrayed are an accurate reflection of what has actually taken place in Nazi Germany. In fact the present German government has boasted of just such incidents as are herein portrayed.

Harmon then broached another topic very much on the mind of the MPPDA:

> Refusal to issue [a Code] seal because of dislike of the content of the film subjects us to legal action as constituting "an unreasonable restraint of foreign commerce." . . . The Association [the MPPDA], as public relations advisor to member companies, may well continue to advise producers not to make such controversial films, and to advise distributors not to distribute such films, but when such a film made by a foreign, non-member producer, is submitted to us for review, it appears that our responsibility is limited to a determination whether or not the film conforms to the Code.[47]

Harmon was giving voice to a pressing concern throughout the industry. Being a front for a cartel, the MPPDA was rightly fearful of indictment as a monopoly in restraint of trade. Under FDR, the federal government had begun to cast a jaundiced eye on the practices of Hollywood's vertically integrated oligopoly. In July 1938 the worst fears of the motion picture industry were realized when the Department of Justice brought suit against the three-tiered system of production, distribution, and exhibition practiced by the major studios.[e] With government lawyers demanding an end to the lucrative racket, the MPPDA thought it prudent to deflect charges of monopoly by a show of equal treatment to the foreign competition.

The MPPDA-PCA decision makers were also not insensitive to a shift in the cultural ground. By early 1939, as *Professor Mamlock* wound its way through the Code bureaucracy, Nazi perfidy was a familiar theme in newspaper articles, radio commentary, and even the newsreels. Warner Bros.' *Confessions of a Nazi Spy* (1939) was nearing completion after a bright green light from the Breen office. Even though the first film to articulate the emerging American consensus on Nazi Germany was from the Soviet Union, official Hollywood could no longer deny expression to so widely held a sentiment.

Partly as a bargaining chip in the ongoing lawsuit brought by the Department of Justice, partly as a sign of the times, *Professor Mamlock* was granted a Code seal. It was the first Soviet-made film to receive the imprimatur of the Breen office, indeed the first time that Amkino had bothered to apply for a Code seal. None of the political content, either anti-Nazi or pro-communist, was tampered with. The only required deletions involved a mild sexual allusion and a glimpse of cruelty during a "third degree" (that is, interrogation) scene at Nazi police headquarters. MPPDA secretary Carl E. Milliken confirmed the official clearance with the standard qualification: "*Professor Mamlock* conformed with all the standards of the Production Code and [our decision] has nothing to do with approval or disapproval with the theme of the picture."[48]

The hurdle of the Breen office may have been cleared, but *Professor Mamlock* still needed to run a coast-to-coast gantlet of municipal and state censor boards. Staffed by political hacks and busy-bodies-about-town, the boards were often far more likely to fold under pressure from a foreign consul or local women's group than was the stiff-necked Breen out in Hollywood. Breen followed codified regulations. Local censors followed their own erratic druthers.

At first sight of the hammer and sickle, many censor boards and police chiefs conspired to impede circulation of Amkino releases. A typical

---

[e] In 1948, in the Paramount Decree, the U.S. Supreme Court would rule that the Hollywood way of doing business was a violation of American antitrust laws and ordered the separation of production from exhibition, thereby tolling the death knell for the classical Hollywood studio system.

instance involved *The Baltic Deputy* (1937), a biopic based on the story of Kliment Timiryazev, a botanist and early supporter of the Russian revolution touted as the "Luther Burbank of Russia." Fearing the Soviet-made paean to "red" propaganda might "incite people to destroy government," the Pennsylvania State Board of Censors banned it. When Amkino took the board to court and its attorney asked chairwoman Mrs. A. Mitchell Palmer why she had banned the film, Mrs. Palmer replied, "The film contains the most magnificent acting I've ever seen, but I don't like communism."[49] Amkino ultimately won the case.

Living up to its reputation as the nation's preeminent chamber of blinkered philistines, the Chicago Board of Censors clamped down hard on the anti-Nazi Soviet imports. It banned *The Oppenheim Family* as propaganda that "exposes to contempt a class of citizens."[50] It banned *Concentration Camp* for being "a vicious propaganda picture of an inflammatory type which could not fail to provoke hatred, bitterness, and dissension."[51] It banned *Professor Mamlock* for being likely to incite a "near riot."[52]

Another group determined to keep anti-Nazi cinema off American screens was the Nazis. German consular officers across America protested to mayors, Nazi-inspired citizens groups appealed to municipal censors, and German-language newspapers editorialized against Amkino insults to the Reich.

Yet despite the pressure from foreign consuls and homegrown Nazis, the support of sympathetic critics and a widespread reluctance to censor political speech (as opposed to immoral images) lent even the Soviet films a layer of protection. Also, by 1939, the same currents that had lifted *Professor Mamlock* to arthouse prominence and Code clearance worked to shield the anti-Nazi films from suppression. Initial bannings by boards were often overturned under pressure from the public or a ruling from a judge. As with the newsreels, the editorial pages of the nation's newspapers rallied to the defense of politically minded films with an alacrity seldom summoned when Hollywood was censored for immorality. Besides, no one could argue that Soviet cinema was too sexy or salacious.

"NAZI SCRAMMERS"

Exiles, refugees, expatriates—the tide of talent that would enliven or, more usually, darken the tone and texture of Hollywood cinema—were the great by-product of the Nazi campaign to cleanse the fatherland of *untermenschen*, subhumans not fit for life in the new Germany. Few of the motion picture artists who arrived in Hollywood after 1933 were wretched or poor, but many were politically aberrant, communist or leaning so, and almost all were racially unacceptable to the Nazis—Jewish, part Jewish, or married to Jews. Many of the refugees were doubly cursed, being ethnically and ideologically repellent to the Third Reich.

The influx of refugees skilled in the art of moviemaking was a backhanded confirmation of the prestige accorded their profession in Nazi Germany. Unlike the American government, whose policy toward creative expression was mainly benign neglect, the Nazis honored intellectuals and artists as avatars of Aryan culture, none more so than those working in the most valued of propaganda media. Talented filmmakers of good stock and reliable opinion were pampered; the rest were persecuted. Purged from Germany and later Austria, producers, directors, actors, writers, musicians, and craftsmen of all sorts were forced to seek work and find succor elsewhere—Paris, London, and, the promised land, Hollywood. As usual, *Variety* came up with a glib coinage for the new migrants in town: "Nazi scrammers."[53]

Dazzled by the picture-perfect climate of California and the well-oiled machinery of the studio system, the transplanted filmmakers were alternately delighted and disoriented, relieved to have escaped from the terror of Nazi Germany and anxious about adjustment to a new life. In assimilating into Hollywood, each confronted problems peculiar to his or her occupational specialty. Some clung fervently to the politics that forced their exodus, others dropped their party affiliations quicker than their accents.

An impediment shared by all the prominent names was that any Hollywood film employing a well-known German refugee was tagged as contraband and forbidden import into Germany. When submitting a film for German release, the Hollywood studios were required to certify that the production was not made by "Jewish emigrants." To the Nazis, "a Jewish emigrant" was defined as a "non-Aryan" who had emigrated after January 30, 1933, and who was considered "to have left the country in silent protest to the present regime."[54] To ship films into Germany, the studios either lied outright on the official forms or wiped the offending name from the credits prior to export.

On July 1, 1933, when the purging of Jews from the German film industry became official, producer Samuel Goldwyn telegrammed reporters. "I

plan to inaugurate a movement here in Hollywood immediately to welcome to our motion picture ranks those artists, producers, writers, and
directors who, because of their Jewish heritage, are being deprived of
a means of livelihood and an outlet for their talent. We not only invite
them here, but what is more important, we need them," he declared,
overlooking restrictive immigration laws that blocked easy entry. "Many
of the people who have been engaged in making pictures in Germany are
among the most capable in the world, and the German government cannot but suffer a grievous loss because of the steps it has taken."[55] Berlin's
loss would be Hollywood's gain—and at a bargain price.

Money being good anywhere, financially solvent producers made the
smoothest transition to filmmaking outside of Germany. After twenty-six
years in the German film industry and sixteen as production head at Ufa,
Erich Pommer landed on his feet first in Paris, working for Fox at the Joinville Studio, later in London, and then, for good, in Hollywood.[56] "Where
else can one find such lovely days?" he enthused during the shooting of
his aptly titled debut for Fox, *Music in the Air* (1934). "The studios are the
last word in efficiency. Here are the best brains in the biz, the best technicians and by far the best facilities for turning out super productions."[57]

In 1934 the theatrical impresario Max Reinhardt was welcomed with
fanfare at Warner Bros., where he was hired to codirect a big-budget all-star
production of William Shakespeare's *A Midsummer Night's Dream* (1935).
To smooth Reinhardt's transition, a codirector was assigned to shepherd
him through the studio system, William (formerly Wilhelm) Dieterle, himself a German import and a former Reinhardt protégé. (A colorful character who wore white gloves on the set and directed in "pig Latin with a
German accent," Dieterle had been under contract at Warner Bros. since
1930.)[58] Reportedly, the combined reputations of Shakespeare and Reinhardt gave actors as cocky as James Cagney (as Bottom) and Mickey Rooney
(as Puck) a case of the butterflies during rehearsals.[59] Reinhardt had his
own adjustments to make in the move from Neubabelsberg to Burbank
when he glimpsed a scene of unseemly modesty on the set. The diaphanous gowns of the girls playing the wood nymphs in *A Midsummer Night's
Dream* should be transparent not veiled, he ordered. He was told that not
even Shakespeare was exempt from the Production Code.

Fluent in the universal language of music, composers also adapted
readily. Franz Waxman was recruited by Erich Pommer to score *Music
in the Air* (1934), secured his reputation with the ethereal strains to *Bride*

of Frankenstein (1935), and became one of the most common credit lines in classical Hollywood cinema, earning twelve Academy Award nominations and two Oscars. Frederick Hollander, who under the name Friedrich Hollaender had written the score for *The Blue Angel* (1930), followed Marlene Dietrich to Hollywood to provide her with theme music and signature songs. Viennese composer Erich Wolfgang Korngold, a former child prodigy hailed as the new Mozart in his home metropolis, first left Vienna in 1935 to score *A Midsummer Night's Dream* for Reinhardt and quickly became a go-to "cleffer" at Warner Bros., earning Oscars for his rousing scores to *Anthony Adverse* (1936) and *The Adventures of Robin Hood* (1938). He left Austria for good weeks before its annexation by the Nazis.

Critics had to be pretty tone deaf not to tune in to the new beat in Hollywood cinema. "Invasion of Hollywood by world's ace composers has gained marked headway in 1936, and some of the most interesting and important musical creations anywhere were composed directly for [the] screen" noted *Variety* in a year-end wrap-up that never mentioned the words "refugee from Nazism" but included a roster of same among the composers whose scores had proven "memorable for music lovers, agreeable to the popular ear, and inspirational to film producers."[60] The German Jewish composers who conducted the soundtracks to the lush Hollywood melodramas of the 1930s and 1940s lent an (ironically) operatic Wagnerian whoosh to the Tin Pan Alley strains of American pop romance.[61]

The linguistically dependent ranks of writers and actors found adjustment more difficult. Few possessed the verbal facility of Billy Wilder, who left Germany in 1932 and came to Hollywood by way of Paris in 1933. Wilder's second-language ear for the lilt of American slang spiced up the dialogue tracks of all his films, though even the witty Wilder always collaborated with a native speaker to fine-tune his screenplays.

Natural chameleons though they were, many actors found the change of habitat wrenching. The screen credits of the marquee stars of Germany and Austria meant nothing to the fan magazines in America. Moreover, as the German voice on radio and in the newsreels came to sound ever more crudely barbaric to the American ear, what had once been a language of husky romance and exotic sophistication took on a guttural and discordant timbre. Refugee actors were caught in a cruel bind. The German-accented character parts they might have been typecast for were also drying up—too sensitive for domestic consumption and too offensive to slip by Nazi censorship. Not until American entry into World War II would a seller's market for German-accented villains restore the fortunes of German thespians, Jew and non-Jew, who could play to Central Casting type. Conrad Veidt, the somnambulist from the German Expressionist classic *The Cabinet of Dr. Caligari* (1920) and the star of *The Wandering Jew* (1933) and *Power* (1934), metamorphosed into a reliable Nazi scoundrel, most memorably as the slithery Major Strasser in *Casablanca* (1942).

Blessed with the mastery of a unique skill set, successful German directors might write their own ticket. The prize catch of all—Ernst Lubitsch—had arrived in 1922, prospered, and showed no desire to return to a nation in perpetual meltdown. In 1932, back in Berlin for a visit, he felt the bad vibrations in the air. Asked by Bella Fromm, the famed diplomatic columnist for the *Vossische Zeitung*, whether he planned ever again to work in Germany, he shook his head. "That's finished," he told her. "Nothing good is going to happen here for a long time. The sun shines every day in California."[62]

Several rungs down from Lubitsch were the directors Ludwig Berger and Reinhold Schuenzel. Berger had been commuting back and forth between Berlin and Hollywood, Ufa and Paramount, since 1928. The talkie revolution pushed him back to Germany, where in June 1933 he had the lonely distinction of being "the only Jewish Ufa director at present," working on one of the last of his Weimar-conceived projects, *Walzekrieg*.[63] When production wrapped, Berger lit out for France, the Netherlands, and Britain, but never found his way back behind the camera in Hollywood. For his part, Schuenzel, the formerly bankable director of *Amphitryon* (1935), found himself suddenly out of favor for considering a project that took a satirical look at dictators. In 1937 he fled Germany for Hollywood and landed a contract with MGM to helm froth such as *Ice Follies of 1939* (1939) and *Balalaika* (1939). (Both Berger and Schuenzel returned to Germany after the war.)

Director Henry Koster, formerly Herman Kosterlitz, was just getting his career off the ground when the Nazis came to power. He worked in Austria, Hungary, and Italy before Joe Pasternak, Universal's overseas production chief, brought him to Hollywood in 1936. He hit pay dirt immediately with *Three Smart Sisters* (1936), where he guided 14-year-old Deanna Durbin to stardom. Koster rode his meal ticket to five more starring vehicles, a franchise that helped keep Universal in the black during the 1930s. A studio workhorse, he enjoyed a 40-picture career in Hollywood.

"The sun shines every day in California": Ernst Lubitsch and his wife, British actress Vivian Gaye, relaxing in San Bernadino, CA, 1939.

The most prominent director to flee Germany was Austrian-born Fritz Lang, the internationally renowned genius behind the sentimental Nazi favorite *Die Nibelungen* (1924), the dystopic science fiction fantasy *Metropolis* (1927), and the crime melodrama *M* (1931). The story Lang told of his escape from Germany was as nerve-wracking as any of the dark thrillers he made in Hollywood: that soon after the Nazis took power, Joseph Goebbels offered to put him in charge of the German film industry. "But my mother was part Jewish!' protested Lang. "I decide who's Jewish and who's not Jewish," hissed Goebbels, whereupon Lang went directly from the propaganda minister's office to the Berlin station and boarded the first train to Paris. (The truth was more prosaic: Lang quietly closed out his affairs, packed up his art collection, and left first class.)[64] Monocled, impeccably dressed, an autocrat on the set, Lang might have been sent over from Central Casting after a call for a tyrannical German director type. His first film for MGM, *Fury* (1936), was a commercial and critical success, a close-to-the-bone social-problem film in which a howling mob tries to lynch a man unjustly accused of kidnapping.

The fresh-off-the-boat immigrants—or, more likely, freshly disembarked from their second-class berths on the Super Chief at Union Station, Los Angeles, the terminal point for the luxury rail liner—rubbed elbows and competed for jobs with the pioneers who had voluntarily left the Weimar Republic in the 1920s and early 1930s. Reportedly, some of the original pilgrims were miffed at being lumped in with the come-latelies. "One of the most remarkable angles on the Hitler thing, as far as filmers are concerned, is the almost unanimous care which former Germans take in pointing out they're not exiles," reported *Variety* in 1933. "Again and again, former German filmers who left the country, complain of being put in the refugee class, pointing out they left of their own volition, they left before the persecution actually started, etc. In some cases it's a matter of thinking they may get back some day; in most it's the business of not wanting to be pitied but standing on their own as directors, writers, and actors rather than as refugee talent that needs bucking up."[65]

Perhaps—but many of the Weimar expatriates joined together and held out a helping hand to their desperate kinsmen. Ernst Lubitsch, Marlene Dietrich, and Carl Laemmle bankrolled escapes, signed affidavits, and put newly arrived talent on the studio payrolls. In 1938 the personal gestures of charity were made official with the establishment of the European Film Fund, through which solvent refugee artists tithed 1 percent of their salaries to sustain refugees down on their luck.

None was more generous or energetic than Paul Kohner, who with Lubitsch cofounded the European Film Fund. Born in 1902 to wealthy and trade-connected parents in the Austro-Hungarian Empire, he met his future in 1920 while interviewing Carl Laemmle. The Universal chieftain was back in his homeland, soaking in the baths at Karlsbad. During the interview, Laemmle offered the 18-year-old a job as his personal assistant. By 1928, Kohner was overseeing Universal coproductions in Germany. When Hitler forced the company to pull up stakes, he fled first to Paris and then returned to Hollywood. In 1938 he opened up the Paul Kohner Agency to broker talent, but his real job in the 1930s was as a one-man refugee relief center for the exiled German community in Hollywood. Wired in to all the casting departments of the majors studios, he procured visas and employment for scores of adrift Germans.[66]

Many of the refugees who landed in Hollywood had known each other since their salad days in Weimar Germany. Socializing and working together, they bonded in a mutual support network. Ernst Lubitsch personally supervised a screen test for Reinhold Schuenzel's 17-year-old daughter Annamarie for a bit part in *The Shop Around the Corner* (1940).[67] Helped along by his friends, Schuenzel himself moved from the director's chair to the other side of the camera. In 1943, doubtless savoring the irony, Lang cast his former colleague and fellow exile as a Gestapo officer in *Hangmen Also Die!* (1943), a dramatization of the assassination of the notorious S.S. Gen. Reinhard Heydrich by the Czechoslovakian underground.

Not all lived out the Hollywood dream. The former German film star Hans von Twardowski took character parts, bit roles, and extra work. Others changed professions: the actor and director Ulrich Steindorf moved into publicity work. Director Joe May, one of the brightest lights of Weimar cinema, floundered in the Hollywood studio system. Brought over by Pommer to direct *Music in the Air,* a box office failure, he was soon relegated to B movies at Universal, working with the Dead End Kids and Lon Chaney Jr. For the ill-starred, the demotion from name-above-the-title to has-been was an ignominious fall made tolerable only by considering the alternative back home.

Before too long, even the Nazis recognized that the hemorrhaging of motion picture talent had to be stanched. Perhaps the racially acceptable artists could be lured back? "German government has officially asked these expatriates (except those of Jewish faith) to come back and take their part in the German film biz of today, no matter what their tie-ups elsewhere," *Variety* reported in 1933.[68] Any artist who failed to return to the Reich was branded the moral equivalent of a Jew. "It is considered unpatriotic—yes, even as treason to the country—if now, in the midst of the great work of rebuilding in the German film world, German artists combine abroad with film companies or film workers who either emigrated from Germany as non-Aryans or who are hostile to Germany or participate in agitation against Germany," warned the *Film-Kurier,* once the German film industry's answer to *Variety,* now a Goebbels mouthpiece. "Such Aryan German film workers employed abroad against

German interests run the risk of being placed beside non-Aryans in the future."[69]

A few non-Jewish, non-left-wing German actors—homesick, afraid of being tarnished as non-Aryans, or having run aground under the Hollywood palms—returned to the fold. Beckoned to Hollywood by a five-year contract with Paramount, Dorothea Wieck, star of *Maedchen in Uniform* (1931), returned in 1934 and enjoyed enormous success in the cinema of the Third Reich. Emil Jannings, who won the very first Academy Award for Best Actor for his work at Paramount in *The Last Command* (1928) and *The Way of All Flesh* (1928), repatriated to Germany with the onset of talkies to become a prize show horse for Joseph Goebbels.

While the refugee community soaked up the sun, learned English, and hustled for work, Hollywood in turn absorbed the nervous tics and night terrors of the refugee sensibility—shadowy and off-kilter, alienated and paranoid, foggy and fearful. The denizens of "Weimar on the Pacific" injected a gloomy *weltanschauung* into Hollywood's bright horizons and happy endings, a touch of evil that in the postwar era blossomed into what sharp-eyed French critics called *film noir*.

Back in the Greater Reich, a few motion picture artists paid the ultimate price for being Jewish or anti-Nazi. In October 1936 the German actor Helmuth Klonka was condemned for high treason and executed.[70] That same year, Werner Krauss, the Austrian director and financier, despondent that Nazi racial laws blocked his productions from Germany, committed suicide in Vienna. "He had made one big mistake," the obituary in *Variety* noted. "He made pictures in Austria with casts which did not get the approval of the German film chamber—that is to say, they were not 100% Aryan."[71] In 1938 the Austrian actor, comedian, and cabaret performer Fritz Grünbaum was arrested and imprisoned in the concentration camp at Dachau, where he died in 1941.

Little wonder that longtime expatriates burned their bridges and pledged new allegiances. "Herr Ernst Lubitsch, one-time Berlin actor, but for years a Paramount director in Hollywood, has finally gotten around, after some eleven years, to the important business of declaring allegiance to the land of opportunity, blue eagles, high salary checks, and double features," trumpeted *Motion Picture Herald* in 1933, when the greatest of all Weimar imports applied to become a U.S. citizen.[72] Marlene Dietrich waited until the fateful year of 1939 to make it official. "I am doggone

"Doggone glad to be a niece of
Uncle Sam": Marlene Dietrich
signs her final U.S. citizenship
papers in Los Angeles, June 9,
1939.

glad to be a niece of Uncle Sam," she told reporters. "The United States
is the most glorious and wonderful country in the whole wide world."[73]

For their part, being all too familiar with the value of identity papers,
the newer arrivals wasted no time in officially signing up for an American passport. Fritz Lang took out his naturalization papers within
months of arriving in Hollywood. Billy Wilder treasured the moment
a sympathetic consular officer in Mexico stamped his passport with a
precious entry visa. After fleeing Nazi Germany, Conrad Veidt became a
loyal British subject, but died a true citizen of Hollywood, succumbing
to a heart attack in 1943 while playing golf at the Riviera Country Club
in Pacific Palisades.

Given conditions at home, few of the exiles suffered from true home-
sickness. The Germany they remembered no longer existed.

In a sense, the film people hounded out of Nazi Germany were lucky. Persecuted from the first days of the Nazi takeover, they got the message early
and fled well in advance of the holocaust that consumed their kinsmen.

Unlike shopkeepers and businessmen, tied down by inventory and contacts, or medical and legal professionals, with clients and credentials, artists were not rooted to real estate or dependent on loyal customers. Itinerant by profession, mobile by inclination, they were a class of professionals ready to hit the road on short notice, carrying little more than a valise and their native talent. Pack a bag, hop a train, walk up a gangplank, and sail into a new life.

8

"THE BLIGHT OF RADICAL PROPAGANDA"

I n the waning days of 1937, Martin J. Quigley, publisher and editor in chief of *Motion Picture Herald* and coauthor of the Production Code, sensed a danger looming over the industry that was more his vocation than business. "There remains in the eyes of the radical propagandists one medium of expression and one influence upon public opinion which thus far vainly excites their envy," he warned. "That medium is the motion picture." Fortunately, Hollywood had "escaped the blight of radical propaganda," but the message mongers were lurking just outside the studio gates, ready "to muscle in, gain an influence over the production of the motion picture, and then use it for the propagation of their own notions of world reform."[1]

Quigley was right to detect deviations from the path of fair-weather entertainment. On screen, Hollywood was inching toward the creation of narratives more in tune with the sentiments of the directors, screenwriters, and actors who packed the meetings of the Hollywood Anti-Nazi League and the Motion Picture Artists Committee. After years of turning a blind eye, the major studios were facing up to the threat from Nazism—fitfully, allegorically, with concessions and compromises, but unmistakably and undeniably.

The ominous news from overseas was a bracing inspiration. An unbroken string of victories lent a frightening momentum to the forward march of the European dictatorships—the invasion of Ethiopia by mechanized Italy, the victories of the fascist-backed Rebels in the Spanish Civil War, and the territorial acquisitions that, without firing a shot, had extended Nazi hegemony from the Saar to the Sudetenland. To read the headlines or watch the newsreels was to see American-style democracy on the wrong side of history.

In January 1938, William E. Dodd, retiring after four and a half years as U.S. Ambassador to Germany, went before the newsreel cameras upon his return to America and spoke with a freedom that the language of diplomacy had heretofore constrained. "Living in Europe these days is profoundly discouraging," he said. "Nazism and fascism are gaining ground everywhere. This is a world crisis, the greatest crisis since Napoleon." Dodd kept up his warnings, on radio (including broadcasts over Warner Bros.' KFWB), and in speeches to the Hollywood Anti-Nazi League and any other group that would listen.

But if some in Hollywood wanted to shout out a warning, commercial and political constraints conspired to keep the medium tongue-tied. In 1936, reviewing *Fires in May*, an anti-Nazi novel by exiled German writer Ruth Feiner, Wolfe Kaufman, *Variety*'s former Berlin correspondent, now safely situated at the paper's New York office, measured the spinelessness of an industry always on the lookout for box office material but prone to flinch at the first sign of controversy. "Too closely related to politics to be picture material," he judged, "but interesting reading for the thinkers."[2] By mutual consent, the thinkers were not interested in Hollywood and Hollywood was not interested in thinking.

Besides the tug of commerce, the bludgeon of what Hollywood called "political censorship" stifled creative options. The phrase referred to the onerous deletions in film content mandated by city and state censorship boards, as distinct from the salutary "self-regulation" performed by the Production Code Administration on behalf of the Motion Picture Producers and Distributors of America. Studio filmmakers accepted the notion of censorship per se and acceded to the moral policing of the Breen office, but they chafed at the suppression of morally sound motion pictures on purely partisan grounds. "I am definitely against filth and vulgarity on the screen, and I am 100% in favor of keeping that sort of thing off the screen," said producer Walter Wanger, a center of gravity for liberal Hollywood opinion, "but I am also 100% against people who try to censor screen entertainment for their own interests."[3]

Of course, some of the people Wanger berated worked for the MPPDA. Spooked by *Blockade* (1938), Wanger's intervention into the Spanish Civil War, and concerned that it might embolden imitators, the MPPDA was reported to be considering the adoption of an amendment to the Production Code prohibiting films "containing controversial subject matter of a political or propaganda nature," a charge the association denied. "The Hays office will never attempt such a ban," an MPPDA official insisted. "The Code doesn't have anything to do with politics or propaganda and an amendment to it ruling out such films hasn't even reached the conversation stages."[4]

Nonetheless, the Hays office had always discouraged the production of politically sensitive motion pictures, not needing the authority of the Code to act on what it considered "the good of the industry as a whole." In 1936, when MGM contemplated a screen version of Sinclair Lewis's novel *It Can't Happen Here*, a dystopic vision of a fascist takeover of America, the Breen office, acting on behalf of headquarters, squashed the notion before the cameras rolled. Likewise, in 1937, despite the enthusiasm of Irving Thalberg for the project, MGM dropped plans to adapt Franz Werfel's best seller *The Forty Days of Musa Dagh*, a searing indictment of the Armenian genocide, after protests from the Turkish and French governments. Unlike city and state boards, who suppressed films after completion, the Hays office strangled projects in the crib.

Outside Hollywood, however, the popular arts were lining up solidly behind the Popular Front. While Hitler blackened the headlines, the theatrical world regularly mounted anti-Nazi stage productions—indeed, sometimes at government expense under the auspices of the Federal Theatre Project. On the radio airwaves, editorial commentary and news reporting sent out anti-Nazi alarms that grew louder and louder as the decade went on. Even the tone of the newsreels became more cautionary and condemnatory when covering Nazi Germany. Only big-screen entertainment seemed oblivious to the grim tidings in the news of the day.

Yet even Hollywood was changing incrementally, pushed along by a personal reason the major studios had for getting into the anti-Nazi business. In pace with its territorial gains, Nazi antipathy toward the American motion picture industry had intensified. From 1933 on, Hollywood had endured an escalating series of bizarre censorship edicts and confiscatory trade policies. By 1937 "the suppression in Germany of American box office hit pictures on unknown pretexts" combined with Nazi consul Dr. Georg Gyssling's meddling in Hollywood production "had aroused American film interests to a high state of resentment against Nazi policies," noted the *Hollywood Reporter* decrying the "Hitler fist"

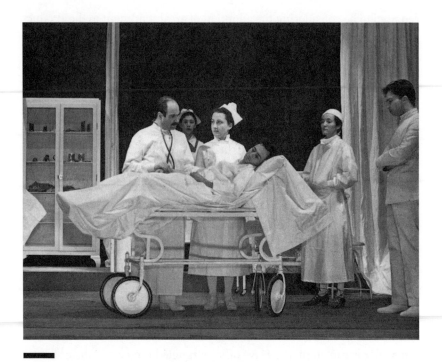

The Popular Front takes center stage: a scene from Friedrich Wolf's anti-Nazi play *Professor Mamlock*, produced by the Federal Theatre Project of the Works Progress Administration, at Daly's Theater in New York, April 13, 1937.

pummeling the industry.[5] On January 1, 1939, the door to Italy was closed completely when the Fascist government took drastic protectionist measures that effectively shut out all Hollywood imports. With more to resent and less to lose, Hollywood's backbone stiffened—or maybe the motion picture industry just shrugged its collective shoulders, figuring that with no percentage in placating the Italians and the Nazis, why not bait them?

As the major studios made tentative incursions into foreign affairs, the actions were cheered or denounced by the interested parties watching from opposite sides of the stands. In a sense, two fifth columns operated behind the scenes in Hollywood—the anti-Nazi activists who sought to inject democratic ideals into Hollywood cinema and the pro-Nazi axis, foreign and domestic, who sought to deflect any criticism, implied or explicit, of Mussolini's Italy and Hitler's Germany. However, not all of the opposition to antifascist moviemaking came from overseas. A third party of native-born opponents staged their protests from the hearing rooms of the United States Congress. When Hollywood fought back against "the Hitler fist" with a few gentle jabs, it was hit with counterpunches from Rome, Berlin, and—in a shot very much below the belt—Washington, D.C.

TROUBLE FROM ROME OVER *IDIOT'S DELIGHT* (1939)

On March 24, 1936, in what looked liked a press agent's plant but was not, the front pages of the New York dailies were filled with the alarming news that Benito Mussolini had nationalized the key defense industries in Italy in preparation for war. "This plan is dominated by one premise," the Italian dictator bellowed, "the inevitability of the nation's being called to war. When? How? Nobody can tell. But the wheels of destiny run fast. This dramatic eventuality must guide all our actions."[6]

That same night, a sold-out crowd packed the Shubert Theater on Broadway for the New York premiere of a new play by Robert E. Sherwood, former film critic, famed playwright, and A-list screenwriter. Mounted by the Theatre Guild, and featuring the first couple of the American stage, Alfred Lunt and Lynn Fontaine, the production was a hot ticket sizzling with advance buzz. Along with Lunt stretching his chops as a music hall hoofer and Fontaine flouncing about in a blonde wig, the playbill promised song, dance, laughter, chorus girls, and social satire literally as timely as the day's headlines. A semi-backstage musical, the plot centered on a theatrical troupe detained by the Italian government in the cocktail lounge of an Alpine hotel. Musical interludes, romance, wisecracks, war profiteering, and international chicanery ensue. "It is definitely anti-Fascist, anti-Nazi, and anti-war, and the audience had an extra thrill because of the prevailing headlines over European news in the papers of the day," noted the *New York Times*.[7]

At the Hollywood office of the Production Code Administration, Joseph Breen's antennae were already tingling. "Please endeavor to see as soon as possible the new Hunt-Fontaine play titled *Idiot's Delight* and telephone me your reaction especially from a policy angle," Breen telegrammed Carl E. Milliken, the New York–based troubleshooter for the Motion Picture Producers and Distributors of America.[8] Perhaps Millikin might combine a bit of business with an evening on the town, Breen suggested, and get back to him with an informal review?

Millikin's review is not recorded in the files of the Breen office, but elsewhere the production met with universal praise. It played for 300 performances on Broadway and enjoyed huge success on the road. It won the Pulitzer Prize for the year's best drama. Naturally, it also attracted the attention of Hollywood producers hungry for a presold property with motion picture potential. Thinking the play a perfect vehicle for Clark Gable and Greta Garbo, MGM scooped up the screen rights and hired Sherwood for the adaptation.

Representatives of the Italian government had also followed the fortunes of *Idiot's Delight* from opening night onward. Upon hearing of the MGM deal, Fulvio Suvich, the Italian ambassador to Washington, immediately contacted Frederick L. Herron, the MPPDA's foreign manager, to communicate his government's displeasure. "Needless to say, if it is made in anything like the form of the stage play, the company producing it will have all their pictures banned in Italy and France, and there will be trouble all over the rest of the world," Herron fretted to Breen. "I imagine that if Metro are going to make it that they will clean it up from the international standpoint, but I think you ought to keep your eyes on the production if and when it occurs because it is full of dynamite."[9] Having already smelled trouble, Breen didn't need Herron to warn him about a possible detonation.

The pressure from foreign governments, continued Herron, was "unfair and ridiculous, but the wall is there and if we expect to sell in those markets we must meet the conditions of such markets. It is their country and they have, of course, a perfect right to say what shall be brought in." After all, U.S. Customs officers and censors in the United States had clamped down on *Ecstasy* (1933), the scandalous German-Czech import that had unveiled Hedy Lamarr dashing *au natural* through nature, "a film acclaimed throughout Europe as a great work of art." Herron poured out his woes to Breen, who was all too familiar with the hyper-sensitivities of foreign nationals:

I had a long talk with the Italian Ambassador in Washington yesterday over many things, among them the trouble over using Bob Sherwood on the scenario of *Marco Polo*. . . . [a] The Ambassador had correspon-

---

[a] Produced by Samuel Goldwyn and directed by Archie Mayo, *The Adventures of Marco Polo* (1938) was a fanciful costume drama starring Gary Cooper as the thirteenth-century explorer who, in a trek from Venice to Peking, discovers spaghetti, gunpowder, and romance. Besides Sherwood's name, it was the errant use of gunpowder in the film that got it banned in Italy.

dence from his Foreign Office in Rome stating that should Bob Sherwood's name appear on that picture, as Marco Polo is considered in Italy
one of their great historical characters, the press of Italy would take the
matter up and the picture if it were shown there be hissed in the theater
and there would be a vicious press campaign that could spread all over
Italy and Italian possessions.

Herron lamented the injustice of the decision, but the Italian ambassador remained unmoved, saying "that Bob Sherwood's name was poison
to the Italians due to the fact that he wrote the stage play *Idiot's Delight*."[10]

Meanwhile, Breen was having problems of his own with the Italian
diplomatic corps on the West Coast. On May 12, 1937, he had lunch with
the Italian consul, Duke Roberto Caracciolo di San Vito, who reiterated
that "his people had been seriously offended" by Sherwood's play, especially the depiction of the Italian officers, and that a screen version would
be "violently opposed" by the Italian government. A former consular officer himself, Breen tried to negotiate with the duke on behalf of MGM.
"After considerable discussion back and forth, the consul authorized me
to state to Metro that if the Company would change the title, and if the
finished picture was inoffensive to Italians, and if, further, as little mention as possible was made of Mr. Sherwood, he felt that he could persuade his government to interpose no further objections to the filming
of this story."

Breen phoned MGM producer Hunt Stromberg and passed on the
Italian's terms. Stromberg refused to sign on, arguing that the title and
playwright were presold assets in the American marketplace and had to
be retained. However, in the spirit of compromise, MGM would be willing to change the title of the film for the Italian release. Moreover, Stromberg promised to make the screen version "thoroughly acceptable to the
Italians and in the [prints] going to Italy, he is willing to delete Mr. Sherwood's name."[11] Practicing a kind of crosstown shuttle diplomacy, Breen
scurried back to the Italian consul with MGM's counterproposal. Both
parties then signed off on the deal.

For Breen and MGM, the pact over *Idiot's Delight* was a job well done.
"Thanks a million for your customarily prompt and marvelous cooperation . . . and if you and I are responsible, via this story, for taking a few
pokes at gentlemen who profit from battle, we'll take time out one these
days to celebrate," Stromberg wrote Breen, expressing gratitude for his

diplomatic initiatives.[12] Having again proven himself Hollywood's indispensible man, Breen must have glowed.

Despite the amicable outcome, however, the near international incident over *Idiot's Delight* was hard to keep secret. "Probably no other subject which has engaged Hollywood attention of late has aroused as much discussion as Robert E. Sherwood's *Idiot's Delight*," reported *Motion Picture Herald*, after noting the all-clear signal from the Breen office. "For a time the planned production threatened international complications. However, all matters have been settled."[13] As usual, the belief was that Hollywood had caved to foreign pressure and defanged the bite of the original. "After much international palavering, *Idiot's Delight* will be filmed with a few slight alterations, such as a new title, a new locale, and a new story," smirked *Daily Variety*. "Outside of that, it will be screened in all its pristine glory."[14]

Just as *Blockade* had to avoid Spanish uniforms, *Idiot's Delight* had to erase any vestiges of Italy, including the Italian language. Rather than resort to gibberish for the dialogue of the soldiers, director Clarence Brown and screenwriter Sherwood hit upon a suitably non-nation-specific lingo to avoid ruffling Italian feathers: Esperanto, with the president of the Esperanto League of America serving as technical advisor.[15] (As with all dialogue on the American screen in whatever language, the Esperanto was then vetted for vulgarity by the PCA.)

The film that resulted from Sherwood's play was not as neutered as *Variety* feared and Italy hoped. Like so many flashbacks from the 1930s, *Idiot's Delight* is haunted by the memory of the Great War, opening with a newsreel montage showing battalions of joyous doughboys marching down Broadway under a shower of ticker tape, a proud nation honoring heroes returning from their gallant crusade Over There. By way of contrast, a ragged army of wounded veterans—amputees on crutches and bandaged men on stretchers, the gristle from the slaughterhouse—disembarks from a troopship to make a less glorious entry into civilian life. As Hollywood tells it, the sequence staged in the studio renders the scarred face of the Great War more realistically than the blithe newsreel record.

Among the walking wounded is Harry Van (Clark Gable), a small-time vaudevillian eager to step back into the spotlight. Versatile though he is—hoofer and huckster, at ease dancing in a chorus line or selling patent medicine on a street corner—his showbiz comeback is not smooth.

While working with a drunken mind reader on the vaudeville circuit in Omaha, he hooks up for a memorable one-night stand with the saucy Irene (Norma Shearer, Garbo being better cast in *Ninotchka* [1939]), a gymnast with a Russian accent that may be fake and a line of patter that certainly is. The couple clicks, but the next morning at the train platform, fate takes them in different directions.

A Slavko Vorkapich montage spins the action two decades forward, tracing the ups and downs of the Jazz Age (for Harry Van, mostly down), the crash of the stock market, and the curse of the Great Depression. Too tenacious to fail for long, Harry lands on his feet fronting a chorus line of six frisky blondes (billed as "les Blondes") on a European tour.

Taking a counterintuitive turn, the effervescent spirit of what seems to be a backstage musical suddenly fizzles. On a train bound to a gig in Geneva, Harry and les Blondes are hauled off at the border, but exactly where and by whom is uncertain. The stranded passengers are ensconced in a grand Alpine hotel, where they will see their fates and backstories intertwine: a young newlywed couple, a raving pacifist, a German scientist, a military man, and a munitions tycoon with a beautiful lady in tow—namely, Irene, the girl from Harry's past, now in blonde wig, putting on aristocratic airs and refusing to recognize her long-ago lover.

The romantic comedy and musical interludes that follow, including a game Gable stretching his safety zone as a song-and-dance man, are foregrounded against the background of war—literally so, for situated below the hotel is a military airstrip. In rear screen projection, roaring airplanes fill the sky like birds of prey, lifting off for bombing raids that the hotel will suffer in kind. As air-raid sirens screech, Harry and les Blondes divert the guests with a sprightly musical number, the pacifist decries a world gone mad, and the munitions tycoon licks his lips at the prospect of windfall profits.

Sherwood's play ended in chaos and death, with Harry and Irene, collateral damage, resigned to their doom, crooning "Onward, Christian Soldiers" as the walls of the hotel cave in around them. ("The din is now terrific," reads Sherwood's curtain-closing stage instructions. "Demolition—bombs, gas-bombs, airplanes, shrapnel, machine guns.") Hedging its bets, MGM concocted two endings for the film, one for domestic consumption, one for international release. The international release is apocalyptic, in tune with the play: as Harry and Irene declare their love, the bombs fall, the hotel crumbles, and the couple are casualties

No Italian accents:
Clark Gable and
Norma Shearer
in MGM's
Idiot's Delight (1939),
Clarence Brown's version
of Robert E. Sherwood's
antiwar play.

of war. MGM previewed the bleak ending and audiences turned thumbs down: no American wanted to see Gable and Shearer blown to bits. The American ending shows the pair in a passionate clinch, resolved to soldier onward—alive.

Idiot's Delight was a solid hit, but the drawn-out negotiations over Sherwood's play meant that its release was delayed until January 1939, vitiating whatever edgy topicality it might have had. By then, the Germans not the Italians were the predatory menace hanging over the European continent. Also, with perverse poetic justice, Hollywood had been forced to withdraw totally from the Italian marketplace after Mussolini nationalized film distribution, so all of MGM's sensitivities to Italian sensitivities were for naught. Besides, the Italians had later decided to preemptively ban *Idiot's Delight*, sight unseen, before its release.[16]

In a postscript to the printed edition of *Idiot's Delight*, written a lifetime ago in the spring of 1936, Sherwood surveyed the harrowing war clouds coughed up by the Italian invasion of Ethiopia, the military occupation of the Rhineland by Hitler, and the Japanese incursions into China, and mused, "What will happen before this play reaches print or a New York audience, I do not know. But let me express here the conviction that those who shrug and say 'War is inevitable,' are false prophets."[17] Three years later, it was Sherwood's hopeful prophecy that sounded idiotic.

TROUBLE FROM BERLIN OVER *THE ROAD BACK* (1937)

A sort-of sequel to *All Quiet on the Western Front*, the film version of which had introduced Hollywood to the ferocity of Nazi film criticism in 1930, Erich Maria Remarque's *The Road Back* was published 1931. Like the original, the novel registered the disgust with war in the aftermath of the Great War. It told the story of a shell-shocked squad of German veterans thrust into the political upheavals and economic chaos of postwar Germany. It might be called a veterans' readjustment story were there a healthy society for the veterans to readjust to.

Although the follow-up did not accrue the sales of *All Quiet on the Western Front*—almost nothing could have—it earned admiration as a worthy successor to the landmark original. "A book that drops like a plummet in the hearts of men," rhapsodized the *New York Times*. "It will be published in twenty-five languages and one must wish that it may be read by every literate man and woman in the world."[18]

Universal grabbed up the film rights, but the daunting expense of the project in the midst of the Great Depression—an estimated $400,000 even without the price tag of $150,000 that came with the obvious choice for director, Lewis Milestone—delayed the project for years. Finally, in 1936, with a screenplay by Charles Kenyon, one of the industry's most reliable script doctors, and British playwright R. C. Sheriff, author of the trench-set deathwatch *Journey's End* (1928), Universal moved firmly into production mode. The studio hoped to relive the prestige and profits from *All Quiet on the Western Front*.[19]

Unlike 1930, however, Hitler had eyes and ears in Hollywood. Tipped off by the trade press, Dr. Georg Gyssling, the vigilant Nazi consul in Los Angeles, contacted the Breen office to raise objections. "It would beyond all doubts lead to controversies and opposition on the part of the German government, as the story gives an untrue and distorted picture of the German people," he wrote. Gyssling urged Breen "to use your influence on behalf of correct relations between the American film industry and Germany" and kill the project.[20]

Having become more than a little sick of Gyssling's interference, Breen ducked his phone calls and ignored his letters. He also gave Universal a friendly heads up.

At Universal, Charles R. Rogers, executive vice president in charge of production, told Breen "the company was not very much concerned about German protests because it was almost impossible for the company to operate in Germany at the present time, and that any business worthwhile worrying about was not being done in Universal in Germany now."[21]

Getting no satisfaction from either Breen or Universal, Gyssling took matters into his own hands and sent out a warning in the form of an epistolary threat to sixty actors signed up to work on the film. To wit:

April 1, 1937

DEUTSCHES CONSULATE
117 West Ninth Street, L.A.
To: (Name of actor)
Universal City, California

Dear Sir:

With reference to the picture, *The Road Back*, in which you are said to play a part, I have been instructed by my government to issue you a warning, in accordance with Article 15 of the German decree of June 28, 1932 regulating the exhibit of foreign motion picture films.

Copy and translation of this article are enclosed herewith.

You will note that the allocation of permits may be refused for films with which persons are connected who have already participated in the production of pictures detrimental to German prestige in tendency or effect in spite of the warning issued by the competent German authorities.

Truly yours,

(signed) Georg Gyssling

Consul

Gyssling had pulled the same stunt the year before with his threatening letter to Isobel Steele, screenwriter-star of *I Was a Captive of Nazi*

Germany (1936). However, *I Was a Captive of Nazi Germany* was an obscure knockoff from an independent producer. *The Road Back* was a prestige literary adaptation from a major studio. Moreover, Gyssling's letter had been sent to the entire cast of *The Road Back*, which guaranteed that shock waves would reverberate throughout Hollywood's talent pool.

Reproduced first in the Hollywood trade press and the Hollywood Anti-Nazi League's *News of the World*, and then in newspapers around the country, Gyssling's letter ignited a furious backlash. Targeting sixty individual actors on stationery embossed with the Nazi eagle was a far more provocative act than applying behind-the-scenes pressure to a no-name independent production. The consul's threat, said the *Hollywood Reporter*, had "aroused American film interests to a high state of resentment against Nazi policies."[22] Actually, not just film interests were aroused. "This isn't a Nazi country, and there's no reason to adopt Nazi standards," huffed the *New York World-Telegram.* [23] The Nazis might bark *streng verboten* at American film people in Berlin, but not in Hollywood—at least not any longer.

At *Motion Picture Daily*, editor Red Kahn, the most reliably anti-Nazi of the trade reporters, hit back hard at Gyssling and his government. Given that "no yardstick can adequately measure the psychopathic vagaries of the Nazi mentality," Kahn wondered "just where is this to end if a crackpot and irrational government, riding the seat of power though ruthlessness and oppression, is to be permitted to waive international and diplomatic courtesy by its unwarranted interference in matters which are none of its business?" Kahn gave credit for the pushback where it was due. "While Universal determined to do the ostrich stunt and preferred a hush-hush policy, certain Hollywood organizations with liberality sprinkled though their backbones, did not."[24]

Of course, the unnamed organization with the stiff backbone was the Hollywood Anti-Nazi League, which, characteristically, had taken point position in the counterattack. Trying hard to conceal its delight beneath its high dudgeon, HANL labeled Gyssling's letter "one of the most insidious examples of Nazi interference in the lives of American citizens." It also sent a telegram to Secretary of State Cordell Hull condemning Gyssling's intimidation tactics and demanding the consul be deported. "This action constituting an infringement on American diplomatic hospitality, we request that you take immediate action toward the removal of the consul and prevention of future occurrences."[25]

Goaded into action, the normally quiescent State Department responded with a formal protest to the German foreign office. It got immediate results: the Nazis backed off. "The German ambassador has instructed the German consul at Los Angeles to refrain from issuing further warnings to American citizens in connection with the production of plays," the State Department informed HANL.[26] Hans-Heinrich Dieckhoff, the new Nazi ambassador in Washington, sweetened the diplomatic victory by issuing a formal apology. He promised that Gyssling's strong-arm tactics would not be repeated. The consul, he said, was merely following orders from former ambassador Hans Luther, who was himself acting on instructions from the Reich Ministry—which Reich Ministry, Dieckhoff did not say.

In truth, Gyssling seems to have been caught in the labyrinthine and sometimes lethal web of Nazi bureaucracy, pinned between Goebbels' Reich Ministry of Popular Enlightenment and Propaganda, the supreme arbiter of all Nazi media matters, and Baron Konstantin von Neurath's Foreign Ministry, nominally in charge of foreign affairs. "I did just what I was advised to do in an order originating in Berlin," Gyssling asserted, denying reports of a rebuke as "just fiction and fabrications not based on any facts."[27]

The threatening letters from the German consul also got Breen's Irish up: it was *he* not the Nazi who laid down the law in Hollywood. While Gyssling flailed, Breen gave Harry Zehner, Universal's liaison with the PCA, the welcome news that "we take pleasure in enclosing Production Code certificate of Approval No. 3137" to *The Road Back*.[28] In a report to Will Hays, he emphasized his personal stamp of approval on the project. "*The Road Back* is an excellent picture. A follow up to *All Quiet on the Western Front*."[29]

As the controversy swirled, production went into high gear. Envisioning another *All Quiet on the Western Front*, and hoping to tap into antiwar sentiment aroused by the turmoil in Europe, Universal spent lavishly but not carelessly on its second Remarque project. Director Lewis Milestone having priced himself out of the running, the studio entrusted the project to its mad doctor of the horror genre, James Whale, the florid director of *Frankenstein* (1932) and *Bride of Frankenstein* (1935), and himself a traumatized survivor of the Great War. Whale ordered three acres of trenches dug on a huge outdoor location and commissioned a 50 by 250–foot matte background, the largest yet built, to simulate the bombed-out moonscapes of no-man's-land. A 120-man technical crew wrangled lights and rigged explosives.[30]

Even with Gyssling muzzled, however, controversy continued to dog the project. Soon after Universal announced completion of the film, *Daily Variety* published a sensational report ("by cable from London") alleging that the print of *The Road Back* slated for release in Germany had been edited to Nazi specifications. J. Cheever Cowdin, chairman of the Universal board, and Gus Schaeffer, the studio's foreign head, were reported to have returned to London from Germany, after a private consultation with Joseph Goebbels. "Following the talk, Goebbels agreed to [a] license [permitting] showing of *The Road Back* on condition that Universal change the ending to glorify Hitler, which it is understood will be done," said the report.

From New York, Universal president R. H. Cochrane angrily denied the meeting with Goebbels or any editing done under the Nazi gun. "A complete falsehood from start to finish," he fumed. "Nothing but malice could have created it." In a cablegram from Europe, Cowdon was equally adamant. "Neither Schaeffer nor I ever met Dr. Goebbels in the first place, and in the second place we have never discussed *The Road Back* with any official in Germany at any time." Cochrane elaborated: "The simple truth is that after showing the picture to the public we decided to add several romantic scenes. Those who have seen both versions say the new one is immeasurably better. Politics and fear had nothing to do with it."[31] Cochrane blamed the report on a disgruntled former employee who had been fired.[32]

Remarque's authorship notwithstanding, Gyssling and the Nazis had little to fear from *The Road Back*. Where *All Quiet on the Western Front* was elegiac and epic, *The Road Back* was toothless and tired. Even so, the Nazis were unhappy with the final cut. For the gala screening held in Washington, D.C., on July 22, 1937, Universal's publicity department (in an obvious setup) sent out special invitations to German ambassador Dieckhoff and his staff. "Members of the goose-stepping embassy staff stayed away in droves," grinned *Variety*, with nary "a single Nazi in the house."[33]

The film the Nazi diplomatic corps shunned opens in the early morning hours of Armistice Day. For a squad of mud-caked, war-weary German soldiers, life in the trenches is grubby and vulgar, full of spit, sweat, grime, bad food, and fear. After years of grueling combat, the men are at the end of their ropes. "It's gotta stop!" wails a psychic wreck. It doesn't, at least not quite then. In the only battle scene in the film, a long tracking shot follows the men over the top, through the concertina wires of no-man's-land, into the mouth of hell.

When news of the Armistice arrives, a montage sequence shows Germans, French, British, and Americans alike celebrating the end of hostilities. To punctuate the utter insanity of war, when the Germans first encounter their former enemy in the persons of a company of fresh-faced, well-provisioned Americans, the first gesture of the Yanks is to offer the Germans cigarettes and chewing gum. "What's the use of fighting decent fellahs like that?" asks a German soldier. "Darn fools we were." Adds a comrade: "And so were they."

Mustered out, the troops enter a politically volatile Germany that has not yet seen the rise of the Nazis, but is certainly being roiled by a group of violent subversives Hollywood is not afraid to indict. "Are you comrades or not?" demands a homefront rabble rouser, marking his band of street thugs not as nascent brownshirts but as communist agitators. Still, the real danger to the well-being of the veterans is the backfire from the past, the psychic meltdown of shell-shocked troops in the grip of what today would be called post-traumatic stress disorder. Warped by four years of killing, the boys are unfit for reentry into civilian life. They wander the streets at night, seeking out each other's company, unable to connect with family, friends, or fiancées. "I must find myself and no one can help me," a shattered survivor tells his girlfriend. Those who did not die on the battlefield have died inside. One crazed veteran is confined in an insane asylum; another, enraged that his unfaithful girlfriend has taken up with a bloated civilian, shoots the man in cold blood. At his trial, the defense pleads mitigating circumstances. "You can't wash four years of killing off the brain with one word—peace!"

In the film's final movement, a newsreel montage tracks the postwar denouement: all the former belligerents are feverishly rearming, all equally culpable, all preparing for a sequel, heedless of the lessons of *All Quiet on the Western Front* and *The Road Back*.

Artistically and commercially, *The Road Back* was no *All Quiet on the Western Front*. Critics strained to find something good to say about the well-meaning, self-serious drama, but they could not deny the tepid response from the crowds. "There is much that is deep and beautiful in *The Road Back*, especially at the present time when banner headlines daily promise the outbreak of another war in Europe in the not too distant future," allowed *Motion Picture Herald*, impressed with Universal's good inten-

Weimar set melodrama I: confronting a clueless home front, a combat veteran (Andy Devine) is forced to surrender his water pistol to his former high school instructor (Al Sheen) in *The Road Back* (1937), James Whale's version of the novel by Erich Maria Remarque.

tions but little else.[b] Attending a matinee at the Globe Theater in New York during its opening week, the reviewer was duty bound to deliver the bad news. "The theater was approximately half filled and the audience was predominantly men, all of whom sat silently as the film unwound, apparently unimpressed at those scenes intended as comic relief, and remained silent as they filed out upon the picture's completion."[34]

Another big-screen version of a well-regarded Remarque novel caused far less of a stir, perhaps because its concern with the backfire from the Great War was subordinate to its wallowing in the passions from a romantic triangle, or quadrangle. Written in 1936, by which time

---

[b] Given a new commentary by screenwriter Gordon Kahn, a montage update of European affairs, and an I-told-you so epilogue, *The Road Back* would be reedited on September 9, 1939, and a new certificate issued for a postwar rerelease.

Remarque was in exile, and published in English in 1937, *Three Comrades* was another psycho-political drama of the residue from the Great War, but the addition of a beautiful girl into the mix put the Hollywood rendering on firmer footing. While the novel was still in galleys, MGM won a fierce bidding war for the film rights only to have second thoughts as it monitored the decline of Universal's *The Road Back*. "*Three Comrades* has political production problems fully as critical, from the showman's angle, as had *The Road Back*," observed *Daily Variety*, by which it meant that overt political reverberations were as problematic for American audiences as for German diplomats.[35] Even so, chastened by his reprimand over *The Road Back*, Gyssling kept mum about the Hollywood version of the subsequent Remarque novel.

Directed by Frank Borzage, *Three Comrades* (1938) is a gauzy period piece, set in Germany after the Armistice but before the uprising of the Nazi Party in Munich in 1923. Like so many interwar flashbacks, it opens precisely on November 11, 1918, Armistice Day, the date scrawled in vapor trails in a skyline establishing shot. In a smoky rathskeller, weary but blissful survivors are toasting the end of the war, raising their glasses to fallen comrades on all sides. The three titular friends—big brotherly Otto (Franchot Tone), idealistic firebrand Gottfried (Robert Young), and strong silent type Erich (matinee idol Robert Taylor) pledge lifelong fidelity on the strength of a bond forged in the crucible of combat. Expert airplane mechanics, they retool for civilian life by opening an automobile repair shop to eke out a living in an economically crippled, spiritually traumatized nation.

One day, taking their beloved souped-up convertible "Baby" out for a cruise in the countryside, a horn-blowing road hog tries to outrace them. The speed demons easily beat out the overweight, arrogant businessman behind the wheel, but his fetching passenger Patricia (a radiant Margaret Sullavan) stops them cold. Defying expectations, the entry of the girl does not break up the male triad, but solidifies it: Otto and Gottfried guide the romantically maladroit Erich through his courtship and protectively embrace Patricia as a sister. Throughout, the usual Code-mandated obscurity falls over the Remarque clarity: Gottfried is an idealist (read: communist) while Patricia's friend (read: sugar daddy) is a Nazi-in-waiting.

In the background of the romantic harmony, the social wreckage of postwar Germany creates a powder keg just waiting for someone to strike the match. Wounded veterans mark time in cafes, roving bands of angry men prowl the streets, and the precious "Baby" is vandalized by thugs. While trying to save his elderly mentor from a howling mob, Gott-fried is shot in the back. Patricia—by now an embodiment of all that was best in bygone Germany—succumbs to that most romantic of terminal illnesses, tuberculosis. In the final image, as fighting again breaks out in their city, Otto and Erich leave Germany for a new life in South America, accompanied by the ectoplasmic forms of Gottfried and Patricia.

Three Comrades was hardly didactic and barely historical, but even three-hankie hokum, if set in Germany, could spark a minor contro-versy. In reviewing the film, *Time* charged that the PCA had compelled the deletion of many anti-Nazi scenes written into the original script by F. Scott Fitzgerald and Edward E. Paramore Jr.—specifically, a scene in which "a poor Jew proclaimed his love for Germany; another in which a rich Jew refrained from cheating three young gentiles; [and] "a scene in which famed books, including Remarque's, were burned by the Nazis." All, claimed *Time*, were deleted.[36]

Weimar set melodrama II: Robert Young, Robert Taylor, Margaret Sullavan, and Fran-chot Tone form a star-crossed romantic quadrangle in MGM's *Three Comrades* (1938), Frank Borzage's version of the novel by Erich Maria Remarque.

Producer Joseph L. Mankiewicz denied the charges: he admitted that the original script contained politically charged material, but pointed out that the 1920–21 setting was prior to the Nazi ascendancy. With the film running long, the studio decided on its own "to delete all sequences which were extraneous to the love story of the film," said Mankiewicz. Neither Breen nor Gyssling played any part in the decisions.[37] Given the primacy of boy-girl stuff in Hollywood melodrama, Mankiewicz offered an all too credible explanation.

A vitriolic review in *Variety*, a rare occurrence for a handsomely mounted A picture from a major studio, had little patience with Hollywood's pat defense: the primacy of entertainment over all else. "There must have been some reason for making this picture, but it isn't in the cause of entertainment," complained John C. Flinn, the paper's high-profile critic. "It provides a dull interlude, and despite all the draught of the star names, it's in for a sharp nosedive at the box office." Flinn argued that time traveling back to the Germany of yore was jarring and off-putting from the jittery perspective of 1938. "In the light of events of the past five years, the background of 1921 in Germany seems like a century ago," Flinn continued. "There is developed in the film no relation between the historical events of that period and the Reich of today. The story is dated and lacks showmanship values of current European movements."[38] Of course, any Hollywood filmmaker who tried to inject the "showmanship values" of "current European movements" into a feature film was impeded by the Breen office and razzed by the reporters at *Variety*. Just ask Walter Wanger.

For all their compromises, however, both *The Road Back* and *Three Comrades* kept faith with the most important of the anti-Nazi blasphemies in the source novels: the Germans were not stabbed in the back but, like the other combatants, had cut their own throats. Even so, the author looked askance at the Hollywood rewrites. After viewing Universal's version of *The Road Back*, he could only mutter, "Well, in any case, it's scarcely Remarquable."[39]

TROUBLE FROM WASHINGTON WITH THE DIES COMMITTEE

In 1938, Martin Dies Jr. was a four-term term Texas Congressman, a Democrat, a disenchanted New Dealer, and man on a mission. In the eyes of Martin Dies, two fifth columns from opposite ends of the ideological spectrum were conspiring to subvert the United States of America. One raised its right arm to Hitler and Nazi Germany under the banner of the German American Bund and the Silver Shirts; the other looked to Stalin and the USSR and plotted sedition at meetings of the Communist Party USA (CPUSA). Both needed to be investigated, exposed, and rooted out of the body politic.

Unlike Joseph McCarthy, a surname forever spat out like a curse, Dies has been largely forgotten to history, but the name of the committee he founded became a permanent part of the lexicon of American culture, the House Committee on Un-American Activities, abbreviated for purposes of pronunciation as HUAC.

Established by Congress in June 1938, HUAC—then called the House Committee for the Investigation of Un-American Activities—was tasked with probing "the extent, character, and objects of un-American propaganda activities" and "all other questions in relation thereto that would aid Congress in any necessary remedial legislation." Dies was appointed chair, and, armed with subpoena power and a squad of G-men, set about implementing his broad mandate. To preempt criticism, he affirmed a commitment to public hearings—his would be no "star chamber proceedings"—and a tightly focused investigation. "This is not going to be any 'shooting in the dark' inquiry," he promised. However, speaking on NBC radio, he left no doubt about who was in his crosshairs. "I cannot understand why the Nazis in the United States do not move to Germany, the Communists, to Russia, and the Fascists, to Italy. The fact that they believe in communism, fascism, or Nazism demonstrates conclusively they do not believe in Americanism."[40]

In point of fact, both the German American Bund and the CPUSA were engaged in deeply un-American activities. The original charge of what quickly became known as the Dies Committee was neither outlandish nor xenophobic. Under the leadership of Fritz Kuhn, a former German machine gunner in the Great War, the German American Bund operated a nationwide network of brownshirt-like paramilitarists who spouted antisemitic venom and agitated for an American Reich. The Bund fit the operative definition of a fifth column, no different, if less brazen and effective, than the Sudeten Deutsch Party that was at that very moment lacerating Czechoslovakia from the inside.

American communists were less enamored of uniforms and regalia, but no less dedicated and far more successful in gaining proximity to the center of American political life. After 1935, under the umbrella of the Popular Front, international communism softened its dogmatic rhetoric and penchant for separatist purity to foster a broader alliance against Nazism. No longer soldiers of an alien ideology emanating from a foreign capital, American communists stressed the native roots of the future revolution. Straining to link the Bolsheviks and the Founding Fathers, Earl Browder, the head of the CPUSA, dreamed up a slick advertising slogan for the brand: "Communism is 20th century Americanism."

Of course, the true mecca for the CPUSA was Moscow not Philadelphia. The pages of the *Daily Worker*, the official newspaper of the American party, and statements by the membership bowed before the cradle of the Marxist revolution, a mythic promised land that more than one member of the Hollywood Anti-Nazi League called Mother Russia. "America rose up and revolted against the tyranny of Old England," declared the actor Melvyn Douglas, very much on message. "The Russian people ended the hundred-year-old tyranny of Czarism."[41]

Even before the Dies Committee hearings, accusations of communist infiltration, often laced with antisemitism, had permeated criticisms of Hollywood. For nativist bigots, the Jewish landlords in the Sodom on the Pacific doubled as agents in a forward operating base for Moscow. Major Frank Pease, a former Hollywood agent, made a second career out of red-baiting and Jew-hating, firing off slanderous telegrams to Hollywood producers and railing against "the Bolshevik temple" built in Hollywood, a phrase that neatly conjoined the alien ideology and non-Christian religion.[42] As prominent actors, screenwriters, and directors moved into the ranks of the Popular Front, their ideological opponents tracked the migration leftward and spouted invective. The Hollywood Anti-Nazi League, the Motion Picture Artists Committee, and kindred celebrity-laden groups found that the magnetic pole that was Hollywood had a minus as well as a plus: the stars attracted attention to the Popular Front cause but attacks on the stars also attracted attention to the attackers. A congressman who went after MGM or Warner Bros. got bigger headlines than a congressman who went after the Farm Security Administration or the Tennessee Valley Authority.

Shortly after its founding in 1936, the Hollywood Anti-Nazi League felt obliged to respond to the accusations. "The League is . . . not surprised that charges of Communist have been directed against it . . . nor is it concerned," declared an editorial in the *Anti-Nazi News*. "We would however regret it if some of our friends and well wishers were to fall into this old

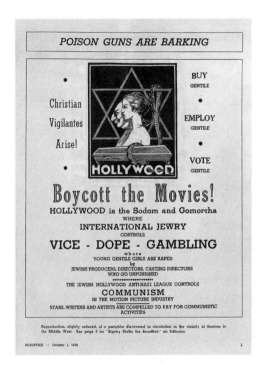

From Berlin to Hollywood: the notorious leaflet dropped from the Garland Building in Los Angeles, September 1938).

Nazi trap. Frightened by the Communist bugbear some of them have rushed to us with the sincerest and best intentions suggesting that we make the league anti-communist as well as anti-Nazi." But HANL refused to be distracted from its core mission, vowing in capital letters: "THIS LEAGUE IS DEDICATED UNALTERERABLY AND EXCLUSIVELY TO FIGHT NAZISM AND NOTHING WILL DIVERT IT FROM THAT ONE AIM." It then affirmed what was patently false: "Not one member of the executive committee is a member of the Communist party."[43]

The whispered love affair between Moscow and Hollywood was amplified dramatically when, beginning on August 12, 1938, Dies brought his gavel down on a series of public hearings that stretched through the dog days of summer. The investigation cast a wide net—over communism and Nazism, labor unions and theater groups, New Deal agencies and paramilitary outfits. The tumultuous political activity of the 1930s provided the committee with plenty of headline-grabbing material. As usual, however, the glamorous workers on the studio soundstages garnered more copy than the prosaic laborers on the shop floors.

"Radical and communist activities are rampant among the studios of Hollywood":
Martin Dies Jr. (D-TX), first chairman and founding member of the House Committee
on Un-American Activities, with his son Bobby, rings down the gavel on hearings in
Washington, D.C., August 13, 1938.

The first day of hearings focused on the German American Bund
and the revelations of the brothers John and James Metcalfe, who had
infiltrated the group and uncovered a "vast spy network" augmented by
a "powerful sabotage machine." The brothers revealed that Fritz Kuhn
boasted of his pull with Adolf Hitler, whom he claimed was grooming
him as the *führer* in a future American Reich.

On the communist side, the less disciplined cadres of the Federal
Theatre Project offered a tantalizing target. Basically a make-work project for playwrights, directors, and actors willing to stage shows in line
with New Deal policies, the FTP favored playbills that smacked of party-
line inspiration featuring cast members who subverted American values
more sacred than capitalism. The committee heard disturbing testimony
about "white girls dancing with colored men" at cast parties and, in one
instance, a black man asking a white singer out on a date.

Yet Hollywood, with bigger names and pocketbooks, was the inevitable destination. On August 14, committee investigator Edward F. Sullivan
fired the first broadside at the motion picture industry. Though Sullivan
devoted most of his testimony to non-Hollywood subversion, notably the

activism of firebrand labor organizer Harry Bridges, West Coast leader of the Committee for Industrial Organization (CIO), the Hollywood angle siphoned off most of the press ink. "Evidence tends to show that all phases of radical and communist activities are rampant among the studios of Hollywood and, although well known, is a matter which the movie moguls desire to keep from the public," he testified. "A number of film celebrities are using their large salaries to finance communistic activities including groups which were conducting agitation campaigns in agricultural regions in California. I might say in passing that a very large number of motion picture stars are strongly opposed to all this subversive activity but, as one very prominent star told me, if he spoke out loud about the situation, he would soon be ditched by the studios and a campaign of vilification would be started against him."

Sullivan did not accuse either the Hollywood Anti-Nazi League or the Motion Picture Artists Committee by name but HANL president Donald Ogden Stewart was happy to pick up the gauntlet. "It is ominous that the Dies investigating committee has adopted the practice of making accusations without revealing facts to substantiate them," he declared in a written statement. "When Hitler is mobilizing a million men at the Czechoslovakian borders, when another investigator of the Dies committee finds that the National Guard is being invaded by the Nazi Bund, and there is an effective German spy ring throughout the country, these charges leveled at an organization devoted to the task of combating Nazism are in themselves a threat to democracy."[44] An indignant statement from MPAC also rejected the "irresponsible attacks" and cheekily demanded "an investigation of the investigation."[45] *Hollywood Now* went over the Sullivan report line by line and concluded: "On the basis of Sullivan's own report, he brands himself as a liar, an anti-Semite, a red-baiter, and a pro-Nazi who is trying to divert attention from Nazi activities by smearing the organizations that fight Nazism."[46]

Seeing the Dies Committee hearings as a danger to all of Hollywood and not just to its leftmost flank, mainstream voices in the industry also spoke out against Dies and company. "Who is this fellow Sullivan who made such a wild bellow in front of the Dies committee the other day in Washington?" demanded Billy Wilkerson from his forum in the *Hollywood Reporter*.[47] Director Willard S. Van Dyke, president of the Academy of Motion Picture Arts and Sciences and vice president of the Screen Directors' Guild, called Sullivan "a very common liar" for tarring Hollywood as a "hotbed of communism." MGM producer John W. Considine sardonically welcomed a complete investigation of the backlots by the Dies Committee so that "the world will realize that we are busy making motion pictures here—we haven't time to act any 'ism'—Nazi, Fascist, or Red."[48] Speaking of isms, the Dies Committee hearings inspired Dorothy Parker to utter one of her most quotable *bon mots*: "The only ism Hollywood is interested in is plagiarism."

Yet as Dies rode to prominence on Hollywood's back, the official voice of the motion picture industry—the MPPDA—was conspicuously silent. Outraged that the MPPDA was leaving it to HANL to defend the integrity of the industry, Billy Wilkerson asked, "Why should an investigating committee sent out from Washington with preconceived notions brand the industry as COMMUNISTIC without having one or a group of creators answering for the industry's protection?"[49]

The answer, besides the fact that wilting at the first sight of political heat was the MPPDA's default mode, was that the association had far more serious Washington-bred problems to deal with than the Dies Committee. Earlier, on July 20, 1938, the Department of Justice had filed a civil suit in New York against the eight major Hollywood studios, charging the industry with monopolistic practices in restraint of trade and seeking to sever the ties between production and exhibition—a stake into the heart of the vertically integrated business. At the same time, in the U.S. Senate, Matthew M. Neely (D-WV) was proposing legislation to ban "block booking," a venerable industry practice in which exhibitors were forced to buy a whole slate of films from a studio, often sight unseen, in order to obtain the top attractions. The Dies Committee hearings were held when both the executive and legislative branches of FDR's New Deal threatened, as an alarmed notice in the *Hollywood Reporter* warned, to "police the industry from camera to projector."[50] Dies might tar Hollywood's image, but the rest of the New Deal seemed poised to deliver a lethal body blow.

At this juncture, the Dies Committee committed an unforced error that changed the game. On August 22, 1938, Dr. James B. Matthews, a former communist organizer now working for the other side, testified that "the Communist party relied heavily on the carelessness or indifference of thousands of prominent citizens in lending their names for its propaganda purposes." In the long-range plans fomented from Moscow, stars were well-meaning dupes with open checkbooks and photogenic faces. "For example, the French newspaper *Ce Soir*, which is owned outright by the communist party, recently featured hearty greetings from Clark Gable, Robert Taylor, James Cagney, and even Shirley Temple." That last name was the gaffe that launched a thousand quips. Matthews hastened to add that he was not accusing the named stars ("No one I hope, is going to claim that any one of these persons in particular is a Communist."), but his disclaimer was lost in the delicious incongruity of the carrot-topped moppet doubling as a red agent for Stalin.

The Dies Committee was drenched in a flood of ridicule. "About everybody in Hollywood except Mickey Mouse, Charlie McCarthy, and Snow White has been signed up for [the] sake of names in some Communist front organization," crowed *Variety*.[51] Picket lines of communist women dressed in short skirts and licking lollypops carried placards reading "Tut! tut! Mr. Dies. Shirley Temple Is Not Subversive." Secretary of Labor Frances Perkins chided the congressman for "the preposterous revelations of your committee in regard to this innocent and likable child."[52] Editorial cartoonists, columnists, and radio wisecrackers relished the image of the subpoenaed tyke being hauled before the Dies Committee for a grilling by the cigar-chomping chairman. Even the conservatives at *Motion Picture Herald* found the notion of America's ten-year-old sweetheart being a Comintern mouthpiece a bit much. "Little Shirley Temple has been 'boring from within' for the Communists, helping the Moscow reds take over the country?" it asked incredulously. "Little Shirley—whose reputation heretofore has been boring from without?"

Humiliated and infuriated, Dies went on radio to set the record straight, angrily comparing Matthews' actual testimony to the press accounts, but no amount of damage control could beat back the derision. "Without question, the Shirley Temple incident was the most reprehensible of the period," recalled Dies years later, still steaming. "The treatment can only be explained as ignorance or deliberate falsehood; those who wrote that Dr. Matthews had called Shirley Temple a Communist left no alterative."[53]

Riding the momentum, HANL announced a rally and issued a challenge:

Because the Dies committee has abandoned its sworn purpose of investigating subversive activity we intend to carry on the fight by holding a mass meeting August 24 in the Philharmonic Auditorium in Los Angeles and we are challenging the Dies committee to present substantiation of these so-called charges at this public meeting so that they may be answered openly and democratically. Failure to meet our challenge can only be interpreted as a misuse by the Dies committee of public funds to aid reactionary Fascist interests, contrary to the law.[54]

Dies, Sullivan, and Matthews never showed up, but some 3,000 Hollywood anti-Nazis packed the auditorium to demand the abolition of the Dies Committee. It was a convivial and rowdy affair, punctuated by laughter, jeers, and sing-alongs. "Fellow subversive elements," began Assemblyman Jack Tenney, president of the musician's union, "I have just heard that Mickey Mouse is conspiring with Shirley Temple to overthrow the government and that there is a witness who has seen the 'Red' card of Donald Duck." Donald Ogden Stewart took the stage to banter and bait. "Folks, I didn't mean to be a Red," he mock-apologized. "I want to tell you how it all happened. Three years ago I was just a good screenwriter—at least I had a three-car garage and a tennis court. Dorothy Parker asked me to join the Hollywood Anti-Nazi League. Then I learned a lot of things about Nazism." Whether carried away by anger at the Dies Committee or the rush of his own rhetoric, Ogden then outed himself ideologically:

> I learned that Nazism had to do with civil liberties and the suppression of labor's rights. The Communist position began to eat into my soul. I found myself questioning editorials in the *Times*. So here I stand before you tonight—one of those things.

The musical portion of the evening was provided by Ray Mayer, Jack Albertson, and Billy Griffith, who sang a number from the MPAC show *Sticks and Stones*, "It Can Happen Over There, But It Can't Happen Here," accompanied by John Green, pianist and composer. The crowd called the quartet back for four encores.[55]

Yet for all the laughter and ridicule heaped upon the Dies Committee, the hearings had done their work. Tarred from the halls of Congress as a launching pad for communist subversion, Hollywood was ever more suspect as a Jewish citadel up to no good. Blaming any spike in antisemitism on the excesses of the New Deal, Dies tried to distance himself from the bigots. On the streets of Los Angeles, however, the antisemitism kicked up by the hearings was literally blown into the faces of pedestrians.

In September 1938, a pro-Nazi fanatic scattered antisemitic leaflets from the top of the Garland Building in downtown Los Angeles. Illustrated with the slick graphics of Reich Ministry propaganda (a hook-nosed Jew, a Star of David, and a serpent entwining an Aryan female), the leaflets boldfaced the usual slurs. "Hollywood is the Sodom and Gomorrha where International Jewry Controls Vice-Dope-Gambling," read the copy. "Where Young Gentile Girls are Raped by Jewish Producers, Directors, Casting Directors." The very skies of Los Angeles were now spewing antisemitic venom.

Red Kahn, who had left his perch at *Motion Picture Daily* to edit the glossy trade weekly *Box Office*, devoted several articles and editorials to the incident. Big names from throughout the industry bombarded *Box Office* with telegrams condemning the rain of Nazi propaganda on the streets of Los Angeles. Pete Harrison suggested that "the vicious propaganda" should be counterattacked from the motion picture screen. "There should be produced a single reel with some of the most prominent moving picture stars delivering a speech to picture audiences, assuring the American people that there is no communism in Hollywood."[56] Yet the fact that the leaflets warranted a refutation was a confirmation of how thickly the air had become permeated with their contents.

On October 3, 1938, NBC gave Donald Ogden Stewart free airtime to respond to the Dies Committee. At 9 p.m., from KECA in Los Angeles, speaking over a nationwide radio hookup in his role as chairman of HANL, Stewart lambasted Dies in what the *Hollywood Tribune* described as "a stinging coast-to-coast broadcast revealing the falsity of the unspeakable accusations against a small group of Americans who are lawfully opposing the obscene doctrines of Hitlerism. His address was a vigorous and forthright attack against the sworn enemies of democracy."[57]

Nonetheless, in the wake of the Dies Committee hearings, some prominent moguls took pains to distance themselves from HANL. "We've got Communists in Hollywood drawing down $2500 a week," claimed MGM chieftain Louis B. Mayer. "Some of them are great writers, who are demanding 'free expression' in their work for pictures. The industry knows who they are and knows too that they are financed and supported by the Third Internationale.[c] The industry has fought them in

---

[c] "The Third Internationale" was another name for the Comintern, the Communist International, founded in 1919 to foment communist revolution worldwide.

the past and stopped them from spreading their pernicious propaganda through motion pictures, which are the greatest molder of public opinion that ever existed."[58] Twentieth Century-Fox head Darryl F. Zanuck asserted that of the 30,000–40,000 workers in the motion picture industry, only a few were rotten apples who gave the rest a bad name. "I do not deny that a few in Hollywood get out the pink shirt now and then. They promptly get splattered over the nation's front pages, and Hollywood is branded communistic," said a frustrated Zanuck. "But actually these people are in an infinitesimal minority. They no more represent the industry than does one drop of water represent a lake."[59]

After finishing the hearings in September the Dies Committee threatened to take its investigation to the scene of the crime—Hollywood—but a lack of funds forestalled the road show.[60] However, it soon revived to prove one of Congress's longest running acts. Throughout 1939 and 1940, despite fierce opposition from the Roosevelt administration, the Dies Committee continued its campaign against un-American activities, left and right, with Hollywood never far from its sights. Chairman Dies kept up the drumbeat in articles for *Liberty* magazine, with scarifying titles like "The Reds in Hollywood" and "Is Communism Invading the Movies?"

But by then it was Washington not Hollywood that was out of synch with the public mood. As war roiled and then erupted in Europe, subsequent congressional investigations, in either the House or the Senate, inspired more defiance than dread from the investigated. "The Dies witch hunt is on again," sneered HANL in 1939, unleashing a metaphor from 1692 that would prove repeatedly serviceable. "It is the same old witch hunt of last year, decked out with a new name and a new 'menace' to attract new attention. This time the quarry is 'pressure groups anxious to get America embroiled in Old World feuds and quarrels,' according to a Dies statement to the press while in Los Angeles."[61] The next year, *Variety* suggested that the Academy of Motion Picture Arts and Sciences should grant Dies a special Oscar for his performance. The classification would read: "For Best Original Melodrama by a Non-Professional."[62]

9

INSIDE NAZI GERMANY WITH THE *MARCH OF TIME*

O nce a featured attraction, the *March of Time* (1935–1951) is remembered today, if remembered at all, as the template for the first mockumentary in American film history, the sly send-up that jump-starts Orson Welles's *Citizen Kane* (1941) scant seconds after the title character gasps his last word. A faux précis of the life of the fictional media baron Charles Foster Kane, the mini-biopic cops a style once instantly recognizable, now a joke lost on the unhip. Truth to tell, a member of the first-run audience who sauntered in a few minutes late might have taken the phony for the original. The fake archival footage doctored to type (Welles and cinematographer Gregg Toland stomped on the raw film stock to mar the celluloid with the scratches and glitches that betoken age), the stentorian bombast of a narrator addressing mere mortals from the clouds of Mount Olympus (voiced by Mercury Player William Allard doing a pitch-perfect imitation of Westbrook Van Voorhis, the *March of Time's* pompous orator), and the circuitous ass-backwards syntax of *Time* magazine-speak ("For forty years appeared in Kane newsprint . . . ") created a note-for-note counterfeit of awesome mimesis. "News—on the March!" blares the voice-over in basso profundo, echoing the signature sign-off of the original: "Time—marches on!"

Debuting on February 1, 1935, distributed monthly by RKO to some 11,000 theaters worldwide, the *March of Time* newsreel, as it was often mislabeled, presented a ripe target for parody: stuffed with its own importance, strutting its print-based lineage, and lording its superior intelligence over the comedy shorts and travelogues it bid to supplant on the motion picture program. Modesty never became the house of publisher Henry R. Luce, the nonfictional media baron who launched an authentic revolution in screen journalism when he adapted *Time* magazine and the *March of Time* radio series for the motion picture theater.[1] One reason was in the title: time. The other was in the journalistic ethos: the *March of Time* embraced the controversial news of the day that the newsreels shunned.

The twice-weekly issues of the five commercial newsreels clocked in at ten minutes or so, barely enough running time for a moviegoer to read the intertitles as a dizzying cascade of images flashed by in rapid-fire review, a smorgasbord of political headlines, photogenic disasters, royal pageantry, glamorous celebrities, adorable critters, sports highlights, fashion tips, and amateur performers with dubious musical talents. On occasion, when the inherent drama or eye-popping spectacle warranted, the newsreel companies expanded from one to two reels with the release of a longer-form "special issue" devoted exclusively to a single momentous event—the trial of Bruno Richard Hauptmann, the kidnapper and murderer of the Lindbergh baby; the explosion of the zeppelin *Hindenburg*; or the Japanese attack on the American warship *Panay* on the Yangtze River—but the release patterns were as unpredictable as the breaking news stories. For in-depth coverage and intelligent commentary, the well-informed citizen read a good newspaper, listened to the radio, or pored over the weekly articles in *Time*, *Liberty*, and *Newsweek*.

In contrast to the drive-by shooting of the newsreels, the *March of Time* took things slow and steady, trading on the aura of gravitas inherited from the parent company. Not being up against a twice-a-week deadline, the editors enjoyed the luxury of time—time for background, context, and rumination. They sifted through archival footage ("library stock" in the jargon of the day) and exploited the still novel mnemonic kick of film footage seen long ago and now replayed to jog the cinematic memory of the moviegoer. In the mid-1930s, the record of the past preserved on newsreel film would fill only a small warehouse—maybe a garage—but the *March of Time* was a pioneering custodian and re-presenter of the past as captured by the motion picture camera.

When library stock or current footage was unavailable, staged reenactments of passable verisimilitude filled in the narrative gaps, sometimes with paid actors, often with the real-life personalities only too flattered to play their part on screen. Intercut with the library stock, the reenacted vignettes may or may not have been mistaken for the real thing by unso-phisticated viewers, but sharp-eyed trade critics noted the reenactments and purists lambasted the playacting.

Hectoring though its Voice of God narration was, off-putting though its puffed-up self-regard might be, the *March of Time* was as responsible as any film title for the First Amendment protections ultimately granted screen journalism. In 1937 the Academy of Motion Picture Arts and Sci-ences expressed its appreciation for the luster the series lent the medium with the award of a special Oscar "for its significance to motion pictures and for having revolutionized one of the most important branches of the industry—the newsreel." The next year, the National Archives in Wash-ington, D.C., hailed the *March of Time* as the "best medium for transmit-ting a record of contemporary life to future generations" and established a special archive to preserve the reels.[2]

Never modest about its own accomplishments, the Luce empire touted the difference its motion picture branch made to screen journalism. In 1936, to celebrate the first anniversary of its cinematic offspring, the edi-tors of *Time* published a slick folio and publicity sheet entitled "Four Hours a Year." Gazing down from on high, the *Time* machine indicted the craven newsreels. "The most stultifying self-imposed censorship ever known to journalism blanketed the existing output" of the newsreel, especially regarding its shameful blacking out of the face of Nazism. "For nearly a year, in 1934, there was an unofficial but strikingly thorough ban on Hitler's voice and picture in U.S. theaters," it pointed out correctly. "Controlled by the fiction-magnates of Hollywood, the newsreel was required only to sidestep trouble." Fortunately, "the public's avid appetite for newsreels"—that is, for authentic, hard-hitting screen journalism—would be served by a bolder reporter. With the "lords of Hollywood" para-lyzed, "*Time* saw its opportunity."[3]

The boast on the *March of Time* title card ("a new kind of pictorial jour-nalism") was not just bluster. Unlike the newsreels, a sidebar chronically averse to agitating an audience prior to the featured attraction, prone to fawn or flinch before government officials or conservative exhibitors, the *March of Time* delighted in roiling the waters. In the context of the 1930s, the topics the series tackled were daring, edgy, and boundary-pushing. "What principally distinguishes *March of Time* is its outspokenness, its fearlessness, its production qualities and its desire to remain impartial, yet painting as accurate a picture as it can of the current topics selected for coverage," judged *Variety*. Abel Green, *Variety*'s editor, placed the screen magazine in a class of its own. "More than a newsreel . . . it's a most skillful visualization of important and little known news happenings."[4]

The auteur of the *March of Time*, the man whose vision and tenacity made the series meet its monthly deadline, was not Henry Luce, the tycoon behind the *Time-Life* media empire, but Louis de Rochemont, a veteran newsreel man turned documentary pioneer. Raymond Fielding, the historian of the *March of Time* series, described him as "the general in the front office, providing the will, the energy, and the central idea which propelled the *March of Time* to success and prominence."[5] Besides command and control, however, he also sold and promoted, shilling the series with the vigor of a studio ad-pub boy.

De Rochemont was hired by Roy E. Larsen, vice president of the *Time* empire, and second only to Luce in influence. In a burst of multimedia synergy, Larsen launched the radio and motion picture versions of the magazine, in 1931 and 1935, respectively. Of the nonprint aspects of the Luce empire, he took a propriety interest. "When it came to the *March of Time* and movies and radio, [Luce] was my partner," Larsen recalled. "In everything else, I was his."[6]

In 1934, Larsen lured de Rochemont away from Fox Movietone to join the editorial staff of *Time* and become vice president and production manager for the project on the drawing board. De Rochemont was then the dashing embodiment of the intrepid globetrotting newsreeler. In 1922 he had covered the destruction of the Smyrna by Kemal Atatürk; in 1924, the opening of the tomb of King Tutankhamen; and in 1930, the British Raj in India. To Larsen's knack for media cross-pollination, he brought a cameraman's eye and practical experience to the job of filmmaking. In September 1937, when Larsen left the *March of Time* to take the reins of *Life*, the company's newly launched platform for photojournalism, de Rochemont became general manager in charge of all motion picture activities. By then, he had also picked up Larsen's gift for promotion.

The *March of Time*'s courtship of controversy was abetted by its relative immunity from censorship, whether external (from the state) or internal (from the studio system). In 1935, when the *March of Time* was launched, the Motion Picture Producers and Distributors of America considered bringing the series under the aegis of the Production Code Administration. After all, the MPPDA reasoned, the use of dramatic reenactments qualified the series for the same scrutiny as other short subjects. Yet its "pictorial journalism" shingle, Lucean lineage, and somber approach made even the Hays office balk. Unique among shorts, the *March of Time* escaped oversight from Joseph I. Breen.[7]

State and city censorship boards were not as deferential. The *March of Time*'s penchant for controversy dismayed official censors while testing the limits of their authority. The right of the boards to censor motion pictures for moral transgressions was conceded, but the censorship of a news medium for political commentary was a gray area contested as an abridgment of free expression. Unaccustomed to dealing with hard-hitting, opinionated screen journalism, the boards vacillated—alternately clamping down and letting slide, bowing to pressure and then folding under backlash.

A typical dustup occurred in the wake of FDR's proposal to expand the membership of the Supreme Court from nine to thirteen members, an ill-fated scheme to pack the judicial branch with justices friendlier to his New Deal agenda. In a report from its April 1937 issue entitled "Number Nine," the *March of Time* aired both sides of the uproar set off by FDR's gambit. The president was shown speaking in favor of the measure in a fireside chat and Sen. Burton K. Wheeler (D-MT) was shown speaking for the opposition. Unimpressed by the evenhandedness, the Kansas State Board of Review, chaired by a staunch New Dealer named Mae Clausen, demanded that the *March of Time* eliminate the remarks by Senator Wheeler. "We feel this dialogue is partisan and biased," Miss Clausen informed the regional RKO distributor, who complied and cut the senator's response—thereby igniting a coast-to-coast firestorm.

As Miss Clausen was deluged with criticism from the nation's newspapers, the *March of Time* garnered reams of front-page coverage and editorial support. "To the best of our knowledge, this is the first time that a statement on a national political issue by an accredited authority like a United States Senator has been censored from the screen by a State Board," responded de Rochemont, before making a calculated comparison. "We are used to censorship like that in our foreign editions (by foreign powers) but it's new to us here." The *New York Herald Tribune* picked up on the theme. "Miss Clausen has functioned precisely as a state censor in Berlin, Moscow, or Rome would have functioned to give her leader the limelight and his critics 'the works.'"[8] Chastened, Miss Clausen backed off and cleared the reel for release.

The pattern was repeated throughout the 1930s: the *March of Time* would spark a controversy, a censor board would attempt to cut or ban the offending issue, the decision would be roundly condemned by editorials around the country, and the besieged board would then hastily, shamefacedly, beat a retreat. The *March of Time* got publicity and esteem; state censorship of screen news got derision and discredit.

In September 1936 the *March of Time* released a report whose forthright editorializing heightened the contrast with the mealy-mouthed newsreels. Entitled "The Lunatic Fringe," the issue dissected a trio of Great Depression–bred demagogues: the geriatric pension fund planner Dr. Francis E. Townsend; the antisemitic radio priest Father Charles E. Coughlin, and the fanatical preacher Gerald L. K. Smith, self-appointed successor to the assassinated Sen. Huey L. Long (D-LS).[a] The segment focused on the megalomaniacal Smith, who obligingly performed for the camera, providing de Rochemont with raw footage aplenty to harpoon the blowhard. In a visual vignette fraught with transatlantic reverberations, Smith sits at a table lighting and blowing out matches, a gesture that dissolves into newsreel shots of Mussolini and Hitler fanning the flames of hatred. Rehearsing his tirades before a mirror, haranguing the viewer in blurry tight close-up, Smith seems more cartoon than menace. Still, "in Gerald Smith's sweating, bombastic oratory, serious commentators see the makings of a Fascist dictator," notes the *March of Time*'s own serious commentator. The coda shows the tireless Smith in a railroad sleeping car yammering at train conductors and disturbing the sleep of weary travelers. As the locomotive screeches down the tracks, Smith's ear-splitting voice is still hollering on the soundtrack.

Following the trail to its source, the *March of Time* shifted its sights from cantankerous domestic demagogues to the more sinister versions overseas. Unlike Gerald L. K. Smith, however, Adolf Hitler was not about to perform like a trained seal for the American newsreels. A personality profile followed by an exclusive interview being impossible, the *March of Time* settled for a behind-the-scenes look at his Reich.

---

[a] In April 1935 the *March of Time* had profiled Long, the self-styled "Kingfish" of Louisiana. Depicted as part country bumpkin, part bayou *führer*, he was said to preside over a "decidedly un-American dictatorship." The state of Louisiana banned the issue. ("Huey a Film Censor Now? Kidding Subject Deleted from 'Time' in N.O.," *Variety*, Apr. 24, 1935: 1, 58.)

From the beginning, the *March of Time* was not content to cede coverage of Hitler and Nazi Germany to radio and newspapers or, like the newsreels, to look away. The Nazi dictator first came under the lens of the *March of Time* in its second issue, released March 1935, when the newsreels were observing a virtual moratorium on Hitler imagery. Titled "Berchtesgaden, Bavaria!," the report is the last and longest segment of a five-segment program. Silhouetted in shadows, sitting glumly, ominously, in a chair, an Adolf Hitler stand-in plots German rearmament and territorial expansion. "In two short years, Adolf Hitler has lost for his country what Germany had nearly regained—the world's sympathy," says Van Voorhis. Shots of Hitler mesmerizing a crowd of 500,000 and of steel mills firing up for munitions production show why this "lone strange man" has made all of Europe nervous and fearful, feelings an American moviegoer in 1935 had good reason to share.

The wide-awake look at Hitler in the *March of Time* contrasted sharply with the willful blindness of the newsreels. The Lucians played up the difference, goading the newsreels for their cowardice and highlighting the fortitude of the screen magazine. "Unplanned, unorganized, unknown to movie audiences, what amounts to a national ban on pictures of Adolf Hitler has been in existence in the United States for many a month," claimed a publicity release from the screen magazine in March 1935. "The motion picture trade is well aware of it, yet no one will admit or deny it. The fact remains but for rare fleeting glimpses, the screens of this country have not shown pictures of Hitler, nor have the movie theater loudspeakers resounded with his voice, for well over a year."[9]

The *March of Time* promised to end the conspiracy of silence. "We feel that Hitler is too important a figure to be ignored," declared Roy E. Larsen. "But for exceptional rare, brief glimpses, Hitler has not been seen on U.S. cinema screens, yet he is the topic of many discussions, his actions are internationally significant. Nothing can give so clear a picture of this, or any man, as talking pictures." The newsreels howled their denials ("It's a lie!" shouted back Cortland Smith, editor of RKO-Pathé) and pointed out that the *March of Time*, having no cameraman of its own in Berlin, relied totally on the newsreels of Fox Movietone for its library stock.[10]

Although not exactly giving blanket coverage to Germany, the *March of Time*, true to its word, kept an eye on the story. In June 1936, in a segment on the former glory of the Austro-Hungarian Empire, Van Voorhis speculated that the territorial greed of Hitler and Mussolini was the main impediment to a restoration of the royal line of the Hapsburgs. During a screening at Radio City Music Hall, a showpiece picture palace whose mainstream clientele was less given to raucous outbursts than the news-hounds of the Embassy Newsreel Theater, the crowd hissed at images of the two dictators.[11]

Seldom did the *March of Time* lose an opportunity to snipe at the Nazis. In June 1937, in a report on "Poland and War," the narration chronicles the many "covetous enemies" that have blighted Poland's tragic history and names the predatory nation most likely to do so again. "All Poles know that Adolf Hitler wants both Danzig and the Polish Corridor."

Already more aggressive and comprehensive than anything in the newsreels, the preliminary encounters served as warm-ups to the most controversial and comprehensive motion picture report on Nazi Germany in the 1930s. Issued in January 1938, the *March of Time*'s "Inside Nazi Germany" was a revelation and a provocation. It exposed what the rest of American cinema kept under wraps.

The behind-the-scenes footage that was the reel's inspiration and exploitation angle was shot by the roving cameraman Julien Bryan. A well-known explorer and lecturer, Bryan took his camera to exotic parts of the world and returned stateside to show the footage and talk about his adventures in a kind of chautauqua-with-film. In 1936, at Carnegie Hall, he presented a show of "all new motion pictures" entitled *Soviet Russia 1935*, a must-see for starry-eyed communists.[12]

Having secured entry into one totalitarian regime, Bryan angled for admission to another. As Bryan told the story, he was attending a function at the German Embassy in Istanbul when a Nazi officer berated him for the anti-Nazi bias in the American newsreels. Sensing an opening, Bryan countered that the newsreels were not permitted access to the marvels of the new Germany. If the Nazis wanted a fair shake, why not allow him into the country?[13]

To Bryan's surprise, the Nazis took the bait. Arriving in Germany in September 1937, he shot some 25,000 feet of footage, all under Nazi supervision, about 1,000 of which (about 11 minutes) was incorporated into the issue.

In the prepublicity buildup for the release, de Rochemont gave the pro-saic arrangement between Bryan and the Nazis a cloak-and-dagger spin. He maintained that Bryan shot the film surreptitiously and then, "after escaping Nazi censorship," smuggled the footage out of Germany by way of Latvia.[14] The magazine branch of Luce's empire printed the same cover story. *Life* repeated the claim that "its editors believe [it] to be the first uncensored film ever brought out of Nazi Germany," a fortuitous happenstance attributed to "Propaganda Minister Goebbels [being] presumably too busy with Mussolini's visit to Berlin [in September 1937] to notice what was getting by his censors."[15] Not much got by Goebbels, but the skullduggery lent "Inside Nazi Germany" the cachet of smuggled goods.

The issue lived up to another part of the publicity buildup. On behalf of the *March of Time*, RKO sent out a press release that cast the issue in starkly anti-Nazi terms. "*March of Time* cameramen survey the scenes unknown to tourists," it bragged. "The propaganda machine is shown functioning. . . . The sequestration of the Jews, banned by state edict from professions and business, is pictorially revealed, as is Hitler's attempt to break down Catholic and Protestant resistance."[16] In truth, "Inside Nazi Germany" contained little in the way of pictorial revelation—Bryan's camera was not hidden and he shot under the watchful eyes of Nazi handlers—but for the first time on screen a magnifying glass was

"Jews are not welcome here": cameraman Julien Bryan stole a quick glimpse of Nazi signage in the *March of Time*'s landmark episode "Inside Nazi Germany," released in January 1938. (Photo by Julien Bryan/Courtesy the United States Holocaust Memorial Museum, Washington, D.C.)

held over a totalitarian nation bent on oppression at home and aggression abroad. That in itself was news.

The issue opens on a note of deceptive serenity, for all the world like one of the chirpy travelogues that the screen magazine often supplanted on the motion picture program. "Show window of Adolf Hitler's Nazi Germany today is its capital city, Berlin," begins Van Voorhis in the patented reverse predicate syntax that *Citizen Kane* lampooned to such devastating effect three years later. Shots of a picture-postcard Germany give the nation its scenic due: the Brandenburg Gate, the Zoological Gardens, and the outdoor cafes along the Ku'damm bustling with beer steins and good cheer, a tourist playground radiating "the air of prosperity" inhaled by "groups of playing, cheerful people."

Looking around casually, "nowhere does the visitor see privation or hunger," admits the Voice, before modulating its chipper tone for a darker inflection: "No sign of dissatisfaction with the Fascist dictatorship which controls their lives . . . a government whose campaign of suppression and regimentation has shocked the world's democracies." Unlike the frothy travelogues on the motion picture bill, where happy natives frolic in colorful costume for smiling American tourists, the *March of Time* promises to peel back the mask over the death's head. "Only those who get behind the scenes know that this outward cheerfulness is the creation of Adolph Hitler's fanatic little propaganda minister Paul Joseph Goebbels." With his mastiff Goebbels, Hitler has "whipped 65 million people into a nation with one mind, one will, and one objective—expansion."

Menacing footage of the rallies at Nuremberg and illustrations mapping out a German African empire paint a clear picture of the Reich's imperial ambitions, but the Nazi vise grip also strangles the life out of the homeland. In the first of several staged sequences, the blade of a guillotine drops on a man prostrate on a chopping block. No less dire is a library shot taken during the Nazi boycott of Jewish goods on April 1, 1933, featuring boisterous brownshirts riding down a Berlin street in a swastika-festooned truck.

In reviewing the racial oppression that animates Nazism, Van Voorhis bellows out a word long banished from the feature film soundtrack. "Still going on as pitilessly, as brutally, as it did five years ago is Goebbels' persecution of the Jews." Though the footage of scrawled signs ("Jude") and stars of David in white paint splayed across storefront windows require no translation, the complete sentences do. "Signposts at city limits bear signs reading 'Jews Not Wanted' and 'Jews Keep Out,'" interprets Van Voorhis. Concealed or temporarily taken down during the 1936 Berlin Olympics, the antisemitic signage wallpapers the Reich. Bryan scored a real scoop for this sequence, sneaking a brief shot of a segregated park bench. Explains the narrator: "Even in parks, if Jews are allowed at all, special yellow benches are set apart labeled, 'For Jews.'" However, Judaism is not the only religion persecuted by a *führer* who will have no other Gods before him. Christian churches are desecrated and nuns are locked behind bars. "To the good Nazi not even God stands above Hitler."

Being itself an organ of multimedia penetration, the *March of Time* obsesses over the all-pervasive reach of Nazi propaganda. In print (the jacket from Hitler's prison memoir, *Mein Kampf,* initiates a montage of the author barking about "a super race headed for a great destiny"); on radio (from the *Volksradio,* the transmission belt for Goebbels' bulletins, snippets from an address by Hitler, untranslated, crackle from the soundtrack); and from the medium before the eyes of the spectator (Nazi newsreels of military might and pageantry), the full range of modern communications is orchestrated to mold the pliable minds of the German masses.

Media-savvy Americans, however, are wise to the tricks of Nazi propaganda. A staged sequence shows a German couple listening to a Nazi propaganda broadcast with the disinformation purveyed over the air translated in subtitles: "La Guardia, New York's Jewish mayor, controls the city's vice and racketeers." The *March of Time* refrains from correcting so obvious a lie. Unlike the propaganda-fed German, the American knows that La Guardia, whose father was Italian and mother Jewish, was an incorruptible civic reformer and a practicing Episcopalian.

So that Depression-weary Americans will not be lured into thinking Germany is a land of abundance, the issue shows how ordinary Germans must scrimp and save to burnish the glory of the Reich. Even garbage scraps are saved "to feed Nazi pigs." The war machine must be fed at all costs.

Yet the menace that is Nazism does not end at the Reich's borders. Nazi "propaganda extends far beyond Fascist frontiers—and today Hitler expects every German everywhere to help spread the Nazi creed." Via an intertitle and a quick edit, the story moves from Nazi Germany to another land where the blight of Nazism is taking root—America itself.

Adopting the Popular Front line, the commentary links Nazism overseas to its domestic fifth column. Here the issue unveils its prize catch, none other than Fritz Kuhn, leader of "the Hitler-inspired German American Bund" and the "loudest mouthpiece in this Nazi propaganda drive." With live synchronous sound, in untranslated German, "*Führer* Kuhn" is shown preaching "orthodox fascist doctrine" to tens of thousands of American Nazis marching in Nuremberg-like pageants. Across a map of the United States, campgrounds dotted with swastikas sprout up like weeds on American soil. Glorying in it all, and not learning from the experience of Gerald L. K. Smith, Kuhn seized the chance to be immortalized by the Luce Empire—strutting for the cameras, collaborating on his own immolation on screen.

Fortunately, a people with native smarts and sturdy backbone resist the invasion. Interviewed upon his return to the United States, former ambassador to Germany William E. Dodd speaks out about the threat from Nazi aggression, but it is ordinary Americans who deliver the most stinging rebuke. In Southbury, Connecticut, the *March of Time* sits in on a town meeting where citizens debate whether the German American Bund should be allowed to build a camp on the outskirts of town. To the applause of his fellow citizens, a man speaks out against "Nazi agents masquerading as American citizens," but the star of the meeting is a feisty Yankee matron. Framed in close-up, she is the picture of New England rectitude, a Puritan goodwife who in another century might have loaded a musket for her husband, or shot it herself. "Mr. Chairman, two of my great-great grandfathers and four of my great grandfathers fought for liberty. So did the other people of this town," she declares in a voice as clear as a bell. "I call upon all of you here to keep the Nazis out!" The town hall crowd cheers. A newspaper headline reveals the decision of the people in a vibrant democracy: the American Nazis are sent packing.

Back in Central Europe, the blessings of democracy—freedom of speech, press, and assembly—are a distant memory. Riding like emperors in an open-air car, Mussolini and Hitler bathe in the worship of their multitudes. Lest anyone snicker at the smug potentates, Van Voorhis reminds viewers that "behind these leaders lies an unbroken succession of Fascist triumphs, military and political." Life inside Nazi Germany can be summed up in three sentences. "Democracy is destroyed. The dictator is a demigod who can do no wrong. Propaganda dominates the nation's mind."

The final peroration—bracing enough in 1938, eerily prophetic in retrospect—pulled no punches. "Nazi Germany faces her destiny with the greatest war machine in history," booms Van Voorhis. "And the inevitable

La Guardia, New York's Jewish mayor, controls the city's vice and racketeers.

A series of images from "Inside Nazi Germany": a reenacted scene of a Nazi storm trooper collecting garbage scraps from a German housewife (*top*); a reenacted scene of a German couple listening to a propaganda broadcast on the *Volksradio* (*middle*); and an authentic shot of a New England patriot speaking out against Nazism at a town hall meeting.

destiny of the great war machines of the past has been to destroy the peace of the world, its people, and the governments of their time." After that oracular prophecy, the triumphal sign-off sounds more like the Voice of Doom than the Voice of God: "Time—marches on!"

"Inside Nazi Germany" clocked in at 18 minutes—approximately the total running time for the three segments usually covered by each issue of the series. Underscoring the importance of the story, the *March of Time* released the exposé as its first ever single-topic issue.

Once the episode was wrapped, de Rochemont held a private screening at the *March of Time* headquarters in New York, allegedly to allow the German authorities to correct misrepresentations, actually to goad them into an official protest that could be milked for free publicity. Dr. Georg F. Krause-Wichmann, the German Vice Consul, and Fritz Kuhn, leader of the German American Bund and preening featured player, showed up. Each responded according to type. An apoplectic Krause-Wichmann demanded the deletion of scenes "prejudicial to the best interests of Germany and likely to be misunderstood by the American public." An appalled Kuhn learned that the message of the medium was all in the editing. "If Hitler sees this film," he moaned, "I'll be ruined!"[17]

De Rochemont was thrilled. "There were storming and rantings," he chuckled. "We fully expect that we will be subjected to retaliations by the triple alliance existing between Italy-Japan-Germany." The producer also fully expected retaliation from opponents at home, but he vowed to stand his ground. "After escaping Nazi censorship in Germany, we have no intention of submitting to Nazi censorship in this country."[18]

In fact, American not Nazi censorship bedeviled "Inside Nazi Germany." Provocative by design, the release incited passionate debate and official pushback—over issues of journalistic integrity (was the film real or staged? made independently or under the eyes of the Nazis?), ideological slant (did the film condemn or promote the Nazi state?), and the very nature of news on film (should the cinematic medium even presume to address thorny geopolitical issues?). "Hardly ever in the history of pictures has any film, placed on exhibition, caused as much comment as the *March of Time* issue depicting the inside story of Germany of 1938," declared publicist Dave Epstein.[19]

Taking the bait, the reliably purblind Chicago Board of Censors voted unanimously to ban "Inside Nazi Germany" on the grounds that it was unfriendly toward a nation officially friendly to the United States.[20] Happy

"If Hitler sees this film, I'll be ruined!": Fritz Kuhn, leader of the German American Bund and featured patsy in "Inside Nazi Germany," meets with Adolf Hitler in 1936, in a photo released by the House Committee on Un-American Activities in August 1938.

to stoke the fires of controversy, de Rochemont lashed back. "We believe that censorship of a painstaking and factual report of this kind is almost unprecedented in the United States," he said. "It puts censorship in Chicago not on the basis of morals or taste but directly on a suppression of news facts. It thus becomes a direct attack on the principles of a free press."[21]

Like every commercial filmmaker in America, de Rochemont accepted the authority of censorship boards on matters of taste and morality—the kind best administered by the Breen office over Hollywood cinema—but he denied the state the power to suppress straight news reporting and political commentary. De Rochemont pledged to appeal the ruling and, if necessary, take his case to court. "Our lawyers are studying the Chicago ordinances relating to films and an appeal will be promptly made," he warned.[22]

De Rochemont lined up a battery of big guns in his corner. He arranged for private screenings in Washington for members of the U.S.

Congress and other powerful politicians, many of whom issued supportive blurbs. Secretary of State Cordell Hull called "Inside Nazi Germany"
"definitely anti-Nazi and a lesson to all Americans." Agreed Sen. Key
Pittman (D-NV), chairman of the Senate Foreign Relations Committee:
"I think it is highly desirable that the picture be seen by every American."
William E. Dodd's seal of approval lent special weight. "The members of
every American family, young and old, who believe in liberty and democracy, should by all means see 'Inside Nazi Germany,'" said the former
ambassador to Germany.[23]

Blistered by de Rochemont's fervent defense, a tide of editorial oppro-
brium, and, most importantly, the displeasure of the city's staunchly
anti-Nazi Cardinal, George Mundelein, the Chicago Board overturned
its initial ruling.[24] "Passed by Censors Uncut!" boasted ads in the Chicago papers the next day. For the *March of Time*, the three-step tango
of banning by a censorship board, followed by blasts of editorial contempt, followed by the board lifting its original ban was the best of all
possible outcomes: after riding a raft of free publicity, the film played
without restriction.

However, by way of collateral comeuppance, the intense scrutiny of
"Inside Nazi Germany" focused attention on a long-standing and heretofore uncontroversial editorial practice: the use of dramatic reenactments
of news events and the impersonations of real people by actors. A stock-
in-trade of the *March of Time* since its inception, dramatic reenactments
had never before much bothered critics or audiences, but the incendiary
topic and high stakes put the untelegraphed transitions from authentic
archival footage to staged reenactments into heightened relief. Ironically,
or appropriately, the *March of Time*'s broadside at the media manipula-
tions of Joseph Goebbels boomeranged back on the media manipula-
tions of the *March of Time*.

Unable to obtain sufficient material to tell the full story, even with Bryan's footage and library stock, the *March of Time* did what it always did
and staged dramatic reenactments. A New Jersey enclave of anti-Nazi German Americans played the part of the Nazis in a snicker-inducing scene
where a Nazi trooper "Heils" after receiving food scraps as well as in the
depictions of the guillotine execution and of the nuns in prison. American
spectators were smart enough to know that the radio broadcast denouncing Mayor La Guardia as a Jewish gangster was a lie, but were they smart
enough to know that the scene itself was staged by the *March of Time*?

Sharp-eyed trade critics had no trouble telling New Jersey from Bavaria. *Variety* tut-tutted over "obviously" staged scenes, singling out "an execution (probably staged) [that] shows what happens to dissenters," and the "absurdity of Nazi campaign to keep German laborers content [that] is vividly illustrated with staged radio sequences."[25]

At this point, Julien Bryan weighed in. He objected to the false publicity purveyed by the *March of Time*—the breathless reports that the film had been smuggled out of Germany—and suggested sensibly that the series simply label the staged reenactments with a subtitled notice. Not wanting to burn his bridges with the Nazis, he stated flatly that the pictures "were taken with the full permission and cooperation of the Nazi government and were not intended in any way to do any 'exposing' whatsoever, but merely to depict the tenor of the German system."[26] Capitalizing on the furor, Bryan put together a lecture presentation on his Nazi footage, which he debuted at Philharmonic Hall in Los Angeles on March 21, 1938. Speaking in Chicago later that year, he again insisted that the pictures were all taken with "the full permission and cooperation of the German propaganda offices."[27]

For one powerful motion picture entity, the mere transmission of Nazi-approved footage proved that the *March of Time* was in bed with the enemy. Warner Bros., the most stoutly anti-Nazi of the major studios, viewed "Inside Nazi Germany" as out-and-out Nazi propaganda. Acting on orders from Harry M. Warner, the studio banned the issue from all 425 of its affiliated theaters.[28] To Warner, the pictures of a well-dressed, well-fed people, marching, singing, and laboring in "iron works and other plants going full blast," overpowered the voice-over condemnations of the regime. "The effect and appeal of the motion picture is to the eye primarily," Warner asserted. "Careful analysis has proven that the words of commentators when used in connection with motion pictures have but a small effect against the great effect of what is shown on screen." Moreover, "nowhere in the picture is there any showing of ministers or priests in jail."[29] Not to mention—Warner didn't—rabbis. "We don't intend to make our screens a medium for the dissemination of propaganda for Germany no matter how thinly veiled that purpose may be."[30]

At that, de Rochemont confessed himself flummoxed. "It is difficult to believe that Harry Warner authorized a statement which explained why his theaters did not run *MOT*'s 'Inside Nazi Germany' by saying that the picture is pro-Nazi propaganda" given the fact that "during the past

24 hours, the German consuls in San Francisco and Buffalo have lodged protests with city officials asking that it be withdrawn from the screen because of the lack of sympathy with their policies." Clergymen, politicians, critics, Nazis, the Chicago Board of Censors—virtually everyone read the film as anti-Nazi.[31]

The bull-headed opposition of Harry M. Warner incited a rare entry into the fray by the grand man of the Time-Life Corporation himself, Henry Luce. "Mr. Warner's assertion that the *March of Time* is 'pro-Nazi propaganda' is ridiculous," Luce scoffed. "Mr. Warner also says that 'movie audiences pay little or no attention to the sound that comes from the screen.' This is an amazing observation to come from the man generally credited with introducing the talking motion picture." Savoring the irony, the print mogul lectured the film mogul on the role of his own medium. Warner may think that the screen's sole purpose was mindless entertainment, but the *March of Time* held loftier ambitions. "Fortunately, Mr. Warner does not control the entire motion picture industry," jibed Luce.[32]

The duel between sound and image recapitulated an already old debate over whether the apparatus of cinema assumes the primacy of the ear or the eye. "A deaf moviegoer might consider the film more pro-Nazi than anti-Nazi," conceded *Life,* before taking the company line and concluding that the volume of the voice-over drowned out the impact of the pictures.[33] Also elevating the auditory over the optical, the Hollywood Anti-Nazi League broke ranks with its patrons at Warner Bros. "To anybody not completely deaf, the *March of Time* reel will fortify all his biases in favor of democracy," said Frank Scully, the well-known author, humorist, and bylined columnist for *Variety,* speaking for HANL's executive board. "What the pictures show as taken inside Germany are, of course, what the Hitler regime wanted shown, but what was shot outside Nazi Germany is enough to have the reel either banned in Germany or cut to ribbons when shown, and in either case none of the dialogue will ever be heard there." Calling the reel "unmistakably anti-Nazi," Scully bestowed HANL's imprimatur: "it should be seen by everybody with a suspicion of what Fascism means."[34]

Finally, a few motion picture professionals resisted the whole notion that the screen should ever treat subjects that might upset the serenity of the moviegoer. Less concerned about whether the film leaned pro- or anti-Nazi, or whether image trumped sound, they fretted over how the motion picture theater—the bucolic oasis tucked away from the woes of the Great Depression and the insanity in Europe—was being hijacked by something so unsettling as political content. Martin J. Quigley of *Motion Picture Herald* was sad to see de Rochemont aligning himself with the Hollywood radicals "who in a headlong rush for a change in political, social, and economic order are in a fever of covetousness to gain the screens of the nation for their stump speeches." Citing the press reports of boisterous hissing and intermittent "Heils!" when close-ups of Hitler filled the screen, Quigley shuddered at the prospect of the nation's theaters being "converted into bedlams of turmoil and dissension" by an incendiary reel that "kindles the embers of violence." After all, huffed Quigley, "theater patrons are supposed to be seated in comfortable opera chairs and not crouched behind barricades."[35] Noting that de Rochemont had taken the precaution of giving the film a sneak preview in the York-ville district of New York to gauge the reaction of a German American audience, *Variety* drolly responded that "No seats were torn up and no disturbances marked [the] showing."[36]

Machts nichts, shrugged exhibitors. "Both Nazi sympathizers and anti-Nazis seem to like ["Inside Nazi Germany"] because the film shows the strength of the Hitler regime while the commentary gives facts which are startling," reported W. French Githens, president of Newsreel The-aters, Inc.[37] However, most audiences—and not just in the politically engaged and disproportionately Jewish demographic in and around New York—rallied to the anti-Nazi message. On the opposite coast, word from the ticket window was emphatically one-sided. "Audience response much applause, thrilled with picture," telegrammed the manager at the Carthay Circle Theatre in Los Angeles.[38] Encouraging reports also filtered back to the *March of Time* home office from Philadelphia (where audiences "nearly tore down the rafters with applause when the good Americans protested against Nazi racism"), Cleveland ("scenes of Americans pro-testing against Nazi activities drew heavy applause"), and Miami ("reac-tion unanimously very favorable").[39] With crowds enthused and business booming, exhibitors raked in the twin rewards of critical plaudits and box office profits.[40]

By way of wrap-up, the *Film Daily* offered the most perceptive comment. "Although the intrinsic news value of the material is not startling in view of substantial front-page accounts of Nazi history, the detached and organized treatment of 'Inside Nazi Germany' presents a coherent picture which brings home the full truth with uncompromising impact for perhaps the first time."[41] Both blueprint and bellwether, "Inside Nazi Germany" was an early harbinger of what would become one of the most popular motion picture genres of the twentieth century, the Nazi-centric documentary.

Released at the beginning of 1938—before the annexation of Austria, before the appeasement at Munich, before the rampage of Kristallnacht—"Inside Nazi Germany" was at once ahead of the cultural curve and on the crest of an oncoming wave. The syndicated columnist and radio broadcaster Walter Winchell, a fierce opponent of Nazism since 1933, lauded the film on his coast-to-coast radio show. "When the patriots of Connecticut are seen and heard outlawing Nazi camps, the audience responds, surprisingly enough, with 100% applause," reported Winchell, who attended several screenings. By the end of the year, 100 percent applause for an anti-Nazi preachment would no longer be surprising.

Another seasoned reporter—Irving Hoffman, the *Hollywood Reporter*'s man in New York—was also monitoring the pulse of the audience. Taking in the charged atmosphere of a packed house at the Embassy Newsreel Theater, his reading preserves the vox populi response to Nazism in the tipping-point year of 1938.

Outside the Embassy, a barker reeled in Broadway passersby with shouts of "Standing Room Only!" and "No Refunds!" Sure enough, the place was mobbed, with standees overflowing into the lobby area for each show, including the midnight screening, and lines snaking down the street. Not since the breathtaking newsreels of the *Hindenburg* explosion on May 6, 1937, had the Embassy drawn such crowds. But if the audience for the *Hindenburg* newsreels had come to gape at a tableau of fiery destruction, the viewers of "Inside Nazi Germany" sought a glimpse into a mysterious country shuttered from motion picture view. The tension in the air—the anticipation of another kind of explosion, this one rumbling up from the crowd—was palpable. To help keep the lid on, a half-dozen uniformed policemen, nightsticks at the ready, circulated around the theater while plainclothes detectives mixed in with the paying customers.

When the houselights dimmed, the familiar brass fanfare trumpeting the *March of Time* had to wait as a title card from the management of the Embassy flashed on the screen:

The issue of *March of Time* you are about to see has caused much controversy. Our policy is to fearlessly present any worthy film produced by a recognized American producer. We therefore present uncensored and impartially the following subject.

A wave of applause greeted the declaration. The *March of Time* then submitted its own preamble:

> The picture you are about to see has been mistakenly branded "a sensational expose." The editors wish to state that the sole object of The March of Time is to present through pictorial journalism the significant events of our time.[42]

Settling in with the Embassy regulars, Hoffman described the action on both sides of the screen:

> With the first shot showing rich and good food being served in the cafes, several spectators were heard to shout, "It isn't true!" The commentator says that this is only a front, but the spectators seem to have beaten him to it. At another point, where bologna is shown, someone yelled, "That's a lot of baloney! Why don't they show you and tell you that it is made out of paper?" And when a half pound of lard was introduced, another spectator yelled, "Twelve million American unemployed haven't even got that!" Goebbels is hissed, Hitler is hissed, and they laugh when a collector [of garbage scraps] and a housewife say, "Heil Hitler!" There are laughter and hisses when the reel shows how false propaganda is delivered over the radio. Fritz Kuhn is hissed. The people of Southbury, Conn., who make a stirring speech against the Nazis, are applauded and so is Ambassador Dodd.

A distinct but vocal minority also made itself heard:

> However, generally, whenever the above reactions just recorded took place, the Nazi sympathizers in the house, numbering from a half dozen to a dozen and a half, applauded and once when the Nazi flag was shown, one yelled, urging the audience to STAND UP.

Drawing his report from attendance at three separate shows, Hoffman witnessed a violent flare-up only once. When a Great War veteran "in the back of the house, leaned over and hit a Nazi sympathizer," a policeman "right on the spot, immediately yanked both of them and told them to fight outside if they wanted to."

Immediately following the *March of Time* issue, as if to reassure audiences that not all was wrong with the world, a heartwarming clip unspooled as balm for the soul. Featuring banjo-eyed singer-comedian Eddie Cantor and superstar moppet Shirley Temple, the vignette made a heartwarming appeal for a cause whose name punned on the preceding title: the March of Dimes, the FDR-inspired charity dedicated to finding a cure for polio. Shirley drew warm applause and affectionate laughter when she suggested everyone watching send in a dime "just like me!" Behind him, Hoffman heard a woman sigh, "It's a pity she has to grow up."[43]

10

"GRIM REAPER MATERIAL"

In 1934, Terry Ramsaye, editor of *Motion Picture Herald* and a former newsreel man himself, sought to disabuse newsreel editors of the notion they were in the news business. "The newsreel is not a purveyor of news and never is likely to become one," he explained. "The newsreel ought to be an entertaining and amusing derivative—just so long as its avenue to the public is through the dramatic screen theater and along with the drama." To aspire to the standards of print journalism or claim the protections of the First Amendment was to reach beyond the proper station of a trivial diversion. "Whether they know it or not, the newsreels, as they call them, are just in the show business, or they should by all means get into it."[1]

More often than not, the content of the newsreels confirmed Ramsaye's low opinion. Working the newsreel beat for *Variety* in the 1930s, Robert Landry wearily endured, week in week out, "a bewildering assortment of important happenings of worldwide consequence side by side with claptrap stunts important only to the press agents who arranged them."[2] No wonder at the first sound of a newsreel fanfare many moviegoers darted into the lobby for a smoke or a visit to the restroom before the start of the serious part of the program, the feature film.

Throughout the epochal 1930s, by common consent, "the greatest human interest story in the history of the newsreels" was neither the trauma of the Great Depression nor the rise of European fascism but the nativity of the Dionne quintuplets. On May 28, 1934, the birth of a litter of five identical baby girls provided a welcome distraction from the punishing economic news, not to say a sense of gratitude from parents without five new mouths to feed. The Quints (as Annette, Cecile, Emelie, Marie, and Yvonne were affectionately known) logged more screen time in the newsreels than the Spanish Civil War. RKO-Pathé News acquired an exclusive contract to film the five and churned out special issues documenting their every burp and coo. The advertising come-ons positively gurgled: "See them from dawn to bedtime . . . feeding . . . sleeping . . . bathing . . . laughing . . . their home . . . their parents . . . their doctor . . . nurses . . . special hospital . . . *and their washline!*" While the newsreel cameras panned diapers flapping in the breeze, the real news of the day was hung out to dry.

Surveys of audience preferences in newsreel content did not encourage a commitment to hard-hitting news coverage. Entertainment fare, fashion parades, and human interest stories rated highest, with women expressing an intense dislike for "strikes, war, crime, and politics." The squeamishness of the distaff side was a constant worry. "Snakes, rats, and mice are taboo in the newsreels because of their effect on women," reported a pamphlet issued by the New York and New Jersey Newsreel Theaters in 1939. "Children, dogs, and other pets, and humorous subjects, are most popular."[3] Reading the returns, William P. Montague, assignment editor for Paramount News, bemoaned the bind of a medium caught between "the prerogatives of a news agency and hence the social obligations of a news disseminating organization," and a clientele that "would only accept their product if it was entertaining—good theater."[4]

Even so, when chasing down a hot story, the newsreels might catch the scent and show a hustle and grit that rivaled the print press. In March 1932 the crime of the century (the kidnap-murder of the 18-month-old baby of Charles and Anne Morrow Lindbergh) and, in January 1935, the trial of the century (the prosecution of the accused perpetrator, Bruno Richard Hauptmann) tested the journalistic mettle of the newsreels. The news of the kidnapping hit screens at the Embassy Newsreel Theater in New York within twenty-four hours of the first wire service alerts. Joining the manhunt, the newsreels sent out an all-points bulletin and—in a first for the medium—screened 8mm home movie footage, blown up to 35mm format, of the baby in his crib.[5] During Hauptmann's trial, the newsreels surreptitiously filmed actual on-the-stand testimony, including a withering cross-examination of the defendant by New Jersey attorney general David T. Wilentz. Outraged at the contempt for court

Bigger than the Spanish Civil War: newsreel darlings the Dionne Quintuplets in *Reunion* (1936), Twentieth Century-Fox's homage to the doctor who delivered Canada's most famous daughters.

decorum—or pretending to be outraged—Wilentz demanded the reels be pulled from circulation. Fox Movietone, Hearst-Metrotone, and Paramount complied; RKO-Pathé and Universal defiantly screened the clips and suffered no legal consequences.[6]

In the most controversial brouhaha over newsreel policy in the 1930s, the medium itself became part of the story. On Memorial Day, 1937, outside the Republic Steel Plant in South Chicago, a violent melee between police and union strikers resulted in the death of ten strikers and the wounding of ninety more. Paramount News cameras recorded what looked to all appearances like a police riot. Eyeing the footage, the *St. Louis Post-Dispatch* described "uniformed policemen firing their revolvers point blank into a dense crowd of men, women, and children and then pursuing and clubbing the survivors unmercifully as they made frantic efforts to escape." The anti-union *Chicago Tribune* countered that the Paramount News cameraman was changing his lens when the police were provoked by projectiles hurled by communist agitators.

Despite its electrifying scoop, Paramount withheld the footage from its regular issue on the grounds that the "horror" of the scenes might incite violence. No newsreel segment with the Memorial Day footage had been edited or issued, no censor board had seen the footage to approve or ban it, and no government agency threatened Paramount with prior restraint. The editors simply slinked away on their own accord. In an example of the "voluntary restraint" that crippled the ability of the news-reels to run with a controversial story, Paramount itself deemed the pic-tures of labor unrest and police brutality as "not fit to be seen." Unlike newspapers, explained Paramount editor A. J. Richard, newsreels were shown to large groups liable to succumb to "crowd hysteria" if exposed to such inflammatory imagery. "Our pictures depict a tense and nerve-racking episode which in certain sections of the country might very well incite local riot and perhaps riotous demonstrations in theaters, leading to further casualties."[7]

The United States Senate disagreed. That July, an investigation into the incident by the Senate Civil Liberties Committee, chaired by Rob-ert M. La Follette (I-WI), requested a print of the Memorial Day footage from Paramount News. On July 2, 1937, the self-censored pictures were screened to a packed Senate hearing room, the first instance of newsreel film being submitted into evidence before either body of the U.S. Con-gress. "This film, having been offered as evidence at a public hearing of the subcommittee, now becomes part of that committee's public record and as such merits the attention and study of the citizens of this coun-try," declared Senator La Follette.[8]

Forgetting its earlier timidity and donning the garments of tribune of the people, Paramount News decided to reap the publicity windfall and release the footage. "More than a month has elapsed since the riot pic-tures were made. A month ago more than 70,000 men were on strike in seven states; feeling ran at white heat," explained Paramount's Richard. "Today, generally speaking, conditions have changed for the better and the feelings of yesterday have subsided." Considering that the pictures had been "presented as evidence in a public hearing" of the U.S. Senate, Paramount News saw no reason not to release a special issue comprised of exclusive pictures of the clash, "made before and during the trouble . . . exactly as they came from the camera as a matter of public service."[9]

The aggressive, gutsy stance of the newsreels over the Hauptmann trial footage and the instinctive, preemptive cowering over the Memorial

Day footage illustrates the difference between a sensational crime story pitting a dastardly villain against an enraged public and an incendiary political story pitting labor against business, but it also shows the newsreels had no clear guidelines or professional ethos about what was fit to screen and what was best left on the cutting-room floor. Following up on the controversy over the Memorial Day footage, *Box Office* asked the editors of the five newsreels to comment on the state of screen journalism and the ethos of self-imposed censorship. The trade weekly was curious about "when newsreels may or may not be subjected to what is commonly known as self-censorship, or self-regulation, or non-circulation" and whether "this form of editing controversial and certain other subjects would prevent official censorship." That is, what exactly did the newsreels self-censor and why?

To a man, the newsreel editors voiced support for the concept of voluntary restraint and said nothing about a professional commitment to aggressive screen journalism. Certainly, "the divorces, the juvenile crimes, the unspeakable incidents of life which must be dealt with by police hospitals and the prisons are 'self-regulated' out of the newsreels," and this sort of editorial discretion was a good thing, went the consensus. "It seems that any editor's job, by its very nature, implies at least some degree of 'self-censorship,' 'self-regulation,' and 'non-circulation,'" said M. D. Clofine, editor of MGM's News of the Day. "This must be particularly true in the case of the newsreel editor whose medium is sold to exhibitors of varied political faiths and social beliefs and reaches millions of people of all ages and classes." Paramount's Richard also praised the internal ties that bound the medium. "To this 'self-regulation' 'self-censorship,' if you please—I attribute the steady growth and tremendous influence of the screen news." Not one of the editors mentioned the Spanish Civil War, Fascist Italy, or Nazi Germany as a news beat that might have been soft-sold by self-censorship.[10]

That willful avoidance was about to change. Though the newsreels remained temperamentally averse to hard-hitting news coverage, the accelerating momentum toward war in 1938 thundered too loudly to ignore. On March 12, 1938, Nazi troops breeched the Austrian border, annexing the nation into the greater Reich in a territorial grab known as the *Anschluss*. Two days later, Hitler marched victoriously into Vienna. Throughout that spring and summer, the fragile democracy of Czechoslovakia was up next on the Nazi chopping block. In October the ax fell.

It was awesome theater and momentous history—made for the motion picture camera and, sometimes, staged for it.

Meanwhile, the Far East was also exploding. Though the remoteness of the battlefield, the Euro-centricity of America, and the fact that the newsreels were all headquartered in New York made the Japanese war on China seem less of an immediate threat, Americans, who were overwhelmingly sympathetic to the Chinese, were not without a rooting interest in the match between the Asian giants. Moreover, the enormous territorial expanse and the absence of clear lines of military authority across China were boons to newsreel access. Amid the chaos on the ground, the newsreels were more liable to elude coercive restrictions. As a result, the most spectacular and bloodiest footage of combat projected on screens in the 1930s—surpassing even the carnage brought back from the Spanish Civil War—was shot in China.

The first combat footage of Americans under fire in China testified to the unique pull of the newsreel medium. On December 12, 1937, Japanese warplanes attacked and sank the U.S.S. *Panay*, a navy gunboat patrolling the Yangtze River. Universal Newsreel, Fox Movietone, and MGM's News of the Day all got gripping footage of the incident: the Japanese aerial attack, sailors returning fire from machine guns mounted on the boat's deck, bombs exploding in the river, and the actual sinking of the gunboat while the crew dove overboard. The after-battle report showed survivors fleeing downriver, tending the wounded, identifying the dead, and dodging Japanese patrols.

Throughout the *Panay* incident, the newsreel cameraman was front and center as audience surrogate, narrating his own daring escapes while keeping the action in focus. Universal Newsreel cameraman Norman Alley, who had been wounded during the attack, was handed a $5,000 check upon docking in San Francisco with his prize footage. To capitalize on the scoop, the turnaround time from photography in China to projection in America set a newsreel speed record. Advertised on marquees above the featured film title, the newsreels were playing in Los Angeles on December 29, 1937, and in New York the next morning. Universal bundled its footage into a special issue, *Bombing of the U.S.S. Panay*, while Fox Movietone and News of the Day highlighted the material in their regular newsreel issues. The American government censored not a foot. "The whole town's talking about those Panay bombing newsreels," reported the *Film Daily*, adding to the chatter. "Looks as if the various newsreel organizations came through with very graphic portrayals." The report concluded with a proud comment on the singular attraction of newsreel imagery: "All the newspaper accounts combined do not make the impression that the sight of these films stirs in the beholder."[11]

Leaving an even deeper impression was the newsreel coverage of the Japanese depredations on the civilian populations of Shanghai and Nanking in 1937. "It is likely that never before in the history of newsreels has there been such gruesome material on display," wrote an appalled Wolfe Kaufman in *Variety*. "The Spanish stuff was largely censored, as [was] true of almost all cases in the past. Here there is no sugar coating. It is war at its cruelest and most vicious, caught by an impartial camera eye. Bodies are strewn right and left. Blood is seen on all sides. Here a headless corpse, there a legless carcass. The scattered pulp of what was once a head is shown. A truckload of scarred and broken and torn bodies, piled carelessly one atop the other, like so much garbage. It's not the kind of stuff to be looked at by anyone with a sensitive stomach. Women are not likely to be able to take it at any time. But, once seen, the effect will take a long time to wear off and the moral lesson is bound to stick." Kaufman called the tableaux of death "Grim Reaper material."[12]

As if wars in Spain and China and the forward march of Nazism in Europe were not enough to spur initiative, the competition from a bigfoot interloper also sharpened the edge of the newsreels in the late 1930s. Since its premiere in 1935, the monthly screen magazine the *March of Time* had played critic's darling to the newsreels' whipping boy. The Academy Award bestowed on the *March of Time* in 1937 "for having revolutionized one of the most important branches of the industry—the newsreel" rubbed salt in the wound. Insulted and chastened, the easygoing, trouble-averse newsreels sought to recoup a measure of self-esteem by downplaying the inane interludes and stepping up the serious coverage. Of course, the newsreels never abandoned the fashion parades, dumb yuks, and sports highlights, but the ratio of fluff to substance began to tilt toward weightier topics. Looking ahead to 1938, Paramount editor A. J. Richard said "the function of the newsreel must be concentrated more than ever on the presentation of spot and live news—economic, political, factual, industrial—to the full extent of the screen time at our command. The injection of vaudeville acts and of entertainment material that properly belongs to shorts does not make a true newsreel."[13]

Whenever the newsreels underwent a personality change, the trade press critics knew whom to credit. The *March of Time* "has a daring that is little by little being approached by the other reels in their handling of highly controversial subjects," *Variety*'s Roy Chartier observed. "For years the standard newsreels were guided by many 'don'ts' for various reasons, but mostly through fear of censorship." The screen magazine had shown the newsreels that their true media kinship was with print journalism not Hollywood entertainment. "Many [newsreel] editors were afraid to try to duplicate in film what newspapers put into print or pictures," said Chartier. "The *March of Time* has definitely acted as an influence in this direction."[14]

The influence, however, was a trend not a transformation. In August 1939, days before German troops invaded Poland to ignite war in Europe, the writer Robert Meltzer broke down the ratio of fluff to substance in a recent program at a newsreel theater:[a]

> About thirty minutes of the hour were taken up with variety shorts showing odd occupations, strange lands, a Parisian hairdresser at work ("he models in hair like a sculptor in clay") and similar edifying *hors d'oeuvres*. Then about fifteen minutes were devoted to the examination of such semi-newsworthy items as the amazing number of uses to which Madison Square Garden is put each year. And then came fifteen minutes of newsreels. Something like ten of these covered the fields of high diving and women's jewelry with commendable thoroughness, which left around five or six minutes in which to cover the war crisis.

Meltzer's critique was more acute because he recognized the potential impact of the newsreel in the media hierarchy, a potential that would only be fulfilled after American entry into World War II. "You may get more complete coverage in reading your newspaper and it may be faster; you

---

[a] Meltzer made uncredited contributions to both Charles Chaplin's *The Great Dictator* (1940) and Orson Welles's *Journey into Fear* (1943). In 1944 he was killed in action in France. To honor Meltzer, the Screen Writers Guild established the Robert Meltzer Award for "the screenplay dealing most ably with the problems of the American scene." In 1951 the guild stopped giving the award. According to director Richard Brooks, Meltzer was "posthumously blacklisted" after he was named before the House Committee on Un-American Activities. In 1991 the Writers Guild of America reestablished the award for "a singular act of courage in defense of freedom of expression and the right of writers." ("WGA Lauds Douglas for 'Plain Guts,' Defense of Writers," *Variety*, Mar. 22, 1991: 1, 10.)

may get your news more quickly yet over your radio; but through neither of these media do you get the immediacy and the full three-dimensional awareness of what is happening that a newsreel can transmit."

Meltzer had a final point to make about the newsreel experience. Listening to his fellow newsreel watchers hiss Hitler and cheer FDR, Meltzer took heart from the vigor of the communal chorus. The participatory spirit was not just an expression of the vox populi, but proof positive that the American demos remained fearlessly opinionated. "This is an extremely important thing," he emphasized. Unlike the newspaper or the radio, while watching a newsreel "you can join in with your fellow men in reacting to world events." Sitting in a theater, and seeing the face of British prime minister Neville Chamberlain, still proud of having negotiated the Munich Pact, "hearing him try to justify his shameless policy of intrigue and betrayal and having your feelings echoed or opposed by everyone else in the house—there's a stirring and in this day extremely important phenomenon. What you experience is a Gallup Poll come to life."[15]

Beginning in 1938, the last full year of nominal peace in Europe, all that the medium could be—as archival memory, as screen journalism, and as an arena for democratic expression—was realized when, after years of lackadaisical, hit-and-miss coverage, the newsreels, at long last, took a cold, hard look at Nazi Germany.

HISTORY UNREELS

The media wraparound of 1938—first, scattershot radio reports, followed by newspaper headlines, then newsweekly articles, and finally newsreel pictures—defines a news-and-information experience light years away from the round-the-clock, wall-to-wall digital sensorium of the twenty-first century. Still, the infrastructure for the Age of Too Much Information was already settling into place. The problem was not the state of the technology but the flow of information. Getting the story—especially the images—was a promethean task for journalists covering Nazi Germany.

Radio, the medium that pervaded the atmosphere of American culture in the 1930s, sparked the communications revolution. Live shortwave transmissions had lately edged aside the newspaper wire services for up-to-the-minute, on-site coverage of foreign affairs. On March 13, 1938, the day after the Nazis invaded Austria, CBS inaugurated its pioneering *World News Roundup*, a series featuring live broadcasts from European capitals. The head of CBS's European division, based in London and then reporting from a tense Vienna awaiting Hitler's arrival, was the soon-to-be-legendary Edward R. Murrow, even then recruiting the stellar lineup of correspondents destined for broadcasting immortality as his dauntless "boys." Despite Nazi censorship and technical glitches, William L. Shirer, Murrow's man in the belly of the Third Reich from 1937 to 1940, struggled to find the words to describe the street-level brutality and global ambitions of Nazism. At NBC, Dr. Max Jordan, a native German speaker with well-placed informants in the Nazi hierarchy, manned the same post for CBS's better-financed rival. Both regularly locked horns not only with Nazi censors but with news directors in New York who seemed more interested in broadcasting live performances of children's choirs than Hitler's speeches in the Reichstag.

As the momentum toward war in Europe escalated, Americans flocked to the electronic medium for breaking news and hourly bulletins—a shift in media allegiance that deeply distressed motion picture exhibitors. During an international crisis, attendance at movie theaters plummeted. On March 12, 1938, broadcasting from Vienna, Max Jordan patched through a live German broadcast of Hitler speaking from his hometown of Linz, a you-are-there moment the other media could never match.[16] The blast of news bulletins and the threat of foreign invasion were very much in the air that year, an emotional link confirmed on October 30, 1938, by the famous Halloween eve broadcast of H. G. Wells's *The War of the Worlds* by Orson Welles's CBS radio series *Mercury Theatre on the Air*. By mimicking the breathless urgency of on-air announcers interrupting regular programming and the static crackling of shortwave reception from overseas—a parodic mode that eerily echoed the real radio bulletins—Welles set off a panic on the eastern seaboard with the fake news that extraterrestrials were invading New Jersey. On the brink of the next world war, *The War of the Worlds* sounded like a remote pickup from the European bureaus of CBS or NBC news.

Not being able to compete with the immediacy or pervasiveness of radio or the detail and comprehensiveness of the newspapers, the newsreels sold themselves as a vital motion picture supplement to news already known and heard. Perhaps only once, in the biggest newsreel scoop of the 1930s, did the medium record a sight that beggared the impact of print or sound, that absolutely had to be seen: the death throes of the *Hindenburg*, the German zeppelin that exploded in flames while coming in for a mooring at Lakehurst, New Jersey, on May 6, 1937. For the newsreels, the tragedy was a rare piece of luck: the scheduled mooring of the vessel was a preplanned, stationary event, so cameras were set up, ready to capture a routine landing when the explosion scorched their lenses. The cameramen rushed back to the newsreel offices in New York where the footage was developed, edited, narrated, and scored in mere hours. The next day—and for days afterward—audiences packed sold-out shows at the Embassy, watching mesmerized as the newsreels unspooled scenes of the conflagration, again and again, in slow motion, from multiple angles.

The next year, the flames from the Nazi vessel must have flickered like foreshadowing: 1938 witnessed three earth-shaking episodes of Nazi aggression the newsreels struggled to capture. Two projected Nazi aggression outward, one turned the violence inward—the annexation of Austria in March, the invasion of the Czechoslovakian Sudetenland in October, and the pogrom against the Jews in November. Cumulatively, the three acts pushed the newsreels to confront a story that since 1933 had mainly been whitewashed, downplayed, or ignored.

Being a territorial grab long expected, the annexation of Austria found the newsreels ready and waiting on the streets of Vienna. On March 14, 1938, as Hitler entered the city, Universal and RKO-Pathé each had a newsreel cameraman in position to record the final hours of Austrian sovereignty, but, as usual, the Nazis controlled access to motion pictures of the Nazis in action. Both men were hauled off to jail by the invaders. After protests by the U.S. Embassy, the cameramen—Universal's Julius Jonak and an unidentified stringer from Pathé—were released. As in Germany, the American newsreel companies had no option but to clear their footage with the Nazis. They also exchanged clips, paying a fee for the dynamic Nazi footage of Hitler riding into Vienna to the cheers of rapturous throngs of newly made subjects of the Third Reich.

On March 21, 1938, newsreel pictures of the *Anschluss* arrived stateside by ship for screenings at the Embassy Newsreel Theater and Trans-Lux Theater on Broadway that same night. "Actual coverage of history-making event, absorption of Austria by the Nazi government, was as carefully and calmly worked out by the camera crews as handling of a big Fifth Avenue parade, with different locations spotted en route of march, newsreel truck going along in procession and other details," *Variety* asserted, neglecting to mention the arrests of the cameramen or the restricted access.[17]

Yet while as dependent as ever on Nazi-approved footage, the newsreels were no longer uncritical conduits for Nazi propaganda. As scenes of Hitler's ride into his hometown of Linz and his prize Vienna unspooled, commentators cautioned spectators to watch skeptically. "The newsreels confess that not all of the photography emanating from Austria is to be believed, telling only part of the story," *Variety* reported, suspecting that not all Austrians were the joyous welcomers panned by the German newsreel cameras. "The narrators talk about the tragedies which followed the 'peaceful' march, and which the cameras can't show." Nazi film or not, however, "it's historical and ought to be seen. Especially that close up of Hitler," seen savoring his first real taste of territorial conquest.[18] Historical it was—but now the footage was branded as filmed or filtered by the Nazis.

After the *Anschluss*, the world spent the rest of the spring and the summer of 1938 nervously awaiting Hitler's next gambit. The smart money was on a jutting piece of real estate in Czechoslovakia that the Nazis called the German Sudeten Territory, an enclave populated mainly by ethnic Germans. The land had been ceded to Czechoslovakia in the Treaty of Versailles, which made it doubly coveted for dominion by the Third Reich. On September 12, 1938, Hitler made a territorial demand that pushed Europe to the brink of war. In a speech before 30,000 ecstatic followers at Nuremberg and millions more by loudspeaker and radio, he demanded that the "oppression of Sudeten Germans must end and the right of self-determination be given to them." Czech president Edvard Beneš was a liar in league with Jews and Bolsheviks, bellowed Hitler. He threatened the use of military force to liberate Sudeten Germans from the yoke of Czech tyranny.

Hitler's speech was carried live by both the CBS and NBC radio networks, with CBS fading out the speech for translations by Edward R. Murrow and NBC providing near simultaneous translation and analysis from Max Jordon. All that month, radio interrupted regular programming for scary updates. Speaking at the Sports Palace in Berlin on September 26, Hitler solemnly assured France and Britain that the Sudetenland was absolutely his "last territorial demand." Handling the broadcast for CBS, William L. Shirer never forgot the "fanatical fire" in Hitler's eyes. "For the first time in all the years I've observed him, he seemed to have completely lost control of himself," Shirer wrote in his diary that night.[19]

Americans heard it all play out on radio. "European war situation has caused one of the biggest ether jams in the history of broadcasting," reported *Daily Variety*, "ether" being archaic trade lingo for the radio airwaves. "Special programs, bulletins, and news flashes cutting into the regular schedules yesterday [September 26th] along with the hour and ten minute talk of Hitler constituted heaviest load of current eventers networks have ever handled."[20] Manning the microphone in New York for CBS, H. V. Kaltenborn kept a 24-hour vigil, sleeping on a cot in the newsroom.[b]

Three days later, desperate to avoid hostilities, British prime minister Neville Chamberlain and French prime minister Édouard Daladier rushed to Munich to negotiate a deal to prevent war. Signed on September 29, formally issued on the 30th, the negotiated agreement—the Munich Pact—sealed Czechoslovakia's fate. In Berlin, NBC's Jordan scooped CBS's Shirer by reading and simultaneously translating the protocols of the pact on live radio. On October 1, Nazi troops crossed the border and absorbed the Sudetenland into the Reich.

Although radio owned the fast-breaking story ("Radio is romancing with destiny these days," wrote Robert Landry), the newsreels claimed a piece of the Czechoslovakian drama.[21] As the crisis raced toward its climax, Landry and his colleagues at *Variety*, with a rising sense of dread and making no attempt at reportorial objectivity, watched the screen and diagnosed the anxiety attacks inside New York's newsreel theaters.

"History unreels here this week" was *Variety*'s succinct description of the Embassy program as the Czechoslovakian crisis intensified in the last weeks of September. The next month, with the Munich Pact signed and Czechoslovakia shredded, the reporters looked on helplessly as Europe hurtled toward the abyss. "History in the making is the way Fox describes the Embassy's feature clip, and history it is," marveled *Variety*. "For here with all the inordinate pomposity dictatorial arrogance could muster, the victory of militarists over democracy is shown, and with no holds barred." Fox Movietone News commentator Lowell Thomas described a

---

[b] The marathon broadcasting session made Kaltenborn's reputation. He would repeat it on screen, after a fashion, appearing as himself monitoring the lengthy filibuster of Jefferson Smith (James Stewart) in Frank Capra's *Mr. Smith Goes to Washington* (1939).

"chastened" Chamberlain and Daladier, "taking the bitter pill of subjugation from Hitler and Mussolini" while signing the Munich Pact, the penmanship lingered over in close-up. In crosscut juxtaposition, the dictators bathe in the adoration of wildly cheering crowds in Berlin while Chamberlain, deplaning at Heston Airport outside of London, waved a white piece of paper over his head.[22]

After Munich, the sense that the war alarums from Europe were not wild fear mongering but an emphatic future tense was taken for granted by *Variety*'s clear-eyed sentinels. "War clouds continue to dominate the reels and well they might since every sector of the globe is experiencing the fever," read the eyewitness report in December 1938. "It's a seething universe, one that's continuing to arm in the event of an emergency, bent upon reaching a peak crisis that will ultimately result in another world conflagration."[23] Chronicling the headlong rush into the fire, the reviewers seem like helpless onlookers to a manmade disaster.

As the newsreels screened the headlines in twice-weekly issues, the monthly *March of Time* continued to set the gold standard for comprehensive motion picture journalism. On April 15, 1938, it released "Nazi Conquest—No. 1," an ominously titled segment making up around 60 percent of its issue. In a nod to "Inside Nazi Germany" (January 1938), the previous exposé, it was billed as "Inside Nazi Austria."

The issue opens with a self-reflexive nod to the venues that served as home base for the *March of Time*: exterior shots of the crowds flocking around the fronts of the Embassy and Trans-Lux theaters in New York. "In a world aflame," Americans have become ravenous newshounds with "an ever increasing interest in world affairs," declares narrator Westbrook Van Voorhis. Either because Americans have also cultivated an ever-increasing interest in how the news is gathered or because the media's favorite story is always its own, the episode gives extensive coverage to a behind-the-scenes look at the business of overseas news gathering, highlighting the enterprising radio reporting of NBC not CBS—doubtless because RKO, which distributed the *March of Time*, was financially underwritten by RCA, NBC's parent company. The vignette stars correspondent Max Jordan, who scoops the competition with the report that German troops have breached the Austrian border, making the nation "a new outpost in the ruthless Nazi realm." Shown in close-up, the pages of *Mein Kampf* are turned so viewers may see their

▬
The face of appeasement:
British prime minister
Neville Chamberlain exits
the Hotel Dreesen in Bad
Godesberg. Behind him is
Nazi foreign minister
Joachim von Ribbentrop,
September 23, 1938.

prophetic significance for the case at hand—and read Hitler's prose as a promise of things to come.[c]

Even in the transformative year of 1938, however, resistance to screen news of the Nazis remained stubborn in some quarters. Bizarrely, Warner Bros. was no happier with "Nazi Conquest—No. 1" than with "Inside Nazi Germany." Again, despite a consensus by "impartial observers" that the *March of Time* review was "an unbiased presentation of Hitler's Austrian coup, ending with the implication that he may seek further expansion and military power, or meet his downfall attempting it," the studio banned the issue from its theaters.[24]

---

[c] Published in 1925, Hitler's prison memoir, the stranger-than-fiction blueprint for the Nazi scheme to take over the world, was then still largely unknown in America. Although Houghton Mifflin purchased the American rights to *Mein Kampf* and published an abridged edition in 1933, the publisher did not release a complete edition until March 1939 through Reynal & Hitchcock. A British edition published by Stackpole Sons was released the same month. The American edition sold 90,000 copies by the end of that year. Both publishers pledged to deny Hitler royalties and donate profits to German refugee relief. ("'Mein Kampf' in Unabridged Form," *New York Times*, Mar. 12, 1939: 94; "Books and Authors," *New York Times*, Dec. 3, 1939: 109.)

The prescient *March of Time* also anticipated the final act of the Czechoslovakian crisis. In July 1938, during preparations for its report "Prelude to Crisis," editor Louis de Rochemont had taken the precaution of asking Czechoslovakian president Edvard Beneš to go before the cameras for an address to the American people should what was feared come to pass. "We have been working hard during the last 20 years and have accomplished a great deal," said Beneš, referring to the fragile democracy enjoyed by the Czechs since the Great War. "We have tried and are still trying honestly to be just, as much as human beings can be. We hope that we shall be able to continue our work in the future, believing that international peace can be saved and honestly maintained by pacific means." On September 19, 1938, Beneš gave the green light to the Paris bureau of the *March of Time* to release the clip, which relayed the go-ahead to de Rochemont.[25] The appeal was quickly edited in to the final cut of "Prelude to Conquest."

Despite its attempts to stay ahead of the story, the monthly screen magazine, even more than the twice-weekly newsreels, was made yesterday's news by the quick-march of history. In the last week of September, just days before war was averted by the capitulation at Munich and thus dated even as it screened, the *March of Time* released its report on the Czechoslovakian crisis. Programmed before the Fred Astaire–Ginger Rogers musical *Carefree* (1938) at Radio City Music Hall in New York, the issue generated the kind of audience response more usually heard at the Embassy. Hitler was boisterously booed and Beneš, leader of the besieged and soon to be engulfed nation of Czechoslovakia, was roundly applauded.[26]

At some point in 1938, whether watching at Radio City, the Embassy, or neighborhood Bijous across America, newsreel audiences seem to have understood what the images of unchecked aggression and martial pageantry portended. Not voice-overs, or intertitles, or barked threats in a foreign tongue, but just the parade of military might and the shots of smug dictators watching from the stands was enough to sense where the parade was heading. In May 1938, flush from the triumph in Austria, Hitler visited Mussolini in Rome, where the Italian dictator staged a colossal festival of war games in honor of his ally. Newsreels showed the two dictators enjoying the show. "While the war games are unspooled with principals apparently in a state of camaraderie, the grim undertones of the reels have their startling effect upon an audience," commented *Variety,* chilled at the sight.[27]

Yet for all the history that unreeled in the newsreels that year, it was the images that could not be obtained that frustrated newsreel editors. "War clouds over Europe, with stress on Austrian and Czechoslovakian situations, dominate new show here [at the Embassy]," reported *Variety*'s Mike Wear the week after the *Anschluss.* "With no really live pictorial news on sudden moves abroad, news weekly lads scurried for latest shots of leaders in wartime preparations or best library material."[28] Looking back over the year's items, Wear summed up the twin dilemmas facing American newsreel journalism in the 1930s. "It was a year of swift happenings," he understated, bemoaning the chronic lack of access and timeliness. "Photographically, the difficulty is making a comprehensive story; topically, the difficulty is securing early shipment." Against the immediacy of radio bulletins and newspaper headlines, the newsreels looked "downright stale" by comparison. Hobbled by a scarcity of pictures, they were left to review news that audiences had already read and heard about, news that was, even as the images flashed on screen, overtaken by events.

As the commercial newsreels and the *March of Time* struggled to create a playbook for screen journalism, a third form of news on screen made no pretense of timeliness, seeking instead to lend perspective and meaning to the dire events of 1938 with a rueful, retrospective vision. A melancholy eulogy for a murdered democracy, the feature-length film *Crisis* (1939) served as a prewar prototype for a motion picture genre that would dominate the second half of the twentieth century—the World War II archival documentary.

The building blocks for *Crisis* were inherited from the handful of archival compilations of Great War footage made in the early 1930s, the pioneering retrieval-reenactment techniques of the *March of Time,* and the agenda-driven reportage of the Spanish Civil War documentaries. Enlivened by segments of instructional animation (maps of Nazi aggression, illustrated with swastikas bleeding over German borders and blackening the territory of other nations), the repurposing of newsreel footage showed that "library material" would never again be left on a studio shelf, shown once and then tucked away to be seen no more. Newsreel footage was becoming a central repository for the cultural memory of the nation.

Crisis was conceived and directed by Herbert Kline, the former editor of *New Theatre and Film* who had served a self-taught apprenticeship on the Spanish Civil War shorts *Spain in Flames* (1937) and *Heart of Spain* (1937). In spring 1938, Kline slipped into Czechoslovakia, gaining the trust of Czech Nazis in the Sudetenland with a forged letter purporting to be from German American Bund leader Fritz Kuhn. After the Munich Pact, assisted by cameraman Alexandr Hackenschmied and stage director Hans Burger, Kline went underground in Prague to complete post-production work. "We worked in fear of discovery and the consequences but got away with it, feeling like actors in an anti-Nazi drama," he recalled years later. With the connivance of anti-Nazi Czech customs officials at the Prague airport, he smuggled the film to Paris "in two suitcases so heavy I could barely lift them on the plane." At Paris customs, Kline switched his story again with a forged letter claiming he was a *March of Time* cameraman carrying harmless travelogue footage of the Czechoslovakian countryside.[29]

Back in New York, foreign correspondent Vincent Sheean, the best-selling author of the Spanish Civil War memoir, *Personal History*, wrote the commentary for *Crisis*, and actor Leif Erickson, a Group Theatre artist-activist just breaking into Hollywood, recorded the brawny narration. An original score, by the Czech composer Walter Susskin, was also added.

Neither newsreel snippets nor a *March of Time* synopsis, *Crisis* was a comprehensive documentary record of the betrayal and destruction of a European democracy. "The newsreels are too hurried, too sketchy to give the public any more than a suggestion of what is going on," Kline told *New York Times* film critic Bosley Crowther. "It takes a careful, reasonable analysis in visual terms which may be understood to give the moviegoing public a conception of the forces impelling a great conflict (such as that in Czechoslovakia)."[30] Covering events from the *Anschluss* to the Munich Pact, the film already assumes the inevitable outbreak of a wider war in Europe and is sending out an urgent alarm.

Crisis opens with a picture of the jacket of Hitler's *Mein Kampf*, further imprinting the work as the sacred book of Nazism in the American mind. An animated map of middle Europe with the Greater Reich, in black, surrounds the eastern edge of Czechoslovakia. The map of Germany morphs into a wolf's head, its jaws open and ready to bite into its territorial prey. Once Austria is consumed by the Third Reich, plucky Czechoslovakia stands next in line for the Nazi predator. The citizens of Prague prepare for the worst, buying up gas masks and equipping baby carriages with bellows for ventilation. "Jew and Aryan fared alike among the babies," notes the voice-over. "They had not yet heard of the Nazi racial laws."

The external threat from the Third Reich is augmented by its fifth column, the SDP, the Sudeten Deutsch Party, lead by the nefarious Konrad Henlein. Like its model, the SDP is a cover for roving gangs of brownshirted thugs, pledged to racial superiority and devoted to Hitler. To soften the sinews of the Czech democracy, "the Nazi propaganda machine" spews tons of leaflets, posters, and pamphlets into the Sudetenland to spawn hatred and sedition.

Wanting only peace, ordinary Czechs reach out a hand of friendship to the Sudeten Germans, many of whom are anti-Nazi refugees from Germany and Austria. There is much to enjoy in a nation of such rich history and gorgeous scenery, where cathedrals and palaces dot the landscape, and the colorful folk ("Catholic, Protestant, Jew") practice traditional arts and crafts and labor in industry and on the farm, abiding in harmony and toiling together for the common good.

Meanwhile, socialist trade unions give aid to anti-Nazi refugees and fight fascism with puppet shows and political theater. To the delight of a packed house, Czech comedians George Voskovec and Jan Werich, actor-playwrights for the Liberated Theater, perform a satirical anti-Nazi revue. The comedians also take the message to children at a trade union camp, singing patriotic Czech songs. (By the time *Crisis* was released, the duo had been forced to flee to New York, where they did publicity for the film.) Viewed from the vantage of 1939, all the bucolic scenes of peace-loving Czechs at work and play unfold as a poignant photo album of a nation-no-more. None of the scenes of indigenous Czech life—the speeches, the performances, and the songs—are subtitled, nor are the clips of Hitler's rants, but the melodious determination of the Czechs and the angry growl of the Germans require no translation.

Tragically, the pastoral ideal is infested with serpents. On May 22, municipal elections take place amid SDP terror tactics, ballot stuffing, and voter intimidation. Hitler seems poised to pounce, but is deterred by a nationwide mobilization called by the Beneš government. As heroic Czechs ("calm and resolute") rally to defend the frontier, the Nazis are temporarily blocked. However, the fifth column agitation continues unabated. When two Sudeten Germans are killed by Czech border guards, the SDP

A series of images from Herbert Kline's pioneering anti-Nazi documentary *Crisis* (1939) (*top to bottom*): opening the book on *Mein Kampf,* illustrating the ravenous appetite of Nazi Germany, and showing the plight of refugee children.

holds a grand funeral procession for the martyrs, replete with banners and torches. A wreath bearing the name of Adolf Hitler is solemnly laid in tribute. "No," says the narrator, "this is not a scene from the Dark Ages. This is the Nazi way."

A new wave of SDP-instigated violence roils the Sudetenland. The cameras miss the action, but not the aftermath: bloodstained sheets and victims battered by truncheons. Finally Beneš declares martial law and outlaws the SDP, closing down its offices and newspapers, but the forceful measures are too little, too late. The capitulation of France and England seals the fate of the democratic republic so unfortunate as to share a frontier with Germany. Desperate to avoid confrontation, Prime Minister Neville Chamberlain scurries first to Berchtesgaden, Hitler's lair, then to Bad Godesberg, and finally to Munich to sign the white piece of paper. "Betrayed and abandoned," Czechoslovakia is invaded by the Reich.

"The human race itself is impoverished and humiliated by these events," mourns the narrator. The outlook for the future is dim, what with men like Chamberlain in England and Daladier in France. We can only hope "that in other lands there may still be men who do not tremble and obey when Adolph Hitler cracks the whip." Considering the political credentials of the production team behind *Crisis*, the reference is more likely to Stalin than FDR.

As the pages of *Mein Kampf* open again, a literal bookend on the tragic tale, the narrator speaks a final admonition, words underscored in script on the screen:

Remember: Peace and freedom and the right to live—they can be possible only in lands where men are determined that the swastika shall not be raised in triumph; that the pages of *Mein Kampf* shall never become supreme law.

Released by veteran foreign film importers Arthur Mayer and Joseph Burstyn, *Crisis* premiered on March 13, 1939, at the 55th Street Playhouse. The night before, Kline had gone on the WABC radio program *We the People* and predicted that Hitler would break the Munich Pact and take Prague—which he did on March 15.

Given the topic and pedigree, *Crisis* had an especially high profile in Popular Front circles—and an inside track to the innermost part of the circle with a special advance screening at the White House. "You must show this film everywhere in our country to help counter the 'America Firsters' propaganda calling me a warmonger!" FDR exclaimed, according to Kline.[31] Better yet, Eleanor Roosevelt plugged the film in her nationally syndicated "My Day" column. "Perhaps the value of this picture for us is the mere realization of the difference which freedom backed by a sense of security gives in comparison with virtual dependency where security can no longer exist," she wrote, a delicate way of rebuking England and France and cautioning America.[32]

The First Lady was not alone in her enthusiasm or ruminations. "Here's a really excellent documentary film that should prove of great historical importance, for it contains phases of the world-stirring crisis that have not been caught by the newsreels," wrote the *Film Daily*, alert to the time capsule endurance of the film. Yes, there was propaganda ("all on the side of the Czechs") but "at least the camera cannot lie, and here are many scenes that will give the intelligent historical student a clearer grasp of many phases that may have escaped his attention, or which newspapers accounts have not covered."[33] *Motion Picture Herald*'s reviewer George Spires, who caught the film under optimal conditions, reported: "The picture, playing to a capacity anti-Nazi audience in New York, was applauded at the finish."[34] *Daily Worker* critic Henry Hart, who saw the film twice in the same venue, dwelled on the grief of those around him. "Sobbing could be heard in the darkness of the theatre as the betrayal of the brave, honorable and intelligent Czech people unfolds and, when the picture was over, tears could be seen in the eyes of men and women, young and old."[35]

According to Kline, the best scene was not in the film: on the night of Hitler's Nuremberg speech, in the town of Opaca, close to the convergence of the German, Czech, and Polish borders, Kline had been tipped to look for trouble. It came soon enough: a group of local Nazi sympathizers surrounded an old Jewish man peddling popcorn on the street corner. In response, a group of Czech youths formed a protective cordon around the old man. Before the Nazis could pounce, a lone Czech policeman defused the situation by lecturing the Nazis about the cowardice of the act. "That was one of the most significant indications I saw of the situation in Czechoslovakia before Munich," Kline recalled. "It was, you might say, the sort of thing that could be easily staged in a studio. I saw it happen. And yet, I couldn't get it in my camera because there was no light."[36]

Yet the newsreels, the *March of Time*, and Kline's *Crisis* shed enough light on the situation in Europe for viewers to see the writing on the wall. Though covered in fits and starts, often with footage filtered by the Nazis, the *Anschluss* and the Czechoslovakia crises gave Americans their first good look at Nazi aggression. However, a more terrible story was unreeling out of sight of the newsreel camera. "Munich was the highlight of 1938 and history," Wear stated in his wrap-up of the year in newsreels, casually mentioning the runner-up. "Jewish persecution scenes, ranked by most newsreel editors as next in importance in foreign affairs, were terrifically ticklish and hard to handle."[37]

"THE PRESENT PERSECUTIONS IN GERMANY"

When the news first flashed over the radio airwaves late in the evening of November 9–10, 1938, the German word *Kristallnacht* had not yet entered the American lexicon. Literally meaning "crystal night," a glib term coined by the brownshirted perpetrators, but now translated as "the night of broken glass," it marks a solemn day of remembrance. The compound noun is an oddly poetic metaphor for the shattering of property, bones, and illusions—a thunderclap moment that made it clear as crystal that the Nazi campaign against the Jews was no off-the-cuff rampage but the orchestration of state policy.

For American journalism also, Kristallnacht marked an epiphany. Jolted awake to the full frenzy of the Nazi pathology against the Jews, newspapers headlined the story, radio flashed bulletins, and editorials condemned the persecutions.[38] Even the newsreels woke up and harkened to the racket. Heretofore, shut out from coverage of Nazi depredations and "terrifically ticklish" about broaching the topic of antisemitism, they had mainly looked the other way.

The match that lit the firestorm was the shooting of the third secretary of the German embassy in Paris, an official with the too-perfect name of Ernst vom Rath, by Herschel Grynszpan, a 17-year-old Polish Jew driven to derangement by his stateless status. When vom Rath succumbed to his wounds at 4:25 p.m. on November 9, the Gestapo sent out secret orders for an orgy of destruction that smashed property and spilled blood in virtually every German and Austrian town with a visible Jewish presence. Joseph Goebbels later claimed that the pogrom was a spontaneous outburst of righteous anger from the German *volk,* a "justifiable and understandable" manifestation of Aryan vengeance against Jewish perfidy, but a lengthy paper trail attests to the calculation behind the anarchy in the streets—which is not to say sundry acts of vandalism, brutality, and murder were not improvised on the spot.[39]

In America the next morning, front-page headlines were already attuned to the sonic atmospherics. "The noise of breaking glass and

Kristallnacht, November
9–10, 1938: the aftermath
of "the night of broken glass"
in Berlin, captured in a wire
service photograph but not
by the American newsreels.

cracking furniture accompanied loud anti-Jewish jeers," read the first report from the Associated Press. "When the smashing crew had passed, it looked like a tornado had swept the street. The pavement was covered with broken glass." Otto D. Tolischus, the Berlin correspondent for the *New York Times,* was also an earwitness to "the shattering of shop windows falling to the pavement, the dull thuds of furniture and fittings being pounded to pieces and the clamor of fire brigades rushing to burning shops and synagogues."[40]

Unfortunately, the most sound-sensitive of the media was well out of hearing range. During Kristallnacht, CBS's European bureau chief Edward R. Murrow happened to be stateside and Berlin correspondent William L. Shirer, heartsick from the fallout from the Munich Pact, had retreated first to Geneva and then to Warsaw. He makes no mention of Kristallnacht in his diary or memoirs. However, NBC's Max Jordan was on the scene in Berlin, "when the antisemitic frenzy reach[ed] its climax," he recalled in his 1944 memoir. Going outside his hotel, he first came across the smoldering ruins of a synagogue and then a fashionable street of Jewish-owned shops where "every single show window had been smashed." He too mentions no direct live broadcast to America.[41] Like all centers of mass communication, the Berlin shortwave transmitter used by the American networks was controlled by Goebbels' Reich Ministry and the copy of radio correspondents was strictly censored prior to broadcast. Even had either correspondent been near an open microphone, the street-level reality would not have gone out over the air.

Radio journalists attempted to conjure the sounds of terror with words. By the next afternoon in America, the news was being read out from wire reports by breathless announcers on NBC's Blue Network:

> This has been a day of terror for the Jews in Germany. All over Hitler's country, Nazi mobs have been beating Jews, wrecking their shops and homes, burning and dynamiting synagogues. It was the worse anti-Jewish outbreak since Hitler came to power. . . . After fourteen hours of violence, propaganda minister Goebbels has finally called a halt, but Goebbels condoned the attacks. . . . Thousands [of Jews] have been arrested, and in Vienna, twenty-five committed suicide.[42]

Regular updates were reported on the hour.

Yet perhaps the din of Kristallnacht came most powerfully into American homes not from stateside announcers reading out wire copy, but from editorial commentary, a relatively new practice. Across the airwaves, commentators raised their voices in full-throated denunciations of the Nazi rampage. "The rage of antisemitic terror in Germany was as good as ordered by the Hitler government," declared NBC's Lowell Thomas. "It's all a deliberate policy, a calculated stroke of terror." On WMCA, former New York governor Al Smith and New York district attorney Thomas E. Dewey condemned the Nazis on a one-hour program later rebroadcast due to popular demand. On WNEW, commentator Richard Brooks recited Marc Antony's funeral oration from *Julius Caesar* with Hitler's name substituted for Brutus'.[43] The radio chorus was blunt, loud, and, with one acid-tongued exception, unanimous.

On November 20, the demagogic radio priest Father Charles E. Coughlin devoted his regular Sunday homily to preaching a familiar set of Nazi canards about the Jews—that the Jews were the agents of Bolshevism, that the Jews caused Germany to lose the Great War, and that the Jews undermined Christian America. Though Coughlin had previously said

as much or worse, this time his screed unleashed a flood of protests. In
New York, WMCA took the unusual step of breaking in after Coughlin's
talk to inform listeners that the priest had made errors of fact. The station later announced it would "not permit a repetition" of Coughlin's
antisemitic incitements.[44]

However vividly Kristallnacht might be rendered in print and on radio,
Americans could neither hear the racket nor see the fires in the newsreels. No newsreel footage of the rampage exists and no newsreel cameraman, American or German, risked his neck for the scoop. An amateur
shutterbug seems to have been the only exception.[d] A Los Angeles doctor
visiting Berlin was reported to have attempted to take motion pictures of

---

[d] Raye Farr, film curator at the United States Holocaust Memorial Museum, knows of only two
brief snippets of motion pictures taken during Kristallnacht. "One is privately owned footage resid-
ing at the Bundesarchiv. It takes place in Bielefeld, and shows locals hanging out the window to
watch the synagogue dome burn; also shots of it collapsing. The other is in Buehl, [showing] moving images of local people and the fire brigade watching the synagogue burn; the firemen train a
hose on the adjacent building's roof. It's 38 seconds long, filmed on 8mm." (Raye Farr to Thomas
Doherty, Oct. 31, 2008.)

smashed shop windows in the city. He was promptly taken into custody and his film confiscated by the Nazis.[45]

Of course, the absence of motion picture verification hardly constituted a mediawide news blackout. The persecution of the Jews under the Nazis in the 1930s was widely known and thoroughly chronicled. Antisemitism was a core tenet of Nazi doctrine, shouted by Hitler at the top of his lungs, trumpeted by Goebbels' propaganda, and visible to any tourist wandering the streets of the Greater Reich. But while news reports and firsthand accounts testified to the systematic discrimination and random violence, motion picture footage documenting the terror was sparse.

Only a few glimpses broke through the Nazi fog. During the brief window of opportunity in early 1933, the literal signs of antisemitism appeared in newsreel coverage of the boycott of Jewish-owned businesses on April 1, 1933. Footage of the Berlin boycott arrived on New York screens precisely two weeks later on April 14, 1933.[46] The clips offered glimpses of scuffling brownshirts, a skull and crossbones with the word "Juden" scrawled above it, storefront placards ordering Germans not to buy from Jews, and signs prohibiting Jews from public accommodations. The select montage of images comprised a core cache of reusable material that was replayed as "library stock" for the rest of the decade. Freeze-framed, the crude sign of the "Juden"-tagged skull and crossbones served as a potent symbol of the poison of antisemitism flowing through the Third Reich.

The only supplement to the newsreels that year was an obscure independent film. Released in April 1933, a 17-minute short entitled *Hitler and Germany* can claim pride of place as the first English-language anti-Nazi documentary. It was produced by the New York–based Film Forum, a self-styled "private society for the discussion and encouragement of unusual motion pictures," a phrase that translated as cadres of left-wing cinephiles sponsoring screenings of Soviet cinema at the New School for Social Research.[47] Modeled on similar groups in Europe, the outfit was bankrolled and presided over by Broadway dramatist Sidney Howard.

A filmed symposium rather than an archival documentary, *Hitler and Germany* recorded a roundtable discussion moderated by Amos Pinchot, an eccentric pacifist-progressive reformer. Pinchot posed questions to a series of notable anti-Nazis and asked each in turn their impressions of the new regime. First to speak was Edward Dahlberg, the American Jewish novelist, just back from Germany, where he told of being attacked on the streets. Dahlberg was followed by Norman Thomas, the prominent socialist and perennial presidential candidate; Clarence Hathaway, a communist stalwart who edited the *Daily Worker*; Peretz Hirschbein, the Russian-born Yiddish-language playwright; Ella Winter, the wife of journalist Lincoln Steffens and secretary of the American Committee Against Fascist Oppression in Germany;[e] and historian Hendrik Willem van Loon, who opined that in a couple of years no one would remember Hitler's name.

Sold as a short subject and recommended only for limited bookings in Jewish or Catholic neighborhoods, *Hitler and Germany* was less a symposium than a one-sided fusillade. "Maybe they couldn't find anyone to take the German butcher's side," figured Wolfe Kaufman.[48] The *Film Daily* worded its review carefully: "Their speeches as a whole represent a protest against the alleged Hitlerite terrorism."[49] At the Cameo, the short played on a bill with Slatan Dudow's Weimer-era communist paean *Whither Germany?* (1932) and then vanished.

After the first part of 1933, the solidification of Nazi control meant that independent motion picture coverage of Nazi Germany by the American newsreels, and especially of the antisemitic outrages, was virtually impossible to obtain. During the 1936 Olympics in Berlin, when the newsreels were given somewhat freer rein, at least beyond Leni Riefenstahl's field of vision, the Nazis stored the antisemitic signage away for the duration so as not to distress the tourists. Print reporters commented on the conspicuous absence but the newsreel camera could not show what was not there. A rare shot of the Nazi wallpaper was captured in 1937 by Julien Bryan who, though closely supervised by his Nazi handlers, managed to sneak a shot of antisemitic signage on park benches for the *March of Time*'s "Inside Nazi Germany" episode of January 1938.

The minimal time the newsreels allotted to coverage of antisemitic incidents in Germany may have been understandable given the medium's utter dependence on footage. Less understandable was the minimal time allotted anti-Nazi protests by Jews in America. Only occasionally did the newsreels cover an anti-Nazi protest organized by Jewish groups. Two factors increased the odds for recognition: if the rally were large enough and in close proximity to newsreel headquarters in New York.

---

[e] Winter married David Ogden Stewart in 1939, three years after Steffens's death.

On March 27, 1933, a huge anti-Nazi rally was held in Madison Square Garden, in coordination with dozens of similar rallies staged nationwide. To an overflow crowd of 20,000—with 35,000 more clogging the streets outside the Garden—former New York governor Al Smith told the cheering throngs he would oppose the bigotry of the Nazis with the same zeal he opposed the Ku Klux Klan. "And it don't make any difference to me whether it is a brownshirt or a nightshirt," he cracked in his gruff New Yorkese.[50] Despite the dramatic images and nationwide significance of the event (nearly one million Jews and their allies participated in anti-Nazi rallies that day), the newsreels mustered little interest in the impressive outpouring of domestic anti-Nazi sentiment. "Luxer was the only house Saturday afternoon to screen the Garden mass meeting in protest of Hitler," Tom Waller noted that weekend, crediting the sole clip to Paramount News. Also on the program at the Trans-Lux that afternoon were segments on a blind man building a house, a one-armed golfer swinging on the green, and a champion pretzel bender. Footage of slugger Babe Ruth signing his new contract with the New York Yankees was given lavish treatment by all the reels.[51]

Those kind of priorities put the newsreels at odds with their prestigious rival in screen journalism. In 1935 the March of Time lambasted the newsreels for the timidity of their coverage of Nazism in general and Nazi persecutions of the Jews in particular. Truman Tally, producer of Fox Movietone News, the newsreel with the best field operation in Germany, admitted the screen magazine had a point but insisted such self-censorship was all in the past. "Of course, there was a time when the reels 'laid off' Hitler to some extent," he explained, attributing the hiatus to a desire not to unduly upset audiences discomforted by reports of Jewish persecutions. Motion Picture Herald elaborated:

> It was indicated by all managers of newsreel companies that there had been occasional protests on the part of Jewish motion picture exhibitors "whose feelings were hurt," but with one exception the newsreels appear to be of the opinion that what the exhibitor chooses to delete under such circumstances is no concern of anyone but the exhibitor himself.[52]

Between the lines of the double-talk, the newsreels were saying that neither audiences nor exhibitors much cared to be shown news of antisemitic terror in Germany. Moviegoing folks, Jew and non-Jew alike, were out for a nice night on the town, and preferred to be walled off from the ugly happenings of the outside world. Thus, even when the newsreels broached the subject of Nazi persecutions, usually with a report on a stateside protest against Nazism, exhibitors often cut the clip to avoid an in-house disturbance or an unpleasant aftertaste that might sour enjoyment of the featured attraction. The same rule applied to coverage of *pro*-Nazi demonstrations. In April 1939 the German American Bund mounted a massive pro-Nazi rally in Madison Square Garden, which the newsreels dutifully covered. In New York, theater after theater reported disturbances from incensed moviegoers. The newsreels quickly eliminated the Bund clips from the issue.[53]

Characteristically, the *March of Time* took a more aggressive and plainspoken stance toward the antisemitism at the heart of Nazi doctrine. The first segment in its seventh issue, released October 1935, reviewed the history of the British protectorate of Palestine and British efforts to colonize the promised land with Jews. "A topic off the beaten trail," noted *Variety*. More offbeat was the reason, besides Zionist zeal, that 50,000 Jews were fleeing Europe. "Shots of Hitler on the soapbox, and of mobs of Nazis making raids on Jewish homes, shops, offices, stores, [are] highly dramatic and, of course, controversial," continued the review, observing, by way of contrast with the newsreels, that the *March of Time* "thrives on controversial items" even though "Nazi elements may yelp at the unflattering picturization."[54] Boasting that "764 Rabbis and 23 Jewish organizations [were] cooperating on the Palestine episode," the publicity for the issue left no doubt about the screen magazine's sympathies—or its target audience.[55]

In "Poland and War" (June 1937), the *March of Time* shows scenes of antisemitic violence in Poland (reenacted), incubated by the antisemitic newspapers (real) of "the club-footed chief of Hitler's propaganda machine," Dr. Joseph Goebbels. "In ghettos, for the first time in many years, pogroms are breaking out," reports narrator Westbrook Van Voorhis, reverting to the house syntax for the indictment: "In the repeated attacks on Jews are seen the workings of Hitler's machine." *Variety* noticed the bluntness and approved: "The *March of Time* by its offscreen narration blames Hitler and his propaganda machine for the horrifying pogroms upon Jews in Poland."[56]

Though "Inside Nazi Germany," the *March of Time*'s most famous episode of the 1930s, condemned "Hitler's relentless campaign against the
Jews" in its commentary and underscored the point in publicity material
that emphasized "the sequestration of the Jews, banned by state edict
from professions and business," such outspokenness remained exceptional.[57] A few weeks before Kristallnacht, the Chicago Board of Censors
snipped scenes of Jewish persecutions from a lecture and screening by
Julien Bryan, the cameraman whose exclusive photography in Nazi Germany was the episode's main selling point.[58]

After Kristallnacht, however, even the Chicago censors lost the habit
of kowtowing to a nominally friendly foreign power. Emboldened by
the new atmospherics and abashed by the criticism in the print press,
the newsreels seized the moment and unloaded on the Nazis—as best
they could given the limitations. "Reflecting the most urgent topic of
the week, the current bill at the Embassy stresses the outbreak of anti-
Semitic terrorism in Germany," reported *Variety*, the conscientious mon-
itor of the newsreel bill. "But since no pictures of the violence are available (there wouldn't have been time enough to get them here even if Nazi
censorship permitted the scenes to be filmed), the newsreels have had
to treat the subject from this end." That is, lacking footage of the actual
pogrom, newsreel editors recruited politicians and religious leaders for
on-camera condemnations, a lineup of luminaries that included former
president Herbert Hoover, former New York governor Al Smith, and former Republican presidential candidate Alf Landon.[59] "American public
opinion is aroused!" proclaimed Lowell Thomas, the voice of Fox Movietone, introducing remarks by Hoover: "The only living ex-president
expresses the official attitude that Nazi violence is both anti-Semitic and
anti-Christian."

Goaded at last into action but still strait-jacketed by lack of access, newsreel editors organized to address the problem. On the morning of November 18, 1938, in a hastily arranged huddle at in the New York offices of the
MPPDA, representatives from Fox Movietone News, News of the Day, Paramount News, RKO-Pathé, and Universal Newsreel met to pool resources
and discuss strategies. According to leaked reports, the purpose of the confab was "to formulate plans for a concerted presentation by each of the
reels of the current persecution in Nazi Germany." On the table was a plan
for all five companies to cooperate on the production of a special issue to

be released first to theaters around the nation and then circulated free of charge to "churches, schools, labor organizations and other outlets."

Faced with the usual brick wall, the well-intentioned venture came to naught. "An insurmountable barrier existed to bar the plans, namely the dearth of film footage available to make a vigorous presentation to the public," lamented the *Film Daily*, which gave a succinct summation of the paucity of imagination and access that had bedeviled the newsreels since 1933 in covering the Nazi war against the Jews:

> Prior to the present persecutions in Germany, the newsreel companies, with the exception of the *March of Time*, which is not strictly in that category, were slow in anticipating the situation which has now developed. Additionally, the Nazi Government has made the taking of authentic scenes of oppression virtually impossible to obtain.[60]

Though Kristallnacht lacked a visceral representation in the newsreel medium, it left a profound impact on the Popular Front. A stepped-up campaign of anti-Nazi activism from within the ranks of the motion picture industry helped fill the vacuum in screen coverage. Locked out from on-location coverage, unable to crack the Hollywood feature film, artist-activists responded to the rising tide of antisemitic violence in the greater Reich with a concurrent surge of political action.

On November 18, 1938, the Hollywood Anti-Nazi League mounted a massive "Quarantine Hitler" rally at Philharmonic Auditorium in Los Angeles. In between impassioned speeches from actor John Garfield and director Frank Capra, a crowd of 3,500 motion picture industry personnel unanimously voted to send a telegram, signed by dozens of prominent Hollywood personalities, to President Roosevelt. "The Nazi outrages against Jews and Catholics have shocked the world," read the plea to FDR. "Coming on the heels of the Munich pact, they prove that capitulation to Hitler means barbarism and terror. . . . We in Hollywood urge you to use your presidential authority to express further the horror and the indignation of the American people."

Chester Bahn, editor of the *Film Daily*, had also had enough. In a boxed-off front-page notice, he announced a new policy for the New York–based trade paper:

> Effective today [November 21, 1938], The Film Daily announces the discontinuance of its long-established Berlin Bureau.

The reason for this decision to withdraw from normal press relations with Nazi Germany should be obvious.

When and if a responsible German Government takes over, re-establishment of the Berlin Bureau will receive careful consideration.[61]

Throughout Hollywood, Kristallnacht spurred a militant anti-Nazi fervor that spread beyond the already energized anti-Nazi core. "This very welcome change of attitude on the part of a few tycoons was unquestionably traceable to news of the most recent Nazi persecutive outrages," reported Ivan Spear in Box Office, though he complained that many in Hollywood's executive ranks still balked at cooperation "with the groups that have been carrying on the valiant fight against the spread of totalitarian doctrines and policies in America."[62] It was into this charged atmosphere that Leni Riefenstahl walked during her ill-fated visit to Hollywood. The town was primed to vent its pent-up fury at the nearest incarnation of the Nazi regime.

However, the most enduring response to Kristallnacht was not a newsreel, a rally, or a telegram, but a song. For the evening of November 10, 1938, just as the wave of antisemitic violence in Berlin was subsiding, the singer Kate Smith had long planned to dedicate her variety show program to the twentieth anniversary of Armistice Day, a solemn look back at the last war as the world stood on the brink of another. She asked her friend, the composer Irving Berlin, for a patriotic anthem suitable for the occasion. Rummaging through his old sheet music, Berlin resurrected a patriotic song originally written for but cut from his Great War musical Yip Yip Yiphank![63] The tune was "God Bless America." Smith belted it with a passion that electrified listeners. An instant sensation, the castoff composition by the Jewish American composer with the Germanic surname became Smith's signature song and America's unofficial national anthem.

Given the terrifying news from overseas, little wonder Americans sought patriotic expression with song-prayers of thanksgiving for their own blessings. By early 1939 the spread of Nazi hegemony, the brutal antisemitic outbreaks, and the plight of pathetic refugees trudging across Central Europe dominated the news of the day across the media, newsreels not excluded. In response, and with no official prompting, the motion picture industry began to play the National Anthem as an integral part of the balanced program: a few big palaces with orchestras played it live; most venues unspooled a Technicolor short featuring a chorus singing over patriotic imagery.[64] When juxtaposed against the nightmarish images from Europe, the contrast could be inspirational. "The showing of [the *March of Time*'s "The Refugee—Today and Tomorrow" (December 1938)] is brought to a rousing pitch by following it immediately with a Technicolor trailer of the Stars and Stripes blowing in the breeze and a recorded choral group giving way to the 'Star Spangled Banner,'" reported a *Variety* reporter at the Embassy Theater. "The audience quickly got to its feet and joined the soundtrack choristers in the anthem's several verses."

Woe to the moviegoer who did not show proper deference. "A few men in the audience, who continued to wear their hats during the rendition, discovered they were in the United States," growled Mike Wear, meaning that the ill-mannered clods were barked at to remove their headgear.[65] No one dared to remain seated.

11

THERE IS NO ROOM FOR LENI RIEFENSTAHL IN HOLLYWOOD

Dancer, athlete, actress, filmmaker, Leni Riefenstahl was the Valkyrie goddess of Third Reich cinema, the lone shimmering star in a constellation of dim hacks. Murnau preferred Camilla Horn for the doomed Gretchen in *Faust* (1926), Lang tapped Brigitte Helm for the metallic siren in *Metropolis* (1927), and von Sternberg anointed Marlene Dietrich as *The Blue Angel* (1929), but an impresario of greater magnitude gave the perennial understudy the role of her lifetime in the director's chair. An authentic genius of the moving image, as graceful with the camera as her body, she choreographed two Nazi pageants that will live as long as images fill motion picture screens, *Triumph of the Will* (1935), a Wagnerian paean to the 1934 Nazi Party rally at Nuremberg, and *Olympia* (1938), a magisterial two-part chronicle of the 1936 Berlin Olympics. Alone of the artists and architects who sculpted idols and built monuments to the Third Reich, she realized her vision in a medium sturdy enough to withstand saturation Allied bombing.

Riefenstahl's life is the stuff of legend, mainly her own. Sifting the facts from the fabrications has proven a nettlesome task for her biographers, but even stripped of her lies the story is remarkable enough.[1]

Born in 1902 in comfortable circumstances in the otherwise working-class district of Wedding on the outskirts of Berlin, she vaulted from her humble origins as a day player at Ufa (unbilled and undraped she appeared in the sexploitation sensation *Ways to Strength and Beauty* [1925]) and into the Weimar spotlight as a nimble dancer flouncing in the diaphanous style of Isadora Duncan. Given star billing on Max Reinhardt's stage, she learned to land on her feet, a skill she never lost. In 1925 she got her 8 by 10 glossy into the hands of director Arnold Fanck. Mesmerized by the portrait, he became her first motion picture mentor.

Fanck was a specialist in, virtually the originator of, the "mountain film," an Ur-German genre played out amid craggy Alpine landscapes, treacherous glaciers, and thundering avalanches. Utterly fearless, game for anything, Riefenstahl mastered the slippery topography, turning herself into an expert mountaineer and skier while risking frostbite and her neck in service to Fanck's snowblind vision. In on-location escapades such as *The Holy Mountain* (1926) and the international hit *The White Hell of Pitz Palu* (1929), she played the snow angel to his ice sculptor.

With her knack for timing and networking, Riefenstahl happened to be present at two key cinematic events of the Weimar era. In 1926, at the Berlin premiere of Sergei Eisenstein's *Battleship Potemkin,* she joined the crowds who sat spellbound before the kinetic vitality of a revolution in filmmaking. Liberated from the gliding camera and painterly set design of the Ufa aesthetic, directors rushed to mimic the Russian's pulsating rhythms and whiplash montage. Three years later, Riefenstahl attended the riotous premiere of *All Quiet on the Western Front* (1930), where she caught her first glimpse of a frothing Joseph Goebbels spitting invective at the screen.[2]

No longer content to let Fanck call the shots—or to bury her in avalanches—Riefenstahl achieved the unthinkable by securing financing to direct and star in her own film. *The Blue Light* (1932) was a Fanck-like high-altitude melodrama about a gypsy girl so in touch with nature, so in tune with the aurora borealis, that the local peasants think she practices witchcraft. Stateside critics marveled at the career change. "Miss Riefenstahl authored and sponsored the production herself," a surprised *Film Daily* noticed, praising her "splendid performance" as the bewitching gypsy.[3] Perhaps, had a Hollywood mogul spotted her star potential and made the right offer, she might have resumed her screen rivalry with Marlene Dietrich at Paramount or, though sheer force of will, broken into the exclusive boys' club of studio directors with Dorothy Arzner.

Riefenstahl's swan song performance as clay in another director's hands was in Universal's *S.O.S. Iceberg* (1933), an on-location spectacular codirected by Hollywood's Tay Garnett and Ufa's Fanck, the last of the big-budget German-American coproductions born of the Weimar era. Garnett handled the melodrama; Fanck the landscapes. Shot in death-defying conditions in Greenland, the subzero action-adventure film built a rescue narrative around astonishing footage of ice calving off the Rink Glacier. Riefenstahl played a tangential character, the aviatrix wife of an Arctic explorer whose research team is cast adrift on an iceberg. The stranded explorers are rescued by the Great War hero Maj. Ernst Udet, famed German air ace, playing himself.

Riefenstahl was soon to be tapped for a bigger part in film history. The story was that Hitler, smitten by her sunlit dance on the beach in *The Holy Mountain*, plucked her from the crowd to channel his cinematic ambitions, much the way Albert Speer gave expression to Hitler's monumental architectural schemes. As a regular guest at Nazi social functions, she dined with the Nazi power elite and sipped after-dinner drinks before screenings of forbidden Hollywood films. Despite the celibate lifestyle attributed to the host, rumors of a romantic liaison between Hitler and Riefenstahl were whispered in Reich Ministry halls and blared in stateside headlines, though by most accounts, and not just her own, the devil's bargain was never consummated, at least not physically. Whatever the exact nature of the attraction, she enjoyed privileged access to the executive in charge of production—very much to the consternation of his jealous male entourage.

Goebbels resented her direct line to Hitler, and, if Riefenstahl is to be believed, her rejection of his sexual overtures, but the propaganda minister was also infuriated by the dismal quality of Nazi cinema. In 1933 he banned the static *Horst Wessel* (1933), a hagio-biopic about the martyred Nazi storm trooper, for "artistic inadequacy," an embarrassment that "neither does justice to the personality of Horst Wessel, reducing his heroic figure through inadequate presentation, nor to the National-Socialist movement which is today bearer of the State."[4] Despite the full backing of the Nazi machine, the Reichsfilmkammer failed to produce a single film with the cross-border appeal of a program filler from Warner Bros. Not blind to her talent, Goebbels suppressed his bureaucratic jealousy and gender bias. Without Riefenstahl, he had precious little to crow about.

In September 1933, Riefenstahl undertook a kind of audition film for the Third Reich, a documentary short of the Nazi Party Congress at Nuremberg entitled *Victory of Faith* (1933), a work afterwards disavowed by the director on aesthetic rather than moral grounds. A year later, during the Sixth Party Congress at Nuremberg, she was given the ranking authority and mammoth resources to construct a 35mm edifice to the

Nazi ethos. Presiding over acres of territory and an obedient cast of thousands, she called the shots for a cinematic spectacle beyond even the means of a D. W. Griffith or Cecil B. DeMille.

The result—the awe-inspiring *Triumph of the Will*—proved that the girl director had morphed into a major artist. Often called a documentary, it is more akin to a concert film, recording a showstopping extravaganza staged for the cameras. Yet the Nazi Party Congress of 1934 was no pseudo-event: something real was happening. Columns of robotic troops planted in geometric patterns, tongues of flame illuminating nighttime parades, and blond youths with clear eyes and taut sinews swirl by in a rapturous revue. Above it all—literally so in the film's devious overture, where the airborne leader swoops down like an eagle from the heavens— is the divine figure of the *führer*, lord ruler of the Nazi universe. All else are mere mortals, extras in his star vehicle.

Unlike the Party Congress at Nuremberg, *Triumph of the Will* was not a metronomic goose step but a sensuous ballet, the tempo of the editing a free-form dance recital. True to her roots, Riefenstahl orchestrated a pageant of pulsating, syncopated movement, vibrant and reverent, festive and purposeful. "Pic is an overgrown newsreel abounding in marching brownshirts, flags, and speeches by Nazi leaders," sneered *Variety,* noting that it tanked even in Berlin.[5] The most important patrons were well satisfied, however. For her cinematic service, Goebbels presented her with the Adolf Hitler prize for Best Picture from 1934.

So vivid in the memory of Nazism today—few archival flashbacks to the Third Reich can resist lifting a clip from *Triumph of the Will*— Riefenstahl's epic was known mainly by reputation and rumor in America in the 1930s. Glimpses of her work flashed by in the American newsreels, without attribution, seemingly snuck in by editors incapable of resisting the allure of the imagery. "Although it is far down in the program, one of the most interesting clips on the show is that of a Hitler rally," observed *Variety*'s Roy Chartier from a seat at the Embassy Newsreel Theater. "Because of the news importance of the Nazi leader and what's happening overseas, this contribution, rather long, should have been up front. Unless, of course, newsreel people want to play down the significance and importance of such material as this, which bearing on Hitler and Nazism, brought scattered applause and sibilation [hisses] Saturday afternoon [October 13, 1934]." Chartier was dumbstruck by the fusion of grand spectacle and cinematic dexterity: "The Hitler celebration, attended by

Leni Riefenstahl ascendant: the Nazi auteur filming a soaring vertical shot at the Nazi Party rally in Nuremberg in 1934 for *Triumph of the Will* (1935). (Courtesy Corbis Images)

700,000 farmers, does not credit the reel maker which supplies it, nor is there any offscreen narration for explanatory remarks. Sound cameras were on the job, screening the rally in detail and efficiently, with a brief speech by Hitler included. The very impressive page from Hitler activity was just ahead of two shorts, which close the show, and may have been placed there with thought of burying it rather than calling greater attention by spotting up [the Nazi clip] near the lead items."[6]

As a titled motion picture, however, *Triumph of the Will* floated under the radar of most Americans in the 1930s—at least most English-speaking Americans. A couple of prints circulated stateside in members-only screenings sponsored by the German American Bund and, in 1939, at least one theatrical screening broke out of the underground circuit. "There's a Nazi controlled theater in New York (96th Street and 3rd Avenue)," revealed Irving Hoffman, the New York–based correspondent for the *Hollywood Reporter,* not deigning to name the 96th Street Theatre, formerly the notorious Yorkville Theatre, "which is a clearing house for German propaganda films that are considered too hot to handle by other Yorkville movie houses." The "hatred-mongering and rabid paean to Nazidom," said Hoffman, "has been kept pretty much of a secret." Word of mouth—in German—whispered news of the film.[a] "Attendance has largely been drawn through the German newspapers and mailing lists of German-American organizations. An announcement on the screen at the conclusion of the picture requests that the audience help spread the picture's 'message' of hate and intolerance by sending others to see it."[7]

The first reference to *Triumph of the Will* in the Hollywood trade press came in March 1935 from an unnamed and by then surely non-Jewish stringer for *Variety* in Berlin. "Called *Triumph des Willens* ("Triumph of the Will"), production and cutting were directed by Leni Riefenstahl acting under party leaders' orders. Miss Riefenstahl ordinarily is known as a film star."[8]

Not any longer. *Triumph of the Will* catapulted Riefenstahl onto the international stage as a creative force to be reckoned with in world cinema. It has been said that there are only two characters in *Triumph of the Will*—Hitler and the masses, *der Führer* and *das Volk*—but the third is the controlling intelligence behind every shot, the auteur, Riefenstahl. Set beside *Triumph of the Will*, wrote the unwillingly awed Carl Dreher, the Austrian-born sound engineer moonlighting as the house expert on Nazi cinema for *New Theatre and Film*, "all other heroic Nazi movies appear dwarfed."[9]

---

[a] On the eve of World War II, only two 35mm copies of *Triumph of the Will* seem to have been extant in the United States: one in the archives of the Museum of Modern Art in New York, the other in the custody of the U.S. Customs Service. Both prints were requisitioned and cannibalized for wartime propaganda films.

Dreher spoke too soon. In the annals of heroic Nazi movies, Riefen-stahl's next venture dwarfed even *Triumph of the Will*. The 1936 Olym-pic Games, held in Berlin from August 1–16, 1936, promised to possess more crossover appeal than a rally for Nazi fanatics. Awarded in 1931 to the soon-to-be-defunct Weimar Republic, the games were to be a media-friendly global showcase for the athletic prowess of a revitalized nation under Nazi rule. The motion picture medium and Riefenstahl were slated to play key roles in fusing the ideal Greek body type to the flesh-and-blood warriors of Nazi myth. "Who else but you could make a film of the Olympics?" Hitler asked her, presumably not rhetorically. Appointed to do for sports what she had done for the party, she was given a free hand to compete for a gold medal in her own event.

The conferring of so singular an honor on a woman, whose gender was ordinarily consigned to children, church, and kitchen in Nazi ideol-ogy, fascinated onlookers beyond the Reich. Even before the wire service reporters, radio correspondents, and newsreel cameramen descended on Berlin to cover the sports story of the decade, the American press corps doted on the sidebar story of the red-haired *fräulein* in command of so much manpower and equipment. In February 1936 a leggy pic-ture of the actress-director on skies in a bathing suit, climbing upward, graced the cover of *Time* magazine—athlete, artist, and pinup girl[b] in the same package.[10]

Unable to imagine a purely professional relationship between the director and the dictator, the press spun outré speculations about the odd couple—he an ascetic vegetarian, she an outdoorsy epicurean. Riefen-stahl was tagged with cutesy nicknames by snarky headline writers: "Hit-ler's honey," the "fuehrer's fraulein," "the czarina of Nazi movieland," and so on. In a sea of drab brownshirts, the splashy redhead made great copy.

Riefenstahl also made enemies, especially among the newsreel cam-eramen and still photographers assigned to cover the Berlin Olympics.

---

[b] In 1998, to celebrate its 75th anniversary and to mark the end of what founding editor-publisher Henry R. Luce had christened "the American century," *Time* hosted a gala for its cover girls and boys at Radio City Music Hall. Watching Riefenstahl, 97 years old, hale and hearty, chatting ami-ably with her fellow honorees, David Remnick from the *New Yorker* could only mutter, "There is no God." Riefenstahl died in her sleep at the age of 101. (David Remnick, "Dept. of Hoopla," *New Yorker*, Mar. 16, 1998: 25.)

"Miss Leni Riefenstahl, [Hitler's] actress friend, is controlling coverage of the Olympic Games," groused *Motion Picture Herald*. "All else is *streng verboten*." National pride mixed with sexist resentment at the girl who dared to invade the all-male preserves and lord her authority over the newsreel boys. If a photographer were caught trespassing, a Riefenstahl flunky handed him a pink slip that read: "Remove yourself immediately from where you are now—Riefenstahl."[11] Forced to sign contracts that limited the amount of footage shot and required to provide a duplicate print to Riefenstahl, newsreel editors deeply resented her appropriation of American footage that later wound up in *Olympia*.

In 1937, as Riefenstahl crouched over an editing board to shape miles of raw footage into a coherent whole, the scent of racial scandal heated up the media obsession with Hitler's tabloid-ordained girlfriend. United Press reported the sensational news that Riefenstahl had been bounced from Hitler's inner circle for an unconscionable transgression: she was Jewish. Goebbels issued a non-denial denial (the report, he said, was "too silly to be denied") and pointed out that a certificate attesting to Riefenstahl's Aryan bloodline was on file at the Reichsfilmkammer.

In America, the Jewish angle only whetted the media appetite for Riefenstahl gossip. "Is Hitler in Love with a Jewess?" teased *Liberty* magazine in July 1938, answering in the affirmative. "The whole story of the curious romance that has blossomed between the Jew-hating Fuehrer and the beautiful Leni Riefenstahl" was revealed by Princess Catherine Radziwill, *Liberty*'s aristocratic European correspondent, who claimed to have the inside dope on *l'amour fou*. "When [Hitler] saw Leni Riefenstahl, something else moved his heart and appealed to his intelligence," confided a breathless Radziwill. Risking all, a heartsick Riefenstahl confessed her Jewess-ness to the lovestruck Hitler, who then gushed, "What does it matter who or what you are since I love you!" Later, when Hitler presents *Olympia* with his Best Picture accolade, he melts, "kissing the hands of Leni Riefenstahl, and murmuring as he did so, 'I love you—oh, *how*, I love you!'"[12]

After two years of postproduction work—a marathon editing session compressing 1,500,000 feet of footage into four hours broken into two parts, "Festival of the Nations" and "Festival of Beauty"—Riefenstahl unveiled her magnum opus.

The Nazi ethos proved disturbingly congenial to the Olympic ideal. Like Nazism itself, *Olympia* harkens back to a golden age when immortals walked the earth. Materializing through the mists of time, sculpted in white marble, Greek statues dissolve into buff Aryans, nude bodies-beautiful without blemish or deformity, hurling javelins, discus, and shot-puts, straining to embody the Platonic-Aryan idea. If the god presiding over the festival in *Triumph of the Will* is Hitler, the god of *Olympia* is Apollo—the athletes are solar-powered deities, muscular perfection in motion, a Greek pantheon come to life as Nazi supermen. The nude female athlete, arms outstretched to the sun, is Riefenstahl.

For the athletic events—track and field, swimming, the marathon—Riefenstahl adapted her perspective and pace to fit the competition—close to the ground and up close for track and field; in the air and free-floating for the pole vaulters and divers; and trudging along at feet-, thigh-, and midsection-level for the long-distance marathoners. Putting Soviet aesthetics in service to Nazi ideology, the editing liberates the athletes from gravity itself, especially in the water sports. Flipping and flying in slow motion and reverse projection, the high divers soar with ecstatic buoyancy, lighter than air. Whatever the event, the contest between the genders is unequal: Riefenstahl's camera caresses the male form, doting on biceps and torsos, muscles stretched tight and blood coursing through veins, seeming to lap up every drop of perspiration.

That Riefenstahl had created a long-form masterpiece was obvious to anyone with eyes. "She has turned out a convincing, exciting, and dramatic record," *Variety* grudgingly conceded.[13] The best certification of her bona fides came from Hitler himself, who in May 1938 personally presented her his award for "the best motion picture achievement of 1937."[14] At the premiere in Paris, the French surrendered unconditionally. "Olympia is more and better than a film," wrote a dazzled cinephile. "It is a glowing poem of images, light and life; it is ageless and almost without nationality."[15]

That August, at the Venice International Film Exposition, where the fix was in, *Olympia* won the Mussolini Cup, the plum prize, beating out Walt Disney's *Snow White and the Seven Dwarfs* (1937), the crowd favorite. Charging "politics," poor sports in America decried the upset as "an Italian effort to please Germany." Harold Smith, European representative for the Motion Picture Producers and Distributors of America, argued that a documentary, not being a legitimate feature film, should not have even been in competition. How else to explain how "an obscure German documentary film" had beaten out the fairy-tale magic of Walt Disney?[16]

Having conquered Germany, France, and Italy, Riefenstahl turned naturally to the nation that ruled world cinema. Like Lubitsch, Murnau, and Lang before her, she would try her luck in Hollywood—not as a hopeful émigré but as a garlanded conqueror. Though her trip to America was officially billed as a private visit, in reality she set sail to secure a stateside distribution deal for *Olympia*. Along with Ernst Jaeger, her old friend and press handler, and Werner Klingeberg, an official with the German Olympic Committee, she brought ten heavy film canisters with three different versions of the four-hour film.[17] On October 29, 1938, Riefenstahl sailed from Bremerhaven aboard the liner *Europa*, little expecting the buzzsaw she would run into at the next port of call.

On November 4, 1938, when the *Europa* dropped anchor in New York, Riefenstahl's arrival had already been heralded by shipboard radio and wirephotos beamed stateside. Speaking for his client, Ernst Jaeger denied the obvious, that Riefenstahl had come to America to publicize *Olympia* and negotiate a distribution deal. No, he said, she had come purely due to her "interest in America and as a sportswoman."[18]

Mere tourist or not, Riefenstahl was Nazism's second most photogenic face. More than that, though, she was a brilliant motion picture artist in thrall to a ruthless dictator, a match that inspired a special measure of loathing from the artists in the Popular Front. The deal she struck with the Nazis wasn't exactly a Faustian bargain—the contract suited both parties—but the willing prostitution of beauty and talent to the coarse and brutal Nazis gave the lie to the notion that truth is beauty and beauty is truth. The previous envoy of Fascist cinema, Vittorio Mussolini, was a dilettante and daddy's boy, a spoiled son of privilege; Riefenstahl was a self-made woman, a charismatic talent. Being the one Nazi filmmaker who was not a second-rater, who was as good, or better, than the Jews purged from Ufa, she intrigued, tantalized, and unnerved. "The gal has charm to burn," gushed gossip monger Hedda Hopper, who was smitten with the lady. "As pretty as a swastika," snarled syndicated columnist Walter Winchell, who was not.

In New York, anti-Nazi activists were waiting with their knives out. The Non-Sectarian Anti-Nazi League to Champion Human Rights sprang into action to isolate Riefenstahl and derail the distribution of the "Hitler-Riefenstahl" film. Founder Samuel Untermyer had stepped down the previous May due to ill health, but after five years the group had logged enough hours walking picket lines and handing out leaflets to operate on automatic. "This visit is part of the Nazi campaign to flood the United States with Nazi doctrines and is in accord with recent statements by German consuls here and German officials abroad in which they attacked American principles and ethics and sought to prove the superiority of Nazism," declared the League.[19]

Studio-affiliated distributors assured NSANL that *Olympia* "won't get to first base in the United States" and that "they would boycott the picture one hundred per cent." Independent bookers were no less antagonistic. Foreign film importer Joseph Seiden rejected *Olympia* on the grounds that any profits from the film would be used "in the furtherance of Nazi propaganda both here and abroad."[20] Even under optimal circumstances, *Olympia* would have been a tough sell in the American market. At twenty reels—approximately 220 minutes, running times of the film varied—it was a dubious attraction even for dedicated sports fans. But the Nazi aura around Riefenstahl wiped out whatever commercial prospects her film might have had. Trafficking in *Olympia* was *streng verboten*.

Outside of the hard core of anti-Nazi activists, however, Riefenstahl herself was often looked upon more as a curiosity than a villain. Initially, reporters were intrigued, even bewitched, by the fetching beauty who blended the exotic allure of Marlene Dietrich and the fiery independence of Katharine Hepburn. "Leni Riefenstahl, an Individualist Even Under Hitler, Expects to Teach 1,000 Beautiful Woman to Ride Horses," headlined a wide-eyed profile in the *New York World-Telgram* trumpeting her presence in the city and plugging her next project, an epic version of Heinrich von Kleist's *Penthesilea*, with Riefenstahl in the saddle as the Queen of the Amazons (hence the need for a thousand female equestrians). She laughed at the inevitable question about her liaison with Hitler, praised the genius of Walt Disney, and denied the rumors that she was Jewish ("I am an Aryan for generations"). "There is one person at least in Nazi Germany who does as she pleases and doesn't take dictation," wrote the male reporter won over by her flirty manner and tentative English. "That would be Leni Riefenstahl."

The date of the love letter to Riefenstahl in the *New York World-Telegram* was November 9, 1938, at which time the news from that night in Nazi Germany had not yet broken.[21] The next day, the front-page banner headline in the paper read: MOBS WRECK 10,000 JEWISH SHOPS IN NAZIS' 14-HOUR REIGN OF TERROR; BURN SYNAGOGUES ALL OVER NATION AS POLICE WATCH.[22]

So perfect for so long, Riefenstahl's timing had failed her. On the night of November 9–10, 1938, while she was still being cast as glamorous celebrity instead of a Nazi henchwoman, the Nazis launched a campaign of antisemitic terror throughout Germany and Austria, the rampage known to history as Kristallnacht. Confronted by reporters, Riefenstahl denied the obvious. The Nazis, she said, would never do such a thing. The reports were false, one-sided, and incomplete.[23]

After Kristallnacht, Riefenstahl's coy act as a political naïf—an artist only, gaze fixed on her muse—fell flat. No longer stroking her with sly gossip items and cute photo captions, the press spat out editorial condemnations and full-throated venom. Henceforth, her working vacation in America was to be a gauntlet of ostracism and insults. Columnists derided her, former colleagues deserted her, and politicians rebuffed her.

Ernst Jaeger would later write an eleven-part series for the *Hollywood Tribune* chronicling Riefenstahl's coast-to-coast hegira, an insider's tell-all written under the trashy title "How Leni Riefenstahl Became Hitler's Girlfriend." With retrospective *schadenfreude*, her now-estranged factotum painted a catty portrait of a diva in distress. As she lugged her film cans from city to city, the high priestess of Nazi cinema was disrespected and disparaged. "The only pictures Leni Riefenstahl could interest Americans in," cracked a refugee director, "would be movies of an autopsy performed on her boyfriend's brain."[24]

Fleeing Judeo-centric New York, Riefenstahl headed south to Washington, D.C. She visited Mount Vernon and the Lincoln Memorial, but no invitation to lunch was forthcoming from FDR and no screening of *Olympia* could be arranged in the capital.

In Chicago, a city with a strong German population, the reception was marginally warmer. She surfaced to screen sections of *Olympia* to a friendly German audience of not more than thirty-five, seven of whom worked for the German consulate.[25] While in Chicago, she made a side trip up to Detroit to meet with Henry Ford, the auto magnate, antisemite, and admirer of the Nazis. It was a rare taste of American hospitality.

Of course, the final destination of Riefenstahl's long march across America was the spot her trip had been homing in on since she boarded the *Europa* in Bremerhaven—Hollywood, where the brilliance of *Olympia* would be recognized by her peers and rewarded with a lucrative distribution contract from a major studio.

When Riefenstahl stepped off the platform at Union Station in Los Angeles ready to vamp for the cameras, the only welcomers were a forlorn party of four led by Dr. Georg Gyssling, the Nazi consul in Los Angeles, who handed her a bouquet of flowers. Dismayed at the absence of flashbulbs, Riefenstahl wailed at Jaeger, "Where is the press?" "But you're supposed to be incognito," he replied. "Ja," she said, "but not so incognito."

The Hollywood Anti-Nazi League was working hard to make her better known, to make her in fact the talk of the town. Redeploying the tactics that had rendered Vittorio Mussolini *persona non grata* the previous year, HANL launched a reverse publicity campaign. It published articles

"Ja, but not so incognito": director Leni Riefenstahl and Nazi consul Georg Gyssling during her ill-fated visit to Hollywood in December 1938. (Courtesy Corbis Images)

in *Hollywood Now*, posted notices on studio bulletin boards, and timed full-page ads for publication in the trade press. On November 29, 1938, HANL purchased space in the *Hollywood Reporter* and *Daily Variety* to alert the citizenry that

> Today Leni Riefenstahl, head of the Nazi film industry, has arrived in Hollywood. There is no room in Hollywood for Leni Riefenstahl. In this moment when hundreds of thousands of our brethren await certain death, close your doors to all Nazi agents. Let the world know there is no room in Hollywood for Nazi agents.

Sections of the ad copy scanned like poetry:

> The Nazi star is at her hotel.
> The man who directed her first picture is barred from his own country.[c]
> The man who discovered her is in a concentration camp.[d]
> The girl's name is Leni Riefenstahl.
> Her answer is "I am not Hitler's girl friend."
> Our answer is . . . There is no room in Hollywood for Nazi agents.[26]

Just a little over a year earlier, a black-tie party for Vittorio Mussolini could be considered a coveted ticket to a swank affair. The annexation of Austria, the seizing of the Czechoslovakian Sudetenland, and the fires of Kristallnacht had converged to change the climate even in far-off California.

Signaling that the antipathy to Riefenstahl was not only personal but institutional, the major studios declared their gates closed. "American films are barred from Germany, so we have nothing to show Miss Riefenstahl that would interest her," explained a studio executive.[27] Asked about the "No Trespassing" signs, Dr. Gyssling denied that his guest was being barred. "I talked with Miss Riefenstahl over the telephone,"

---

[c] The man who directed her first picture was Arnold Fanck, auteur of *The Holy Mountain*. The reference is probably to G. W. Pabst, who with Fanck codirected *The White Hell of Pitz Palu*. Pabst fled to Paris after the Nazis came to power but rejoined the fold in 1940 when the Nazis conquered France.

[d] Actor-director Luis Trenker, Riefenstahl's costar in *The Holy Mountain*, is usually credited with "discovering" her when he gave a picture of her to Fanck. He was never in a concentration camp.

Gyssling said, "but she made no request for me to arrange any visits. She said nothing of being rebuffed and I am sure she would have spoken of the incident if it had occurred."[28] Everyone knew better. "So far as Hollywood is concerned," gloated *Variety*, "she is just another tourist whom it is too busy to show around or be seen with."[29] Chimed in the *Hollywood Reporter*: "Leni Riefenstahl has found out just how hard being a bosom pal of Adolph Hitler has made the going in Hollywood."[30]

Surprised to be "thus personally attacked," Riefenstahl issued an aggrieved statement. "Immediately upon my arrival in New York, I told the press that my trip was absolutely private and that I had no official mission to fulfill. Furthermore, I would like to state that I have never had an official position in Germany, and therefore I could not be head of the Nazi film industry. I am a free creative artist. As a consequence of my work in *The Blue Light*, I was assigned to direct both great artistic documentary films of the Olympic games."[31] To help with damage control, she tried to hire Dick Hunt, a prominent Hollywood press agent. Hunt turned her down flat and, being a press agent, informed the press of his principled rejection.[32]

While Riefenstahl holed up in a bungalow at the Beverly Hills Hotel and stewed, folks around Hollywood competed in gestures of ostentatious ostracism. Phil Selznick turned her away from his nightclub. Silva Weaver, fashion editor of the *Los Angeles Times*, called off a cocktail party. Actors that Riefenstahl had been on friendly terms with in Germany avoided eye contact and refused to do lunch.

A few tone-deaf—or just plain ornery—actors and filmmakers broke ranks and met Riefenstahl on the sly, out of sight of photographers. She spent a quiet evening with Vilma Banky and Rod LaRoque, acquaintances from *S.O.S. Iceberg*. Harboring no grudge about his loss to Riefenstahl at the Venice Film Festival, Walt Disney escorted her around his animation shop, showing off storyboards to his next full-length animated feature, *Fantasia* (1940). Winfield Sheehan, former head of Fox, and his wife, Viennese opera singer Maria Jeritza, sheltered Riefenstahl at their home in Palm Springs. Sheehan had been on the outs in Hollywood since he had left Fox in 1935 after its merger with Twentieth Century Pictures, and his taste in houseguests did not enhance his popularity.

Riefenstahl's most prominent local booster was the powerful gossip columnist and harridan-about-town Hedda Hopper, who blabbed harmless tidbits about the stars but kept the best secrets to herself for leverage.

She met Riefenstahl, was enchanted, and saw *Olympia*, and was impressed. Mounting her high horse, Hopper chastised Hollywood for its hypocritical inconsistency in the welcome given two different emissaries from European fascism. "Last year Hal Roach entertained Il Duce's favorite son, Vittorio, at a great gala party. Our glamorous stars were proud to be photographed with him," she pointed out, forgetting Mussolini's own chilly reception the morning after, not to mention the seismic shifts in history that had occurred since. "Now Leni Riefenstahl, supposed to be Hitler's erstwhile girlfriend, can't even get a peek through a keyhole." *Olympia*, opined Hopper, was made "without propaganda" and featured a winner's circle of great American athletes, notably track star Jesse Owens, the African American Mercury who won four Gold Medals. "Why shouldn't we be allowed to see them?" she demanded.[33]

Box Office columnist Ivan Spear typed out a terse reply. "Those who head the industry that liberally supports Mesdame Hopper, and who are familiar with what the policies and bigotries of Leni and her Aryan playmates have cost the studios, individually and collectively, would have a ready and convincing answer to Hedda's query—if they took it seriously enough to feel it warranted a reply."[34]

On January 7, 1939, Dr. Gyssling hosted a reception in Riefenstahl's honor at his tony residence on 1801 North Curson Avenue. Over 200 guests feted the actress-director in a well-catered affair totally bereft of star power. "And not a single Hollywoodian among the 200, which indicates pretty clearly the rapid approach toward unanimity of the film capital's feelings concerning Herr Hitler and his playmate," exulted Spear.[35]

If not quite run out of town on a rail, Riefenstahl was all but cold-shouldered out to Union Station for an ignominious exit from the American film capital. On January 13, 1939, as a delegation from the German consulate stood and saluted stiffly in the chill morning, she boarded the Santa Fe Chief for the trip back East. The train reservations were made under an assumed name. She said she had enjoyed the climate and scenery, but kept mum about her very public shunning, saying only "I hope next time it will be different when I come, yes?"[36]

No, growled HANL, the trade press, and the metropolitan dailies. With one voice, they bid the Nazi filmmaker good riddance. *Daily Variety* wished her a quick trip back to "Adolf Hitler's domain, along with the films of the Berlin Olympics, which she brought here to sell but which she couldn't give away, even with a set of dishes." Bestowing his mock

A FOUR-STAR SNUB   by Ellis

Pariah: a cartoon from the *Daily Worker* welcomes Leni Riefenstahl to Hollywood.

year-end Oscar awards, columnist Ed Sullivan awarded an apt booby prize: "An Iron Cross to Leni Riefenstahl for the daffiest junket of the year, her tactless trip to Hollywood."[37]

For turning the Nazi goddess into a social leper, the Hollywood Anti-Nazi League bathed in the praise of a grateful community. "The Anti-Nazi League is to be complimented on its activity directed against Leni Riefenstahl and the concurrent actions of the studios in denying her entrance," the *Hollywood Reporter* editorialized. "If Germany bars Hollywood's product why shouldn't Hollywood bar this German film representative? But without the blast of the Anti-Nazi League, apparently nothing would have been done."[38] No longer a cadre of fringe leftists, the group had come to occupy the center of cultural-political gravity in Hollywood.

On January 18, 1939, after a sullen train trip to New York, Riefenstahl boarded the German liner *Hansa* to head for friendlier shores. Before the ship sailed, she invited the press aboard for a final confab. As Riefenstahl nibbled *hors d'oeuvres* and autographed pictures, she spoke through an interpreter, who translated her remarks only after careful consultation about the answers.

It was a pity that the American people ("sportsmen all") would be deprived of the chance to see *Olympia*, she sighed. Yes, the Hollywood producers behaved abominably, as might be expected, but the "better class" of Californians had treated her marvelously. She looked forward to returning to America at the earliest opportunity.

Yet the wounds from her flaying in Hollywood were still raw. Riefenstahl bristled at her "unfair" treatment from the motion picture industry and singled out the social and professional pressure brought to bear by the Hollywood Anti-Nazi League. "If anyone talked to me, they would lose their job," she claimed. "Is that American?"

"What would happen if a Jewish producer brought some film with him to Germany?" a reporter asked.

"Do you think America is all Jewish?" she snapped.

Riefenstahl wondered if any of the reporters had seen *Olympia*. None of them had. "That is the trouble. You don't realize the film is very good. If you would know my picture, you would understand my work." Exasperated at the injustice of it all, she could contain her frustrations no longer. "Only the bad things you write!" she cried. "Why don't you write the good things?"[39]

Back on European soil, Riefenstahl vented her frustrations less diplomatically. "I was welcomed everywhere in the United States but in Hollywood—where the film industry is controlled by Jews and anti-Nazi leagues."[40]

12

"THE ONLY STUDIO WITH ANY GUTS"

On the evening of December 8, 1938, with the fires from Kristallnacht out in Germany but the anger in America still burning, a group of well-heeled anti-Nazi activists gathered at the Beverly Hills home of actor Edward G. Robinson to weigh options and plan a response. Circulating among the stars, screenwriters, and producers—and sampling the libations—was the town's resident wise guy, Groucho Marx. Raising his glass, and for once not his eyebrows, he announced, "I want to propose a toast to Warners—the only studio with any guts."[1]

Groucho, who with his brothers was under contract to MGM, was toasting Hollywood's other fraternal outfit for initiating production on a domestic espionage thriller called *Confessions of a Nazi Spy,* the first frontal assault on Nazism from a major studio, indeed the first time the four-letter word that had streaked across newspaper headlines and blared from radio bulletins since 1933 had been boldfaced in the title of a studio film. From the executive offices to the backlots, the news electrified the motion picture industry. "While making the rounds on the Hollywood front yesterday, we couldn't help but feel the spark which had been set off by the Warners declaration that it would film the Nazi spy story in the raw, with no punches pulled, even insofar as real names were concerned," wrote Billy Wilkerson, editor-publisher of the *Hollywood Reporter.* "One top executive of a rival studio went so far as to tell us that the Warners mob had more guts than a lot of other outfits rolled together."[2]

In truth, the decision was a gutsy gambit, but not out of line with company policy. Of all the studios that made up the winner's circle known as the Big Five, Warner Bros. alone wore the badge of anti-Nazism as proudly as the WB-emblazoned shield that was its emblem. Up until the outbreak of war in Europe, MGM, Paramount, RKO, and Twentieth Century-Fox figured business was business. Only Warner Bros. dissented, putting its money where its politics were. It cut off relations with Germany in 1933, contributed funds to an array of anti-Nazi causes, donated airtime for anti-Nazi broadcasts on KFWB, its flagship radio station, and injected anti-Nazi sentiments into its short subjects and feature films.[3] No for-profit company did more than Warner Bros. to alert Americans to what Nazism was and where it would lead.

The story of Hollywood's most famous bloodline moguls—level-headed chieftain Harry, backstage mediator Albert, tech geek Sam, and obnoxious front man Jack—is only partly the story of a smoothly operating dream factory run by a dysfunctional family. It is also the story of how the ideological commitment of two Hollywood moguls—eldest brother Harry M. and youngest brother Jack L.—helped make anti-Nazism synonymous with pro-Americanism. Prior to 1939, the connection was not self-evident.

Like many Hollywood brand names, the Warner brothers were of Eastern European Jewish heritage: father Ben, who emigrated from Poland in 1880, was so eager to erase memories of the Old World that the real family name was jettisoned before his boat docked in the New.[4] In 1903, noticing how enthusiastically customers plunked down coins for a nickelodeon treat, the brothers got in on the ground floor of a growth industry—first exhibition, then distribution, finally production. By dint of hustle, hard work, and chutzpah, the quartet soon secured a precarious niche in the wide-open, wildcat business. Setting up shop in Hollywood in 1912, incorporated in 1923 under a logo officially writ as "Warner Bros. Pictures, Inc.," they made the studio payroll mainly on the back of one of the most talented and least temperamental stars of the silent era, the canine matinee idol Rin Tin Tin, a German shepherd rescued from the battlefield by an American doughboy during the Great War.

In 1925 the mechanically fixated Sam persuaded his skeptical siblings to invest in a new-fangled technology that bid to expand the sensory range of the motion picture medium. The result was *The Jazz Singer* (1927), the epochal first sound film that was also, fittingly, a story of Jewish assimilation and all-American aspiration. (The original program for the film included a Yiddish-English glossary to help gentiles with the intertitled vernacular.) In a melancholy twist of fate, the Warner brothers did not attend the gala Broadway premiere to witness their triumphal breakthrough: Sam died the day before the film opened.

The Jazz Singer propelled the company from Poverty Row to the big time, but the house style was never as opulent or otherworldly as the product conjured on rival backlots. The Warner Bros. look was lean and hungry, urban and hardscrabble, clouded by cigarette smoke and bathed in noirish lighting, often to hide the bare-bones sets. The roster of contract players suited the atmospherics. Over at MGM, Clark Gable and Greta Garbo embodied the celestial glamour of the studio that boasted "more stars than there are in heaven," but at Warner Bros. the actors were more down-to-earth, streetwise and smart-mouthed, typified by the likes of James Cagney and Bette Davis, guys who knew the backstreets and gals who had been around the block. They didn't need to stretch too far to play taxi drivers, waitresses, truck drivers, shopgirls, bootleggers, and dime-a-dance dames on the make.

In the mid-1930s, the studio hit its stride. A series of "great man" biopics, notably *The Story of Louis Pasteur* (1936) and *The Life of Emile Zola* (1937), lent prestige and earned Best Picture Oscars, but its trademark genres were gritty crime mellers, fast-paced action pics, and multiple-hankie women's weepies. Not least, in a series of moody, hard-hitting melodramas such as *Black Fury* (1935), *Black Legion* (1936), and *They Won't Forget* (1937)—spiritual descendents of the even sharper-edged pre-Code firebombs *I Am a Fugitive from a Chain Gang* (1932), *Heroes for Sale* (1933), and *Wild Boys of the Road* (1933)—the studio pioneered a cycle of "social consciousness" films that fessed up to the fact that something called the Great Depression lurked just outside the theater lobby.

On and off screen, another quality set Warner Bros. apart. In film content and political affinities, it was the most frankly Jewish and fiercely anti-Nazi of all the Hollywood studios. In 1933, after Phil Kaufman, its Berlin branch manager, was pummeled in a back alley by Nazi brownshirts, Warner Bros. became the first studio to sever economic ties with the lucrative German market.[a] The brothers also showed their colors by supporting the Hollywood Anti-Nazi League, hosting fund-raisers, and

---

[a] The studio's last big hit in the German market was *I Am a Fugitive from a Chain Gang*, the story of a man unjustly sentenced to a brutal prison camp by a callous and duplicitous state government.

shaking down employees for "donations" to the cause. At first allegorically, then more explicitly as Europe headed toward the brink, the studio agitated for racial tolerance at home while warning of the racist menace abroad.

To a company man, Warner Bros.' corporate rivals opted for a more conciliatory approach. Despite frustration with Nazi censorship and economic restrictions—the banned pictures and the blocked currency— each of the other four major studios was willing to meet the Nazis halfway, or further. After 1933, German filmgoers with a taste for Hollywood cinema did not have a full menu to choose from, but they did not starve for lack of fare.

RKO officially bolted soon after Hitler came to power, but even with no offices in Berlin or formal middlemen for distribution it closed deals and collected money. "RKO has sold a few pictures into Germany in the past couple of years, but strictly on a cash and carry basis," *Variety* noted in 1937. "If any German distrib offers to buy an RKO pic, paying dollars for it, he can have it. Otherwise, no dice." Thus, as the distributor of Walt Disney's desirable roster, RKO was ready to haggle with the Nazis had not its American client driven so hard a bargain. When Germany's legions of cartoon fans clamored for *Snow White and the Seven Dwarfs* (1937), the animator set strict terms. "Walt Disney wants a cash guarantee on the line before he releases the picture and Germany doesn't want to put up American dollars," said an RKO executive in 1939. "Until then, there won't be a deal."[5] There wasn't.

RKO's cash-on-demand policy ceded the bulk of the market to Paramount, Twentieth Century-Fox, and MGM, each of whom jostled for a piece of a shrinking pie. In the three-way competition, Paramount and Fox held an advantage over MGM, long top dog in Hollywood's corporate hierarchy, because both studios produced newsreels in Germany, a side business that allowed them to circumvent restrictions on exporting hard currency earned from their feature films. Profits from commercial features playing in Germany could be spent domestically to produce the newsreels and then the footage could be exported and sold overseas— a roundabout way to sidestep Nazi financial restrictions, and hardly a financial windfall, but better than letting the funds sit in a Reich bank. The arrangement, *Variety* pointed out, meant Paramount and Fox were, unlike MGM, "not piling up coin internally." For its part, MGM, despite the blocked currency and confiscatory transfer fees, didn't "want to leave the field, such as it is, solely to Paramount and 20th."[6] Throughout the decade, the three studios bent to Nazi demands in order to smooth the course of commerce and keep the product flowing.

MGM was often reported to be "about ready to kiss the German market goodbye," but the studio was never quite able to break off a relationship that paid, however measly the dividends. Working with the Nazis, however, required compromise and, sometimes, capitulation. In 1936, when pressure from the Non-Sectarian Anti-Nazi League to Champion Human Rights forced MGM to withdraw the shorts *Sports on Ice* (1936) and *Olympic Ski Champions* (1936) from the program at the Capitol Theatre in New York, MGM balked at pulling the films nationally. "Obviously, any official action nationwide would bring immediate reprisals against Metro product in Germany, where the company is still operating," explained *Variety*.[7]

If not a quid pro quo, the bilateral arrangement between MGM and the Third Reich amounted to a suspiciously convenient chain of causality. In 1936 the elliptically anti-Nazi film *Are We Civilized?* (1934), an independent production from Raspin Productions, Inc., was booked into Baltimore's Valencia Theater, a house aligned with the Loew's circuit, MGM's corporate parent. Dr. Hans Luther, the German ambassador to the United States, lodged an official protest with Secretary of State Cordell Hull. Loew's New York office promptly canceled the booking. "Loew didn't want to become involved in the exhibiting of the flicker because Metro pix are still being sold in Germany," noted *Variety*. A week after canceling the Baltimore booking of *Are We Civilized?*, a slate of twelve MGM pictures was cleared for release in Germany.[8]

Not that all was smooth sailing for MGM in Nazi Germany. Douglas Miller, the acting commercial attaché at the U.S. Embassy in Berlin, felt that MGM was being treated more harshly than Paramount and Fox because "Metro was considered to be a Jewish firm abroad, while Paramount and Fox were considered as Aryans"—presumably because solid Anglo-Saxon nouns like "Paramount" and "Fox" sounded less semitic than Mayer and Goldwyn, the two surnames in the MGM acronym. Knowing that Paramount was founded by Adolph Zukor and Fox by William Fox, née Wilhelm Fried, both Jews born in the Austrio-Hungarian Empire, attaché Miller could only comment: "As a matter of fact, Jewish influence is strong in all these American moving picture companies." Frits Strengholt, the non-Jewish Dutchman who headed MGM's

Berlin office, was also, in Nazi terms, a troublemaker. According the Miller, "while honest and trustworthy, [Strengholt] is an unbending fellow who tries to stand on his rights, whereas the representatives of the other American companies have been more successful in personal contacts with local officials, and have cultivated these more extensively."[9]

To serve as a counterweight to the uppity Strengholt and to help grease the skids with the Nazi authorities, MGM put the nephew of German foreign minister Konstantin von Neurath on the payroll of its Berlin office.[10] As late as June 1939, MGM was still trying to placate the Nazis by playing host to a group of German newspaper editors on a "good will" visit to America, even providing a VIP tour of the MGM lot at Culver City. Though the editors swooped in and out before the Hollywood Anti-Nazi League could launch a protest, MGM was the only studio that by then would have laid out a welcome mat for emissaries from Joseph Goebbels.[11]

In March 1938, when the Nazis rolled into Austria, the studios faced the same personnel crisis in their foreign offices as when the Nazis took over Germany in 1933. Each responded according to type. "It looks like the end of the Austrian market," said a spokesman at Universal, reluctant to say too much until hearing from its branch manager in Vienna, William Satori, a native-born Austrian who had recently taken out citizenship papers in the United States.[12] (Satori escaped Austria, worked stateside for Universal during the war, and returned to Europe in the postwar era for Monogram and Allied Artists.) Felix Bernstein, MGM's Jewish sales manager in Austria, was immediately removed. "[It is] anticipated that Metro will name a new sales chief who is acceptable to [the] Nazi-dominated governmental body," Variety reported, matter of factly.[13] (Bernstein landed on his feet in Hollywood with a sweet assignment for a Viennese Jew: technical advisor on MGM's Florian [1940], an equestrian biopic chronicling the exploits of a magnificent white Lipizzaner stallion owned by Emperor Franz Josef of Austria.) Paramount stood ready not only to ship its Jews out of Vienna but its Catholics as well "to conform with ideas of the new Nazi regime." The manager of RKO's Vienna office, Michael Havas, was transferred to Rome. For a time, the whereabouts of Twentieth Century-Fox's legal representative in Vienna, Dr. Paul Koretz, was unknown and his "safety is in doubt." (Koretz escaped, making his way to London to head up Fox's story department, and thence to Hollywood during the war.) No longer needing a branch office in Vienna, Fox did business with the Greater Reich from its main office in Berlin.

Reporting on the annexation of Austria, *Variety* issued a resigned, non-judgmental assessment. "Expect usual number of anti-Semitic moves directed against the picture business." It was also expected that the usual antisemitic moves would not deter MGM, Paramount, and Twentieth Century-Fox from adapting to new market realities. "Of course, [their] offices have reduced their staffs considerably and dismissed all Jewish executives," noted *Motion Picture Herald*. The casual "of course" is the giveaway: unlike 1933, when surprise and shock greeted the policy of Aryanization, by 1938 it was the predictable and acceptable cost of doing business with the Nazis.[14] "Within a few days of the annexation, nearly every Jewish exhibitor, particularly the owners of first-run theaters, was taken into custody on trumped up charges of being in arrears on tax payments," reported an on-site correspondent for *Motion Picture Herald*, a stringer who wisely took only the byline of "Special Correspondent." "The notice 'Under Aryan Management' or 'Under the Commissariat of the Reichsfilmkammer' is seen at the entrance of almost all cinemas owned hitherto by Jewish exhibitors."[15]

Fox, Paramount, and MGM all hung on despite the fact that the financial compensations from the German market were steadily diminishing. Due to ever-tightening currency restrictions, the studios that stayed behind found it harder and harder to squeeze money out of the Reich. "Some major film officials estimate that little more than 10–15% of the total rental money actually is withdrawn to this country because of the blocked-[Deutsche]mark situation as well as the disparity in value between the mark in the Reich and in the U.S.," reported *Variety* in mid-1939. "Added factor is the premium charged for such withdrawn coin. Blocked marks is the method employed by the Nazis whereby they earmark a certain part of coin for a stay in Germany. Major film companies admit there is little they can do about the situation."[16]

Thus, in an irony better appreciated in retrospect, even as Nazi bellicosity and violence toward Jews in Germany escalated, the trademark product of Jews in America remained up on marquees throughout the Third Reich. Before German Jews were banned from motion picture theaters in the aftermath of Kristallnacht, the scholar, film buff, and diarist Victor Klemperer, an avid fan of the cinema since the glory days of German Expressionism, often took refuge from the insanity of the Third Reich by treating his wife and himself to a night at the movies. He winced at the propaganda newsreels, but even from a seat in

Dresden, an import from Hollywood was not considered exotic fare. In 1937 he caught screenings of MGM's earthquake disaster film *San Francisco* (1936), whose seismic upheavals must have reverberated metaphorically, and Universal's Mississippi riverboat musical *Show Boat* (1936), whose subplot about miscegenation in the Deep South abided with Nazi racial laws. A "very pleasant film evening," he said of *Showboat*, "thoroughly American in music, dance, fights, gum chewing." Of *San Francisco*, his only comment was a wistful "all too American," seemingly glad, if for only two hours, to be in a city besides Dresden.[17]

Yet as the 1930s wore on, fewer and fewer American films crossed Nazi borders. By 1937, only thirty pictures a year entered Germany, with the studios having to submit to the censors about three or four times that number to meet their quota. In the first half of 1938, a mere thirteen films passed inspection.[b] Given the sparse profits and near-confiscatory monetary policies, many industry insiders questioned why the major studios continued dealing with the Nazis at all. Politics and morality aside, the economic rewards were paltry. Glancing over the slim pickings, *Variety* figured that for Paramount, Twentieth Century-Fox, and MGM, "it might be just as well to forget the headaches in the German sales."[18]

Nonetheless, in the end, the three studios were willing to suffer the mental anguish to stay in the game. Taking the long view, their unwavering commitment to the German market was less about the immediate lure of hard cash than about maintaining a foothold in a market that had lately been so profitable and, with a change of regime, might well be again. As a hedge against the future, it was thought best to keep the distribution infrastructure in place on the off chance that the market should open up again. The moguls did not expect the Third Reich to last for a thousand years.

At the beginning of 1939, the Nazis turned the financial screw an additional notch by leveling a tax of 75 percent on exported funds, but even

---

[b] The figures from the German side differ. In his study *Hollywood unterm Hakenkruez* (*Hollywood under the Swastika*), the German film scholar Markus Spieker breaks down the number of Hollywood films released in Germany per year as: 43 in 1933, 47 in 1934, 35 in 1935, 30 in 1936, 33 in 1937, 41 in 1938, and 26 in 1939. The titles include a disproportionate number of mediocrities and outright turkeys, giving credence to Hollywood suspicions that the Nazis more readily passed the worst films to sour German audiences on Hollywood and funnel them into domestic productions. (Markus Spieker, *Hollywood unterm Hakenkreuz: Der Americkanische Spielfilm im Dritten Reich* [Trier: WVT Wissemschaftlicher Verlag Trier, 1999], 348–60.)

then Fox, Paramount, and MGM refused to quit the field. "Today [January 1939] the business of the remaining three is described in New York as almost negligible," puzzled *Motion Picture Herald*, when, for the first time in memory, not a single American feature was playing in Berlin's first-run theaters. The trade weekly estimated that each studio recouped "no more than between $15,000 to $50,000 from the market"—a pittance.[19] From the period of January to May 1939, only five Hollywood films entered the Reich. "Hitler Hates Us," joked a headline in the *Hollywood Reporter*.[20]

Only at Warner Bros. was the feeling mutual.

THE WARNER BROS. PATRIOTIC SHORTS

In September 1938, trade reporter Vance King was roaming the Warner Bros. lot when he was accosted by none other than Harry M. Warner. Why, Warner demanded, had King never mentioned the series of patriotic shorts his studio had been making since 1936? A chagrined King said he had never seen one. Warner would remedy that oversight immediately. The studio kingpin marched the reporter into a projection room and ordered up a sampling.

After the private screening, Warner took his captive audience aside for an exclusive interview about his labors of love. To be sure, the shorts had met with "tremendous success," but Warner Bros. was not merely peddling program filler, it was serving the needs of the nation. "In producing [the patriotic shorts], we feel that we are making more than a commercial product," Warner insisted, warming to his topic. "We believe that we are rendering a service to the entire nation through the presentation of subjects that inspire greater patriotism."[21]

Like other major studios, Warner Bros. maintained a shorts department that produced 10- to 20-minute short subjects (also known as one- or two-reelers) to round out the exhibitor's balanced program and to keep soundstages humming during the downtime between the production of feature films. All of the major studios released trademark shorts and cartoons, usually stitched together in-house, sometimes farmed out to independents—MGM had the *Fitzpatrick Travelogues* and Pete Smith specialties, Columbia had the Three Stooges, and Warner Bros. had its Merrie Melodies cartoons and Broadway Brevities.

In May 1936, Warner Bros. assigned the minor budget line a major task. The studio announced a commitment to a series of patriotic short subjects whose source material would be drawn from the colorful pageant of American history. A special production unit comprised of supervising producer Gordon Hollingshead, producer Brian Foy, and director Crane Wilbur was assigned to oversee the series, which was initially dubbed "the American Parade." To devote more resources to the enterprise, Warners cut back on the production of its musical shorts.[22] To ensure historical accuracy, research for the series, so said Warner Bros.' publicity department, would be "done in Washington in government files."[23]

Shot in brighter-than-life Technicolor and lavished with front office attention, the patriotic shorts waved two flags—the nation's and the studio's. As such, they were sent out in style. Radio City Music Hall showcased each of the series in its program lineup, thereby guaranteeing attention from New York critics and audiences. Beginning in October 1938, each Wednesday and Saturday evening on KFWB, the studio broadcast radio versions of the shorts on a new series called *Our America*.[24] The later slates of shorts were also released under the company name— Warner Bros.—not under the Vitaphone logo as had been the policy with shorts since the onset of sound.

To establish the civic bona fides of the enterprise, Warner Bros. enlisted the cooperation of educators. On September 1, 1938, at the Warners Hollywood Theater, 1,000 teachers convened for a special screening highlighting the shorts. The versatile actor John Litel, a non-marquee name called on to impersonate a series of colonial greats in powdered wigs and long stockings, read a message on behalf of Harry M. Warner. "Educators have encouraged us in our efforts to bring these notable historical moments to life," wrote Warner. "Their help has inspired us to put more time, effort, and money into them. The result is a series of shorts of which we, at Warner Brothers, are proud not merely because they are interesting to audiences, but because they represent part of our contribution to a better understanding of the ideals and the achievements of those patriots who laid the foundation of our United States of America."[25] Three months later, in response to numerous requests from American Legion posts and other patriotic organizations, Warner Bros. formally established an "Americanization" department to coordinate screenings of the shorts with educational and civic groups. Department head Jack Holmes went on multicity tours to publicize the series and arrange screenings.[26]

The first of the lineup was *Song of a Nation* (July 1936), based on the backstory to "The Star Spangled Banner," composed by Francis Scott Key under the rocket's red glare of the bombardment of Fort McHenry during the War of 1812. The planned slate of capsule history lessons was also to include *The Louisiana Purchase*, *The Fall of the Alamo*, *Patrick Henry*, *The Declaration of Independence*, *The Burr-Hamilton Duel*, *John Paul Jones*, *Thomas Edison—The Wizard*, and *The Hoosier Youth* (about the Indiana boyhood of Abraham Lincoln).[27] In the next years, some of the scenarios fell by the wayside and new ones were added, but the titles in the inaugural package give a good sense of the animating vision: presold passages from American history that every schoolchild would be familiar with but that Warner Bros. would punch up with action, drama, and primary colors.

The second and best known of the initial run of releases was *Give Me Liberty!* (December 1936), a fanciful account of the behind-the-scenes marital crisis that nearly silenced the ringing declaration by Patrick Henry in the Virginia House of Burgesses in 1775. In Warner Bros.' retelling, Henry (played by the reliable John Litel) manages to overcome the misgivings of his pacifist wife to rally his countrymen to the cause of rebellion against British tyranny. Savoring his big moment, Litel wraps his voice around the speech, building slowly in intensity before slamming home the rallying cry that most moviegoers could mouth the words to: "I know not what course others may take, but as for me—give me liberty, or give me death!"

During a special screening of *Give Me Liberty!* for the Academy of Motion Picture Arts and Sciences, the stirring recitation inspired prolonged applause, an accurate augur of the Academy Award given the film that year for Best Short Subject in Color. "I was afraid the audience would find this tiresome, but most of them must have learned Patrick Henry's oration in school because [*Give Me Liberty!*] aroused a great deal of interest," reported a pleasantly surprised theater manager.

Other entries were *Under Southern Stars* (February 1937), about the death of Confederate general Stonewall Jackson, and *Romance of Louisiana* (March 1937), about the Louisiana Purchase, but the most celebrated—and curious—was *The Man Without a Country* (November 1937). Based on a short story written in 1863 by Edward Everett Hale, a work of pure fiction meant to inspire loyalty to the Union during the Civil War, it marked a departure from the highly touted scholarly rigor of the series.

However, the liberties with the historical record served a larger histori-cal purpose. Lt. Phillip Nolan (John Litel) is a young naval officer whose ambition for advancement leads him to conspire with the adventurer Aaron Burr in a plot to set up an independent fiefdom west of the Mis-sissippi in 1805. Dragged before a court-martial for his role in the hare-brained scheme, the hot-headed Nolan blurts out a shocking blasphemy. "Damn the United States!" he cries. "I hope I may never see or hear of the United States again!"

Nolan gets his wish. A Navy court-martial condemns him to an eternal exile at sea, never again to set eyes upon or hear about the homeland he cursed. Nolan's shipmates are forbidden from so much as uttering the sacred name of the United States in range of his hearing. His devoted, long-suffering fiancée petitions president after president to pardon him, but the verdict of military justice is final. Not even Abraham Lincoln will extend his legendary mercy to the wretched heretic. Sixty years later, pen-itent and punished, the ancient mariner lies on his deathbed. Under his pillow is an American flag, sewn from scraps of colored cloth collected over the years.

The Man Without a Country grabbed the second Oscar in a row for the series, winning the 1937 Academy Award for Best Short Subject in Color. It also earned an asterisk mark in Production Code history for being granted a verbal dispensation that would not be heard again until Rhett Butler's brusque kiss-off of Scarlett O'Hara in *Gone With the Wind* (1939)—the use of the word "damn" on the soundtrack of a Hollywood film.

However, despite the Academy kudos and the studio chest-thumping, the Americanism series had little as yet to do with American values. The first entries sent out a nonpartisan glow of free-floating patriotism. The evenhanded selection of Stonewall Jackson to be an honored bust in the pantheon of American heroes indicates how remote from ideology the chapters from American history might be. According to Warner Bros., the Confederacy was a cause as deeply American as the Union.

Likewise, *The Man Without a Country* pledges allegiance to an America utterly detached from its founding principles. The film salutes a proto-fascist doctrine of unconditional fealty to the nation state as enforced by uniformed officials determined to mete out every last lash of a harsh sentence. The opening crawl for the film reads: "May this story serve as it has in the past to awaken in the hearts of all men a deeper love for their homeland, a greater homage to their flag." American patriotism is yoked to icons and talismans—the Stars and Stripes, the name of the nation—but not to religious tolerance, freedom of expression, or the autonomy of the individual. The country the man is without might just as well be Nazi Germany.

Subsequent entries in the series would be more explicit about the self-evident truths held by American patriots, more tied to themes of religious and ethnic tolerance. They would also be positioned more pointedly, if still always allegorically, in opposition to Nazism.

The 1938–39 season called for five inspirational parables: *Teddy Roosevelt and His Rough Riders*, *Remember the Alamo*, *American Cavalcade*, *The Declaration of Independence*, and *Lincoln in the White House*. In part because the series was becoming more transparently present-minded, in part because the geopolitical crises of 1938 made the embrace of traditional American values a shelter from the chaos and danger abroad, the next round of patriotic shorts attracted greater attention. As events in Europe grew more ominous, the lessons from the American past sounded less like a distant trumpet and more like a call to arms.

Where better to begin than *The Declaration of Independence* (October 1938)? The story behind the parchment is built around the action-packed exploits of Caesar Rodney, Delaware delegate to the Second Continental Congress, a dashingly handsome rebel who eludes Tories and Redcoats to arrive in Philadelphia in the nick of time to cast the deciding vote on July 4, 1776. "We have champions in England," Virginia delegate Richard Henry Lee tells his colleague Thomas Jefferson as the men travel by coach to the Second Continental Congress before taking a swipe at the contemporary 75th U.S. Congress. "It's the conservatives in our own congress that I'm worried about." In the most pointed historical note, Jefferson (John Litel again) is shown attempting to include his condemnation of the slave trade into the original draft of the Declaration. "I'm sorry but that antislavery clause must come out," insists John Adams, protecting the profits his New England constituents receive from the traffic in slaves. Ever pragmatic, Ben Franklin agrees. Jefferson reluctantly relents and scratches out the lines, muttering "it only puts off the trouble to another day."

Released in the wake of the signing of the Munich Pact, the story of the signing of the Declaration of Independence benefited by way of comparison. Radio City Music Hall manager W. G. Van Schmus wrote Harry M. Warner to pass on word from the field. "You would be amazed and

gratified at the reception, with applause not only at the end but breaking out spontaneously during the course of the picture," he enthused.
"The subject is one that should be thoroughly familiar to all of us, and
yet, somehow, is not. It has been treated with such imagination and dramatic effect it makes a profound impression. I am happy to have the privilege of showing it on our screen."[28] Few observers missed the connections between 1776 and 1938. "There is that about the state of the world
today which makes for a considerable national consciousness," observed
Motion Picture Herald editor Terry Ramsaye, who couldn't resist a snarky
description of the short as "an action picture with a suspense sequence."
Box Office also picked up the link across the centuries. "It transcends the
realm of accepted screen entertainment in that it not only is intensely
absorbing, but provides more than a little food for thought at a time
when personal liberty is being made the target of reactionary groups."[29]

Inevitably, the series went to the other great wellspring of patriotic
sustenance in American history. A ripe example of the rampant Lincoln-
philia that enraptured so much of Great Depression America, *Lincoln in
the White House* (February 1939) was a tributary in a river of devotion that
also included Robert E. Sherwood's popular Broadway play, *Abe Lincoln
in Illinois*, and Fox's twinpack, *Young Mr. Lincoln* (1939) and *Abe Lincoln
in Illinois* (1940). Directed by William McGann, written by Charles L.
Tedford, and starring veteran Lincoln impersonator Frank McGlynn Sr.,
the film tracks Lincoln from his inaugural address on March 4, 1861, to
the Gettysburg Address on November 19, 1863. Whether playing with his
son Tad (cherubic child actor Dickie Moore), showing mercy to a court-
martialed Union private, or asking a Union band to play "Dixie, " the warm
humanitarianism and conciliatory spirit of the Great Emancipator exists
in the same lean frame as his frontier fortitude and moral rectitude. The
recitation of Lincoln's 272-word elegy to the Union dead at the site of the
pivotal battle of the Civil War, presumably with members of the audience
joining in for at least the first and last lines, was the emotional highpoint.

Variety's Abel Green, no easy audience, succumbed fully to the patriotic spell. "If visual education ever assumes the wide importance its
advocates have been urging, this excerpt alone is surefire for every classroom," he wrote.[30] "A must for American screens," decreed the trades.
"Here is a picture that is not only an honor but a duty for every theater to
show. . . . Harry Warner has done the industry and the nation a genuine
service in this memorable instance."[31]

The official release date for *Lincoln in the White House* was February 12, 1939—the anniversary of Lincoln's birthday—and Radio City Music Hall was accorded first honors. "The blasé Music Hall audience salvoed this film like it was the 4th of July," reported Abel Green. "It's a natural, of course, now amidst the world strife between democratic and demagogic advocates, but at all times it is forthright entertainment and sound Americanism."[32] "This subject should be played in every theater in the country, regardless of run or size," lectured *Box Office*. "It is not only a subject for February 12, but one that comes at a time ripe for maintaining the spirit of Americanism."[33]

By far the most explicit colonial-era broadside at Nazism concerned a Founding Father who was neither Deist nor Protestant. After Patrick Henry, Thomas Jefferson, and Abraham Lincoln, the hero of *Sons of Liberty* (April 1939) would be a name unfamiliar even to history buffs: Haym Salomon, the Jewish American financial backer of the American Revolution. The audacity of the topic—and uncertainty over how to handle it—is indicated by its stop-and-start production history. Originally slated as a follow-up to *The Man Without a Country* under the title *His Country First*, *Sons of Liberty* was for a time considered for feature-length treatment. Then the "Jewish angle" was to be downplayed in favor of a story built around George Washington. Then it was reconceived as a four-reeler, then a three-reeler, and finally a two-reeler with Salomon as the hero.

Clocking in at 23 minutes, *Sons of Liberty* glitters with all the sheen of a big-budget feature production: a Technicolor format, a prestige director (Michael Curtiz, straight from *The Adventures of Robin Hood* [1938] and *Four Daughters* [1938]) and a top-tier cast fronted by Claude Rains, Donald Crisp, and Gale Sondergaard. "Warner Bros. produced it like a feature!" blared trade ads, truthfully. "Warner Bros. promoted it like a feature!"

No sentient moviegoer in 1939 would have missed the echoes of the day's headlines. The first shot shows a tableau of huddled refugee masses in eighteenth-century garb. "The first Americans were Europeans who came to the New World in search of liberty. In the dangerous days of the Revolution, these people of many races and many creeds, long oppressed in their own native lands, dedicated their lives, their fortunes, and their sacred honor to the creation of a free America" exposits the opening script, offering an interpretation of American history that erases the Puritan errand into the wilderness in favor of a secular vision of America as the last best hope of mankind. "Persecution and intoler-ance drove my family into exile," says Salomon (played by the dignified British import Claude Rains), explaining his zeal for the rebel cause. "I came to America in search of liberty and I found it here. And now that liberty is threatened I want to join those who are fighting to secure it."

The Sons of Liberty are united by more than a desire to cast off the yoke of tyranny. Arrested by the British and tossed into a holding cell for rebel prisoners, Salomon is informed by a Yiddish-accented friend that a fellow prisoner ("a good Christian lad") condemned to be hanged is in need of religious comfort. The youth cannot remember the words to the Twenty-third Psalm. Salomon approaches him and begins to recite the psalm ("The Lord is my Shepherd, I shall not want"). Thus prompted, the lad chimes in and the two patriots recite the psalm together. Now, at peace with God, the condemned man can go to his death with the solace of a heavenly reward. Calling the youth to the gallows, a Redcoat guard barks out his name: "Nathan Hale!"

Salomon escapes from prison and continues his revolutionary ser-vice—a good thing too because the fate of the embryonic nation hangs in the balance. Desperately in need of funds to pay the disgruntled Conti-nental army, George Washington knows where to turn. He dispatches an emissary to Salomon with an urgent plea.

The Jewish patriot is at temple observing the holiest day on the Jewish calendar, Yom Kippur, the Day of Atonement. When Washington's mes-senger barges through the doors of the synagogue, Salomon heeds the summons.

"Haym—have you forgotten this is the Day of Atonement?" chides the rabbi.

"I'm sorry, rabbi, but this is very urgent," says the messenger, explain-ing his appeal comes directly from General Washington.

When the rabbi hears the name of Washington, he is stunned into reverential submission. "An appeal from General Washington must be heeded," he says. "God will forgive us."

Salomon pleads with the congregation to dig deep for the necessary donations. "Centuries of bitter persecution have taught us the value of liberty," he reminds his kinsmen. To sustain the noble cause, the congre-gation willingly empties its pockets.

Though liberty will be secured through the courage and generosity of the Jewish American patriot, a postwar denouement shows that Haym

Salomon has reaped no personal profit from the American Revolution—
on the contrary. In 1785, on his deathbed, the observant Jew and steadfast
patriot refuses to sign the legal documents that will secure his patrimony
for his children, it being the Sabbath, when no business may be conducted. The banker Washington turned to in the nation's hour of need
dies penniless. His dying wish to his wife is "to raise our children to be
good Americans."

While eulogizing a forgotten Jewish American patriot and making an
implicit plea for America to welcome refugees from Nazism, *Sons of Liberty* also had to tread carefully around an inconvenient historical fact. The
tale of colonial rebellion against a harsh tyrant risked vilifying the enemy
of the eighteenth century (the British) at the expense of the ally of the
twentieth century (also the British). Conveniently enough, as the funds
raised from Salomon and the Jewish congregation are being rushed to
Washington, it is a cavalry of Hessians not British Redcoats that attacks the
coach transporting the money. (Fortunately, Washington's men intercept

"Raise my children to be good Americans": Claude Rains as Hyam Salomon, Jewish
hero of the American Revolution, in Warner Bros.' patriotic short, *Sons of Liberty* (1939).

and rout the German mercenaries.) No less important, American audiences cannot be left with the impression that the stereotypical ethnic niche carved out by Jews—money and financing—is their sole contribution to the Revolutionary War. Among the congregation at the Yom Kippur service, one man has sacrificed two sons to the Revolution, another has lost an arm. Jewish blood, not just Jewish money, has been spent in the cause of American liberty.

Critical response to *Sons of Liberty* was ecstatic. At a press screening in New York, hardened scribes from the trade press applauded "spontaneously and sincerely." The Veterans of Foreign Wars endorsed it, Jewish groups endorsed it, and the trade press reached for superlatives. "There has never been a short subject of finer merit," stated the *Showmen's Trade Review*. "Transcendently magnificent," exclaimed the *Film Daily*. "With isms running amuck in a troubled world, this short is like a beacon of light in the darkness."[34] Only *Variety* refused to join the chorus. "Obviously a compromise," it demurred. "[The film] reflects a certain hesitation and confusion of counsel. While not without some effectiveness as propaganda in favor of tolerance and projected with restraint, the short is extremely sketchy in continuity and time elements." Not to mention religion. "A synagogue interior and a 'rabbi' addressed by title, are the sole non-secular connotations."[35]

In ballyhooing the patriotic shorts, Warner Bros.' public relations department did not have to fake sincerity. "We sincerely believe this series is an important one, particularly so in these troubled times when the nation is faced with 'isms' of all kinds," Norman H. Moray, the studio's sales manager for short subjects, announced.[36] Jack and Harry also sent personal letters to exhibitors encouraging them to get behind the shorts. "We're interested in showing what's been going on here since 1612 and keeping it going on," Jack Warner declared in 1939. "Yes, you could call it defensive Americanism—we aim to do our part in preserving the United States as is and in making Americans conscious of their heritage."[37]

The planned slate for 1939–40 called for five titles: *The Monroe Doctrine, Nathan Hale, The Father of His Country, Old Hickory,* and *Teddy, the Rough Rider.* "Warners are sinking heavy dough into these classy shorts . . . each planned for one hundred grand less distribution costs," reported the *Film Daily*, " . . . all being made with featured cast, writers, and directors . . . on the same magnificent scale as those patriotic shorts that have preceded them."[38]

A few exhibitors squawked about doing their patriotic duty. "We've got 530 theaters, lots of them running double features too, but they've got standing orders to run the Americanism shorts if they've got to kill the second feature to do it," said Jack Warner. "Any exhibitor who hasn't enough love for the rights of man to run an Americanism short isn't an American"—or, Warner did not need to add, in business with his studio.[39]

THE ACTIVIST MOGULS

Until the watershed breakthrough of *Confessions of a Nazi Spy*, the anti-Nazism of Warner Bros. on screen was implicit and allegorical. Off screen, however, the studio telegraphed its message in capital letters. Out front and in public, Harry M. and Jack L. Warner made anti-Nazism company policy and personal business. They wrote checks, sponsored events, lent their names to petitions, and put the squeeze on colleagues and employees for donations. In the ranks of Hollywood's Popular Front, directors, screenwriters, and actors were common enough. The two Warner brothers were the only active moguls who were also staunch anti-Nazi activists.

Low-key family man Harry, the eldest brother and senior partner, was based in New York, with the Wall Street moneymen and the executive board of the Motion Picture Producers and Distributors of America, his formal title being president of Warner Bros. Pictures, Inc. Irascible, randy Jack, the youngest brother, ran the day-to-day operations on the Burbank lot, taking an ego-stroking "executive producer" credit on Warner Bros.' features, his byline arching over the company logo or under the title as the executive "in charge of production." The two squabbled over nearly everything—money, films, authority—but on Nazism they saw eye to eye.[c]

KFWB, the company's radio station established in 1925, amplified the anti-Nazism message. Some of the loudest radio salvoes against the Nazis were fired not by the Hollywood Anti-Nazi League but by Warner Bros., the group's main corporate patron. Typical was a special titled "Four Years of Hitler," broadcast over KFWB on January 30, 1937, featuring

---

[c] In 1957, Jack would seize control of the company after betraying Harry in a sleazy stock deal.

lyricist Oscar Hammerstein, comedian George Jessel, and screenwriter Dudley Nichols offering responses to Hitler's rants.

Warner Bros.-owned and affiliated theaters were also in synch with directives from the front office. Harry monitored the programming in the studio's theaters and expunged anything that smacked of Nazism. In 1936 he banned the special newsreel issues of the first Max Schmeling–Joe Louis championship bout from all Warner Bros. theaters.[40] The African American fighter Louis, the Brown Bomber, had lost to Schmeling, the great Aryan hope, for the heavyweight championship of the world, a fight card with more geopolitical than pugilistic significance. Two years later, in the most anticipated rematch of the 1930s, Louis flattened the Nazi in the first round, knocking him out in two minutes and four seconds. Warners expressed no objection to bookings of *The Louis-Schmeling Fight* (June 1938), a newsreel short that stretched out the fight coverage to seventeen minutes.

The studio's open-armed embrace of a non-motion picture star from Germany also made clear where the brothers stood. In March 1938, in a departure from the low regard in which writers were usually held around Warner Bros. (it was Jack who dubbed his stable of screenwriters "schmucks with Underwoods"), Harry and Jack underwrote and sponsored a visit by the famed German novelist Thomas Mann, the exiled author whose Weimar era books had served as kindling for the Nazi book burnings in 1933.[d] Mann had come to Hollywood to speak at an anti-Nazi rally at the Shrine Auditorium on "The Coming Victory of Democracy." Jack hosted a $100-a-plate dinner for Mann, with the proceeds—an estimated $10,000—going to the Hollywood Anti-Nazi League. "The limited invitation list will be the envy of all admirers of Mann, who with Albert Einstein is the most prominent critic of the Hitler regime," bragged *Hollywood Now*.[41]

On April 1, 1938, the day Mann was scheduled to speak, the Hollywood Anti-Nazi League devoted its "Talent in Exile" show on KFWB, scheduled from 6:30 to 7:00 p.m., as a kind of warm-up act for the speech. Actor

---

[d] Jack Warner also courted another famous refugee from the Nazis. In 1938 the studio cabled its London office to open negotiations with Sigmund Freud, hoping to lure the founder of psychoanalysis to Hollywood to supervise the "scientific details" of *Dark Victory* (1939), the forthcoming Bette Davis melodrama about a woman with only five months to live. Freud, alas, declined. ("Warners Wants Freud Aid in 'Dark Victory,'" *Daily Variety*, July 25, 1938: 3.)

J. Edward Bromberg played Dr. Edmund Nobel, one of Austria's most famous child specialists, who had reportedly committed suicide during the Nazi invasion of Austria;[e] singer-actress-activist Helen Gahagan sang songs by banned German composers; and cartoonist Milt Gross spoke on the artist's role in defending democracy.[42]

Jack Warner's soiree for Mann marked something of a turning point for up-front, no-apologies incursions into politics around Hollywood. Mere actors and screenwriters may not have had the executive status or real-world acumen to justify their involvement in serious affairs of state, but when money-minded moguls cast their lot with the artists of the Popular Front, they lent credibility to what might otherwise be written off as feather-brained idealism. "Though up to now producers have tried hard to turn their backs on political upheavals abroad, figuring it was bad biz to air their own political biases while trying to sell the foreigners a bill of goods, conditions have changed so much that many are in favor of saying, 'Nuts to the foreign market, let's be ourselves,'" Variety reported.[43] Of course, Warner Bros. had been saying nuts to the Nazis since 1933.

Closing ranks with the Popular Front, however, meant that Harry and Jack needed to protect their right flank. The Dies Committee hearings of August 1938 had given a congressional megaphone to what had long been whispered in country clubs and circulated in antisemitic leaflets: that Hollywood, the Jewish fiefdom, was a hotbed of Bolshevism, that the moviemaking of the moguls was an un-American activity. While tearing into the swastika, the brothers took care to wrap themselves in Old Glory.

The perfect occasion for Warner Bros. to show its colors was provided by the most red, white, and blue-plated organization in America. In September 1938, the month after the Dies Committee staged its first round of hearings, the American Legion held its annual convention in Los Angeles. The leaders of the motion picture industry fell over themselves honoring the conventioneers.

All week, Hollywood treated the veterans like visiting royalty—welcoming the leadership to the studios, feting the conventioneers with parties, dinners, and teas, and providing star-guided tours of the soundstages and backlots. A huge parade with Frank Merriam, Governor of California; Daniel J. Doherty, National Commander of the Legion; and a phalanx of motion picture executives jammed traffic from Hollywood to

---

[e] Nobel actually escaped from Austria and died in London in 1946.

the San Fernando Valley. Other tributes included a gala "Motion Picture Night" at Olympic Coliseum, banquets at swank hotels, and special teas for the legionnaires and their wives hosted by Jeanette MacDonald, Marion Davies, and Shirley Temple. At the Paramount Theater, comedienne Martha Raye played mistress of ceremonies for a special screening of Paramount's *Sons of the Legion* (1938), a one-hour homage that, if it hadn't been made to order for the convention, might have been. "It has plenty of flag waving, bugles blowing, lectures on Americanism, and occasional shots of marching Legionnaires," noted the *Hollywood Reporter*. "Perhaps it is a little on the propaganda side."[44]

In paying tribute to America's veterans, Warner Bros. surpassed both its studio rivals and the city fathers of Los Angeles. Jack and Harry provided A-list escorts and privileged access to anyone wearing an American Legion cap. On September 19, 1938, the brothers opened the gates of the Burbank studio and gave the starstruck veterans the run of the soundstages and backlots. "One of the great motion picture studios capitulated to a force of 35,000 Legionnaires and their friends," beamed *American Legion Magazine*, the organization's glossy monthly, aglow at the memory. "For five hours a procession of visitors, by invitation, streamlined through the Warner Bros. lot in Burbank, and at the conclusion screen luminaries filled a studio grandstand to give the Legionnaires a rousing cheer."[45] With newsreel-like speed, Warner Bros.' shorts department produced a one-reeler commemorating the festivities and presented it as a souvenir.

The centerpiece of the Warner Bros. tribute was a grand luncheon honoring the Legion's officer corps. After an exchange of pleasantries and introductions, Harry M. Warner took to the podium to salute his guests—and to fire back at the Dies Committee's allegations that communism was on the march in Hollywood. Though the object of ridicule in Popular Front circles, the hearings had left a nasty residue. Prior to coming to town, the Legion had sent the Hays office a letter listing the names of suspect stars whom they emphatically did *not* want to meet.[46]

After praising the Legionnaires as bulwarks of "true Americanism," Warner belittled the "cheap accusation" that communism was rampant in Hollywood. On the contrary, Hollywood cinema and American values were locked in a beautiful friendship, each having "brought peace and happiness to us when nearly the rest of the world is miserable and afraid." Warner did not mince words:

The only ism is Americanism: joyous veterans and their families given the run of the Warner Bros. lot during the American Legion convention held in Los Angeles (*top*) and Harry M. Warner, Legion Commander Daniel J. Doherty, and Jack L. Warner at the luncheon in honor of the Legion's officer corps, September 19, 1938 (*bottom*). (Courtesy of the American Legion National Headquarters)

Certain bigots representing malcontents who want to ruin what they cannot rule whisper that Hollywood is run by isms. They lie when they say it. Let them show us the slightest proof. You may have heard communism is rampant in the picture industry. I tell you this industry has no sympathy with communism, fascism, Nazism, or any other ism— except for Americanism. We collectively and as individual studios are doing much, all we can do in fact, to teach the principles of true democracy to the outside world. I defy our accusers to prove this industry is run by isms. We have no need for regimented thinking in this country. We need no dictators to rule our private lives. Within the industry I am known as a man who calls a spade a spade. I tell you, whatever faith you may observe, we must all be Americans first, last and always.

Warner then circled in on his real target:

In recent years, since various foreign governments have fallen in to the bloody hands of dictators, autocrats and tyrants, other organizations have grown up within our own borders. These groups are inspired, financed, and managed by foreign interests, which are supplying a never ending stream of poisonous propaganda aimed, directly and indirectly, at the destruction of our national life. Those who seek to sow the seeds of discontent, of intolerance, and national destruction, are our common enemies, and we can never relax in our vigilance against them if America is to fulfill her splendid destiny.[47]

Warner's fusillade received a thunderous ovation from the Legion officers.[48] In the days that followed, the speech was also applauded coast-to-coast in the popular press. Newspapers quoted at length from Warner's remarks and editorials lauded his sentiments. To keep the momentum going, the studio printed 150,000 pamphlets of the talk.

Throughout 1938 and 1939, both brothers gave interviews and speeches reiterating the sentiments in Harry's speech to the American Legion. "We are descendents of immigrants and we know why our father came to America," Jack explained. "Possibly we have a more acute appreciation of these ideals than those who accept American freedom as a matter of course. We believe that anyone who is anti-Semitic, anti-Catholic, anti-Protestant or anti-anything that has gone into the building of this country is anti-American."[49]

Earlier in the decade, trying to wrap Marxism-Leninism in native garments, Earl Browder, the head of the Communist Party USA, had sought to rebrand his product with a catchy slogan that the targeted consumers never quite bought: "Communism is twentieth century Americanism." Better salesmen with better wares, Harry M. and Jack L. Warner sold anti-Nazism as twentieth-century Americanism.

"THE PICTURE THAT CALLS A SWASTIKA A SWASTIKA!": *CONFESSIONS OF A NAZI SPY* (1939)

Like everyone with a professional interest in Hollywood, Dr. Georg Gyssling, the German consul in Los Angeles, was an avid reader of the motion picture trade press. On October 27, 1938, the *Hollywood Reporter* ran an item that caught his eye: "Krims Covers Spy Trial for Warners Picture."

The short piece recounted the outlines of a sensational spy case splashing across the New York tabloids and unspooling in the newsreels.[50] In January 1938, tipped by MI5, the British internal intelligence agency, the FBI uncovered a Nazi espionage ring that had been operating with impunity in and around New York. That June, a federal grand jury indicted eighteen persons, including known Nazi officials, on charges of conspiracy to steal military codes from the U.S. armed forces. Most of the indicted had already slipped through the fingers of federal authorities, jumping a liner back to Germany, but in late November three of the accused were brought to trial and found guilty. "The important point is that the American public must be made aware of the existence of this spy plot, and impressed with the dangers," said U.S. district attorney Lamar Hardy, casting the trial less as a criminal prosecution than a teachable moment. "Our government and citizens must be awakened to the fact that it is imperative that we have an efficient counter-espionage service to protect us against such vicious spy rings as this."[51]

Leon G. Turrou, the FBI agent in charge of the case, sold his inside story to the *New York Post* for $25,000 and published a book, *Nazi Spies in America*, in collaboration with reporter David G. Wittels, who had covered the trial for the paper. It was during the trial phase that Warner Bros. dispatched screenwriter Milton Krims to New York to follow the testimony for a possible motion picture project. The case was packed with film-friendly elements: cloak-and-dagger espionage, fifth column sedition, a passable Mata Hari, and the timely suspicion that the Nazis were no longer a remote threat but a clear and present danger.

Wise to the location of the levers of Hollywood power, Gyssling contacted Joseph I. Breen at the Production Code Administration. "My dear Mr. Breen," he began, easing from faux solicitude to veiled threat. "Will you kindly see to it that the matter which is mentioned in the enclosed clipping of the *Hollywood Reporter* of October 27, 1938 will not result in difficulties such as we have unfortunately experienced before?"

Gyssling was referring to the difficulties experienced over *I Was a Captive of Nazi Germany* (1936) and *The Road Back* (1938), the two films that ignited his nastiest flare-ups with Hollywood over depictions of Germany, new and old. Ever since his appointment in 1933, the Nazi consul had badgered the Hollywood studios over any perceived slight to German honor, usually contacting Breen first, who in turn wearily passed the objections on to the offending studio. The year before, Gyssling had been chastened by a rebuke from Nazi ambassador Hans-Heinrich Dieckhoff, for sending a threatening letter to sixty actors performing in *The Road Back*. A serious overreach, Gyssling's widely publicized fulmination resulted in a diplomatic incident when Secretary of State Cordell Hull protested the intimidation tactics. A provocation as raw as *Confessions of a Nazi Spy* roused him again to action—but via the backchannel route through Breen, not with a public denunciation of the project or a threatening letter to the cast. Ready to tussle and reap the advance publicity, Warner Bros. leaked Gyssling's letter to Breen to the trade press, whereupon the story hit the wire services.[52]

After Warner Bros. reasserted its commitment to the project, a miffed Gyssling wrote Breen again. "I would greatly appreciate it, if you would let me know, whether this firm"—one can almost hear the Aryan distaste in his throat—"has really the intention to make a picture like that."[53]

After nearly five years of playing middleman to the Nazi consul and the Hollywood moguls, Breen was fed up. "My dear Dr. Gyssling," he responded in kind, "I have sent [your inquiry] along to the Warner Brothers studio, with the request that, if they care to do so, they communicate with you directly in the matter in which you wrote."[54]

Breen might wash his hands of the Nazi, but he still needed to launder the most politically incendiary project that had crossed his desk since he set up shop in 1934. On the day before Christmas 1938, Warner Bros. producer Robert Lord sent the "temp script" over to the Breen office for a preliminary once-over. "It goes without saying that this script must be kept under lock and key when you are not actually reading it because the German American Bund, the German Consul, and all such forces are desperately trying to get a copy of it," Lord cautioned Breen, who hardly needed reminding. "I know you appreciate the gravity of the situation and will do your utmost to cooperate with us."

Breen did his utmost. Working through the Christmas holiday, he delivered a formal response before year's end. Hollywood's censor had good news for Warner Bros. "[T]he nation involved—Germany—seems to be represented honestly and without fraud or misrepresentation, and the 'institutions, prominent people, and citizenry' of the nation represented 'fairly,'" he concluded, citing the apt section of the Code. "The activities of this nation and its citizenry, as set forth in this script, seem to be supported by the testimony at the trial and the evidence adduced by the United States Attorney and the federal operations." (After sending his formal response to Warner Bros., Breen continued mulling the implications of Code-sanctioned anti-Nazism for the rest of the day. He composed a second letter on the question of what he italicized as *general industry policy* and worked up a five-page synopsis of the project for Will Hays. Neither document was sent up the chain of command.)[55]

The restatement of the distinction between "fairly" and "sympathetically"—a parsing that had been on the books since 1936—broke the logjam blocking the passage of anti-Nazi material through the Breen office. Breen had previously granted a Code seal to *I Was a Captive of Nazi Germany*, but that was an obscure independent film, and would later clear Amkino's *Professor Mamlock* (1938), but that was an obscure foreign film. *Confessions of a Nazi Spy* was a high-profile provocation from a major studio: the Code seal and the Warner Bros. shield flashed a bright green light signaling that anti-Nazism, if based on credible evidence, was now a fit subject for Hollywood cinema. Again, the Code could not be blamed if Hollywood flinched before the Third Reich.

Hoping not just to slip through but to widen the loophole, Lord sent Breen a list of citations from the federal trial. "Some time in the future in case you are questioned, here is a list of our sources of inspiration in the Nazi story," he offered, playing the helpful research assistant.[56]

Within the ranks of the Breen office, the break with precedent was dramatic enough to incite a rare instance of internal dissent. In an in-house memo, Code staffer Karl Lischka, a former journalist for the Catholic press and a friend of Breen's since the 1920s, stated his objections for the record. "Supposing everything in this story is true and fair, it still looks like an impending mistake. I fear it will be one of the most memorable, one of the most lamentable mistakes ever made by the industry," Lischka predicted. "Will there be a Storm over America?" he asked, using an early title for the project. "There will be a Hurricane!"[57]

Lischka's forecast was flat wrong: the winds of change were blowing in another direction. Warner Bros. had an emergent cultural zeitgeist at its back, one it had nurtured with its Americanism shorts, its radio broadcasts on KFWB, and in allegorical anti-Nazi feature films like *Black Legion* (1936) (against homegrown racist vigilantism), *The Life of Emile Zola* (1937) (against antisemitism), and *They Won't Forget* (1937) (against mob rule and lynch law).

Given the sensitivity of the subject matter, the early versions of the shooting script for *Confessions of a Nazi Spy* were handled with the security protocols usually reserved for top secret documents. The tensions did not dampen Robert Lord's sense of humor when he selected a diversionary title for the hush-hush project—though not everyone in the loop was amused. "Dear Bob," wrote Walter MacEwen, assistant to Hal B. Wallis, head of production for Warner Bros. "Mr. Hays and Mr. Breen are afraid the title 'Hot Lips' has too much of a sex connotation for use on the Krims assignment. Can you suggest something else—seriously?"[58] Besides "Hot Lips," *Confessions of a Nazi Spy* also went under the pseudonyms "I Spy," "The World Is Ours," and "Storm over America."

However glib Lord might be, Hal Wallis was dead serious about keeping the project on a strict need-to-know basis. Hearing that Lord and director Anatole Litvak had shared the script with actors Francis Lederer and Paul Lukas, Wallis issued a stern reprimand. "I don't have to tell you the dynamite that is in this story and I see no reason for allowing a lot of actors to be familiar with the contents of our script."[59]

When production commenced, *Confessions of a Nazi Spy* was shot on a closed set marked with deceptive signage to misdirect potential saboteurs dispatched from either Nazi Germany or the German American Bund. Accidents during production—a falling light from a catwalk nearly brained actor Edward G. Robinson—took on sinister overtones. Warner Bros.' internal security was beefed up and placed on high alert.[60] In typical Hollywood fashion, the secretive atmosphere surrounding the film was then leaked to the press: publicizing the secrecy for publicity value.[61]

To lend verisimilitude to its espionage thriller, the studio that had banned the *March of Time*'s Nazi exposés lifted the screen magazine's two trademark techniques—the Voice of God narrator for exposition and the use of newsreel footage for flashbacks to the recent past. Hired for voice-over duties was radio actor John Deering, whose no-nonsense baritone would be heard to equally authoritative effect later that year in *The Roaring Twenties* (1939). "Be sure that [Deering] has plenty of volume on the track and that he comes through clear, sharp, and loud," Wallis instructed the sound engineers at Warner Bros. "We want plenty of body to the whole thing so that we get the forceful effect as they do in the *March of Time*."[62] Earlier Wallis had considered hiring *March of Time* narrator Westbrook Van Voorhis himself to do the voice-over. In a nod to the central role radio was playing in the breaking news from Europe, Deering is shot in blackened silhouette before a microphone, as if broadcasting an urgent news bulletin.

Two departures from Hollywood convention immediately set the film apart. First, except for a single title card, there were no opening credits. All the actors and artists agreed to forgo upfront billing for a cold opening. (The cast credits and main artists were run at the end of the film.) Second, the standard legal disclaimer professing that "all characters are fictional and any similarity to real persons living or dead is purely coincidental" was omitted. The characters and incidents were real and named, and the story was factual not fictional. There was nothing purely coincidental about *Confessions of a Nazi Spy*.

Breathless and didactic, *Confessions of a Nazi Spy* is an oddball hybrid, a spy thriller and courtroom drama sprinkled with elements of marital discord (America's head Nazi is a philandering husband with a jealous wife). The probe into Nazism begins at a raucous meeting of a group that can only be the German American Bund, where the crowd is being harangued by Dr. Karl Kassel (Paul Lukas), a slithery academic type more in the mold of the skeletal Joseph Goebbels than the burly Fritz Kuhn. "America is founded on German blood and culture!" he shrieks. Listening dubiously in the audience, a brave member of the American Legion stands up to oppose the Nazi's nativism with dialogue lifted nearly verbatim from Harry M. Warner's speech to the American Legion: "We don't want any isms in this country except Americanism!" he thunders. When a loyal German American raises his voice to defend the Legionnaire, the American brownshirts launch a wild, chair-throwing melee.

Yet Dr. Kassel's hate-mongering reaches receptive ears. Hopped-up on the Third Reich rhetoric, the twitchy, delusional Kurt Schneider (Francis Lederer, himself a refugee from Nazi Germany) is a vainglorious German-born loser who offers his services to Nazi intelligence, dragging along his good-natured but dim army buddy Werner (Joe Sawyer) as hapless wing man. Schneider is an amateur and a bumbler, but he delivers the top secret goods to his Nazi masters.

For the typical moviegoer in 1939, more eye-and-ear-opening than the plot or the politics of *Confessions of a Nazi Spy* was the visual drapery and sonic atmosphere. The insignia, salutes, and catchphrases of Nazism—huge swastikas, giant portraits of Hitler, and throngs of rabid Americans in Nazi garb shouting "Seig heil!," arms upraised in the Nazi salute as the Horst Wessel song rings out on the soundtrack—had never before been seen and heard in a major feature film. In American territory, the Nazi set design, the German beer halls, the German accents, and the free-wheeling operation of Nazi military men and espionage agents in New York conjured an elaborate fifth column crisscrossing America, a cancer eating away at the body politic.

With the Nazi contagion spreading, Kassel returns to headquarters in Germany to get his marching orders directly from a high-ranking Nazi official who is never named but is a dead ringer for Joseph Goebbels.[f] While Dr. Kassel is in transit, a flashbacking montage reviews the history of Nazi Germany in the six years since 1933. Narrated by Deering in his best Vorhissian timbre, the rapid-fire cascade of images keeps pace with the accelerating momentum of Nazi aggression. For the cinematic blitzkrieg, the Warner Bros. montage unit unleashed its full arsenal of special effects: wipes, animation, dissolves. The newsreel-laden history lesson would serve as a template for the techniques used by Frank Capra in his *Why We Fight* series (1942–1945) during World War II.

As Warner Bros. rolls out its own anti-Nazi propaganda, the techniques of Nazi propaganda—the insidious methods deployed to bore from within—are an obsessive concern. The Goebbels surrogate instructs

---

[f] Dr. Goebbels' body double is played by Martin Kosleck, under his birth name Noccolia Yoshkin, a doppelgänger who would go on to make something of a specialty of playing Goebbels in wartime cinema.

An education in propaganda: a Joseph Goebbels lookalike (Martin Kosleck) orchestrates the ideological invasion of America in Warner Bros.' *Confessions of a Nazi Spy* (1939).

Dr. Kassel to dress up Nazism "in the American flag" and spread the Big Lie coast-to-coast. Smuggled stateside as cargo in German ocean liners, a blizzard of toxic paper ("vitriolic, scurrilous propaganda") rains down on America like disease-bearing ticker tape: dropped from planes and tossed out of windows, flyers, pamphlets, and posters choke America in a cloud of foreign-bred hatred. The litter is tossed from the upper floors of office buildings, plastered on walls, and even stuffed into the lunchboxes of American schoolchildren.[g]

However, whether printed or spoken, the Nazi propaganda is close-mouthed about the people the regime most despises. Nazi agents in American refer darkly to "subversive elements" and an "insidious international conspiracy of desperate subhuman criminals," but the word *Jew*

---

[g] The montage reenacts the real event that left the Hollywood community shaken and angered. In September 1938 a local pro-Nazi nutcase tossed antisemitic flyers from the Garland Building in downtown Los Angeles.

is never uttered or spotted in the signage—no shouts of "Jews out!" or caricatures of hook-nosed perverts. "Nazi" was emblazoned in the title, but "Jew" was not heard on the dialogue track.

The G-man who brings down the spy ring is Ed Renard (Edward G. Robinson), who breaks the case when the jealous wife of Dr. Kassel finds her husband is tomcatting around with a young blonde acolyte. It is not FBI vigilance or military intelligence that exposes the Nazi network operating under the nose of federal authorities ("the FBI does not have a counter-intelligence program," sneers a Nazi), but a lucky break. Unlike most Hollywood paeans to G-men, which reassured Americans that the awesome apparatus of federal law enforcement was maintaining domestic tranquility, *Confessions of a Nazi Spy* depicts a nation whose watchmen are asleep at the switch.

In the final reel, the remaining Nazi spies stand before the bar of justice in a New York courthouse. Winding up his summation to the jury, the district attorney looks into the eyes of the other jury—in the theater seats—for a direct-address history lesson. As he indicts Nazi aggression and the sinister propaganda that softens up the American people, another brisk newsreel montage illustrates his words.[h] The jury—on screen and presumably off—renders its unanimous verdict of guilty.

With the Nazis convicted and the threat, for the moment, contained, the prosecutor and the FBI agent go to a nearby diner to ponder the nature of Nazism. "You see these Nazis operating here and you think of all those operating in Germany, and you can't help feeling that they're— well—absolutely insane," marvels a disbelieving agent Renard, shaking his head. "We see what's happened in Europe. We know what they're trying to do here. It all seems so unreal—*fantastic*—an absurd nightmare." Yet "when you think of its potential menace, it's terrifying." As Renard speaks, the diner owner and a pair of regular American guys shoot the breeze about the dire headlines from overseas. "This ain't Europe," snorts the diner owner. The common sense and firm courage of the average Joe will protect America from the Big Lie that is Nazism.

Or will it? Against the well-coordinated and ruthless machinations of Nazi espionage, the hapless state of American counterintelligence offers

---

[h] In May 1940, Warner Bros. recut the last reel for a reissue, adding a newsreel montage that updated events with footage reviewing the invasions of Denmark, Norway, Luxemburg, Belgium, the Netherlands, and France.

a pitiful line of defense. J. Edgar Hoover's G-men may have neutralized the threat from the gangsters of the early 1930s, but up against the agents of Nazism the feds are undermanned and outmaneuvered. The stateside Nazis kidnap suspected turncoats and sneak them back in to Germany, easily escaping the porous security at American ports. American diplomatic protests are ignored. It *can* happen here.

After production wrapped on *Confessions of a Nazi Spy*, the ad-pub boys for Warner Bros. went into overdrive, ballyhooing the gutsy patriotism of "the picture that calls a swastika a swastika!" No mere commercial venture, "it was Warners' American Duty to Make It!" As for exhibitors: "It Is Your American privilege to Show It!" Sadly, the blather of previous ad-pub hyperbole had diminished the power of words like "great" and "colossal," but *Confessions of a Nazi Spy* really was great:

> Great in the sense that Warner Brothers have given Hollywood the voice of protest. They have dramatized the protest of the American people. THERE HAS NEVER BEEN AN AMERICAN PICTURE LIKE CONFESSIONS OF A NAZI SPY.[63]

A gala premiere was scheduled for April 27, 1939, at Warners Beverly Theater. "Are you nervous about the *Nazi Spy* preview?" quizzed the *Hollywood Reporter*.[64] Anticipating trouble—perhaps a domestic replay of the Nazi trashing of *All Quiet on the Western Front*—Warner Bros. took no chances. The Los Angeles Police Department was out in force, supplemented by forty members of the studio's private security force. Stationed inside, plainclothesmen scanned the crowd for troublemakers, ready to leap on any Bund minion planted in the audience to screech "Judenfilm!"

The precautions were unnecessary. The only sounds from the adoring crowd were the bursts of applause that rippled throughout the screening. At the close, a rousing cheer and thunderous ovation lasted for the duration of the end credits. "The heaviest police guard handled one of the quietest preview crowds in recent motion picture history," reported *Daily Variety* under a resonant headline: "Big Police Guard at Nazi Preview but All's Quiet."[65]

Telegrams of congratulations poured in to the studio. "Last night, the motion picture had a Bar Mitzvah," Warner Bros. producer Lou Edelman told Jack Warner. "It came of age."

Buoyed along by an admiration not wholly aesthetic, the reviews were five-star hosannas. "Daring, fearless, provocative, gripping with an intensity seldom seen in screen offerings, *Confessions of a Nazi Spy* will be one of the most discussed and argumentative films of current time," *Daily Variety* predicted. "It is as timely as this morning's scare-heads; as disturbing as an impending catastrophe."[66] Most satisfyingly, the film earned plaudits from forums more usually given to smug condescension. "Picture biz is getting a new hunk of applause and hurrahs from a new quarter as a result of the production of *Juarez* and *Nazi Spy*," the trade paper continued. "Arty and radical magazines throughout the country have gone hook, line, and sinker for both films."[67]

The German American Bund, the unbilled villains in *Confessions of a Nazi Spy*, fought back with slurs and disinformation. "Motion pictures of this type disgust American audiences and destroy foreign markets for American-made pictures, and deprive our thousands of unemployed actors, technicians, and extras of opportunity to work," it claimed in a leaflet signed by a bogus group called the Committee of Unemployment, Hollywood Actors and Technicians. The flyer urged workers in the film industry to oppose "the control of the Jews" in their unions and to "demand that your union leaders take immediate steps to end these un-American Jewish practices." Alleging libel, Bund chief Fritz Kuhn filed a $5,000,000 lawsuit against the film and demanded an injunction prohibiting distribution.[68] (The injunction was denied and the libel suit was ultimately dismissed—to the displeasure of Warner Bros., which was eager to go to court. By then, in 1940, Kuhn was in jail for embezzling Bund funds.)

German consular offices across America also tried to suppress *Confessions of a Nazi Spy*, but the diplomats found that since the revelations from the New York espionage case, their stock as envoys of a "friendly government" had fallen precipitously. In a letter of protest sent to Secretary of State Cordell Hull, Dr. Hans Thomsen, the German chargé d'affaires, denounced the film "as an example of the pernicious propaganda that has been 'poisoning' German-American relations." The State Department tersely informed Dr. Thomsen it had no legal right to bar the distribution of the film.[69] Hermann Gasttriech, Nazi vice consul in Kansas City, charged that "the picture tends to incite discontent and racial feeling and violates the American principles of justice and equality for all regardless of race or creed."[70] The Kansas City Censor Board, not known for cutting-edge commitment to freedom of expression, ignored the dip-lomatic protest and passed the film.

Given the reviews and the buzz around Hollywood, Warner Bros. expected a huge payday from *Confessions of a Nazi Spy*. However, for all the brouhaha and ballyhoo, the cloak-and-dagger production process and the precedent-shattering Code imprimatur, the headlines generated by the film did not generate lines at the box office. The financial returns for the film were only so-so—not a failure, but not the breakout hit Warner Bros. had banked on.

Seeming a bit defensive about defensive Americanism, Jack Warner insisted that *Confessions of a Nazi Spy* was not just good patriotism but good business as well. "Naturally the success of the revolutionary type of picture, which drew sharp protests from the Nazi government and Nazi sympathizers in this country, has not been pleasing news to certain peo-ple and they have been instrumental in spreading rumors that *Confes-sions of a Nazi Spy* is not a successful picture," he explained. Yet despite the disinformation, just as Warner Bros. had pioneered talkies and Tech-nicolor, the studio would stay in the vanguard of timely, socially con-scious cinema. "*The Story of Louis Pasteur, The Life of Emile Zola, Juarez,* and countless other films of a definitely progressive nature, is guiding us in our determination to stick to our policy of showing the public what exists in the world today."[71]

As proof, Warner announced starting dates for *The Bishop Who Walked with God,* a dramatization of the plight of Berlin pastor Martin Niemöller, the courageous anti-Nazi cleric imprisoned in the Sachsenhausen con-centration camp, and *Underground,* a thriller set in Nazi Germany. "Efforts have been made to persuade us to call off these pictures just as efforts were made to discourage us before we filmed and released *Nazi Spy,*" said Warner. "We do not intend to heed these. We produced the *Nazi Spy* picture because we believed first that it would supply dramatic entertainment and second because we felt it exposed conditions concern-ing which every American and every free man everywhere should be informed. The public now has rendered its verdict both in this country and abroad and we are pleased to report that *Confessions of a Nazi Spy* will be one of the most successful pictures Warner Brothers has produced this year."

Of course, unqualified success would have inspired imitators. But though *Confessions of a Nazi Spy* had cleared the way for anti-Nazi pictures with the full approval of the Code, the market was still blocked by the cold calculus of commerce. A flood of anti-Nazi screenplays "swirling around studio story editors" was "getting a comparatively cold shoulder," puzzled *Variety*. Despite the good material, the "jittery status of international relations has stymied the market." That is, if peace suddenly broke out, nations wary of getting in the middle of an ideological tiff between the Nazis and the Americans would close their markets to anti-Nazi pictures. In fact, so went the reasoning, "with [the] crisis over, even U.S. would not look favorably on such productions from either official or audience point of view. On the other hand, if war comes, [the] trend of production may change overnight and the pictures [would] be of little market value." Even allowing for the unusually speedy turnaround of an A picture like *Confessions*, the lag time between temp script and release prints was a geopolitical lifetime. "Already on the shelves of most of the major studios are story properties dealing with headline news of the day which they are afraid to make—not because of the subject matter as such but through fear sudden change will ruin the market."[72] Playing it conservative for once, Warner Bros. shelved the Pastor Niemöller project and relegated *Underground,* released the next year, to B-picture status.

Given that a film as timely as today's headlines always risked being outdated by tomorrow's, reprinting yesterday's headlines remained the safer strategy. Indeed, proving that Hollywood allegory could drive home a point more strongly than Hollywood agitprop, Warner Bros.' most effective anti-Nazi film of the 1930s was set in Mexico in the 1860s. Premiering just two days before *Confessions of a Nazi Spy*, budgeted at a reported $2,000,000 and boasting a cast of thousands, *Juarez* had all the trappings of a prestigious Warner Bros. biopic—built around a great man from history, set in a sartorially resplendent locale, and starring the ethnically versatile Paul Muni in the title role—but, even more than the pleas for tolerance in *The Life of Emile Zola* or the democratic aspirations of the men of Sherwood Forest in *The Adventures of Robin Hood* (1938), it was a journey through the past with its eye on the present. Pitting the will to power of a megalomaniacal, expansionist European dictator against the common decency and stoic courage of a New World democrat born of the peasantry, the story of Mexican resistance to French imperialism unfolded as a parallel universe radiating lines of convergence to the here and now. Also lending the pageant a flavor more Germanic than Hispanic was the crew of anti-Nazi refugee talent behind the screen: directed by William Dieterle, the Weimar import who never repatriated; scored by Erich Wolfgang Korngold, the Viennese composer who had traveled back and forth between Hollywood and Austria since 1935 but by 1938 had no country to return to; based in part on a play by Franz Werfel, whose novels fed the pyre in the Nazi book burnings; and coadapted by producer-writer Wolfgang Reinhardt, son of exiled theatrical impresario Max.[i]

Contrary to Hollywood convention, the *mano a mano* in *Juarez* is an ideological face-off, not a personal bout: Juárez never shares screen space with his two nemeses, the "supreme autocrat" behind "an overwhelming war machine," Napoleon III and the usurper-monarch Maximilian. "Democracy," scoffs Napoleon (Claude Rains), determined to bring the uppity Mexican Republic to heel. "Government of the cattle, by the cattle, and for the cattle!" Throughout *Juarez*, democratic governance is debated, invoked, and uttered like prayer.

After a rigged election and voter coercion, the blueblood pretender from Austria, Maximilian von Hasburg (Brian Aherne), and his wife, Empress Carlotta (Bette Davis), arrive in Vera Cruz to assume sovereignty over their new kingdom, only to be greeted by symbolically cawing vultures and defiant graffiti ("Viva Juárez!"). Already a breed destined for extinction, the childless couple are dupes of wealthy landowners and ruthless schemers, out of their depth in the high-stakes poker games of modern Europe.

The would-be overlord of Mexico certainly looks the part: Maximilian is a magnificent specimen of Aryan physicality, "tall and fair with blue eyes and a beard yellow like the silk of corn." So regal is his bearing and golden are his locks that he is said to inspire worship from the dark and primitive locals, who gaze upon him as if he were the reincarnation of the "blond god of the Aztec Indians."

In coloring, caste, and character, Juárez is Maximilian's mirror opposite. With his swarthy complexion, helmet of jet-black hair, austere funereal attire, and plain manners, he embodies a radical revision in the notion of a great leader. So biologically unfit for the role of president is Juárez that his ambitious second in command suggests, to avoid the war for Mexican independence degenerating into a "a racial struggle," that Juárez step down in favor of a man descended from a purer European bloodline, namely himself. True, says the president calmly, he is a "poor

---

[i] Wolfgang Reinhardt's last credit as writer-producer was *Hitler: The Last Ten Days* (1973).

ugly figure of an Indian indeed to oppose one like Maximiliano—one so magnificent," but he is the people's democratically elected tribune and he will not shirk his duty. Decked out in Lincolnesque garb, gazing for inspiration into a portrait of Lincoln that hangs on his wall, and clutching a letter of support from his spiritual *compañero*, Juárez is presented as a Latino Great Emancipator who hopes to bring to Mexico the democratic liberty that Lincoln is fighting for up north. The trope of breeding and bloodlines flows throughout the narrative, but the racial order of *Juarez* overturns the hierarchy of Nazi eugenics.

Yet—as if the thrust of Hollywood narrative is unable to maintain a consistent focus on political ideology despite its best intentions— the emotional spine of the story bends away from the conflict between democracy and tyranny and toward Maximilian's personal psychodramas. Maximilian himself is no racist—he appoints a Mexican Indian to his general staff—but his outdated notions of monarchal privilege and *noblesse oblige* put him on a collision course with the locomotive of history. Ultimately deserted by his French patrons, he may either flee Mexico to save his royal skin or stay and rally his few loyal followers. Dignified, devout, and, in the end, quietly courageous, he refuses to abdicate the throne and save himself. His death by firing squad at the hands of the rebels, though a just verdict rendered under constitutional law, is a somber moment, not a joyous triumph. While back on European soil Carlotta goes batty, Juárez, who has refused to commute Maximilian's death sentence, comes to pay his respects at the coffin of the man who would have been king. He mutters two words: "Forgive me." Maximilian is not evil: he is well intentioned, honorable, and totally out of his element. He is Neville Chamberlain positioned between FDR and Hitler.

Critics saw the parallels and praised the democratic impulse. "Ideologically the new Warner film is faultless," judged Frank S. Nugent in the *New York Times*. "With pardonable opportunism they have written between the lines of Benito Juárez's defiance the text of a liberal's scorn for fascism and Nazism."

Premiering in both Hollywood and New York on April 25, 1939, *Juarez* was initially showcased less as an allegorical anti-Nazi film than as a gesture of solidarity with the nations of the Western Hemisphere. The film depicts the United States as a Good Neighbor to its friends south of the border, a stalwart supporter of the democratic aspirations of the Mexican Republic. To the delight of Warner Bros., ambassadors from twenty-

An ideological *mano a mano*: the swarthy, Lincolnesque Benito Juárez (Paul Muni, *top*) sends the blond, Austrian-born Emperor Maximilian von Hapsburg (Brian Aherne, *bottom*) to his death in *Juarez* (1939), Warner Bros.' anti-Nazi allegory about the Mexican Revolution.

one South and Central American nations accepted invitations to attend the premiere. As "scores of celebrities from the mink and monocle set" arrived for the gala New York opening, the dignitaries stepped up to CBS microphones to greet listeners in their home countries, the network having arranged special shortwave hookups. During the screening, "thunderous clapping greeted the timely speeches of Benito Juarez," noted the *Hollywood Reporter*. "The conclusion of the film brought cheers that seemed to last years."[73]

As a measure of the excitement the film generated in Popular Front circles, the *Hollywood Tribune*, an alternative weekly founded in 1939 to "endorse and express the policy of protection of America's democracy, [and] antipathy toward Fascism, Nazism, [and] personal dictatorship," rallied behind *Juarez*.[74] Calling it "the first political document ever to be filmed in Hollywood," the paper commissioned bicoastal reviews from Donald Ogden Stewart (from Hollywood) and the author and struggling screenwriter Meyer Levin (from New York). "As one who worked two years on Marie Antoinette (I refer to the picture of course), I bow to the makers of *Juarez*," Stewart wrote, joshing at his own expense about his less than revolutionary service on MGM's bloated biopic of the pouty French queen. He welcomed the arrival of two new screen stars—History and Democracy—and praised the studio that gave them top billing. "Warner Bros., with this picture, gave the lie once and for all to the canard that the movies are for twelve year olds." Levin linked the film to another Hispanic culture lately plowed under by Fascism. "None will miss this meaning in *Juarez* for the film contains direct speeches whose application to modern times is as obvious as the European mobilization headlines that hit the audience emerging from the theater"—an audience, figured Levin, "maybe somewhat wiser than when they went in to the theater, which is a rare thing to say about people coming out of a movie."[75]

Together, the makeshift anti-Nazi double bill of *Juarez* and *Confessions of a Nazi Spy* was also a balanced sampling of the studio's genres of choice—the ornate biopic and the sensational social consciousness film. The former purveyed allegorical meaning, the latter in-your-face didacticism. *Juarez* played everywhere without incident, but a few theaters that booked *Confessions of a Nazi Spy* reported minor disturbances, threatening letters, and slashed seats.[76] Warner Bros., however, was not without a defense against brownshirt thuggery. Returning in kind the studio's hospitality, members of the American Legion stood guard outside Warner Bros. theaters playing the film.

13

HOLLYWOOD GOES TO WAR

On August 23, 1939, the romance of American communism collided with the realpolitik of the Soviet Union. Adolf Hitler and Joseph Stalin had come to an arrangement. In Moscow, Nazi foreign minister Joachim von Ribbentrop and Soviet foreign minister Vyacheslav Molotov signed a mutual nonaggression pact that carved up Poland, surrendered Finland, and lit the fuse for a European war. Flashed worldwide by wire photo, pictures of the cozy diplomatic scene struck like a lightning bolt— or, to the staunch anti-Nazi, a knife in the heart.

In America, literally overnight, the Hitler-Stalin Pact fractured the sense of common purpose that had unified the disparate ranks of the Popular Front. Heeding marching orders from the Comintern, the Moscow-based nerve center for revolutionary action, American communists pledged fealty to the hastily revised party line. Stupefied by the betrayal, liberals bolted from the new orthodoxy.[1] At the 1939–40 New York World's Fair, the film programming at the Russian Pavilion reacted to the seismic shift in the geopolitical terrain. The Soviet-made anti-Nazi film *Professor Mamlock* (1938) was yanked from the screen and replaced with *Lenin in 1918* (1939), a hagiographic biopic binding the founder of the Soviet state to his strong right arm and anointed successor, Joseph Stalin. "Just a routine change of program," insisted Soviet officials.[2]

Many Popular Front groups were also forced to change their programs. Few fell into line as compliantly as the Hollywood Anti-Nazi League. With the selfsame fervor lately mustered to oppose Nazism, HANL now opposed the policies it had once advocated so passionately—a peacetime draft, a strong national defense, and American intervention in European affairs. "The League affirms positively that the United States should in no way become involved in the war," editorialized *Hollywood Now*, as the Luftwaffe strafed Poland.[3] Even the party liners found it hard to look former allies in the eye and defend the 180-degree turnabout with a straight face. "I didn't think myself into an acceptance of the pact as much as I felt that there must be a reason for it," Donald Ogden Stewart reflected years later. "Russia was the only country of Marxism, and I didn't think I could abandon Stalin without surrendering my life raft."[4]

On December 15, 1939, the Hollywood Anti-Nazi League dropped the "anti-Nazi" from its masthead and officially changed its name to the Hollywood League for Democratic Action. In context, "democratic action" meant isolationist paralysis.

In January 1940, with Poland crushed but "brave little Finland" still hanging on against Soviet aggression, the renamed League launched a "vigorous protest against loans to Finland or other belligerents" and passed a resolution affirming same. "The Hollywood League for Democratic

Shattering the Popular Front (*left to right*): in Moscow, German foreign minister Joachim von Ribbentrop, German undersecretary of state Dr. Friedrich Wilhelm Gaus, a beaming Josef Stalin, and Soviet foreign minister Vyacheslav Molotov, at the signing of the Soviet-German Non-Aggression Pact, August 23, 1939.

Action composed of 4,000 members, wishes to go on record as unalterably opposed" to financial aid to Finland or other warring nations—notably France or Great Britain—as "a flagrant evasion of that neutrality which the administration has pledged the American people." Making common cause with Republican Party isolationists, the League declared: "These bills violate the spirit and essence of our neutrality by involving America in European affairs. Such loans will endanger the peace of this nation."[5]

By then, Hollywood's red-blooded political action group had become an anemic shell of its former self. While Stewart and his comrades clung to their life raft, the liberals who had swelled the ranks of the Hollywood Anti-Nazi League leapt overboard. Membership shrank and donations dried up. Soon, the executive officers were reduced to pleading for basic operating funds. "This issue [of *Hollywood Now*] will reach you after a hectic week during which our staff set aside important work in order to try to raise enough money to make a small payment to the printer," the League informed its dwindling readership. "The crisis isn't over—not by a long shot. If you want to see *Hollywood Now* continue in business, you must furnish it with the necessary money. We put this bluntly because that's the way things shape up."[6]

Only party discipline and an eye for the big picture kept the true believers in line. The screenwriter Dalton Trumbo, a dutiful party liner, published an anitwar novel, *Johnny Got His Gun,* about a young American doughboy from the Great War, his face, arms, and legs blown off, who pleads in Morse code to be put on exhibit as a warning to future generations.[7] A belated variation on *All Quiet on the Western Front,* the tract was designed to remind readers of the horror and waste of the Great War. Americans who argued for defense appropriations and intervention overseas, Trumbo declared, held opinions that "constitute a treasonable state of mind."[8]

Of course, the new party line followed by the League also applied to Hollywood feature films. Apparently, the Hays office had been right all along: interventionist themes and anti-Nazi plotlines had no place in American motion picture entertainment. Like Washington, Hollywood should butt out of European affairs.

Ironically, however, even as the Hollywood Anti-Nazi League was parroting Soviet foreign policy, the major studios had been roused to action. In the 1939–1941 interim between the Hitler-Stalin Pact and the Japanese attack on Pearl Harbor, a slate of unabashedly anti-Nazi melodramas moved through the studio pipelines—works that kindled a revived American patriotism, that called for a strong national defense, and that named Germany as the wolf at the door. Hollywood was finally making the kind of films that the Hollywood Anti-Nazi League had been demanding since 1936—only now the rebranded League was no longer in the business of anti-Nazism.

Hollywood, however, had decided anti-Nazism was indeed its business. Even the most conservative moguls were not insensitive to the shift in the zeitgeist—that with the outbreak of war in Europe, a nation of isolationist temper could also be pro-defense and anti-Nazi. True to industry form, a decisive factor in the sensibility turnabout was commercial. The considerations that had constrained Hollywood since 1933—the profits from the German market and the hope that relations might return to normal in a post-Hitler Germany—had become moot. Hollywood made anti-Nazi films because, after September 1939, there was no good reason not to.

On September 1, 1939, when war broke out in Europe, Hollywood's first concern was the futures market—namely, how the fighting would impact box office revenues from overseas. The major studios took in around a third of their total profits from foreign markets, with 17 percent of the revenue stream drawn from England, France, and Poland, at the time the major belligerents. Optimistically—too optimistically as it turned out—the projected shortfall from the warring nations was estimated to be a mere 25 percent of the peacetime take.[a] A trade analysis indicated that the Axis powers had already been written off as profit centers. "Germany, of course, has long since been deemed a lost market for U.S. films, save for skeleton organizations maintained by Metro, 20th-Fox, and Paramount. For another reason, all the majors bowed out en masse from Italy Jan. 1 [1939]."[9] (On that date, Mussolini nationalized all aspects of the Italian film industry, including the business of foreign distribution, precipitating a total American withdrawal.) Fixated on the ticket window, *Variety* was not fretting over the fate of Poland. "Outbreak of European war would be a blow to American

---

[a] At the time, the industry could not have foreseen the scope of Germany's future hegemony over markets in Norway, Denmark, the Netherlands, Belgium, and France or the financial compensations from a flush domestic market during the war years.

picture distribution in the foreign field," it lamented. "Greatest threat to profitable operations in warring countries would be the clamping down on coin restrictions."[10]

Motion picture personnel in Nazi-occupied Europe faced greater threats than blocked currency. From the safety of Paris, Boris Jankolowicz, head of the Warner Bros. branch office in Warsaw, sent back a ghastly account of how seriously the Nazis took cinema. Jankolowicz had trekked over 300 miles "with only the clothes on his back and a few scraps of food" to escape the Nazi *blitzkrieg*. He reported that Polish exhibitors who had screened *Confessions of a Nazi Spy* (1939) were hanged from the rafters of their own theaters.[11]

On the domestic front, before the booming economy of the war years pumped up weekly attendance figures to 85–90 million moviegoers per week, Hollywood's audience was diverted by the real-life drama purveyed by another medium. With the news from Europe surpassing the danger and suspense of any scenario on screen, many Americans spent evenings huddled by their radios rather than at the corner Bijou. The war of the worlds was being broadcast for real.

Defying the turn to the radio dial, one motion picture theater boasted a full house—the Embassy Newsreel Theater. Audiences flocked to the Times Square landmark to catch a glimpse of what they had heard over the air and read about in the newspapers. Even dated library shots showing war preparations filmed days or weeks earlier braced jittery patrons. Watching a newsreel while the war overseas raged was "much more dramatic and intense," *Variety* felt. "That's visible in the drawn expressions of the people in the film as well as the bated reception by the newsreel audience." In late 1939, a lengthy segment in MGM's News of the Day recapped the events that had led up to the war, including the Munich Crisis of September 1938, when war was averted by the appeasement of British prime minister Neville Chamberlain and French prime minister Édouard Daladier. The newsreel flashed the shot of Chamberlain deplaning at Heston Airport, clutching the white piece of paper that guaranteed "peace in our time." Throughout World War II, and ever after, the image of the frail old man waving the treaty paper like a flag of surrender would be photographic metonomy for how Europe's weak-willed democracies cowered before the Nazi war machine. That afternoon at the Embassy marked the first time that audiences viewed the clip with rueful, retrospective knowledge, the first time that the bitter epithet "Munich" became a codeword for appeasement. "It draws hollow laughter in light of current events," reported *Variety*.[12]

What might be thought of as the anti-Embassy—the pro-Nazi Yorkville Theatre, rechristened the 96th Street Theatre, after its cross-street—continued to operate, catering to a German clientele fired up by Nazi military victories across Europe. Benefiting from a surge in pan-German patriotism, the theater initially underwent a spurt in attendance and a concurrent upswing in picket lines. With a collection box for "German War Relief" placed conspicuously in the theater lobby, Nazi propaganda films such as *Sieg im Westen* (1940), a newsreel celebration of the *blitzkrieg* into Poland, and *D III 88: The German Air Force Attacks* (1940), a male-bonding aviation melodrama, made up some of the war-minded entertainment programming. Newsreel shots of Hitler and the swastika inspired "wild cheering" reported an unbylined firsthand account in *Variety* that must have been written by Wolfe Kaufman given the droll comment that followed: that a crowd cheering Hitler in New York was "slightly amazing within a mile of 100 spots where Adolf would be slung from a lamppost before he could mutter 'Lebensraum.'"[13] The 96th Street Theatre and its programming were shuttered after American entry into World War II.[b]

In this atmosphere, the precedent of *Confessions of a Nazi Spy* seemed to open a door that had long been shut in the face of a producer who had been pitching an anti-Nazi melodrama since 1933. Sensing his moment was finally at hand, the ever hopeful Al Rosen sought to breathe new life into his dormant scenario. "Hollywood's celluloid problem child, the long-projected and comparably long-deterred filming of *The Mad Dog of Europe*, again is occupying the limelight," reported *Box Office*, days after the release of the pathbreaker from Warner Bros. *Daily Variety* chimed in with a canine pun: "Rosen's 'Dog' Rebarks."[14]

---

[b] In March 1940, Leni Riefenstahl's *Olympia*, with an English-language narration and fifteen seconds of Hitler, finally secured a stateside booking, playing in two parts at the 86th Street Garden Theatre, another home for German cinema. Yorkville's third major venue for German cinema was the 86th Street Casino Theatre, which in December 1941 decided that a state of war between the United States and Germany compelled a shift in box office strategy. Shuttering the Nazi-made programming the house had welcomed since 1933, it switched over the marquee to official Soviet films, launching the rebranding with *General Suvorov* (1941), a timely melodrama distributed by Artkino about the Russian field marshal who defeated Napoleon's invading armies. ("Slight Switch," *Variety*, Dec. 24, 1941: 2, 54.)

Attempting to revive his pet project in a more propitious business climate, Rosen did what he always did—hyped the production in press interviews, met with investors, and secured endorsements from religious leaders. "Al Rosen Announces the Forthcoming Production of *The Mad Dog of Europe*," promised his latest round of trade press ads. "[It has been] endorsed by outstanding Catholic periodicals whose editors have read the shooting script, and carefully planned for the past four years, with the keen intuitive ability he has demonstrated in the past." The updated shooting script remained credited to Herman J. Mankiewicz and Lynn Root, but Rosen now took a screenwriting credit as well. The would-be film was still described as "dealing with true conditions in Germany under Hitler rule," buttressed by 3,000 feet of newsreel film purporting to show concentration camps and street riots.[15]

Despite Rosen's keen opportunism, he was shut out again—or rather beaten to the punch. Producers Distributing Corporation, a bargain-basement outfit hardscrabble even by Poverty Row standards, churned out an anti-Nazi exploitation picture entitled *Hitler—Beast of Berlin* (1939) and rushed it into theaters by November. *Variety* panned its artistic merits ("There are doubtless powerful pictures to be made on the anti-Nazi theme, but this isn't one") while hailing its commercial acumen ("From a monetary standpoint, this picture should be a spectacular success. . . . Its treatment is precisely the sort calculated to inflame mob passions during a period of growing hysteria.").[16] Rosen must have gritted his teeth as he followed the grosses and read the tagline for the film that now made *The Mad Dog of Europe* redundant: "The Mad Monster of Europe Is Loose!" Unfortunately for Rosen, it was not he who released it.

Though less rabid than either *Hitler—Beast of Berlin* or the aborted *Mad Dog of Europe*, the anti-Nazi feature films released by the major studios in the interregnum between September 1, 1939, and December 7, 1941, were no less forthright in their condemnation of Nazism. The most devastating of the shots was fired by a filmmaker with good reason to take Nazism—and its *führer*—personally. In gestation officially since 1937 and probably since 1933, Charles Chaplin's *The Great Dictator* (1940) had the great comedian playing his evil doppelgänger for laughs, but not just for laughs, in a dual role as a Jewish barber and a megalomaniacal tyrant. For the first time on screen, the actor spoke fluent English in an end-reel tirade against all that Nazism stood for. (Reflecting the change in MPPDA policy and his esteem for the comic genius, Chaplin's anti-Nazi film was cheered on by Joseph Breen himself.) Also taking advantage of the new atmosphere, Walter Wanger finally made *Personal History*, Vincent Sheean's memoir of the Spanish Civil War, transferring the action to Europe and the London blitz for Alfred Hitchcock's *Foreign Correspondent* (1940).

Having already led the charge with *Confessions of a Nazi Spy*, Warner Bros. kept mostly in the back of the field. Jack Warner made good on his promise to produce *Underground* (1940), a Berlin-set thriller about German resistance to the Nazis, but where *Confessions of a Nazi Spy* was a class A production with a massive publicity campaign, *Underground* was a B-level programmer given a lackluster rollout. The contemplated project about the life of the heroic Protestant pastor Martin Niemöller never came to fruition. Taking the lesson from *Juarez* (1939), the studio preferred allegorical attacks to another frontal assault on Nazism.

In fact, the two most effective anti-Nazi features from Warner Bros. released before America's entry into World War II were set during World War I. Both William Keighley's *The Fighting 69th* (1940) and Howard Hawks's *Sergeant York* (1941) blotted out the antiwar legacy of the interwar Great War films and restored America's crusade Over There to the status of a patriotic cause worth fighting for in the run-up to the sequel. Accompanying the Great War revisionism were pointed lessons in ethnic and religious tolerance. In *The Fighting 69th*, after a Jewish recruit changes his name to join the fabled Irish Catholic regiment, a Catholic chaplain returns the favor by filling in for a Jewish rabbi, reading a prayer in Hebrew for the dying Jewish doughboy. For its part, *Sergeant York* abided no conscientious objection to war in a conversion narrative affirming that a born-again Christian could reconcile faith and patriotism by rendering unto Caesar what is Caesar's and unto God what is God's. Backdating the anti-Nazi allegory even further, the Errol Flynn swashbuckler *The Sea Hawk* (1940) cast Warner Bros.' most valuable star property as a dashing privateer for Queen Elizabeth, dueling against the expansionist, totalitarian forces of the Hitlerian Spanish monarch Charles I on behalf of plucky, besieged, and freedom-loving England.

Oddly enough, the most affecting of the prewar anti-Nazi films came not from Warner Bros. but from MGM, the studio most deeply immersed in trafficking with the Nazis during the 1930s. Directed by Frank Borzage, who helped ensure that *Three Comrades* would have no reference at all to the nascent Nazism in the Weimar Republic, *The Mortal Storm* (1940) reviewed the history of the period between 1933 and 1939 that had been mainly overlooked by the Hollywood cinema produced between 1933 and 1939. The first-act curtain raises on the fateful date of January 30, 1933, a day of some significance and as yet no irony to the beloved Professor Viktor Roth (avuncular character actor Frank Morgan), the personification of bewhiskered Teutonic scholarship, an educator with none of the stuffiness or foibles of Emil Jannings in *The Blue Angel* (1929) and all of the brilliance and kindheartedness of Semyon Mezhinsky in *Professor Mamlock*. By screenwriterly coincidence, January 30th is Herr Professor's sixtieth birthday: telegrams of congratulation pour in from afar, a testament to the universal esteem in which he is held. That night, around the dinner table with friends and family, Professor Roth basks in the glow of a happy home and warm hearth, the well-earned reward of a life devoted to "tolerance and good humor."

The fete is interrupted by a maid with a momentous bulletin from the radio. "Something wonderful has happened! We have just heard. They have made Adolf Hitler chancellor of Germany!" she blurts, giddy with excitement.

Germany's slide into oppression is not incremental. As a *gemütlich* German town is swathed in the regalia of Nazism, the university, once a citadel of learning, morphs into a military camp. A phalanx of thuggish student-brownshirts sits menacingly in the lecture hall and shouts down Professor Roth when he affirms the biochemical unity of all bloodstreams. A reenactment of the Nazi book burning of May 10, 1933, shows cartloads of books consigned to the fire. Illuminated by tongues of flame, Roth watches as the treasures of German culture—Heinrich Heine, Albert Einstein, Erich Maria Remarque—are torched like so much kindling. Nazism blankets the land, enveloping all, smothering dissent. When peer pressure does not coerce conformity, a boot in the face will serve. For recreation, brownshirts pummel a gentle, kind-hearted family friend named Mr. Werner.

Meanwhile the contagion spreads to Roth's own home. Under director Borzage's expert hand, the convivial bustle of the opening sequences is peeled away by degrees, the joyous voices silenced, the social contacts curtailed. The now deserted Roth house resembles a mausoleum. It is as if the cozy neighborhood sheltering the Hardys, MGM's ur-American family, had been wiped out by a plague.

Unapologetic message mongering: led by former star pupil Fritz Marberg (Robert Young), brownshirts take over the classroom of kindly Professor Roth (Frank Morgan) in MGM's interwar anti-Nazi film *The Mortal Storm* (1940).

The word that is still unspoken in *The Mortal Storm* is "Jew," but by 1940 only the dimmest moviegoer would have failed to read the signs. The name, physiognomy, and accent of the beaten Mr. Werner mark him for what he is. Professor Roth identifies himself as "non-Aryan" and what kind of non-Aryan is made clear when his wife visits him in a concentration camp and a "J" adorns his sleeve. *The Mortal Storm* sailed through the Breen office.

After the thunderbolt of the Hitler-Stalin Pact, another vertiginous news bulletin rescrambled the domestic political scene when, on June 22, 1941, Nazi Germany betrayed its cosignatory and invaded the Soviet Union. Immediately, American communists reversed their earlier reversal and took up an anti-Nazi, pro-interventionist stance with renewed vigor. While driving through Connecticut, Donald Ogden Stewart heard a radio announcer read the news and burst into tears—not out of sympathy with the Russian people but out of relief. "I was once more on the 'right' side, the side of all my old friends," he recalled. "I could continue believing in my remote dream, the country where the true equality of man was becoming a reality under the philosophy of Marxism and Leninism and the leadership of the great Stalin."[17] With the Nazis again a common ideological enemy and soon a military one, a wartime version of the Popular Front reassembled and congealed, but the liberals remembered where the real allegiances of their comrades would always reside.

By September 1941, Hollywood's explicitly anti-Nazi and implicitly pro-interventionist stance had incited a reaction from isolationist elements within the U.S. Senate.[c] Alarmed at Hollywood's polemicist streak, a subcommittee of the Senate Interstate Commerce Committee, under the chairmanship of D. Worth Clark (D-ID) and the instigation of Burton Wheeler (D-MT) and Gerald Nye (D-ND), launched a series of hearings into alleged Hollywood war mongering. "The movies control one of the most important sources of information the people have," declared Senator Clark. "We should ascertain whether they are being used to deluge the people with propaganda tending to incite war."[18] The conversation of the senators, both on the senate floor and in public forums, was tinged with enough nativist antisemitism to justify comparisons with the regime the industry under investigation was condemning on screen. Senator Nye in particular was given to outbursts against "foreign born" persons "of the Jewish faith" plotting to sucker America into another European war.[19] To defend itself, the industry hired the highest profile of establishment lawyers—Wendell Willkie, the Republican nominee for president in 1940.

In the course of the widely publicized hearings, Willkie and the moguls routed the senators. In passionate testimony, a defiant Darryl F. Zanuck of Twentieth Century-Fox spoke for his colleagues: yes, Hollywood was making anti-Nazi films, what of it? Zanuck, a Methodist from Yahoo City, Nebraska, invoked every Hollywood film from *The Birth of a Nation* (1915) to *The Grapes of Wrath* (1940) to prove Hollywood a noble defender of the American way of life. As the gallery erupted in applause, he declared that

---

[c] The Dies Committee was still making charges of communist subversion in Hollywood and had lately targeted the leadership of Actors Equity for special investigation. However, the invasion of Russia by the Nazis in June 1941 helped derail the hearings. Concurrently, Martin Dies' unsuccessful campaign for a seat in the U.S. Senate also took the wind out of his sails. ("Soviet-Nazi War Stymies Probe of Equity Reds," *Variety*, Aug. 13, 1941: 3, 25.)

Hollywood pictures sold Americanism "so strongly that when dictators took over Italy and Germany, what did Hitler and his flunky Mussolini do? The first thing they did was to ban our pictures and throw us out. They wanted no part of the American way of life."[20]

Senators Clark, Wheeler, and Nye had no better luck intimidating the foreign-born mogul in their sights. A few days before Zanuck's testimony, on September 25, 1941, Harry M. Warner was summoned for a daylong grilling. With Willkie at his side, Warner read a lengthy statement before deftly parrying the questions-cum-accusations from the committeemen. Warner was unapologetic and unbowed. He asserted his deep hatred for Nazism and pledged to do everything in his power to destroy Hitler. He praised the besieged British ("England is fighting for every right-thinking person in the world") and lobbied for FDR's National Defense program. His films were not propaganda, he explained, but all-too-true depictions of a world at war. "In truth, the only sin of which Warner Bros. is guilty is that of accurately recording on the screen the world as it is or as it has been," he said. "I cannot conceive of how any patriotic citizen could object to a picture accurately recording the danger already existing within our country. Certainly it is not in the public interest for the average citizen to shut his eyes ostrich-like to attempts of Hitler to undermine the unity of those he seeks to conquer." Warner also gently reminded Senator Nye that two years earlier he himself had personally endorsed *Confessions of a Nazi Spy*. Warner too was interrupted repeatedly by applause from the gallery.[21] Outmaneuvered and outperformed by their witnesses, the committee adjourned.

As America moved toward December 7, 1941, two of the players most central to the motion picture dramas of 1933–1939 had left the scene. One was forcibly removed, the other passed away naturally.

On June 16, 1941, FDR severed diplomatic relations with Nazi Germany and ordered its embassy and consular offices shuttered. In Los Angeles, a wistful Dr. Georg Gyssling closed up shop. "Of course I regret leaving the United States," said Gyssling, who had been consul in L.A. since Hitler had come to power and whose 13-year-old daughter, Angelika, had been born in America. "I have thousands of friends here. I hope someday to return."

Gyssling set about packing up the furniture and burning official correspondence and secret papers. "The huge fireplace in the German Consulate at 403 S. Mariposa Avenue was clogging with the ashes of burned confidential documents yesterday [June 28, 1941]," reported the *Los Angeles Times*.[22] Back in the fatherland, Gyssling continued to serve the Nazis as a political and cultural affairs officer, devoting himself to broadcasting and specializing in North American affairs. He survived the war, avoided prosecution at the Nuremberg trials, and died in Spain in 1965.[23]

The German-born transplant who really did have thousands of friends in the United States was also gone. Carl Laemmle had officially retired in 1936, after selling Universal Pictures, but Hollywood's beloved Uncle Carl continued to preside over the industry as a kind of mogul emeritus. In 1937, at a huge outdoor barbeque at his mansion overlooking Beverly Hills and Benedict Canyon, he welcomed scores of well-wishers—all decked out in white aprons and chefs' toques—to celebrate his seventieth birthday. Though nominally retired, after thirty years in the business he could not help but scan the trade papers for a hot new project. "I am keeping my eyes open and when a good story comes along, one like *All Quiet on the Western Front*, I will make it into a picture," he promised. In a pensive mood, he confided a desire he had long harbored, assuming his health held up. "I have never been to Jerusalem," he mused, "and it is one place I would like to visit. And if I feel up to it, I will make a trip there next month."[24]

In the summer of 1938, Laemmle took his car, chauffeur, and secretary for a two-month vacation through Europe. He visited England, France, Switzerland, and Norway. Germany, the land of his birth, and Austria, now part of the Reich, were not on the itinerary.[25] Nor was Jerusalem.

Always antsy, Laemmle devoted himself to enough charity work to keep two secretaries busy. As in the 1920s, when the people of his hometown of Laupheim faced starvation, he took a special interest in the well-being of his German countrymen, now suffering under another lethal threat. He signed affidavits, put up cash bond, and shepherded scores of refugees through the hurdles of American immigration policy, not just relatives but any desperate kinsman. In early 1939, *Variety* observed him working feverishly "to bring every refugee out of Laupheim now living there."[26]

On August 24, 1939, as the headlines in the morning newspapers heralded the Hitler-Stalin Pact, Carl Laemmle died at his home in Beverly Hills. He was seventy-two years old. "The Laemmle servants, some of whom had been with him for thirty years, were inconsolable," read a forlorn account in the *Hollywood Reporter*, and the hired help was not alone.

The death of the benevolent old man cast a pall over the town.[27] For many in Hollywood, who foresaw where the war clouds in Europe would ultimately settle, the passing of one of the industry's founding fathers marked a shift in generations and perspective. Soon enough, Hollywood too would be at war, marshaled as a weapon in the arsenal of democracy.

Laemmle's passing was also a reminder of what Germans and Germany had meant in Hollywood a lifetime ago, before 1933. At 12:30 p.m., during Laemmle's funeral service at the Wilshire Temple B'Nai B'Brith, every studio in Hollywood stood silent for five minutes. Over 2,000 mourners attended the service. That evening, Warner Bros. paid homage to their competitor with a memorial program on KFWB. More than lip service, the eulogies and tributes that poured in had the ring of heartfelt affection.[28] "It is reported he left an estate of four millions," wrote Terry Ramsaye in *Motion Picture Herald*. "He gave away more than that before."[29]

Earlier that week, Universal had reissued Laemmle's proudest legacy, *All Quiet on the Western Front*. The film was billed as "The Uncensored Version," a deceptive label that required an asterisk: "uncensored by war or military authorities." Naturally, the 1939 rerelease had been vetted by the Breen office for conformity with the Production Code, not operative during the film's original release in 1930, but American military authorities had never attempted to censor the film, and the version censored by the Germans had not been shown in America. John Deering, the voice of *Confessions of a Nazi Spy*, narrated both a special prologue and an epilogue comprised of newsreel clips reviewing the history of the Great War and what had transpired since 1930: the rise of the Nazis and the cupidity of the European powers, a grim survey highlighted by the now iconic newsreel footage of the book burning in Berlin in 1933 overseen by Joseph Goebbels. Among the volumes being tossed into the pyre was, of course, Erich Maria Remarque's *All Quiet on the Western Front*.

EPILOGUE
The Motion Picture Memory of Nazism

World War II buffs and film geeks—often an overlapping category—cherish stories of serendipitous cinematic discovery. Somewhere in Germany, the grandson of a deceased Wehrmacht veteran, while rummaging through the old man's things in the attic, comes across a cache of dusty film canisters. Unspooled, the reels show color footage of Hitler in Munich in 1939, just weeks before the outbreak of war in Europe, or of Operation Barbarossa, the invasion of the Soviet Union, taken from atop a tank barreling eastward. Or perhaps the lucky find comes from a more custodial source, a warehoused print left on a shelf in an obscure archive, mislabeled and forgotten, until happenstance reveals the existence of pristine 35mm footage of the Warsaw Ghetto taken by Nazi cameramen in 1942. Scanned and sifted by a historian-filmmaker, the material—perhaps only twenty or thirty minutes of new stuff—is precious enough to become the centerpiece of a full-blown documentary. Add music and narration, fill in the continuity gaps, recruit talking heads for context and exposition, and another title is added to the motion picture memory of the Nazi-infested twentieth century: respectively, *Good Morning, Mr. Hitler* (1993), *Mein Krieg* (1990), and *A Film Unfinished* (2010).

"Fascinating fascism" is the phrase critic Susan Sontag coined to describe the allure of Nazism on screen—the hypnotic tug that the visuals of the Third Reich exert on the eyeballs.[1] Without benefit of special effects or CGI sweetening, the talismanic drawing power of the signs and symbols that dressed up Germany between 1933 and 1945 seem to forever bedazzle spectators: the Teutonic pageantry and Spartan physiques, the stern eagles in profile, the medieval Germanic typeface, the skulls on the insignia of the black S.S. uniforms, the pagan rituals performed by flicking torchlight, the throngs of ecstatic acolytes swept by search lights; and, above all, the crisscross slashes of the *hakenkreuz*, the swastika—on banners, flags, and armbands, on everything from dinnerware to stilettos, set off in red, black, and white, the colors of the spectrum that, advertising executives and depth psychologists say, exert the strongest attraction for the human eye.

The visual syntax of Nazism came to life most vibrantly on the motion picture screen, and it is on the motion picture screen that, long after its historical demise, the Third Reich still breathes and moves, forever animate. The occasion for Sontag's alliterative tag, after all, was the cinema and still photography of Leni Riefenstahl, the Third Reich's only pantheon auteur, who via editing, set design, lighting, and mise-en-scène set the standard for the primal call of Nazism on screen.

The Germans bathed in that motion picture imagery from the late 1920s until 1945, but only with the outbreak of world war was the mythos made universal—by force in the countries the Nazis occupied, by way of inoculation in the United States. After America's entry into World War II, the scenes from Nazi propaganda became a featured attraction in the nation's theaters and required viewing for millions of men and women in the U.S. armed forces. Hijacked for purposes of education and morale, the signage from Nazi newsreels and feature films unfurled alongside the patriotic bunting of America at war. Especially in the groundbreaking *Why We Fight* series (1942–1945), supervised by Maj. Frank Capra at the Special Services Branch of the U.S. Army, the films of the Nazis were recast for American purposes. Scouring the library stock of the five commercial newsreels, which were themselves now avidly covering the Nazis and rerunning sequences from their back issues, the military filmmakers, most of whom were pressed into service from the soundstages and editing rooms of the Hollywood studios, undertook a comprehensive campaign to collect, collate, and re-present motion pictures of the Nazis. Considering the colossal shadow Hitler had cast since 1933, the record the newly commissioned archivists had to draw on was distressingly sparse. In time, however, the extant newsreel material was supplemented by footage confiscated from domestic sources and captured from the Nazis. Inevitably, Riefenstahl's majestic *Triumph of the Will* (1935)

Archival imprinting: a majestic tableau from Leni Riefenstahl's *Triumph of the Will* (1935), the go-to source for motion picture images of the Nazis in full *sturm und drang*. (Courtesy Photofest)

served as the ur-source for the most dynamic images of the Nazis in full *sturm und drang*. All the Nuremberg rallies were covered by the motion picture cameras, but none was covered with such starstruck genius as the pageant in 1934.

Tutored by the scant precedent from the 1930s (notably, the *March of Time*, the Spanish Civil War documentaries, Herbert Kline's *Crisis* [1939], and the montage sequences in *Confessions of a Nazi Spy* [1939]), and making it up as they went along, Capra and his generation of documentarians in uniform constructed a durable set of generic conventions for the Nazi-centric World War II documentary: a generous sampling of stark archival footage; a *March of Time*–like Voice of God thundering on the soundtrack; bold exclamations blazing across the screen; maps illustrated with seas of swastikas flooding out of German borders and bleeding across Europe; and a narrative trajectory that was both a moral imperative and a foreign policy. Hammered home again and again was the great lesson of the

1930s: aggression undeterred is aggression encouraged. Munich was the codeword, Neville Chamberlain waving a white piece of paper the freeze-framed synecdoche.

The end of the war generated a montage of imagery that was even more indelible than the spectacles from the 1930s or the grisly combat footage from the battlefields of Europe. In late April and early May 1945, footage of the liberation of the Nazi concentration camps taken by British and American motion picture units arrived on screens in America and the British Isles. Each of the American newsreels devoted extensive coverage to the Nazi murder mills and, at the request of Gen. Dwight Eisenhower, Supreme Commander of the Allied Expeditionary Forces, the newsreels were shown in virtually every motion picture theater in the United States. In the issue from Universal Newsreel, an American GI opens the door of a crematorium oven to reveal the charred remains of a body within. "Don't turn away! Look!" barks the announcer, Ed Herlihy, knowing the delicate sensibilities of an audience long sheltered by the Production Code. Yet for each viewer who turned away, how many felt compelled to look?

That November, when the Allies compiled evidence of Nazi war crimes for the Nuremberg trials, the brief for the prosecution included not only wrenching eyewitness testimony and a voluminous paper trail but, for the first time in the history of jurisprudence, a motion picture was called to the stand to bear witness. "We will show you their own films," Justice Robert H. Jackson, chief U.S. prosecutor, promised the tribunal in his opening statement. "You will see their own conduct and hear their own voices as these defendants reenact for you some of the events in the course of their conspiracy." Drawing mainly on the concentration camp footage taken by U.S. and British military cameramen, the prosecution assembled a body of evidence that could stand up to any cross-examination. The legacy of Joseph Goebbels and his Reich Ministry of Popular Enlightenment and Propaganda having taught the wartime generation skepticism toward motion picture images, the Americans took pains to stamp the material as authentic and to assure disbelieving viewers that nothing had been faked. Lt. Ray Kellogg, a Navy photographer who worked at Twentieth Century-Fox as a "special photographic effects" expert, provided an affidavit, appended to the top of the film, attesting that none of the footage submitted into evidence had been doctored. Culled from some twenty hours of atrocity footage ("cinematic evidence of a caliber which has been reported as even making high Army officers unable to stomach it," *Variety* reported), the 90-minute précis was shown to the eight judges on a screen behind the witness chair. Lieutenant Kellogg, who had worked on the hellish special effects sequences for Fox's *Dante's Inferno* (1935), remarked that "the Nazi's real-life infernos were never like anything Dante or Hollywood could conjure."[2]

Not that Hollywood would ever balk at conjuring Nazism. Between the fascinating fascism of the Third Reich ascendant and the macabre death tableaux of the concentration camps, the motion picture residue from Nazism was impossible to shake. Moreover, the cache of incriminating material grew exponentially over time, as elusive German newsreels from the 1920s and 1930s entered the marketplace of available imagery and private stock became public. The three-act dramaturgy of the Nazi empire—the Weimar buildup, the regime hegemonic, and the Götterdämmerung ending—was too extensively filmed and cinematically hypnotic to be packed away into warehouses, never to be projected again.

A good deal of the documentary material wove its way into Hollywood feature films—setting the scene, adding verisimilitude, tugging at the memory of the postwar audience. Indeed, the settings and scenarios of World War II provided an unexpected jolt to production. In 1949–50 the motion picture industry discovered, somewhat to its surprise, that the late war would continue to be a reliable profit center. Unlike World War I, whose grim legacy made for downbeat melodrama that, *All Quiet on the Western Front* (1930) aside, was rarely lucrative, World War II generated a consistent run of crowd-pleasing box office hits. *Battleground* (1949), *Sands of Iwo Jima* (1949), *Task Force* (1949), and *Twelve O'Clock High* (1949) comprised but the first wave of a rolling tide. The exhibitor's traditional aversion to war pictures as too violent, too gritty, and too light on boy-girl romance to attract the female audience—the most important demographic for classical Hollywood cinema—turned out to be a mentality inherited from the last war.

Throughout the Cold War, World War II shadowed the superpower face-off as an omnipresent screen presence, with the Nazi precedent always uppermost in the minds of decision makers and citizens alike. By comparison, the Japanese enemy receded in screen memory, with the war in the Pacific ranking a distant second in the Hollywood lineup. The dramatic elements proffered by Hitler's Asian ally were intrinsically less motion picture friendly: the cultural isolation, the racism, and the exterminationist cast of the fighting, all played out in a terrain lacking a ready pool of white females for romantic liaisons. Successful World War II films set in the Pacific such as *From Here to Eternity* (1953) and *Mister Roberts* (1955) could do away with the person of the Japanese enemy. Not so with the Nazis, always front and center in (to offer a very partial sampling) *To Hell and Back* (1955), *The Longest Day* (1962), *The Great Escape* (1963), *Von Ryan's Express* (1965), *The Dirty Dozen* (1967), *The Bridge at Remagen* (1969), and *Patton* (1970).

With the arrival of television, the small screen transmitted the motion picture memory of Nazism with no less dedication than the big. Whether broadcasting Hollywood feature films or creating special made-for-television shows (NBC's *Victory at Sea* [1952–53] was an early landmark), Nazism maintained a prominent prime-time profile throughout the era of three-network hegemony. As early as 1956, when Henry Salomon's *The Twisted Cross* (1956), a one-hour documentary survey of the Third Reich, was telecast on NBC, publicists for the show were already boasting of the lure of "hitherto impounded" Nazi newsreel footage to entice viewers jaded by the same old library footage. Already too, critics were complaining about "a subject that has been rehashed for years."[3]

Rehashed or not, the enduring fascination with Nazi newsreels was confirmed over three nights in 1968, when ABC broadcast a three-hour documentary version of William L. Shirer's *The Rise and Fall of the Third Reich*, the magisterial history that the former CBS correspondent in Berlin had labored on for years. His firsthand account, published in 1960, was a sensation, ultimately selling nearly a million copies in hardback. Produced by David L. Wolper, sponsored by Xerox Corporation, and costing $750,000, the film racked up solid Nielsen ratings on the strength of a no-nonsense presentation of archival footage, much of it new to the eyes of American audiences, and interviews with a few select eyewitnesses to history. Ernst "Putzi" Hanfstaengl, the factotum who in 1933 had tried to shake down Cornelius Vanderbilt Jr. for $5,000 for an exclusive interview with Hitler, cheerfully recalls his salad days with the future *führer*. Sitting down at a piano and playing a few bars, he reveals that a moody Hitler could be soothed by the strains of "Russian Lullaby"—a melody composed by Irving Berlin. Director Jack Kaufman sorted through a treasure trove of German newsreels that had originally been seized by American troops in 1945 and then deposited at the National Archives, only to be returned to Germany in 1963 by President John Kennedy. "For two and a half weeks I locked myself on a castle in the Rhine and was enthralled at what seemed like endless miles of official Nazi film that I'm sure has never before been seen on television," recalled Kaufman.[4]

More long-lived and epic in scope was a British import, the Thames Television production of *The World at War* (1973–74), a 26-part series that bid to be the definitive motion picture review of the twentieth century's most convulsive chapter. Like *The Rise and Fall of the Third Reich*, it had the actuarial advantage of on-camera interviews with friends and associates of Hitler and many of the power players in the Allied command. It also reinforced a new documentary tradition by refusing to privilege the Great Men of the war and soliciting testimony from common soldiers and civilians caught in the cyclone of history.

For the rest of the twentieth century, and beyond, the Nazi-centric documentary and narrative feature film retained cultural currency—rarely dropping in value, always a good investment. Appropriately, the turn of millennium saw a sharp upward spike in the graph. With the World War II generation dying off but their offspring fully devoted to commemoration, every tributary of American culture—literature, scholarship, film, television, museums, national parks, the Washington Mall—competed in offering a heartfelt salute to the warriors who defeated the Nazis. In 1998, Tom Brokaw's best-selling *The Greatest Generation* kicked off a national ritual of genuflection whose highest-profile motion picture tributes were Steven Spielberg's *Saving Private Ryan* (1998), a visceral combat film by the most successful filmmaker in Hollywood history, and, on television, HBO's *Band of Brothers* (2001), a reverent miniseries based on historian Stephen Ambrose's chronicle of an infantry company from boot camp to the invasion of Normandy to the liberation of the concentration camps.

In the digital age, the collection and repackaging of images of the Nazis remains a growth industry, sustaining documentary features, Hollywood action films, DVD box sets, and specialty cable channels. On YouTube and on websites for rabid World War II buffs, the motion picture memory of Nazism is instantly accessible via streaming and peer-to-peer sharing. The regalia of Nazism holds on to its value too, with auctions on eBay garnering top dollar for anything embossed with a swastika.

Ultimately, the glut of imagery inspired (thus far) the most extravagant of all big-screen meditations on the motion picture memory of Nazism: auteur-provocateur Quentin Tarantino's *Inglourious Basterds* (2009). Set

The talismanic power of Nazism on screen: Mélanie Laurent in Quentin Tarantino's counterfactual romp, *Inglourious Basterds* (2009).

in a counterfactual fantasy world removed from history but not from the fascination with the cinematic legacy of Nazism, it is a Nazi-obsessed movie about other Nazi-obsessed movies, an affectionate *homage* to the many hours of cinematic pleasure the Nazis have given moviegoers. The intoxication with the iconography of the Third Reich is unblushing and obsessive: wallpapered with swastikas, outfitted in S.S. and Wehrmacht battledress, fixated on name-dropping the stars of Nazi filmdom (Leni Riefenstahl, G. W. Pabst, and Emil Jannings), and dominated by a deliciously sinister villain nicknamed "the Jew Hunter." Joseph Goebbels (portrayed not by Warner Bros.' preferred body double, Martin Kosleck, but by Sylvester Groth) struts about as a wannabe mogul. "He sees himself more as David O. Selznick," comments an expert on German cinema, recruited as part of a commando team sent into Nazi-occupied France to orchestrate a mass assassination of the Nazi leadership, including Hitler, scheduled to climax at a motion picture theater in Paris, ground zero for

rampant cinephilia. At play in the field of Nazism, wallowing in the pleasure of the text, director and audience share a matinee lark. Nowhere do
the real images of Nazism crash the party and wrench the spectator back
into history—no clips from *Triumph of the Will* or the newsreels of boycotts, book burnings, and concentration camps.

"Films beget films," the film historian Jay Leyda famously observed,[5]
and no films have seeded more descendents than the footage from the
twelve-year Reich. The preceding study has contemplated the emergence
of those images before they became imprinted and all-pervasive, when
they were fresh and new, when the early apprehensions of Nazism first
filtered into the American consciousness through Hollywood cinema.
It has also considered how a great art-industry confronted a profound
moral quandary—cooperating with, looking away from, and, ultimately,
facing up to a menace beyond its imagination.

THANKS AND ACKNOWLEDGMENTS

H ollywood and Hitler, 1933–1939 ends where most studies of Hollywood
and Nazism begin, with the outbreak of World War II. Its animating impulse was to sharpen the focus on a blurry chapter in motion
picture history—when Hollywood, in the grip of the Great Depression,
first mediated Nazism as a business, an ideology, and, finally, a threat.
Believing that today's high cinematic profile of Nazism is a perceptual
trick, a kind of false film memory, I wanted to recapture what was seen
on screen at the time and to gauge how Americans, filmmakers and
moviegoers alike, responded. Much of the task was purely archaeological—
excavating forgotten films and eavesdropping on audiences.

To conjure the Hollywood past, the films have been at the center of the
inquiry, but I have also relied on a rich repository of archival sources: on
accounts in the motion picture trade press, especially the witty reportage
from *Variety*, the *Hollywood Reporter*, and the other Hollywood-dependent
periodicals; on the files of the Production Code Administration, Hollywood's in-house moral police force, and its parent outfit, the Motion Picture Producers and Distributors of America; on memos from U.S. government bureaucrats; and on the commentary and reporting from the
major newspapers and magazines of the day. Thinking it best not to over-
lay what we know now onto what they knew then, I have tried, with a few
unavoidable exceptions, to keep away from after-the-fact memoirs and
the mammoth bulk of secondary scholarship written on the 1930s and
Nazism. Nor have I flash-forwarded to the postwar backfires. Many of
the members of the Hollywood Anti-Nazi League and others who fought

against Hitler in the 1930s—the "premature anti-fascists" as they ruefully dubbed themselves—would later run afoul of the House Committee on Un-American Activities and kindred Cold War watchdogs, private and public, who detected only communist subversion in the work of the Popular Front. That is an important story but not the one told here. Finally, in looking at the movie-minded men and women who first faced up to or flinched before Nazism, I have strived to keep perspective and cultivate humility. To generations with a clear picture of the Nazis, it is hard to imagine anyone would ever have had any dealings with them. Although I like to think that, had I been there as a mogul or moviegoer, I would have been both preternaturally farsighted and scrupulously moral, I am not so sure.

* * *

One of the nice things about finishing a book, besides actually finishing the book, is getting to thank the people who helped, guided, encouraged, kibitzed, and listened along the way. I owe a special debt of gratitude to my dear friend Greg Burk, who read the manuscript with care and understanding, correcting gaffes and telling me, gently, when his eyes glazed over: thanks, Greg, I owe you big. Steven J. Ross also gave the manuscript a scrupulous and extraordinarily helpful reading, for which I am extremely grateful. Being, like so many Americans, linguistically challenged, I was fortunate to have friends who shared their fluency. Miranda Neubauer and Fritz Neubauer tracked down the postwar German genealogy of Nazi consul Georg Gyssling. Olga Gershenson and Irina Murtazashvili offered expertise in Russian, and Olga provided an eloquent on-the-spot subtitling during a living room screening of *Professor Mamlock*. Scholars are always dependent on the kindness of archivists and I have been the fortunate recipient of the generous guidance of Sharon Rivo and Lisa Rivo of the National Center for Jewish Film at Brandeis University; Sandra J. Lee at the Warner Bros. Archives at the University of Southern California; Barbara Hall, Kristine Krueger, and Faye Thompson at the Margaret Herrick Library of the Academy of Motion Picture Arts and Sciences; Robert Clark at the Franklin D. Roosevelt Presidential Library; Rosemary Hanes, Zoran Sinodad, and Josie Walters-Johnston at the Motion Picture Division of the Library of Congress; Lindsay Zarwell, Ronald Coleman, Megan Lewis, Bruce Levy, and Raye Farr at the United

States Holocaust Memorial Museum; Benjamin Singleton at the Moving Image Research Collections at the University of South Carolina; Kathy McLeister at the Theatre Historical Society of America; Drew Adan at the Beinecke Rare Book and Manuscript Library at Yale University; Kevin Flanagan, Howard Trace, and Debra Bookhart at the American Legion National Headquarters; Charles Silver of the Department of Film at the Museum of Modern Art; Jane Klain at the Paley Center for Media; and Rainer Rother at the Deutsche Kinemethek. Nicola Mazzanti and Bruno Mestdagh at the Cinémathèque royale de Belgique and Roel Vande Winkel helped tremendously with their late-breaking discovery of a print of *Hitler's Reign of Terror*. At Columbia University Press, Associate Director and Editorial Director Jennifer Crewe, editorial assistant Kathryn Schell, and ace copy editor Roy Thomas were, as usual, total professionals and supportive collaborators. The serenely competent Eve Neiger was a lifesaver, lending her sharp eye and digital skills to the acquisition and spiffing-up of illustrations. A particularly precious resource—time—was provided by the Shaw Foundation Professorship at Nanyang Technological University in Singapore, for which I am deeply thankful to Benjamin Detenber, Stephen Teo, Bradley Freeman, and especially Adam Knee for his crucial role as middleman and cross-cultural facilitator. For tea, sympathy, factoids, and not nodding off as I rambled on, I am grateful to Joyce Antler, Jerry Cohen, Richard Gaskins, Haden Guest, Andrew Hudgins, Catherine Jurca, Paul Lesch, Robin Lichtenstein, Charles Maland, Steve Mayer, Erin McGraw, Ross Melnick, Ed Monsour, Dane Morrison, Nancy Palmer, Kerk Phillips, John Raeburn, Steve Rothman, Jonathan Sarna, Colin Shindler, Abraham Shragge, David Sterritt, David Weinstein, Steve Whitfield, and Anne Woodrum. As always, to my wife Sandra, kind editor and life companion, I owe more than I can say.

▬▬

NOTES

PROLOGUE: *JUDENFILM!*

1. Col. Jason S. Joy's Resume, Apr. 8, 1930 (*All Quiet on the Western Front*, Production Code Administration files, Academy of Motion Picture Arts and Sciences, Margaret Herrick Library, Beverly Hills, CA; hereinafter, PCA files).

2. Col. Joy's Resume, Feb. 15, 1930 (*All Quiet on the Western Front*, PCA files). See also Andrew Kelly, *All Quiet on the Western Front: The Story of a Film* (London: I. B. Taurus, 1998), 120–21; and Jerold Simmons, "Film and International Politics: The Banning of *All Quiet on the Western Front* in Germany and Austria, 1930–1931," *The Historian* (August 2007): 40–60.

3. "Berlin Riot Over 'All Quiet' as Much Anti-Semitic as Anything Else—Forcing New Censor Law," *Variety*, Dec. 12, 1930: 7.

4. "'All Quiet' Clicks in Berlin," *Film Daily*, Dec. 7, 1930: 2.

5. Joseph Goebbels, *Tagebücher, Band 2* (1930–1934) (Munich: Piper, 1992), 542–43.

6. "Ask 'All Quiet' Ban," *Hollywood Reporter*, Dec. 10, 1930: 1, 3.

7. Laemmle, quoted in John Drinkwater, *The Life and Adventures of Carl Laemmle* (New York: Putnam's, 1931), 216–17.

8. "Laemmle Collects $4,000,000 in Cash and Looks Forward to Takin' It Easy," *Variety*, Apr. 1, 1936: 5.

9. "Laemmle Will Film Remarque War Film," *New York Times*, Aug. 6, 1929, 8; "Mr. Laemmle Returns," *New York Times*, Oct. 6, 1929, X8.

10. "Ignoring Old Taboos, Laemmle, Jr., Banks on Fresh Ideas to Hold Fans," *Variety*, Mar. 29, 1932: 2, 31.

11. Drinkwater, *Life of Carl Laemmle*, 239.

12. "'All Quiet' May Bring Martial Law," *Film Daily*, Dec. 11, 1930: 3.

13. "Germany Bans 'All Quiet,'" *Los Angeles Times*, Dec. 14, 1930, B11.

14. "'All Quiet' Admired in Vienna, Tho Again Inspiring Wild Political Riots," *Variety*, Jan. 7, 1931: 7.

15. "Berlin Riot Over 'All Quiet' as Much Anti-Semitic as Anything Else—Forcing New Censor Law," *Variety*, Dec. 12, 1930: 7; "'All Quiet' Gets German Ban," *Hollywood Reporter*, Dec. 12, 1930: 1; "Germany Bans 'All Quiet' as Political Move, Orders Check on Propaganda; U Shifts Plans," *Variety*, Dec. 17, 1930: 7, 43.

16. Internal Report on *All Quiet on the Western Front* from the Foreign Department of the Motion Picture Producers and Distributors of America, Dec. 29, 1930 (*All Quiet on the Western Front* file, PCA files).

17. "Results of Prohibition of All Quiet on the Western Front," Dec. 18, 1930 (*All Quiet on the Western Front*, PCA files).

18. Will Rogers, "Will Rogers Suggests Film Show America Losing War," *New York Times*, Dec. 13, 1930, 20.

19. W. R. Wilkerson, "Tradeviews," *Hollywood Reporter*, Dec. 16, 1930: 1.

1. HOLLYWOOD—BERLIN—HOLLYWOOD

1. Eisenstein, quoted in Yon Baran, *Eisenstein* (Bloomington: Indiana UP, 1966), 74.

2. Sime Silverman, "*Variety*," *Variety*, June 30, 1926: 10.

3. "'Variety' Amazes Broadway, $34,450 1st Week at Rialto," *Variety*, July 7, 1926: 7.

4. "Fans Want Happy Ending Says Lubitsch," *New York Times*, Dec. 23, 1923, III28.

5. Ibid.

6. "A Fortune for Stories," *New York Times*, Sept. 11, 1927, X5.

7. "The German Goose—or the Golden Eggs?" *Moving Picture World*, July 24, 1926: 213; Bill Reilly, "Germany Cures the Bacon—We Get It," *Moving Picture World*, Aug. 7, 1926: 337.

8. Graham Petrie, *Hollywood Destinies: European Directors in America, 1922–1931* (London: Routledge and Keegan Paul, 1986), 170.

9. Max Magnus, "German Observers Hold New Quota Would Paralyze Nation's Own Biz," *Variety*, July 19, 1932: 23.

10. "Ufa to Rule Films Under Hitler With Hugenberg in New Cabinet; See Relaxed Quota, Break for U.S.," *Variety*, Feb. 21, 1933: 13.

11. "Germany: 'We Demand!'" *Time*, July 10, 1933, 16–18.

12. "Nazis Must Control Pix," *Variety*, Feb. 27, 1933: 15.

13. "Germany Orders Radical Film Trade Reforms to Advance Native Product; Cuts Sales Costs, Ends Overseating," *Variety*, May 30, 1933: 19.

14. "Nazis Must Control Pix," *Variety*, Feb. 27, 1933: 15.

15. "Nazis Urge Best Quality in Films," *Motion Picture Herald*, Apr. 14, 1934: 53.

16. "Nazis Must Control Pix,'" *Variety*, Feb. 27, 1934: 15.

17. "Nazi Propaganda Minister Orders Tighter 'Aryanization' of Show Biz," *Variety*, Mar. 20, 1934: 54.

18. "Await German Ruling on Jewish Salesmen," *Variety*, Apr. 25, 1933: 13.

19. "Nazi-Controlled 'Film Kurier,' Berlin Film Trade Paper, Pans Variety's German Picture News," *Variety*, May 23, 1933: 13, 46.

20. "New German Quota Law Bars Jews in Production; Old Ratio Stands, Elastic Clause Gives Govt. Leeway," *Variety*, July 4, 1933: 11.

21. "Nazi Racial Bar Reaches Films; Goldwyn Invites Workers to U.S.," *Motion Picture Herald*, July 8, 1933: 11.

22. "Call for Immediate Return of German Players Is Reported," *Motion Picture Herald*, Sept. 30, 1933: 33.

23. "Pommer Declines German Studio O.K. With String to It, Waits Fox Start," *Variety*, May 9, 1933: 13.

24. Cecelia Ager, "U's New Directional Importation Analyzes World Mart's Film Tastes," *Variety*, Feb. 26, 1936: 2.

25. "Alfred Rotter Killed in Nazi Kidnap Plot," *Variety*, Apr. 11, 1933: 13.

26. "Nazis Urge Best Quality in Films," *Motion Picture Herald*, Apr. 14, 1934: 53.

27. "Hitler Thing Deadly," *Variety*, July 18, 1933: 31.

28. Wolfe Kaufman, "Hitlerized Show Biz," *Variety*, June 19, 1934: 1, 48.

29. "Hitler's Policies, Ufa's Pull, Forcing German Indie Producers to Vienna," *Variety*, Mar. 28, 1933: 13. See also "Nazi Rule Driving Big German Players to U.S., *Hollywood Reporter*, Dec. 29, 1934: 1, 3.

30. "U.S. Foreign Film Trade Up 16 P.C. Filling Gap of German Breakdown," *Variety*, May 23, 1933: 13.

31. "Rich European Film Markets Soon for U.S. as Tariff Walls Topple," *Variety*, May 16, 1933: 13, 27.

32. "Nazi Rule Puts German Film Industry on Rocks," *Hollywood Reporter*, December 1, 1934: 1, 7.

33. Jack Alicoate, "The Screen," *Film Daily*, Jan. 6, 1934: 1.

34. Richard J. Evans, *The Coming of the Third Reich* (New York, Penguin, 2003), 381.

35. "U.S. Producers May Urge Hays Office to Force an Official Nazi Ruling on American Pix," *Variety*, Apr. 3, 1934: 13.

36. "Nazis Ban Lace Pants," *Variety*, Oct. 30, 1934: 1.

37. "Germany Bars 'Dream' Even Before It's Made," *Variety*, Nov. 6, 1934: 5.

38. "Reich Censors Tough on U.S. Pix," *Variety*, June 3, 1936: 13.

39. "Kontingent Main German Obstacle, Otherwise U.S. Prospects Brighten," *Variety*, June 27, 1933: 17.

40. "Reich Censors Tough on U.S. Pix," *Variety*, June 3, 1936: 13.

41. "Ban Par's 'Songs' in Germany; Slap at Marlene Also," *Variety*, Mar. 20, 1934: 15.

42. "Call for Immediate Return of German Players Reported," *Motion Picture Herald*, Sept. 30, 1933: 33.

43. "Nazis Ban Chaplin Pic," *Variety*, Mar. 11, 1936: 3. For a full account of the ideological temper of the actor he dubs "the first political movie star," see Steven J. Ross, *Hollywood Left and Right: How Movie Stars Shaped American Politics* (New York; Oxford UP, 2011), 11–49.

44. "Smuggled Pamphlet Bares Hitler Hate," *Hollywood Reporter*, Sept. 25, 1933: 4; "Chaplin Hitler Crack Has Teutons Frothing," *Hollywood Reporter*, Sept. 26, 1933: 7.

45. "Nazis Ban Chaplin Pic," *Variety*, Mar. 11, 1936: 3.

46. Douglas Miller to Ferdinand L. Mayer, May 14, 1936. Record Group 151, Records of the Bureau of Foreign and Domestic Commerce, National Archives, College Park, MD.

47. "German Nixes," *Variety*, Jan. 27, 1937: 11.

48. N. D. Golden to Col. Frederick L. Herron, Sept. 26, 1933. Record Group 151, Records of the Bureau of Foreign and Domestic Commerce.

49. "Reveal Nazi Reprisals," *Hollywood Reporter*, July 25, 1936: 1, 2.

50. James P. Cunningham, "Asides and Interludes," *Motion Picture Herald*, July 22, 1933: 17.

51. Louise Brooks, *Lulu in Hollywood* (New York: Knopf, 1982), 97.

52. Jack Alicoate, "Berlin . . . as We See It," *Film Daily*, Sept. 1934: 1, 2.

53. "Nazi Victim Is Proprietor of Theater in Rochester," *Variety*, Mar. 14, 1933: 3.

54. "Nazis Oust U.S. Film Men," *Variety*, Apr. 18, 1933: 1.

55. "Hitler Lowdown Being Checked by Hays with Wash.," *Variety*, Apr. 11, 1933: 13.

56. "U Taking No Chances with the Nazis on Its $450,000 Production," *Variety*, May 2, 1933: 3.

57. George R. Canty, Weekly Report No. 43, Apr. 22, 1933.

58. Heinrich Fraenkel, "Berlin," *Variety*, May 9, 1933: 60.

59. "U's Berlin Personnel Producing in Paris," *Variety*, Dec. 12, 1933: 12; "American Filming in Paris Booms, All Majors Plunging on Product; German Policy Big Factor in Move," *Variety*, Dec. 19, 1933: 11, 63.

60. "'U' Forced to Sell All Its German Interests," *Hollywood Reporter*, July 16, 1934: 1, 5.

61. "Nazis Oust U.S. Film Men," *Variety*, Apr. 18, 1933: 17; "Par Leaving Germany with Notice to 150 Employees in Berlin; WB Only Other Am. Co. on Way," *Variety*, June 6, 1933: 17; "Kahn Kameo Co.," *Variety*, Oct. 23, 1934: 49.

62. "Par Leaving Germany with Notice to 150 Employees in Berlin; WB Only Other Am. Co. on Way," *Variety*, June 6, 1933: 17.

63. "All U.S. Pictures May Come Out of Germany," *Hollywood Reporter*, Apr. 20, 1933: 1.

64. George R. Canty, Weekly Report No. 43, Apr. 22, 1933.

65. "U.S. Filmers Protest Restrictions in Germany, but Carry on Trade," *Variety*, Apr. 25, 1933: 13.

66. "Hitler Lowdown Being Checked by Hays with Wash.," *Variety*, Apr. 1, 1933: 13.

67. "Nazis Oust U.S. Film Men," *Variety*, Apr. 18, 1933: 1, 17; "Withdrawal of U.S. Films from Germany on May 15 Is Threatened," *Motion Picture Herald*, Apr. 29, 1933: 17.

68. "WB European Manager Dies," *Daily Variety*, Dec. 4, 1933: 2.

69. Jack L. Warner with Dean Jennings, *My First Hundred Years in Hollywood* (New York: Random House, 1964), 249. Though often cited as the animating reason for the anti-Nazism of Warner Bros. in the 1930s, the circumstances of Kaufman's death, as related by Jack Warner in his memoir, are inaccurate in several details, not the least of which is his identification of "our Warner Brothers man in Germany" as Joe, not Phil, Kaufman. "Like many another outnumbered Jew, he was trapped in an alley," Warner wrote. "They hit him with fists and clubs, and kicked the life out of him with their boots, and left him lying there." Warner's version of Kaufman's death is now considered apocryphal. "Phil Kaufmann Passes,

WB European Head," *Variety*, Dec. 5, 1933: 11; "Kaufman, Warner European Manager, Dies in Stockholm," *Motion Picture Herald*, Dec. 9, 1933: 30. "Phil Kauffman Dies; Warner Foreign MGR," *Film Daily*, Dec. 4, 1933: 1. None of the obituaries in the trade press mentions his beating by the Nazis the previous April. Nor do they agree on the spelling of his last name.

70. "Withdrawal of U.S. Films from Germany on May 15 Is Threatened." *Motion Picture Herald*, Apr. 29, 1933: 17.

71. "New European Film Map," *Variety*, Sept. 18, 1934: 17. Warner Bros. is named as "the first absolutely complete withdrawal from [Nazi Germany] by an American firm," but the trade paper suggests that even Warner Bros. pictures were still available "theoretically if anyone wants to buy them outright, but there are no accredited distributors in the country." There were also no buyers.

72. "Germany's Kontingent Boost to 8G Brings Talk of U.S. Quitting Reich," *Variety*, Nov. 20, 1934: 13.

73. "U.S. Film Units Yield to Nazis on Race Issue," *Variety*, May 9, 1933: 13.

74. Ibid.

75. "Withdrawal of U.S. Films from Germany on May 15 Is Threatened," *Motion Picture Herald*, Apr. 29, 1933: 17.

76. "Fear of Nazi Agents and Homeland Danger Silences Coast Jews," *Variety*, Apr. 25, 1933: 3.

77. "Withdrawal of U.S. Films from Germany on May 15 Is Threatened," *Motion Picture Herald*, Apr. 29, 1933: 17.

78. "U.S. Producers May Urge Hays Office to Force an Official Nazi Ruling on American Pix," *Variety*, Apr. 3, 1934: 13.

79. "U.S. Film Units Yield to Nazis on Race Issue," *Variety*, May 9, 1933: 13.

2. HITLER, A "BLAH SHOW SUBJECT"

1. "Hitler Lowdown Being Checked by Hays with Wash.," *Variety*, Apr. 11, 1933: 13.

2. N. D. Golden to Col. Frederick L. Herron (undated but April 1933). Record Group 151, Records of the Bureau of Foreign and Domestic Commerce, National Archives, College Park, MD.

3. "All U.S. Pictures May Come Out of Germany," *Hollywood Reporter*, Apr. 20, 1933: 1.

4. "American Film Withdrawal from Nazi Germany Would Be Strictly Individual Co. Action, Says Hays," *Variety*, June 24, 1936: 5.

5. "Inside Stuff—Pictures," *Variety*, Dec. 5, 1933: 51.

6. "Hitler, Pro or Anti, a Blah Show Subject," *Variety*, Nov. 7, 1933: 1.

7. "Inside Stuff—Pictures," *Variety*, Oct. 17, 1933: 52.

8. "Inside Stuff—Pictures," *Variety*, Dec. 12, 1933: 50.

9. McCarthy, "*The House of Rothschild*," *Motion Picture Herald*, Mar. 10, 1934: 49.

10. Joseph I. Breen to Will H. Hays, Sept. 17, 1934 (*The Wandering Jew* file, Production Code Administration files, Academy of Motion Picture Arts and Sciences, Margaret Herrick Library, Beverly Hills, CA; hereinafter, PCA files).

11. "'Bengal Lancer' $70,000, Par's Best Gross in Two Years, Draining Town; 'Evergreen' $65,000; 'Symphony,' 25G," *Variety*, Jan. 15, 1935: 9.

12. Abel Green, "*The Wandering Jew*," *Variety*, Jan. 15, 1935: 13.

13. "Power," *Harrison's Reports*, Oct. 13, 1934: 162.

14. "Religious OK on 'Power' Causes Loew's to Change Its Views and Book Film," *Variety*, Oct. 23, 1934: 2.

15. Aaronson, "*The Wandering Jew*," *Motion Picture Herald*, Oct. 28, 1933: 59.

16. Wolfe Kaufman, "*Wandering Jew*," *Variety*, Oct. 24, 1933: 32.

17. "Hitler, Pro or Anti, a Blah Show Subject," *Variety*, Nov. 7, 1933: 1.

18. "Sam Jaffe, Par Washup After Sternberg Row," *Variety*, July 19, 1932: 2; Barbara Hall, *An Oral History with Sam Jaffe* (Beverly Hills: Academy of Motion Picture Arts and Sciences, 1992).

19. "Inside Stuff—Pictures," *Variety*, July 18, 1933: 68.

20. "16 Papers to Print Story of 'Mad Dog,'" *Hollywood Reporter*, Aug. 2, 1933: 3.

21. "Jaffe to Col. as General Executive," *Hollywood Reporter*, Sept. 29, 1933: 1.

22. "Kultur—and 'Mad Dog,'" *Motion Picture Herald*, Nov. 11, 1933: 8.

23. "Doubling for Hitler," *Hollywood Reporter*, Oct. 21, 1933: 3.

24. "Rosen Zanzi for Hays," *Daily Variety*, Oct. 16, 1933: 1.

25. "Al Rosen's $1,022,000 Suit Over 'Mad Dog,'" *Variety*, Oct. 31, 1933: 21; "Hays Group Sued by Rosen on 'Mad Dog,'" *Hollywood Reporter*, Oct. 24, 1933: 3.

26. "Rosen in War on Hays," *Daily Variety*, Oct. 24, 1933: 6.

27. "Kultur—and 'Mad Dog,'" *Motion Picture Herald*, Nov. 11, 1933: 8; "Rosen to Film Hitler Story Despite Fears," *Washington Post*, Oct. 15, 1933: 15.

28. "Rosen Seeking Jewish Aid for His 'Mad Dog,'" *Variety*, Oct. 24, 1933: 2.

29. "Rosen All Set to Start Hitler Pic," *Variety*, Jan. 2, 1934: 4.

30. "Rosoff Reported Behind Rosen's Anti-Hitler Pic," *Variety*, Jan. 16, 1934: 5; "Hollywood Inside," *Daily Variety*, Jan. 15, 1934: 2.

31. See *Daily Variety* for Feb. 7, 1934: 1, and for Feb. 8, 1934: 1.

32. "Rosen Goes Ahead on Hitler Picture," *Hollywood Reporter*, Feb. 9, 1934: 5.

33. Joseph I. Breen to Sol Lesser, Nov. 25, 1936 (*Mad Dog of Europe* file, PCA files). Breen was forwarding a copy of his original 1934 memo to Rosen to RKO producer Sol Lesser when RKO was considering the project.

34. Col. Frederick L. Herron to Joseph I. Breen, Oct. 30, 1936 (*Mad Dog of Europe* file, PCA files).

35. Cornelius Vanderbilt Jr., *Farewell to Fifth Avenue* (New York: Simon and Schuster, 1935), 96.

36. "Van Newsreels Vienna," *Variety*, May 30, 1933: 19.

37. The circumstances surrounding the encounter with Hitler are related in Cornelius Vanderbilt Jr., "Under the Sign of the Three H's," *Redbook*, June 1933, 30–31, 98–101, and, with slightly different wording, in Vanderbilt Jr.'s memoir, *Farewell to Fifth Avenue*, 191, 175–81, 193–94.

38. "Vanderbilt Bringing Camera Evidence of German Jew Turmoil," *Variety*, May 23,1933: 3; "Van Newsreels Vienna," *Variety*, May 30, 1933: 19.

39. "Insiders Outlook," *Motion Picture Daily*, June 23, 1933: 2.

40. "Hitler Film Packs New York Mayfair," *Hollywood Reporter*, May 1, 1934: 1.

41. Mr. Norr to Maurice McKenzie, "Re Film: *Hitler's Reign of Terror*" (*Hitler's Reign of Terror* file, PCA files).

42. George R. Canty to J. C. White, June 16, 1934. Record Group 151, Records of the Bureau of Foreign and Domestic Commerce.

43. "Denied License by Censor, Call 'Hitler' News Film," *Film Daily*, May 1, 1934: 1, 3.

44. "'Hitler's Reign, Only $2000, Bad," *Variety*, May 8, 1934: 9.

45. "Hitler's Reign of Terror," *Film Daily*, Apr. 27, 1934: 7.

46. "Vanderbilt Scoop on German Riot Pix," *Hollywood Reporter*, July 16, 1934: 1.

47. "Hitler's Reign Flops in Frisco," *Variety*, May 22, 1934: 10.

48. Hal Burton, "Path to German Prison Told by Isobel Steele," *Chicago Daily Tribune*, Dec. 28, 1934, 11.

49. Hal Burton, "Jailed By Nazis, Girl Arrives in U.S. with Story," *Chicago Daily Tribune*, Dec. 27, 1934, 1.

50. "Girl Held by Nazis 4 Months Returns," *New York Times*, Dec. 27, 1934, 7.

51. Dr. Georg Gyssling to Columbia Pictures Corporation, Sept. 11, 1933 (*Below the Sea* file, PCA files).

52. Dr. Georg Gyssling to Joseph I. Breen, June 6, 1937 (*The Lancer Spy* file, PCA files).

53. "New German Film Edict Applied to American Picture at Source," *Motion Picture Herald*, July 25, 1936: 15.

54. Joseph I. Breen to Alfred T. Mannon, July 22, 1936 (*I Was a Captive of Nazi Germany* file, PCA files).

55. Alfred T. Mannon to Joseph I. Breen, July 29, 1936 (*I Was a Captive of Nazi Germany* file, PCA files).

56. Joseph I. Breen to Will H. Hays, Aug. 5, 1936 (*I Was a Captive of Nazi Germany* file, PCA files).

57. "Mild Bronxing Given Anti-Nazi Pic on B'way," *Variety*, Aug. 5, 1936: 4.

58. "Captive of Nazi Germany," *Variety*, Aug. 5, 1936: 17.

59. William Weaver, "*I Was a Captive of Nazi Germany*," *Motion Picture Herald*, Aug. 8, 1936: 42.

60. "Nazi Captive Themer Tedious on B'way," *Daily Variety*, Aug. 3, 1936: 2.

61. Frank S. Nugent, "Romanticist Forever!" *New York Times*, Aug. 9, 1936: X3; Frank S. Nugent, "The Screen," *New York Times*, Aug. 3, 1936: 3.

3. THE NAZIS IN THE NEWSREELS

1. Tom Waller, "Newsreels," *Variety*, Apr. 4, 1933: 14.

2. Don Carle Gillette, "Newsreels Get a Lease on Life," *Film Daily*, Oct. 5, 1934: 1.

3. "Movietone Mussolini Film," *Film Daily*, Mar. 3, 1933: 2.

4. "SRO Crowds Welcome Opening of Embassy Newsreel Theatre," *Exhibitors Herald-World*, Nov. 9, 1929: 21; Phil M. Daily Jr., "Along the Rialto," *Film Daily*, Nov. 6, 1929: 2; Sime Silverman, "Embassy," *Variety*, Nov. 6, 1929: 6.

5. "Keeping 'Messages' Out," *Variety*, Nov. 9, 1938: 3.

6. Irving Hoffman, "Reviewpoints," *Hollywood Reporter*, Oct. 18, 1937: 2.

7. Jane Cobb, "Newsreels," *New York Times*, Apr. 28, 1940: 104.

8. Tom Waller, "Embassy," *Variety*, Jan. 31, 1933: 13; Tom Waller, "Newsreels," *Variety*, June 6, 1933: 13.

9. Sime Silverman, "Newsreel," *Variety*, July 9, 1930: 41.

10. "SRO Crowds Welcome Opening of Embassy Newsreel Theatre," *Exhibitors Herald-World*, Nov. 9, 1929: 21.

11. Terry Ramsaye, "Shorts Are in Season," *Motion Picture Herald*, May 13, 1933: 33.

12. Don Hancock, "Newsreels in a Cloud," *Film Daily*, Apr. 7, 1934: 8.

13. "Panay Newsreels Prove B.O. on B'Way," *Variety*, Jan. 5, 1938: 4.

14. "Newsreelers Know When to Lay Off," *Variety*, Apr. 21, 1937: 27.

15. Charles Peden, *Newsreel Man* (New York: Doubleday, Doran, 1932): 17.

16. Tom Waller, "21 Big Newsreel Stars," *Variety*, Dec. 8, 1931: 1, 23.

17. Tom Waller, "Newsreels," *Variety*, Nov. 3, 1931: 37.

18. "How Germany Stands in Czechoslovakia," *Variety*, Jan. 12, 1932: 11.

19. Tom Waller, "Embassy," *Variety*, Mar. 29, 1932: 42; Tom Waller, "Embassy," *Variety*, Apr. 19, 1932: 35.

20. Tom Waller, "Newsreels," *Variety*, Dec. 6, 1932: 13.

21. Tom Waller, "Embassy," *Variety*, Feb. 14, 1933: 13.

22. Tom Waller, "Newsreels," *Variety*, May 16, 1933: 16.

23. "Pix Reaction Is Anti-Hitler," *Variety*, Mar. 28, 1933: 1.

24. "Boycott of German Pictures Is Deplored," *Motion Picture Herald*, Apr. 1, 1933: 16.

25. Tom Waller, "Newsreels," *Variety*, Mar. 28, 1933: 14.

26. Tom Waller, "Newsreels," *Variety*, Aug. 21, 1934: 19.

27. "Nazis Off Cal Screens," *Daily Variety*, Sept. 23, 1933: 1.

28. "Hitler Doesn't Entertain 'Em," *Variety*, May 8, 1934: 3.

29. "German Film's Fisticuffs," *Variety*, May 16, 1933: 1.

30. Tom Waller, "Newsreels," *Variety*, July 25, 1933: 12.

31. Tom Waller, "Newsreels," *Variety*, Mar. 13, 1934: 17.

32. Roy Chartier, "Embassy, N.Y.," *Variety*, Dec. 25, 1935: 53.

33. Scho, "Newsreels," *Variety*, Aug. 19, 1936: 56–57.

34. "Movie of the Week: *The March of Time*," *Life*, Jan. 31, 1938: 24.

35. Roy Chartier, "Embassy, N.Y.," *Variety*, Mar. 27, 1935: 14; "Embassy, N.Y.," *Variety*, Apr. 3, 1935: 31.

36. "German Rules for Newsreels," *Variety*, Nov. 6, 1934: 13.

37. "Charge Newsreels Favor Hitlerites," *Hollywood Reporter*, Oct. 25, 1933: 7.

38. "Inside Stuff—Pictures," *Variety*, Sept. 5, 1933: 75.

39. "Embassy, N.Y.," *Variety*, Jan. 29, 1936: 29.

40. Tom Waller, "Newsreels," *Variety*, Sept. 5, 1933: 16.

41. Quoted in Saul Friedlander, *The Years of Persecution: Nazi Germany and the Jews, 1933–1939* (London: Phoenix, 1997), 22.

42. Tom Waller, "Newsreels," *Variety*, Apr. 18, 1933: 20.

43. "German Pyre," *Motion Picture Herald*, May 6, 1933: 8.

44. Tom Waller, "Newsreels," *Variety*, May 30, 1933: 14.

45. Thomas Sugre, "The Newsreels," *Scribner's*, Apr. 1937, 9–18.

4. THE HOLLYWOOD ANTI-NAZI LEAGUE

1. "Prince Löwenstein In," *Daily Variety*, Apr. 24, 1936: 15.

2. "Films' Anti-Nazi Dinner," *Variety*, Apr. 22, 1936: 2; "Dinner Reservation Rush," *Hollywood Reporter*, Apr. 25, 1936: 2; "Rambling Reporter," *Hollywood Reporter*, Apr. 27, 1936: 2; "Rambling Reporter," *Hollywood Reporter*, Apr. 28, 1936: 2; "350 Hear Lowenstein Tell of Hitlerism," *Daily Variety*, Apr. 27, 1936: 4.

3. Prince Hubertus zu Löwenstein, *Towards the Further Shore: An Autobiography* (London: Gollanz, 1968), 175.

4. "Hollywood Fights Nazism," *Anti-Nazi News*, Oct. 20, 1936: 1.

5. "Inside Stuff—Pictures," *Variety*, May 6, 1936: 6.

6. Donald Ogden Stewart, *By a Stroke of Luck! An Autobiography* (New York: Paddington Press, Ltd., 1975): 218; 240. "It must be remembered that I contributed very little to the running of the League besides my name and an occasional speech," Stewart insisted. "All the daily grind of collecting dues, planning meetings and radio programs, and getting out the newspaper was done by four or five devoted members who were, I had been told, members of the Communist Party."

7. "Rambling Reporter," *Hollywood Reporter*, June 29, 1939: 2.

8. From the 4th Report of the California Committee on Un-American Activities: 249, 250.

9. Theodore Draper, "The Man Who Wanted to Hang," *The Reporter*, January 6, 1953: 26–30. Draper provides a fascinating character sketch of Katz, who was hanged for treason in Prague in 1952. See also Löwenstein, *Towards the Further Shore*, 171–72.

10. Löwenstein, *Towards the Further Shore*, 175; Stewart 226. The full and bizarre story of Otto Katz is told in Jonathan Miles, *The Dangerous Otto Katz: The Many Lives of a Soviet Spy* (USA: Bloomsbury, 2010).

11. William L. Stidger, "Hitler Planning to Be Kind to the Jews?" *Liberty*, May 30, 1936: 16–17; "Vox Pop: Row on Hitler Planning to Be Kind to Jews," *Liberty*, July 11, 1936: 64.

12. "Nazi Policies Rapped by Filmites at H'wood Meet," *Daily Variety*, July 24, 1936: 8.

13. Walter Barusch, "Industry 'Fascistic and Infantile,' Western Writers' Left Wing Says," *Motion Picture Herald*, Nov. 21, 1936: 31.

14. Big Names Set for Broadcasts," *Anti-Nazi News*, Feb. 20, 1937: 1, 4.

15. Minutes of the Cultural Committee of the Hollywood Anti-Nazi League, Nov. 16, 1936 (Margaret Herrick Library, Academy of Motion Picture Arts and Sciences, Beverly Hills, CA).

16. "Big Names Set for Broadcasts," *Anti-Nazi News*, Feb. 20, 1937: 1, 4.

17. "Radio Bringing New Members to HANL," *Hollywood Now*, July 15, 1938: 4.

18. "Vandal Raid on Office Bolsters Anti-Nazi Work," *News of the World*, Apr. 10, 1937: 1, 2.

19. "Vandal Raid on Office Bolsters Anti-Nazi Work," *News of the World*, Apr. 10, 1937: 2.

20. "Burglary of Anti-Nazi League Bobs up in Leo McLaglen Case," *News of the World*, Nov. 19, 1937: 1.

21. "Hollywood Gets Rid of McLaglen," *News of the World*, Apr. 9, 1938: 1.

22. "League Moves to New Offices," *News of the World*, Apr. 30, 1938: 2.

23. "Birthday Greetings!" *News of the World*, June 4, 1938: 1.

24. Ivan Spear, "Spearheads," *Box Office*, Nov. 11, 1938: 21, 40.

25. "Films and Newspapers Greatest Industries, Ickes Declares," *Daily Variety*, Oct. 20, 1938: 8.

26. "Anti-Nazis Turning to New Interests," *Box Office*, Oct. 29, 1938: 38-C.

27. Walter Barusch, "Industry 'Fascistic and Infantile,' Western Writers' Left Wing Says," *Motion Picture Herald*, Nov. 21, 1937: 31.

28. Louis B. Mayer's atypical—and pioneering—Republican affinities are discussed in Steven J. Ross, *Hollywood Left and Right: How Movie Stars Shaped American Politics* (New York: Oxford University Press, 2011) 51–88.

29. "Pix Republicans Did Not Attend Roosevelt Rally," *Variety*, Sept. 27, 1932: 2.

30. "Hollywood Inside!" *Daily Variety*, Sept. 22, 1936: 2.

31. Manngreen, "Lights! Camera! But No Action," *Daily Worker*, June 27, 1938: 7.

32. "Eddie Cantor," *Hollywood Now*, June 11, 1938: 2.

33. "Protests and Benefits in Show Business Follow Nazi's Attacks," *Motion Picture Herald*, Nov. 26, 1938: 17.

34. Quoted in Ivan Spear, "Spearheads," *Box Office*, Aug. 13, 1938: 37.

35. "Hollywood Stars Send Two Ambulances to Aid Spain," *Daily Worker*, Sept. 17, 1937: 9.

36. "Curb on Player 'Isms," *Hollywood Reporter*, Oct. 14, 1937: 1, 2.

37. Frank Pope, "Tradeviews," *Hollywood Reporter*, Oct. 16, 1937: 1, 2.

38. "May Film Folks Fight Fascism?" *News of the World*, Oct. 23, 1937: 2.

39. Frank Pope, "Tradeviews," *Hollywood Reporter*, Oct. 29, 1937: 1, 6.

40. See, for example, "Anti-Fascists Have Two Social Events," *Box Office*, July 6, 1938: 37.

41. "Sticks and Stones," *Daily Variety*, Aug. 15, 1938: 3.

42. "Committee of 56 Will Fete Benes," *Box Office*, Mar. 4, 1939: 82.

43. "Minority Oppression Abroad Spurs Anti-Fascist Action, *Box Office*, Nov. 26, 1938: 35, 38.

44. "Dr. Smith, Frank Capra Denounce Nazi Pogroms," *Hollywood Now*, Nov. 25, 1938: 2.

45. Ivan Spear, "Spearheads," *Box Office*, Nov. 20, 1938: 21, 40.

46. "A Mistaken Move," *Variety*, December 14, 1938: 5.

47. Frank Pope, "Tradeviews," *Hollywood Reporter*, Oct. 18, 1937: 1, 8.

48. "Hollywood Asks Nazi Boycott; Aid Refugees," *Motion Picture Herald*, Dec. 17, 1938: 62.

49. "Coast Notables Hurl Invectives at Nazis," *Box Office*, Dec. 17, 1938: 15.

50. "17 Film Personalities Go on Newsreel Record Against Nazis," *Hollywood Reporter*, Dec. 22, 1938: 2; "Newsreels Record Formal Signing of Declaration," *Hollywood Now*, Dec. 23, 1938: 7.

51. "Coast Notables Hurl Invectives at Nazis," *Box Office*, Dec. 17, 1938: 15; "Committee of 56 Actively Pushing Berlin Trade Break," *Box Office*, Dec. 31, 1938: 5.

5. MUSSOLINI JR. GOES HOLLYWOOD

1. "Inside Pictures," *Variety*, Aug. 20, 1932: 43.

2. W. R. Wilkerson, "Tradeviews," *Hollywood Reporter*, Sept. 11, 1938: 1.

3. "Young Mussolini as Prod'r Opens Roman Hollywood," *Hollywood Reporter*, Apr. 21, 1937: 1, 21.

4. "Wanger-Mussolini-Gianinni's Italian Film Production Deal," *Variety*, July 1, 1936: 4.

5. Cecelia Ager, "Wanger Discusses Europe's New Youth, Fascism, Ideals—and Pix," *Variety*, July 8, 1936: 2, 26.

6. "Wanger's Duce Deal Still On," *Variety*, July 14, 1937: 3.

7. Vittorio Mussolini, "Hollywood closed down for a year . . . would be blessed," *Motion Picture Herald*, Oct. 2, 1937: 21.

8. "Advertisement," *Hollywood Reporter*, Oct. 4, 1937: 8.

9. "Il Duce, Jr. as 'Czar' of Pix in Italy?" *Variety*, Dec. 2, 1936: 1.

10. "Young Mussolini as Prod'r Opens Roman Hollywood," *Hollywood Reporter*, Apr. 21, 1937: 1, 2.

11. Read Kendall, "Around and About in Hollywood," *Los Angeles Times*, Oct. 12, 1937: A8.

12. Bill Ornstein, "Roach Bullish on Il Duce; Will Produce with Junior," *Motion Picture Daily*, Sept. 24, 1937: 1, 17.

13. "Mussolini Gets Protection," *Film Daily*, Sept. 24, 1937: 1.

14. Bill Ornstein, "Roach Bullish on Il Duce; Will Produce with Junior," *Motion Picture Daily*, Sept. 24, 1937: 1, 17.

15. "20 Pictures a Year, Hal Roach Plan for Italy," *Film Daily*, Sept. 24, 1937: 1, 12.

16. "Film Folk Snub Mussolini; He Flies East," *Chicago Tribune*, Oct. 9, 1937: 7.

17. "Mussolini's Son on Way to Hollywood," *Box Office*, Sept. 18, 1937: 15.

18. Bill Ornstein, "Roach Bullish on Il Duce; Will Produce with Junior," *Motion Picture Daily*, Sept. 24, 1937: 1, 17.

19. "RAM Not Assured of Metro as Outlet," *Box Office*, Oct. 2, 1937: 10.

20. "Hal Roach Announces Big Deal as Mussolini Partner," *Motion Picture Herald*, Oct. 2, 1937: 21–22.

21. "Son of Il Duce Arrives to See Films Made Here," *Los Angeles Times*, Sept. 26, 1937: 1.

22. "H'wood Extends Icy Paw to Young Mussolini; Under Heavy Guard," *Variety*, Sept. 29, 1937: 2.

23. "Mussolini Vague About Plans at Press Conference," *Daily Variety*, Sept. 28, 1937: 4.

24. "Mussolini Senior Visits Hitler; Mussolini Jr. Visits Hollywood," *News of the World*, Oct. 2, 1937: 1, 2.

25. Ed Sullivan, "Looking at Hollywood," *Chicago Tribune*, Oct. 2, 1937: 17.

26. Phyllis Marie Arthur, "Gals and Gab: Roach Fetes Mussolini," *Daily Variety*, Sept. 29, 1937: 3.

27. Ed Sullivan, "Looking at Hollywood," *Chicago Tribune*, Oct. 4, 1937: 19.

28. Isabel Sheldon, "Mr. and Mrs. Hal Roach Mark Anniversary at Birthday Party for Son of Il Duce," *Los Angeles Times*, Oct. 3, 1937: D6.

29. "Advertisement," *Hollywood Reporter*, Sept. 24, 1937: 9.

30. "Advertisement," *Daily Variety*, Oct. 3, 1937: 8.

31. "H'wood Still Het Up over Mussolini, Jr.; Will Take Rap on Pix Anyway?" *Variety*, Oct. 6, 1937: 2.

32. "Mussolini Says Deal with Hal Roach Stands, but—," *Motion Picture Herald*, Oct. 16, 1937: 17–18.

33. "RAM Not Assured of Metro as Outlet," *Box Office*, Oct. 2, 1937: 10.

34. Red Kahn, "Insider's Outlook," *Motion Picture Daily*, Sept. 29, 1937; reprinted in *News of the Day*, Oct. 2, 1937: 2.

35. "Rambling Reporter," *Hollywood Reporter*, Sept. 29, 1937: 2.

36. Robert P. Post, "Roosevelt Urges 'Concerted Action,'" *New York Times*, Oct. 6, 1937: 1, 17.

37. "Mussolini's Son and Roach to Hollyw'd," *Box Office*, September 25, 1937: 20.

38. "Mussolini Deal Off, Duce's Son Chilled by Reception; Roach Out 12 Grand," *Daily Variety*, Oct. 7, 1937: 1, 6.

39. Ed Sullivan, "Looking at Hollywood," *Chicago Tribune*, Dec. 24, 1937: 9.

40. "Il Duce's Phone Call to Vittorio in H'wood Climaxed Italo-U.S. Idea; Too Much Opposish to Roach Plan," *Variety*, Oct. 13, 1937: 5, 52; "Public Headache No. 1," *Daily Variety*, Oct. 8, 1937: 3.

41. James P. Cunningham, "Asides and Interludes," *Motion Picture Herald*, Oct. 9, 1937: 33.

42. "Mussolini Deal Off, Duce's Son Chilled by Reception; Roach Out 12 Grand," *Daily Variety*, Oct. 7, 1937: 1, 6. See also "Roach-Italy Deal Cold," *Hollywood Reporter*, Oct. 7, 1937: 1, 3.

6. THE SPANISH CIVIL WAR IN HOLLYWOOD

1. "Movies Are Guilty of 'Escapism,' Can Be Proud of It, Hays Finds," *New York Times*, Mar. 29, 1938: 23.

2. Joseph I. Breen to Walter Wanger, June 21, 1938 (*Personal History* file, Production Code Administration files, Academy of Motion Picture Arts and Sciences, Margaret Herrick Library, Beverly Hills, CA; hereinafter, PCA files).

3. "Walter Wanger Blames Falling Boxoffice on Too Much Screen Censorship," *Variety*, June 28, 1939: 2, 54.

4. George Orwell, *Homage to Catalonia* (1938) (rpt., New York: Harcourt, Brace, World, 1952), 149, 232.

5. "Frontier Films," *New Theatre and Film* (Mar. 1937): 50.

6. "'Liberal News Reel, Frankly Propaganda," *Variety*, Apr. 21, 1937: 27.

7. Dorothy Parker, "Film Writer Assails Nazi Book Burnings," *Daily Worker*, May 29, 1938: 13.

8. "Joan Crawford Spain's Sweetie," *Hollywood Now*, June 25, 1938: 2.

9. "Anti-Nazi Censorship," *Variety*, June 8, 1938: 26.

10. "Left Leanings Don't Mean We're Reds, Say Hollywood Leftists," *Variety*, June 2, 1937: 2.

11. Harry Chapin Plummer, "'Advice' on 'Alcazar' Film Called Belied by Facts," *Motion Picture Herald*, Jan. 16, 1936: 18.

12. Ivor Montagu, "An Open Letter to Darryl Zanuck," *New Theatre and Film* (Mar. 1937): 27–29.

13. "Ufa's 'Alkazar' But 20th-Fox Heeds Beefs," *Variety*, Nov. 18, 1936: 3.

14. "Anti-Fascist and Anti-War Bodies in U.S. Keen on Supporting 2 New Pix," *Variety*, Nov. 25, 1936: 3.

15. Joseph I. Breen to John Hammell, Mar. 11, 1937 (*The Last Train from Madrid* file, PCA files).

16. "Hays Finally OK's Par's 'Madrid' Script," *Variety*, Apr. 7, 1937: 4.

17. Joseph I. Breen to Will H. Hays, May 31 1937 (*The Last Train from Madrid* file, PCA files).

18. "*Last Train to Madrid*," *Hollywood Reporter*, June 5, 1937: 3.

19. "Fascist Foes Plug MG, 'Gun,' Par 'Madrid,' Spike 'Alcazar,'" *Daily Variety*, Nov. 25, 1936: 2.

20. "Wanger, 74, Dies; Money Showman Tho 'Erudite,'" *Variety*, Nov. 20, 1968: 5, 40.

21. "*Walter Wanger's Vogues of 1938*," *Daily Variety*, Aug. 4, 1937: 3. For a complete biography, see Matthew Bernstein, *Walter Wanger: Hollywood Independent* (Berkeley: U of California P, 1994).

22. Joseph I. Breen to Will H. Hays, Feb. 28, 1937 (*Blockade* file, PCA files).

23. Joseph I. Breen to Walter Wanger, Feb. 3, 1937 (*Blockade* file, PCA files).

24. Joseph I. Breen to Walter Wanger, Jan. 4, 1938 (*Blockade* file, PCA files).

25. E. R. O'Neill, Memo on Blockade, May 3, 1939 (*Blockade* file, PCA files).

26. Joseph I. Breen to Walter Wanger, Feb. 7, 1938 (*Blockade* file, PCA files).

27. Joseph I. Breen to Walter Wanger, Feb. 22, 1937 (*Blockade* file, PCA files). Wanger also needed to watch his literature. "Please also delete the title of the book *Madame Bovary*."

28. "UA Says 'Blockade' Will Be Released on Scheduled Date," *Motion Picture Herald*, May 28, 1938: 74.

29. Dan Blackwell, "Film City Packs Theatre for 'Blockade' Preview," *Daily Worker*, June 14, 1938: 7; Alfred O'Malley, "Blockade," *Daily Worker*, June 19, 1938: 5.

30. William R. Weaver, "*Blockade*," *Motion Picture Herald*, June 11, 1938: 37.

31. John Ross, "'Blockade' Film Tells People's Stirring Story," *Hollywood Now*, June 25, 1938: 2; "Here and Now," *Hollywood Now*, June 11, 1938: 2.

32. Andrew Collins, "*Blockade* Powerful Film of Wartime in Spain," *Daily Worker*, June 17, 1938: 7; "*Blockade*," *Daily Worker*, June 18, 1938: 7.

33. "Strange Shows on the Screen," *The Catholic News*, June 18, 1938.

34. Winchell Taylor, "Secret Movie Censors," *The Nation*, July 9, 1938, 38–40.

35. "Legion of Decency, Seeing Picture Dive, Restates Policy," *Motion Picture Herald*, Aug. 27, 1938: 43.

36. John C. Flinn, "Film Industry Watching 'Blockade' as B.O. Cue on Provocative Themes," *Variety*, June 22, 1938: 55.

37. Patrick Scanlon, *The Brooklyn Tablet*, June 24, 1938.

38. "Supreme Board Protest to Will Hays Asks Propaganda Tag on Blockade," *Six-Twenty-One* (July 1938): 4.

39. "'Blockade' Defense Mapped by MPAC," *Box Office*, July 23, 1938.

40. "Public Backs Stars in Censorship Fight," *Hollywood Now*, July 16, 1938: 2.

41. "Blockade Starts Free Speech Fight," *Hollywood Now*, July 2, 1938: 2.

42. "Defends 'Blockade,'" *Box Office*, July 2, 1938: 24-E.

43. "Daring Strokes for 'Blockade' in Frisco," *Box Office*, Aug. 6, 1938: 33.

44. "Pulpit Attack Cancels 'Blockade,' Loew's Ad Squarer in Church Paper," *Variety*, July 6, 1938: 4; John C. Flinn, "Film Industry Watching 'Blockade' as B.O. Cue on Provocative Themes," *Variety*, June 22, 1938: 55.

45. "Wanger Blasts Foreign Censorship of U.S. Films," *News of the World*, May 20, 1938: 1.

46. "*Blockade*," *Harrison's Reports*, June 11, 1938: 94.

47. "Pepping Up the Nex Pix," *Variety*, July 19, 1939: 1.

48. Joseph I. Breen to Rev. Daniel A. Lord, S.J., Sept. 18, 1938 (Midwest Jesuit Archives, St. Louis, MO).

49. Joseph I. Breen to Dr. Charles J. Turek, Aug. 4, 1938 (*Blockade* file, PCA files).

50. Arthur E. DeBra to Joseph I. Breen, Sept. 28, 1938 (*Blockade* file, PCA files).

51. Walter Wanger, "Is Hollywood on the Spot?" *Liberty*, Sept. 10, 1938: 18.

52. John Dored, "Newsreel War Crews Now in the Making," *Motion Picture Herald*, Aug. 29, 1936: 38.

53. Robert Landry, "Embassy, N.Y.," *Variety*, Oct. 14, 1936: 56.

54. "Advertisement," *Film Daily*, Aug. 3, 1936: 8.

55. "Americans Filming the Spanish Civil War, Despite Rigid Ban," *Motion Picture Herald*, Aug. 8, 1936: 57.

56. John Dored, "Newsreel War Crews Now in the Making," *Motion Picture Herald*, Aug. 29, 1936: 38.

57. "Americans Filming the Spanish Civil War, Despite Rigid Ban," *Motion Picture Herald*, Aug. 8, 1936: 57.

58. "Embassy Newsreels, N.Y.," *Variety*, Mar. 24, 1937: 66.

59. [Terry Ramsaye], "Hearst Name Off Reel," *Motion Picture Herald*, Nov. 14, 1936: 8.

60. Ibid.

61. Joris Ivens, "Notes on Hollywood," *New Theatre and Film* (Oct. 1936): 20.

62. The invaluable source on this pair of films remains Russell Campbell, *Cinema Strikes Back: Radical Filmmaking in the United States, 1930–1942* (Ann Arbor MI: UMI Research Press, 1982), 165–92.

63. Herbert Kline, *New Theatre and Film, 1934 to 1937: An Anthology* (New York: Harcourt Brace Jovanovich, 1985), 363, 307 .

64. Campbell, *Cinema Strikes Back*, 165–92.

65. "Theatre Arts Committee to Show New Film on Spain at Waldorf," *Daily Worker*, July 10, 1938: 13.

66. "Artists Seek Funds for Loyalist Spain," *Daily Variety*, Sept. 8, 1937: 6.

67. "New Film of Lincoln Brigade," *Hollywood Now*, Sept. 2, 1938: 4.

68. "Spain Film Showing on Sept. 28," *Hollywood Now*, Sept. 16, 1938: 3.

69. "New Film of Spain Made in Barcelona Area," *Hollywood Now*, Mar. 3, 1939: 4.

70. "*Spain in Flames*," *The Nation*, Mar. 27, 1937, 341.

71. "*Spain in Flames*," *Variety*, Feb. 3, 1937: 15.

72. Dorothy Gates, "*Spain in Flames* Details History of Fascist Coup," *Daily Worker*, Jan. 28, 1937: 7.

73. "Birds of a Feather!" *Motion Picture Herald*, July 4, 1936: 7.

74. "Advertisement," *Daily Worker*, May 20, 1937: 7.

75. William R. Weaver, "*Spain in Flames*," *Motion Picture Herald*, Feb. 13, 1937: 56–57.

76. "Readers Urge Support of Anti-Fascist Film," *Daily Worker*, Feb. 1, 1937: 7.

77. "Check List," *New Theatre and Film* (Apr. 1937): 49.

78. Archibald MacLeish to Edna Ferber, Jan 6, 1937 (Joris Ivens Papers, Academy of Motion Picture Arts and Sciences, Margaret Herrick Library, Beverly Hills, CA).

79. Ernest Hemingway, "Heavy Shell-Fire in Madrid Advance," *New York Times*, Apr. 10, 1937, 9.

80. "Documentary Film Appetite Growing Says Joris Ivens," *Motion Picture Herald*, Apr. 1, 1939: 64.

81. John T. McManus, "Down to Earth in Spain" *New York Times*, July 25, 1937, 134.

82. "Hemingway Previews Spanish Pic to Hollywood," *Variety*, July 14, 1937: 4.

83. Frank Scully, "Hemingway's War Film on Cast Grosses $15,000 from Audience of 15," *Variety* July 21, 1937: 5, 66.

84. "*The Spanish Earth*," *Box Office*, Oct. 23, 1937: 25, 26.

85. David Platt, "Spanish Earth Is Great Dynamic Portrayal of Heroic People's Front Fighting Fascism," *Daily Worker*, Aug. 20, 1937: 9.

86. Joseph F. Coughlin, "*Spanish Earth*," *Motion Picture Herald*, Sept. 4, 1937: 42.

87. "Press Protests Ban on Picture," *Motion Picture Herald*, Feb. 20, 1937: 23.

88. Roy Chartier, "*Spain in Flames*," *Variety*, Feb. 3, 1937: 15; "Inside Stuff-Pictures," *Variety*, Feb. 17, 1937: 6.

89. "Pennsy Suppresses," *Variety*, Mar. 17, 1937: 25.

90. "*Spain in Flames*," *The Nation*, Mar. 27, 1937, 341; "Governor Earle in Flames," *The Nation*, Apr. 16, 1937: 396.

91. "'Spain in Flames' Ok'd in Pennsy on Grounds It's a Current Newsreel," *Variety*, Dec. 1, 1937: 27.

92. "Governor Earle Gives 'Red' Film His Blessing," *Motion Picture Herald*, Oct. 16, 1937: 38.

93. Ibid.

94. "A Reluctant Okay Given Spanish Film," *Box Office*, Oct. 16, 1937: 21.

95. "Documentary Film Appetite Growing Says Joris Ivens," *Motion Picture Herald*, Apr. 1, 1939: 64.

96. Antony Beevor, *The Battle for Spain: The Spanish Civil War, 1936–1939* (New York: Penguin Books, 1982), xxv–xxvi.

7. FOREIGN IMPORTS

1. Phil M. Daily, "Along the Rialto," *Film Daily*, July 29, 1936: 4.

2. "Anti-Nazi 'Kampf' Pic Banned in St. Louis," *Variety*, Apr. 28, 1937: 9.

3. "Keep 'Messages' Out," *Variety*, Nov. 9, 1938: 3.

4. "Foreign Films Mystery Boom," *Variety*, Oct. 11, 1932: 18.

5. Max Magnus, "German Observers Hold New Quota Would Paralyze Nation's Own Biz," *Variety*, July 19, 1932: 62.

6. Wolfe Kaufman, "Foreign Films in U.S.," *Variety*, Jan. 3, 1933: 13.

7. "Foreigns Losing Pull for U.S. Screen," *Variety*, Sept. 13, 1932: 14.

8. "100 German Cinemas in U.S. Drop to 6; Bars Up All Over Continent," *Variety*, May 23, 1933: 13.

9. "Advertisement for *Maedchen in Uniform*," *Variety*, Feb. 21, 1933: 22.

10. "Pix Reaction Is Anti-Hitler," *Variety*, Mar. 28, 1933: 1; "Hitlerism Forces Standstill of U.S. Film Trade in Germany," *Motion Picture Herald*, Apr. 15, 1933: 10.

11. "Hitler Thing Deadly," *Variety*, July 18, 1933: 31.

12. "Boycott of German Pictures Is Deplored," *Motion Picture Herald*, Apr. 1, 1933: 16.

13. "German 'M' Pulled," *Variety*, Apr. 11, 1933: 4.

14. "Nero Film Head Quits Germany; Has Eye on U.S.," *Variety*, Apr. 25, 1933: 13.

15. "Inside Stuff—Pictures," *Variety*, Sept. 19, 1933: 43.

16. "100 German Cinemas in U.S. Drop to 6; Bars Up All Over Continent," *Variety*, May 23, 1933: 13.

17. "Sees German Film Ban Hurting Wrong Parties," *Film Daily*, Apr. 3, 1933: 1, 2.

18. Wolfe Kaufman, "Yorkville, N.Y." *Variety*, Oct. 17, 1933: 14.

19. "*S.A. Mann Brand*," *Film Daily*, May 29, 1934: 6.

20. "Hitlerjunge Quex," *Variety*, July 7, 1934: 25.

21. "2-Way Boycott Socks Yorkville, N.Y.; Jewish Owned and Showing Nazi Pix," *Variety*, July 17, 1934: 1, 52.

22. "*A Trip Through Germany*," *Variety*, June 12, 1935: 12; "Embassy, N.Y.," *Variety*, June 12, 1935: 14.

23. Richard A. Hawkins, " 'Hitler's bitterest foe': Samuel Untermyer and the Boycott of Nazi Germany, 1933–1938," *American Jewish History*, Mar. 1, 2007: 21–30.

24. "Masking of Nazi Films as French Is Charged as New Boycott Looms," *Motion Picture Herald*, Nov. 7, 1936: 13.

25. "German-Made French Talker Jerked When Boycott Threatens," *Variety*, Oct. 28, 1936: 7; "Tabu on German-Made French Talkers in N.Y.," *Variety*, Oct. 21, 1936: 20.

26. "'Amphitryon' Bows Anew to Gotham Anti-Nazi Ire," *Box Office*, Apr. 3, 1937: 20. See also A. L. Finestone, "Boycott of Nazi Films May Reach Court Soon," *Box Office*, Aug. 14, 1937: 112, 30.

27. "Masking of Nazi Films as French Is Charged as New Boycott Looms," *Motion Picture Herald*, Nov. 7, 1936: 13; "Anti-Nazis Persuade MGM to Drop Films Which They Brand 'Pro-Nazi,'" *Motion Picture Herald*, Nov. 14, 1936: 31.

28. Harry Waldman, *Nazi Films in America, 1933–1942* (Jefferson, NC: McFarland, 2008) tracks Nazi efforts to penetrate the U.S. market in the 1930s. Waldman asserts that "nearly 500 Nazi films were shown in America's theatres," a number that seems impossibly high.

29. For a dissenting view, see Waldman, *Nazi Films in America, 1933–1942*.

30. "Der Katzensteg," *Variety*, Jan. 26, 1938: 23.

31. "Jugende von Heute," *Variety*, Nov. 9, 1938: 19.

32. Wolfe Kaufman, "Foreign Films in the U.S.," *Variety*, Jan. 6, 1937: 33.

33. "German Films Enter Despite Duty Tilt," *Box Office*, Apr. 1, 1939: 32.

34. Wolfe Kaufman, "Foreign Films in U.S.," *Variety*, Jan. 1, 1935: 41.

35. "Eva," *Variety*, Jan. 12, 1938: 27.

36. Wolfe Kaufman, "The International Show Biz Scene," *Variety*, Jan. 6, 1937: 21. See also Kaufman, "Foreign Films in the U.S.," *Variety*, Jan. 1, 1935: 41.

37. "231 Foreign Films Released in the U.S. in 16 Months by 37 Distributors," *Motion Picture Herald*, May 13, 1939: 17.

38. Phil M. Daily, "Along the Rialto," *Film Daily*, Apr. 15, 1932: 4.

39. B.R.C., "The Screen," *New York Times*, May 24, 1939: 33.

40. "Concentration Camp," *Variety*, Mar. 22, 1939: 30.

41. "The Oppenheim Family," *Variety*, May 31, 1939: 14.

42. Frank S. Nugent, "Der Kampf," *New York Times*, Sept. 11, 1936: 29.

43. Charles E. Dexter, "'Prof. Mamlock' a Weapon in Anti-Fascist Fight," *Daily Worker*, 15, 1937: 7.

44. Peter Kenney, "Professor Mamlock," *Daily Worker*, Nov. 19, 1938: 7.

45. "'Mamlock' Strong Indictment of Nazi Regime," *Hollywood Reporter*, Mar. 15, 1939: 4.

46. David Platt, "'Blockade' and 'Professor Mamlock' Chosen as the Leading Films of the Year," *Daily Worker*, Jan. 2, 1938: 7; "Choice on the Left," *Motion Picture Herald*, Jan. 14, 1939: 7.

47. Francis S. Harmon to Will H. Hays, Feb. 14, 1939 (*Professor Mamlock*, Production Code Administration files, Academy of Motion Picture Arts and Sciences, Margaret Herrick Library, Beverly Hills, CA; hereinafter, PCA files).

48. "Professor Mamlock," *Motion Picture Herald*, Mar. 4, 1939: 8.

49. "Salacious Ads on Theatre Fronts Draw Censor's Ire in Two States," *Motion Picture Herald*, Jan. 15, 1938: 13.

50. "Chi Bans Russian Anti-Nazi Film, 'Oppenheim Family'; Other Reactions," *Variety*, June 7, 1939: 5.

51. "Fight Ban in Chicago on 'Concentration Camp,'" *Box Office*, Mar. 18, 1939: 37.

52. "Chi's Censorial Frowns," *Variety*, Nov. 23, 1938: 15.

53. "Nazi Exile Doing O.K.," *Variety*, Sept. 9, 1933: 19.

54. George R. Canty to Fritz Keller, Nov. 12, 1934. Record Group 151, Records of the Bureau of Foreign and Domestic Commerce, National Archives, College Park, MD.

55. "Nazi Racial Bar Reaches Films; Goldwyn Invites Workers to U.S.," *Motion Picture Herald*, July 8, 1933: 11.

56. Pommer's pre- and post-Nazi life is traced in Ursula Hardt's marvelously titled *From Caligari to California: Erich Pommer's Life in the International Film Wars* (Providence, RI: Bergham Books, 1996).

57. "Eric Pommer Goes Native Son and the Hard Way at That," *Variety*, Sept. 1, 1934: 3, 25.

58. "Dieterle's Shirttails and Dirty Hands Keep Director Irritated," *Variety*, Oct. 20, 1931: 4.

59. "Inside Stuff—Pictures," *Variety*, Dec. 18, 1934: 20.

60. Jack Jungmeyer, "Development of Music in Pix During Year," *Variety*, Jan. 6, 1937: 52.

61. Lutz Koepnick, *The Dark Mirror: German Cinema Between Hitler and Hollywood* (Berkeley: U of California P, 2002), 37–42.

62. Bella Fromm, *Blood and Banquets: A Berlin Social Diary* (New York: Harper, 1942), 61.

63. Heinrich Fraenkel, "Berlin," *Variety*, June 6, 1933: 60.

64. Patrick McGilligan effectively debunked Lang's "gussied-up" version of events in *Fritz Lang: The Nature of the Beast* (New York: St. Martin's Press, 1997), 174–81.

65. "Inside Stuff—Pictures, *Variety*, Nov. 14, 1933: 45.

66. Karen Thomas's fascinating documentary *Cinema's Exiles: From Hitler to Hollywood* (2009) tells the story of Paul Kohner and many other German refugees.

67. Alta Durant, "Gab," *Daily Variety*, Oct. 24, 1939: 3.

68. "Nazis' Threat to Blacklist Expatriates," *Variety*, Apr. 8, 1933: 1.

69. "Nazi Move for Big Circuit Is Reported," *Motion Picture Herald*, Sept. 16, 1933: 27.

70. "Film Actor Executed," *Variety*, Oct. 14, 1936: 19.

71. "Film Producer Commits Suicide; Forced to Wall by Aryan Laws," *Variety*, Nov. 18, 1936: 11. This Werner Krauss is not to be confused with the ideologically versatile actor of the same name who played the title role in *The Cabinet of Dr. Caligari* (1920) and Rabbi Loew in Veit Harlan's Nazi-approved version of *The Jew Suss* (1940).

72. James P. Cunningham, "Asides and Interludes," *Motion Picture Herald*, Nov. 4, 1933: 27.

73. "Actress Marlene Dietrich Gets Final Citizenship Papers," *International News* photo caption, June 9, 1939.

8. "THE BLIGHT OF RADICAL PROPAGANDA"

1. Martin J. Quigley, "Radicalism—An Industry Peril," *Motion Picture Herald*, Dec. 11, 1937: 17–18.

2. Wolfe Kaufman, "Fiction and Films," *Variety*, Apr. 1, 1936: 58.

3. "Wanger Blames Falling Boxoffice on Too Much Screen Censorship," *Variety*, June 28, 1939: 2, 54.

4. "'Propaganda' Curb Rumor Is Scouted," *Box Office*, Aug. 20, 1938: 78.

5. "Hitler Fist at H'wood," *Hollywood Reporter*, Apr. 6, 1937: 1, 2.

6. Arnaldo Cortesi, "Mussolini Nationalizes Key Defense Industries, Holding War Is Certain," *New York Times*, Mar. 24, 1936: 1, 6.

7. "'Idiot's Delight' Opens in Capital," *New York Times*, Mar. 10, 1936: 26.

8. Joseph I. Breen to Carl E. Milliken, Mar. 23, 1936 (*Idiot's Delight*, Production Code Administration files, Academy of Motion Picture Arts and Sciences, Margaret Herrick Library, Beverly Hills, CA; hereinafter, PCA files).

9. Frederick L. Herron to Joseph I. Breen, Jan. 7, 1937 (*Idiot's Delight* file, PCA files).

10. Frederick L. Herron to Joseph I. Breen, May 7, 1937 (*Idiot's Delight* file, PCA files).

11. Internal Memorandum re *Idiot's Delight* by Joseph I. Breen, May 12, 1937 (*Idiot's Delight* file, PCA files).

12. Hunt Stromberg to Joseph I. Breen, May 12, 1938 (*Idiot's Delight* file, PCA files).

13. "In the Cutting Room," *Motion Picture Herald*, Dec. 17, 1938: 48. See also "Fascists Threaten MGM if 'Idiot's Delight' Filmed," *Hollywood Now*, Sept. 6, 1938: 1.

14. George E. Phair, "Retakes," *Daily Variety*, Oct. 5, 1938: 2.

15. "Takes to Esperanto in 'Idiot's Delight,'" *Motion Picture Herald*, Nov. 19, 1938: 55.

16. "Hollywood's Anti-War Pix Bothering Il Duce," *Hollywood Now*, Aug. 26, 1938: 2.

17. Robert Emmet Sherwood, *Idiot's Delight* (New York: Scribner's, 1938), 189.

18. J.D.A., "Remarque's Farewell to Arms," *New York Times*, May 10, 1931: BR1.

19. "'Road Back' Upped by U; Remarque Tempted," *Daily Variety*, Sept. 30, 1936: 2.

20. Dr. Georg Gyssling to Joseph I. Breen, Sept. 30, 1936 (*The Road Back* file, PCA files).

21. Joseph I. Breen to Harry Zehner, May 26, 1937. (*The Road Back* file, PCA files).

22. "Hitler Fist at H'wood," *Hollywood Reporter*, Apr. 6, 1937: 1, 2.

23. Red Kahn, "Insider's Outlook," *Motion Picture Daily*, June 16, 1937 (reprinted in *News of the World*, June 26, 1937: 6).

24. Red Kahn, "Insider's Outlook," *Motion Picture Daily*, May 12, 1937: 2 (reprinted in *News of the World*, May 30, 1937: 7).

25. "Nazis Threaten U.S. Actors," *News of the World*, Apr. 10, 1937: 2.

26. "Nazis Pledge Nix on Blacklisting of U.S. Thesps," *Daily Variety*, June 15, 1937: 2.

27. "U.S. Stops Nazis' Intimidation of Hollywood Motion Picture Stars," *Motion Picture Herald*, June 19, 1937: 1; "German Consul Denies Rebuke, Received in Actor-Warning Row," *Los Angeles Times*, June 16, 1937: 1.

28. Joseph I. Breen to Harry Zehner, May 26, 1937 (*The Road Back* file, PCA files).

29. Joseph I. Breen to Will H. Hays, May 31, 1938 (*The Road Back* file, PCA files).

30. "Inside Stuff—Pictures," *Variety*, Feb. 3, 1937: 6.

31. "U's New Finish for 'Road Back': Palate Germany?" and "U Denies Nazi Angle," *Variety*, July 7, 1937: 4.

32. "U's New Finish for 'Road Back': Palate Germany?" and "U Denies Nazi Angle," *Variety*, July 7, 1937: 4; "Universal Denies Hitler Instigated Change in 'Road,'"

Motion Picture Herald, July 17, 1937: 41; "Denies Politics Cause 'Road Back' Changes," *Box Office*, July 17, 1937: 7.

33. "Nazis Nix D.C. Preem of U's 'Road Back,'" *Variety*, July 28, 1937: 2.

34. Fred Baehler, "*The Road Back*," *Motion Picture Herald*, June 26, 1937: 88.

35. "Metro Spying 'Road Back,' Biz for 'Comrades' Fate," *Daily Variety*, June 26, 1937: 2.

36. "Three Comrades," *Time*, June 6, 1938: 41–42.

37. "Anti-Nazi Censorship," *Variety*, June 8, 1938: 26.

38. John C. Flinn, "*Three Comrades*," *Variety*, May 25, 1938: 12.

39. "Rambling Reporter," *Hollywood Reporter*, Oct. 23, 1938: 2.

40. "Maps Wide Inquiry into Propaganda," *New York Times*, June 19, 1938: 26, "'Isms' Advocates Should Go Home, Rep Dies Declares," *Washington Post*, July 5, 1938: X24.

41. "Melvyn Douglas Says," *News of the World*, May 29, 1938: 1, 3.

42. "Self-Styled 'Hollywood Technical Directors Institute' Also Wants Eisenstein Out of Country," *Exhibitors Herald-World*, June 28, 1930: 11.

43. "Why Only Nazism," *Anti-Nazi News*, Nov. 20, 1936: 2.

44. Vance King, "Hollywood Anti-Nazis Repudiate U.S. Agent's Cry of 'Communist,'" *Motion Picture Herald*, Aug. 20, 1938: 28.

45. "Two Studio Groups Lash at Prober's 'Communist' Label," *Box Office*, Aug. 20, 1938: 22.

46. "Mr. Sullivan's Report," *Hollywood Now*, Aug. 19, 1938: 1, 2.

47. W. R. Wilkerson, "Tradeviews," *Hollywood Reporter*, Aug. 17, 1938: 1, 2; W. R. Wilkerson, "Tradeviews," *Hollywood Reporter*, Aug. 23, 1938: 1, 2.

48. "Anti-Nazi League Derides 'Red' Attack on Industry," *Box Office*, Aug. 27, 1938: 34.

49. W. R. Wilkerson, "Tradeviews," *Hollywood Reporter*, Aug. 23, 1938: 1, 2.

50. "U.S. Expects Film Surrender," *Hollywood Reporter*, July 21, 1938: 1, 6.

51. "Washington's Red-baiting Probes Regarded as One-Ring Circus," *Variety*, Aug. 24, 1938: 2.

52. Jack Beall, "Dies Body May Be Remembered for Its Attack on Shirley," *Washington Post*, Sept. 4, 1938: B5.

53. Martin Dies, *Martin Dies Story* (New York: The Bookmailer, 1963), 134.

54. "Filmsters Deny Dies 'Red' Charge, Challenge Debate," *Hollywood Reporter*, Aug. 18, 1938: 3.

55. "Demand President Roosevelt Dissolve Dies Committee," *Hollywood Now*, Aug. 26, 1938: 1, 4.

56. "How Bigotry Can Best Be Fought," *Harrison's Reports*, Oct. 15, 1938: 165.

57. "Stewart Will Answer Congressman Dies," *Daily Variety*, Oct. 1, 1938: 4; James J. Geller, "Donald Ogden Stewart," *Hollywood Tribune*, July 31, 1939: 13.

58. "L. B. Mayer, Feted in Frisco Civic Function, Pans Hollywood's Pinkos," *Variety* Oct. 14, 1936: 5.

59. "Zanuck Hits 'Pink Shirts'; Pledges Pix to Americanism," *Daily Variety*, Sept. 21, 1938: 5.

60. "Dies Definitely Abandons West Coast Hearings," *Hollywood Reporter*, Nov. 26, 1938: 2.

61. "Same Old Witch Hunt," *Hollywood Now*, May 5, 1939: 4.

62. "An Oscar for Dies," *Variety*, Feb. 21, 1940: 3.

9. INSIDE NAZI GERMANY WITH THE *MARCH OF TIME*

1. The best guide to the *March of Time* remains Raymond Fielding, *The March of Time, 1935–1951* (New York: Oxford UP, 1978).

2. "March of Time in Fifth Year," *Motion Picture Herald*, Mar. 11, 1939: 25.

3. "March of Time Criticizes Other Reels, Cites $1,000,000 Gross," *Motion Picture Herald*, July 18, 1936: 67.

4. "Newsreels and World Affairs," *Variety*, Jan. 6, 1937: 6; Abel Green, "March of Time," *Variety*, Mar. 13, 1935: 15.

5. Fielding, *The March of Time*, 90.

6. James Barron, "After 59 Years, Roy Larsen, 80, Retires as Executive of Time, Inc.," *New York Times*, Apr. 20, 1979, B4.

7. " 'Time' Reels' Controversial Subject Matter of Concern to Hays Org.," *Variety*, Oct. 9, 1935: 4.

8. "Inside Stuff—Pictures," *Variety*, May 5, 1937: 21.

9. "Newsreels Answer March of Time on Pictures of Hitler," *Motion Picture Herald*, Mar. 23, 1935: 30.

10. Ibid.

11. Robert Landry, "*March of Time*," *Variety*, June 24, 1936: 29.

12. Advertisement in *New Theater* (Mar. 1936): 33.

13. Julien Bryan's papers, including the extant material on "Inside Nazi Germany," are archived at the United States Holocaust Memorial Museum, Washington, D.C.

14. "Press Supports Warner's Charge March of Time Reel Is Pro-Nazi," *Motion Picture Herald*, Feb. 19, 1938: 34.

15. "Movie of the Week: *The March of Time*," *Life*, Jan. 31, 1938: 24.

16. "Press Supports Warner's Charge March of Time Reel Is Pro-Nazi," *Motion Picture Herald*, Feb. 19, 1938: 33.

17. "Nazis Squawking over M. of T. Films," *Variety*, Jan. 19, 1938: 6; "M of T's 'Inside Nazi Germany' Barred in Chicago," *Film Daily*, Jan. 18, 1938: 10.

18. "Nazis Hint Invoking Treaty to Bar March of Time in 3 Nations," *Motion Picture Herald*, Jan. 22, 1938: 15–16.

19. Dave Epstein, "Nazi Propaganda," *Hollywood Reporter*, Feb. 5, 1938: 4.

20. "March of Time in Jams," *Hollywood Reporter*, Jan. 20, 1938: 1, 2.

21. "M of T's 'Inside Nazi Germany' Barred in Chicago," *Film Daily*, Jan. 19, 1938: 1, 10.

22. "M of T Will Fight Chi. Nazi Reel Ban," *Film Daily*, Jan. 20, 1938: 1, 8.

23. "Warners, MOT, Public Battle over Nazi Pic," *Daily Variety*, Jan. 22, 1938: 4.

24. "Chi Okays It," *Variety*, Jan. 24, 1938: 11.

25. "Pros and Cons on 'March of Time's' Nazi Subject Boosts B.O. All Over," *Variety*, Jan. 26, 1938: 11; "Embassy Newsreel, N.Y.," *Variety*, Jan. 26, 1938: 53.

26. "Photog of M. of T.'s Nazi Reel States He Didn't Have to Smuggle Films Out," *Variety*, Feb. 16, 1938: 7.

27. "Chi's Censorial Frowns," *Variety*, Oct. 23, 1938: 15.

28. "WB Circuit Bans March of Time Reel," *Hollywood Reporter*, Jan. 21, 1938: 1.

29. "The March of Time," *News of the Day*, Feb. 4, 1938: 4.

30. "Warners, MOT, Public Battle over Nazi Pic," *Daily Variety*, Jan. 22, 1938: 4.

31. Ibid.

32. "Time's Prexy Says Pro-Nazi Charge Against M of T Reel Is 'Ridiculous,'" *Film Daily*, Jan. 24, 1938: 1, 3.

33. "Move of the Week: *The March of Time*," *Life*, Jan. 31, 1938: 24.

34. "Anti-Nazi League Okays Time Reel," *Hollywood Reporter*, Jan. 27, 1938: 12. A rare editorial in the *Hollywood Reporter* weighed in with Harry Warner: "Time Reel Is Favorable Propaganda for Nazism," *Hollywood Reporter*, Jan. 26, 1938: 2.

35. Martin Quigley, "The Exhibitor's Screen—How Shall It Be Used?" *Motion Picture Herald*, Feb. 5, 1938: 7–8.

36. "Pros and Cons on 'March of Time's' Nazi Subject Boosts B.O. All Over," *Variety*, Jan. 26, 1938: 11.

37. Chester B. Bahn, "March of Time Nazi Reel Causes Industry Stir," *Film Daily*, Jan. 21, 1938: 1, 10.

38. "M of T Will Fight Chi. Nazi Reel Ban," *Film Daily*, Jan. 20, 1938: 1, 8.

39. The reactions are culled from a two-page advertising spread by the *March of Time* in *Motion Picture Herald*, Feb. 5, 1938: 58–59.

40. Chester B. Bahn, "March of Time Nazi Reel Causes Industry Stir," *Film Daily*, Jan. 21, 1938: 1, 10.

41. "*The March of Time*," *Film Daily*, Jan. 20, 1938: 6.

42. The title card prose was reported in "Fearlessly" and "M of T Special Forward," *Film Daily*, Jan. 21, 1938: 10.

43. Irving Hoffman, "Reviewpoints," *Hollywood Reporter*, Jan. 25, 1938: 2.

10. "GRIM REAPER MATERIAL"

1. Terry Ramsaye, "News and Corpses," *Motion Picture Herald*, Sept. 1, 1934: 7, 8.

2. Robert Landry, "Embassy, N.Y." *Variety*, Oct. 14, 1936: 56.

3. As reported in Irving Hoffman, "Tales of Hoffman," *Hollywood Reporter*, Feb. 11, 1939: 3.

4. "To Entertain Is Film Industry's Only Mission, Quigley Tells Forum," *Motion Picture Herald*, Sept. 4, 1937: 23.

5. Tom Waller, "Newsreels," *Variety*, Mar. 8, 1932: 36.

6. "Cochrane of U Defies Wilentz on Clips of Bruno," *Daily Variety*, Feb. 6, 1935: 1, 10.

7. "Steel Men to Live in Pullman Cars," *New York Times*, June 8, 1937, 8.

8. "Paramount Releases Steel Strike Films," *Motion Picture Herald*, July 10, 1937: 27.

9. Ibid.

10. "Definition of an Editor's Responsibility," *Box Office*, July 31, 1937: 5–6.

11. "All Along the Rialto," *Film Daily*, Dec. 31, 1937: 4.

12. Wolfe Kaufman, "Embassy, N.Y.," *Variety*, Sept. 15, 1937: 17, 19.

13. "Richard Forecasts Longer Newsreel," *Motion Picture Herald*, Dec. 18, 1937: 62.

14. Roy Chartier, "The Newsreels," *Variety*, Jan. 1, 1936: 43.

15. Robert Meltzer, "The Newsreel Goes Round and Round and Out Comes—A Fur Coat," *Hollywood Tribune*, Sept. 4, 1939: 8.

16. Max Jordan, *Beyond All Fronts: A Bystander's Notes on This Thirty Years War* (Milwaukee: Bruce Publishing, 1944), 193–94, 220–35.

17. "U and Pathé Newsreelers Released; Vienna Films In," *Variety*, Mar. 23, 1938: 4.

18. Shan., "Embassy Newsreel, N.Y.," *Variety*, Mar. 30, 1938: 60.

19. William L. Shirer, *Berlin Diary: The Journal of a Foreign Correspondent* (New York; Penguin Books, 1979), 142.

20. "Hollywood Inside," *Daily Variety*, Sept. 27, 1938: 2.

21. Robert Landry, "Today and Tomorrow," *Variety*, Jan. 4, 1939: 113.

22. "Embassy, N.Y.," *Variety*, Sept. 21, 1938: 47; Mike Wear, "Embassy, N.Y." *Variety*, Oct. 19, 1938: 17.

23. "Embassy Newsreel, N.Y.," *Variety*, Dec. 14, 1938: 57; "Embassy Newsreel, N.Y.," *Variety*, Nov. 16, 1938: 45.

24. "Inside Stuff—Pictures," *Variety*, Apr. 20, 1938: 10.

25. "Newsreels in U.S. Turn 'War-Minded,'" *Motion Picture Herald*, Sept. 24, 1938: 14, 15.

26. Mike Wear, "March of Time's Czech Reel," *Variety*, Sept. 28, 1938: 53.

27. "Embassy Newsreel, N.Y.," *Variety*, May 25, 1938: 45.

28. Mike Wear, "Embassy Newsreel, N.Y.," *Variety*, Mar. 23, 1938: 52.

29. Herbert Kline relates the production history of *Crisis* in Kline, *New Theatre and Film, 1934 to 1937: An Anthology* (New York: Harcourt Brace Jovanovich, 1985), 338–40.

30. Kline, quoted in Bosley Crowther, "Matter of Fact," *New York Times*, Mar. 12, 1939, 154.

31. Kline, *New Theatre and Film*, 339.

32. Eleanor Roosevelt, "May Day," Mar. 7, 1939, United Features Syndicate, Inc. (available online at the Eleanor Roosevelt Papers Project, George Washington University).

33. "Crisis," *Film Daily*, Mar. 20, 1939: 10.

34. George Spires, "Crisis," *Motion Picture Herald*, Mar. 25, 1939: 44.

35. Henry Hart, "A Letter About 'Crisis' Documentary Film on Nazi Invasion of Czechoslovakia," *Daily Worker*, Mar. 23, 1939: 7.

36. Kline, quoted in Bosley Crowther, "Matter of Fact," *New York Times*, Mar. 12, 1939, 154.

37. Mike Wear, "Newsreels and World News," *Variety*, Jan. 4, 1939: 110.

38. Deborah E. Lipstadt, *Beyond Belief: The American Press and the Coming of the Holocaust* (New York: Free Press, 1986), 96–111, chronicles the vociferous reaction of the

American press to Kristallnacht and the universal chorus of condemnation in the nation's editorial pages.

39. Richard J. Evans, *The Third Reich in Power* (New York: Penguin Books, 2005), 808.

40. "Damage in the Millions," and Otto D. Tolischus, "Bands Rove Cities," *New York Times*, Nov. 11, 1938, 1, 4.

41. Jordan, *Beyond All Fronts*, 170–71.

42. Lowell Thomas Reports, Unpublished Script, Blue Network Master Books, NBC Collection, Recorded Sound Section, Library of Congress, Nov. 10, 1938.

43. Ibid.; "Follow Up Comment," *Variety*, Nov. 23, 1938: 26.

44. "Coughlin's Hot Potato," *Variety*, Nov. 23, 1938: 25.

45. "Los Angeles Man in Custody," *Los Angeles Times*, Nov. 11, 1938: 2.

46. Tom Waller, "Newsreels," *Variety*, Apr. 18, 1933: 20.

47. "Seeks Unusual Films," *New York Times*, Dec. 1, 1932, 25.

48. Wolfe Kaufman, "*Hitler and Germany,*" *Variety*, Apr. 25, 1933: 14.

49. "*Hitler and Germany,*" *Film Daily*, Apr. 4, 1933: 8.

50. "55,000 in Protests of Hitler Attacks," *New York Times*, Mar. 28, 1933, 1, 12.

51. Tom Waller, "Newsreels," *Variety*, Apr. 4, 1933: 14.

52. "Newsreels Answer March of Time on Pictures of Hitler," *Motion Picture Herald*, Mar. 23, 1935: 30.

53. John C. Flinn, "Film Showmanship," *Variety*, Apr. 26, 1939: 3.

54. Robert Landry, "March of Time (no. 7)," *Variety*, Oct. 23, 1935: 13.

55. *Variety*, October 30, 1935: 31.

56. Shan., "Embassy Newsreel, N.Y.," *Variety*, June 30, 1937: 53.

57. "Press Supports Warner's Charge March of Time Reel Is Pro-Nazi," *Motion Picture Herald*, Feb. 19, 1938: 33.

58. "Chi's Censorial Frowns," *Variety*, Oct. 23, 1938: 15.

59. "Embassy Newsreel, N.Y.," *Variety*, Nov. 23, 1938: 45.

60. "Newsreels Huddle on Nazi Outrages," *Film Daily*, Nov. 17, 1938: 1; "Footage Dearth Stymies Newsreels' Nazi Expose," *Film Daily*, Nov. 21, 1938: 10.

61. Chester Bahn, "Film Daily Closes Berlin Bureau," *Film Daily*, Nov. 21, 1938: 1.

62. Ivan Spear, "Spearheads," *Box Office*, Jan. 28, 1939: 39.

63. There are several different versions of the "God Bless America" story, most of which inaccurately place the date of the show on Armistice Day itself. See Laurence Bergeen, *As Thousands Cheer: The Life of Irving Berlin* (New York, Viking Penguin, 1990), 370–72.

64. "Embassy, N.Y.," *Variety*, Jan. 18, 1939: 45; "Chi's Anthem Singing," *Variety*, Feb. 15, 1939: 6.

65. Mike Wear, "Embassy, N.Y.," *Variety*, Jan. 25, 1939: 53.

11. THERE IS NO ROOM FOR LENI RIEFENSTAHL IN HOLLYWOOD

1. To fact-check Riefenstahl's own accounts, see Steven Bach, *Leni: The Life and Work of Leni Riefenstahl* (New York: Knopf, 2007), and Rainer Rother, *Leni Riefenstahl:*

The Seduction of Genius (London: Continuum, 2002). Ray Muller's essential documentary *The Wonderful, Horrible Life of Leni Riefenstahl* (1993) includes some on-camera denials by Riefenstahl of the written record. Riefenstahl's version is related in Leni Riefenstahl, *A Memoir* (New York: St. Martin's Press, 1992).

2. Andrew Kelly, *All Quiet on the Western Front: The Story of a Film* (London: I. B. Tauris, 1998), 122–23; Riefenstahl, *A Memoir*, 65–66.

3. "*The Blue Light*," *Film Daily*, May 8, 1934: 8.

4. "Hitler Gets Cold Feet on Picture Glorifying Horst Wessel, Nazi Hero," *Variety*, Oct. 31, 1933: 11. The ban was later lifted so the producers could recoup their investment, but only under the condition that Wessel's name not be used. It was released under the title *Hans Westmer* (1933).

5. "The Winnah," *Variety*, May 8, 1935: 15.

6. Roy Chartier, "Newsreels," *Variety*, Oct. 16, 1934: 14.

7. Irving Hoffman, "Tales of Hoffman," *Hollywood Reporter*, July 6, 1939: 3.

8. "Nazi Congress as Feature Pic," *Variety*, Mar. 13, 1935: 13.

9. Carl Dreher, "Parade Ground Art—The German Film Under Hitler," *New Theatre and Film* (June 1936): 34.

10. "Sport: Games at Garmish," *Time*, Feb. 16, 1936.

11. James P. Cunningham, "Hitler Makes U.S. Olympic Films Advertise Germany," *Motion Picture Herald*, Aug. 8, 1936: 13–15; "Hitler's Riefenstahl Watching U.S. Reels," *Motion Picture Herald*, Aug. 22, 1936: 73.

12. Fulton Oursler, "Is Hitler in Love with a Jewess?" *Liberty*, July 9, 1938: 58; Princess Catherine Radziwill, "Is Hitler in Love with a Jewess?" *Liberty*, July 16, 1938: 21–23.

13. "Italians, Nazis Split Venice Awards," *Variety*, Sept. 14, 1938: 13.

14. "German Award," *Motion Picture Herald*, May 7, 1938: 8.

15. Riefenstahl, *A Memoir*, 231.

16. Smith, quoted in Joseph D. Ravotto, "'Politics' Charged in Venice Festival," *Motion Picture Herald*, Sept. 10, 1938: 63; Terry Ramsaye, "International," *Motion Picture Herald*, Sept. 17, 1938: 7.

17. For an in-depth look at her trip to America, see Cooper C. Graham, "'Olympia' in America, 1938: Leni Riefenstahl, Hollywood, and the Kristallnacht," *Historical Journal of Film, Radio, and Television* 13.4 (1938): 433–50.

18. "Anti Nazis Protest Visit to Circulate Olympic Film," *Motion Picture Herald*, Nov. 12, 1938: 19.

19. "Trade, Public Balk, at Nazi 'Olympia,'" *Box Office*, Nov. 12, 1938: 16.

20. "Anti Nazis Protest Visit to Circulate Olympic Film," *Motion Picture Herald*, Nov. 12, 1938: 19.

21. Morris Gilbert, "Leni Riefenstahl, an Individualist Even Under Hitler, Expects to Teach 1,000 Beautiful Women to Ride Horses," *New York World-Telegram*, Nov. 9, 1938: 3.

22. Edward W. Beattie Jr., "Mobs Wreck 10,000 Jewish Shops in Nazis' 14-Hour Reign of Terror," *New York World-Telegram*, Nov. 10, 1938: 1.

23. Riefenstahl, *A Memoir*, 237.

24. Irving Hoffman, "Tales of Hoffman," *Hollywood Reporter*, Nov. 15 1938: 3.

25. Arch Ward, "In the Wake of the News," *Chicago Tribune*, Nov. 22, 1938, 23.

26. "The Female of the Species," *Hollywood Now*, Dec. 2, 1938: 1.

27. "Hitler 'Girl Friend' Barred at Studios," *Daily Variety*, Nov. 30, 1938: 1.

28. "Hitler's Girlfriend Gets Snub from Hollywood," *Daily Worker*, Dec. 2, 1938: 1, 8.

29. "Leni Riefenstahl Still Getting Film Business' Brushoff," *Variety*, Dec. 7, 1938: 1.

30. "Rambling Reporter," *Hollywood Reporter*, Nov. 30, 1938: 2.

31. Ernst Jaeger, "How Leni Riefenstahl Became Hitler's Girlfriend," *Hollywood Tribune*, June 23, 1939: 13.

32. "Miss Riefenstahl Is Surprised," *Box Office*, Dec. 3, 1938: 20.

33. "Hedda Hopper's Hollywood," *Los Angeles Times*, Jan. 13, 1939: A19; "Hedda Hopper's Hollywood," *Los Angeles Times*, Dec. 5, 1938: 26.

34. Ivan Spear, "Spearheads," *Box Office*, Jan. 21, 1939: 29.

35. Ivan Spear, "Spearheads," *Box Office*, Jan. 14, 1939: 39.

36. "Nazi Retreat from Hollywood Chilled by Frigid Farewells," *Daily Variety*, Jan. 14, 1939: 3.

37. Ed Sullivan, "Looking at Hollywood," Jan. 17, 1939: 13.

38. "Hollywood Closes Doors to Hitler's Emissary," *Hollywood Now*, Dec. 2, 1938: 1, 4.

39. "Leni Riefenstahl Sails," *Motion Picture Herald*, Jan. 21, 1939: 8; James Golding, "Riefenstahl's Exit Is Not Exactly Gay," *Box Office*, Jan. 21, 1939: 24.

40. "Leni Riefenstahl in January," *Hollywood Now*, Feb. 3, 1939: 2.

12. "THE ONLY STUDIO WITH ANY GUTS"

1. "Anti-Nazi League Meets," *Hollywood Reporter*, Dec. 8, 1938: 7; "Rambling Reporter," *Hollywood Reporter*, Dec. 10, 1938: 2.

2. W. R. Wilkerson, "Tradeviews," *Hollywood Reporter*, Dec. 7, 1938: 1.

3. The anomalous anti-Nazism of Warner Bros. Pictures has attracted a good deal of scholarly attention. See Christine Ann Colgan, "Warner Brothers' Crusade Against the Third Reich: A Study of Anti-Nazi Activism and Film Production, 1933 to 1941" (Ph.D. diss., University of Southern California, 1985).

4. Told from the perspective of Harry's granddaughter, Cass Warner's documentary *The Brothers Warner* (2008) provides an informative family history of the brothers.

5. "He Sailed Without 'Snow White,'" *Box Office*, Apr. 1, 1939: 32.

6. "Metro about Ready to Bow Out of Germany if Par-20th Will Likewise," *Variety*, July 22, 1936: 35.

7. "Sure Seaters Concur on Anti-Nazi Film Stand in U.S.; Jerk M-G Olympix," *Variety*, Nov. 11, 1936: 11.

8. "Loew Cancels Anti-Nazi Pic; Squawks," *Variety*, Sept. 2, 1936: 7; "MG's German 12," *Variety*, Sept. 9, 1936: 13.

9. Douglas Miller to American Embassy, Apr. 23, 1936. Record Group 281, Records of the Bureau of Foreign and Domestic Commerce, National Archives, College Park, MD.

10. George B. Canty, Confidential Memorandum to Mr. White, Jan. 26, 1935.

11. "Ten Nazi Editors Are Guests at Metro Lot," *Box Office*, June 24, 1939: 74–75.

12. "Companies Halt Films to Austria," *Motion Picture Herald*, Apr. 2, 1938: 20.

13. "Bernstein Out as M-G Austria Rep; Nazi Move," *Variety*, Mar. 23, 1938: 13.

14. "Anschluss Shifts Austrian Film Biz Under Berlin Office Direction," *Variety*, Mar. 30, 1938: 5.

15. Special Correspondent, "Anschluss Shuts Austrian Studios; Only Three American Offices Open," *Motion Picture Herald*, June 4, 1938: 20.

16. "Foreign Coin Curbs Held Biggest Bugaboo for Yank Picture Firms," *Variety*, June 7, 1939: 11.

17. Victor Klemperer, *I Will Bear Witness, 1933–1941: A Diary of the Nazi Years*, trans. Martin Chambers (New York: Modern Library, 1999), 211–38.

18. "Prospects for German Industry Not Bright, U.S. Attache Finds," *Motion Picture Herald*, Jan. 15, 1938: 35–36; "20th-Fox's Move to Dub German Dialog in Italy (Because of Low Costs) Important to All U.S. Pix," *Variety*, Apr. 7, 1937: 13.

19. "'Totalitarian' States Put Further Squeeze on Hollywood's Films," *Motion Picture Herald*, Jan. 28, 1939: 17.

20. "Hitler Hates Us," *Hollywood Reporter*, June 30, 1939: 1.

21. Harry M. Warner, quoted in "Patriotic Films," *Motion Picture Herald*, Sept. 17, 1938: 35.

22. "WB Drops Short Tuners," *Daily Variety*, Dec. 9, 1937: 16.

23. "Hollywood Insider," *Daily Variety*, Aug. 23, 1938: 2.

24. "Warner Shorts Heard on New Radio Program," *Motion Picture Herald*, Oct. 8, 1938: 14.

25. "Warner Stresses Education Value of Shorts," *Motion Picture Herald*, Sept. 10, 1938: 70.

26. "Warners in Tieup with Legion Posts," *Motion Picture Herald*, Dec. 17, 1938: 34.

27. "WB Skeds Historical Series Themed on American Sagas," *Daily Variety*, May 19, 1936: 2.

28. Van Schmus, quoted in Terry Ramsaye, "It Moves," *Motion Picture Herald*, Nov. 26, 1938: 7.

29. "Declaration of Independence," *Box Office*, Oct. 15, 1938: 32.

30. "Lincoln in the White House," *Variety*, Jan. 18, 1939: 12.

31. "Lincoln in the White House," *Motion Picture Herald*, Jan. 14, 1939: 49; Phil M. Daily, "Along the Rialto," *Film Daily*, Jan. 9, 1939: 2.

32. "Lincoln in the White House," *Variety*, Jan. 18, 1939: 12.

33. "Lincoln in the White House," *Box Office*, Jan. 14, 1939: 95.

34. "Sons of Liberty," *Motion Picture Herald*, Mar. 25, 1938: 48; "Advertisement for Sons of Liberty," *Box Office*, Mar. 27, 1938: 11; "Sons of Liberty," *Film Daily*, Mar. 23, 1939: 10.

35. "Inside Stuff—Pictures," *Variety*, June 21, 1939: 12.

36. "Warner Short Answers 'isms,'" *Motion Picture Herald*, Oct. 15, 1938: 30.

37. "Americanism, Motion Pictures, and a Warner Creed," *Motion Picture Herald*, Jan. 28, 1939: 12.

38. Phil M. Daily, "Along the Rialto," *Film Daily*, June 1, 1939: 2.

39. "Americanism, Motion Pictures, and a Warner Creed," *Motion Picture Herald*, Jan. 28, 1939: 13.

40. "WB's Schmeling Ban," *Variety*, July 1, 1936: 1.

41. "Jack Warner to Be HANL Banquet Host," *News of the World*, Mar. 12, 1938: 1.

42. "League on KFWB at 6:30 Tonight!" *News of the World*, Apr. 1, 1938: 1.

43. "Jack Warner's Dinner to Exiled Thos. Mann May Touch Off a Militant Anti-Hitler Campaign in Hollywood," *Variety*, Mar. 23, 1938: 2.

44. "Sons of Legion," *Hollywood Reporter*, Sept. 9, 1938: 3.

45. Alexander Gardiner and Boyd B. Stutler, "Now Showing: Legion," *American Legion Magazine* (Nov. 1938): 56.

46. "Rambling Reporter," *Hollywood Reporter*, Aug. 22, 1938: 2.

47. "H. M. Warner Condemns All Isms," *Variety*, Sept. 21, 1938: 2.

48. "Red Charge Is False, Warner Tells Legion," *Motion Picture Herald*, Sept. 24, 1938: 16.

49. Douglas W. Churchill, "Hollywood Pledges Allegiance to America," *New York Times*, Jan. 15, 1939, X5.

50. "Embassy Newsreel, N.Y.," *Variety*, Oct. 26, 1938: 44. "Now we will enter the trial courtroom with a Paramount cameraman," declared the announcer as a photographer marches briskly into the revolving door of the court building—only to be ejected through the other side of the same door, propelled by a court marshal.

51. Hardy, quoted in Leon G. Turrou, *Nazi Spies in America* (New York: Random House, 1938), 285.

52. "Rambling Reporter," *Hollywood Reporter*, Dec. 10, 1938: 2.

53. Dr. Georg Gyssling to Joseph I. Breen, Dec. 6, 1938 (*Confessions of a Nazi Spy* file, Production Code Administration files, Academy of Motion Picture Arts and Sciences, Margaret Herrick Library, Beverly Hills, CA; hereinafter, PCA files).

54. Joseph I. Breen to Dr. Georg Gyssling, Dec. 7, 1938 (*Confessions of a Nazi Spy* file, PCA files).

55. Joseph I. Breen to Jack L. Warner, Dec. 30, 1938; Joseph I. Breen to Jack L. Warner, Dec. 30, 1938; Joseph I. Breen to Will H. Hays, Dec. 30, 1938 (*Confessions of a Nazi Spy* file, PCA files).

56. Robert Lord to Joseph I. Breen, Jan. 25, 1939 (*Confessions of a Nazi Spy* file PCA files).

57. Karl Lishka, memo, Jan. 22, 1939 (*Confessions of a Nazi Spy* file, PCA files).

58. Internal memo from Walter MacEwen to Robert Lord, Nov. 16, 1939 (Warner Bros. archives, University of Southern California, Los Angeles, CA).

59. Internal memo from Hal Wallis to Robert Lord and Anatole Litvak, Jan. 6, 1939 (*Confessions of a Nazi Spy* file, Warner Bros. archives, USC).

60. Hedda Hopper, "Dramatic Story Behind Spy Film," *Los Angeles Times*, Apr. 23, 1939, C3.

61. "A.F.A. Releases Story of '*Confessions of a Nazi Spy*,'" *Hollywood Now*, Mar. 10, 1939: 2.

62. Hal Wallis to Nathan Levinson, Mar. 24, 1939 (*Confessions of a Nazi Spy* file, Warner Bros. archives, USC).

63. "See 'Confessions of a Nazi Spy,'" *Hollywood Now*, May 5, 1939: 1.

64. "Rambling Reporter," *Hollywood Reporter*, Apr. 24, 1939: 2.

65. "'Nazi Spy' Must Attraction Scoring Boxoffice Bullseye," *Hollywood Reporter*, Apr. 28, 1939: 3; "Big Police Guard at Nazi Preview but All's Quiet," *Daily Variety*, Apr. 28, 1939: 22.

66. "Confessions of a Nazi Spy," *Daily Variety*, Apr. 28, 1939: 3, 22.

67. "Hollywood Inside," *Daily Variety*, May 12, 1939: 2.

68. "Deny Kuhn Injunction," *Variety*, June 21, 1939: 2.

69. "Can't Bar 'Spy' Hull Tells Nazis," *Motion Picture Herald*, June 1, 1939: 42.

70. "Nazi Consul Fails to Stop 'Confessions,'" *Hollywood Now*, May 12, 1939: 1.

71. "'Confessions' to Run in France, Cuba," *Hollywood Now*, June 23, 1939: 2.

72. "Hollywood Inside," *Daily Variety*, May 2, 1939: 2.

73. "'Juarez' Opening Sparkles B'way to a Fare-thee-well," *Hollywood Reporter*, Apr. 26, 1939: 1, 7.

74. Frank S. Nugent, "Juarez," *New York Times*, Apr. 26, 1939: 27.

75. "Donald Ogden Stewart (Hollywood): Meyer Levin (New York)," *Hollywood Tribune*, Apr. 28, 1939: 2, 19.

76. "Slashed Seats During 'Nazi' Engagement," *Variety*, June 21, 1939: 2.

13. HOLLYWOOD GOES TO WAR

1. The traumatic impact of the Hitler-Stalin Pact on Hollywood's Popular Front is recollected in many memoirs and oral histories from the era, both left and right. See, for example, Douglas Bell's interview with MGM producer Richard Goldstone in Bell, *An Oral History with Richard Goldstone* (Beverly Hills: Academy of Motion Picture Arts and Sciences, 1991), 152–53.

2. "Soviet Film Replaced," *Motion Picture Herald*, Sept. 2, 1939: 8.

3. "A Program for Peace," *Hollywood Now*, Sept. 22, 1939: 2.

4. Donald Ogden Stewart, *By a Stroke of Luck! An Autobiography* (New York: Paddington Press, 1975), 247–48.

5. "League Attacks Finnish Loans," *Hollywood Now*, Jan. 26, 1940: 1.

6. "Pardon Our Bluntness," *Hollywood Now*, Dec. 1, 1939: 4.

7. Dalton Trumbo, *Johnny Got His Gun* (New York: Lippincott, 1939). Though written before the Hitler-Stalin Pact, the timing of the antiwar tract for isolationist purposes was perfect: it was published in September 1939. In the 1971 motion picture, Johnny taps out "Kill me."

8. Dalton Trumbo, "Trumbo Hits War Market," *Hollywood Now*, Jan. 19, 1940: 1, 3.

9. "Films' 8–9% Foreign Loss," *Variety*, Oct. 4, 1939: 1, 18.

10. "War Jitters Clip Show Biz," *Variety*, Aug. 30, 1939: 1, 18.

11. "Exhibs of 'Nazi Spy' in Poland Hung By Nazis," *Variety*, Apr. 24, 1940: 2.

12. "European War Crisis Films Shown At Embassy, N.Y., 56–72 Hours Later," *Variety*, Aug. 30, 1939: 16.

13. "German Picture House in Yorkville Passes the Hat for Nazi Winter War Relief; Hitler a Popular Kid," *Variety*, Oct. 23, 1940: 3.

14. " 'Mad Dog of Europe' Project Stirs Again," *Box Office*, Apr. 15, 1939: 62–63; "Rosen's 'Dog' Rebarks," *Daily Variety*, Apr. 13, 1939: 2.

15. "The Mad Dog of Europe," *Box Office*, Apr. 22, 1939: 26-G.

16. "*Beasts of Berlin*," *Variety*, Nov. 22, 1939: 16.

17. Stewart, *By a Stroke of Luck!*, 257.

18. "Willkie Named Film Counsel," *Daily Variety*, Sept. 2, 1941: 1, 6.

19. "Willkie Gagged by Senate Rules as Probe Opens," *Daily Variety*, Sept. 10, 1941: 10.

20. "Zanuck Speech Given Big Hand Even by Isolationists," *Daily Variety*, Sept. 29, 1941: 8.

21. "H. Warner on Grill All Day," *Daily Variety*, Sept. 26, 1941: 1, 8–9.

22. "German Consul Burns Records, Closes Offices," *Los Angeles Times*, June 29, 1941, 1; "Nazi Consul Here Receives a Notice of Closing Order," *Los Angeles Times*, June 18, 1941, 4.

23. I am grateful to Fritz Neubauer and Miranda Neubauer for accessing information from the handbook of the German foreign service and translating same for the information on Gyssling's post-Hollywood career.

24. "Laemmle at 70, Champing at the Bit for Another Whirl at Making Films," *Variety*, Jan. 13, 1937: 4.

25. "Laemmle to Auto Tour Europe This Summer," *Variety*, June 1, 1938: 2.

26. "Laemmle Would Evacuate His German Home Town," *Variety*, Feb. 1, 1939: 1.

27. " 'Uncle Carl' Laemmle Dies at Home, Aged 72," *Hollywood Reporter*, Sept. 25, 1939: 1, 6.

28. "Entire Industry Mourns Passing of 'Uncle Carl,' " *Hollywood Reporter*, Sept. 26, 1939: 1, 7.

29. Terry Ramsaye, "Laemmle's Death Takes Pioneer 'Independent' of IMP Film Days," *Motion Picture Herald*, Sept. 20, 1930: 19, 21.

EPILOGUE: THE MOTION PICTURE MEMORY OF NAZISM

1. Susan Sontag, "Fascinating Fascism," *New York Review of Books*, Feb. 6, 1975.

2. Kellogg, quoted in Abel Green, "Pix as Evidence in Nazi Trials," *Variety*, Oct. 3, 1945: 1, 24.

3. J. P. Shanley, "TV: The Time of Hitler," *New York Times*, Mar. 15, 1956, 46; Walter Ames, "Hitler's Downfall Seen in TV's 'Twisted Cross,' " *Los Angeles Times*, Mar. 14, 1956: B9.

4. Kaufman, quoted in Jack Hellman, "Light and Airy," *Daily Variety*, Feb. 19, 1968: 8.

5. Jay Leyda, *Films Beget Films* (New York: Hill and Wang, 1964).

INDEX